The Lost Plays of Greek Tragedy

Also available from Bloomsbury

Greek Tragedy: Themes and Contexts, Laura Swift
Hellenistic Tragedy: Texts, Translations and a Critical Survey, Agnieszka
Kotlinska-Toma
Ovid: A Poet on the Margins, Laurel Fulkerson
The Plays of Aeschylus, A. F. Garvie
The Plays of Euripides, James Morwood
The Plays of Sophocles, A. F. Garvie

The Lost Plays of Greek Tragedy

Volume 1: Neglected Authors

Matthew Wright

Bloomsbury Academic
An imprint of Bloomsbury Publishing Plc

BLOOMSBURY
LONDON · OXFORD · NEW YORK · NEW DELHI · SYDNEY

Bloomsbury Academic

An imprint of Bloomsbury Publishing Plc

50 Bedford Square	1385 Broadway
London	New York
WC1B 3DP	NY 10018
UK	USA

www.bloomsbury.com

BLOOMSBURY and the Diana logo are trademarks of Bloomsbury Publishing Plc

First published 2016

© Matthew Wright, 2016

British Library Cataloguing-in-Publication Data
A catalogue record for this book is available from the British Library.

ISBN:	HB:	978-1-47256-776-5
	PB:	978-1-47256-775-8
	ePDF:	978-1-47256-778-9
	ePub:	978-1-47256-777-2

Library of Congress Cataloging-in-Publication Data
Names: Wright, Matthew (Matthew Ephraim), author.
Title: The lost plays of Greek tragedy / Matthew Wright.
Description: New York ; London : Bloomsbury Academic, 2016– |
Includes bibliographical references and index.
Identifiers: LCCN 2016019105 (print) | LCCN 2016019691 (ebook) |
ISBN 9781472567765 (hardback) | ISBN 9781472567758 (pbk.) |
ISBN 9781472567789 (epdf) | ISBN 9781472567772 (epub)
Subjects: LCSH: Greek drama (Tragedy)–History and criticism. | Lost literature–Greece.
Classification: LCC PA3136 .W75 2016 (print) | LCC PA3136 (ebook) |
DDC 882/.0109–dc23
LC record available at https://lccn.loc.gov/2016019105.

Cover image © Allan T. Kohl/Art Images for College Teaching

Typeset by RefineCatch Limited, Bungay, Suffolk
Printed and bound in India

Contents

Acknowledgements

I began working on this book during a very happy year at Vassar College, where I was Blegen Research Fellow in 2011–12. Special thanks are due to Curtis Dozier, Rachel Friedman, Rachel Kitzinger, Bert Lott, Barbara Olsen and Robert Brown, for giving me the warmest possible welcome and providing plenty of encouragement and intellectual stimulus.

Back in Exeter, I have been helped and guided in all sorts of ways, as ever, by Richard Seaford and John Wilkins – to whom, on the occasion of their retirement, I dedicate this book in return for many years of friendship and collegiality.

M.E.W.

Exeter

December 2015

Prologue

Their ghosts are gagged, their books are library flotsam,
Some of their names – not all – we learnt in school
But, life being short, we rarely read their poems,
Mere source-books now to point or except a rule,
While those opinions which rank them high are based
On a wish to be different or on lack of taste.

Louis MacNeice, 'Elegy for Minor Poets'

There are already so many books about Greek tragedy that the appearance of yet
another might seem to call for special apology or explanation. What marks this
one out as different is that, whereas nearly all the others deal with the thirty-two
tragedies that still survive today, I am concerned exclusively with the tragedies
that no longer exist. Many hundreds of tragedies were performed, in Athens and
further afield, during the classical period, and even though almost all of them
are lost, a certain amount is known about them through fragments and other
types of evidence. Nevertheless, this material is not easily accessible to the
general reader, and it has not always been fully discussed or integrated into
scholarly accounts of the tragic genre.[1] What I aim to provide here is the first
comprehensive study of all the lost plays and neglected authors of Greek tragedy,
which gathers together and presents the evidence in a thoroughly accessible and
reader-friendly way. I also make available a complete English translation of the
fragments for the first time.

The amount of material to be discussed proved too much for a single book,
and so what you are holding in your hands right now is Volume 1: 'Neglected
Authors'. It discusses the tragic genre from its sixth-century origins down to
c. 322 BCE (the conventional end point for the 'classical' period), and it includes

---

[1] All existing books, articles and editions deal with individual authors or fragments, or are aimed
exclusively at specialists. Selected fragments are discussed by (e.g.) Snell (1971), Knox (1985),
Cropp (2005), McHardy et al. (2005), but no general study exists. The complete fragments of
Aeschylus, Sophocles and Euripides have recently been made available in the Loeb Classical Library,
but there is no English version of the fragments of the other tragedians. Most (not all) of the
fragments from *TrGF* 1 are translated into German by Kannicht et al. (1991), and Lévêque (1955)
offers French versions of Agathon's remains. (See also Appendix 4 below.)

every playwright known to us from that period except the three who are nowadays the most famous. I would have continued beyond this date but for the appearance of Agnieszka Kotlińska-Toma's excellent new book *Hellenistic Tragedy*, to which readers are enthusiastically directed.[2] Volume 2 (forthcoming) will be devoted to the lost plays of Aeschylus, Sophocles and Euripides. Between them the two volumes will offer a fresh perspective on Greek tragedy, showing that careful study of the lost works can lead to a reappraisal of the whole genre – or, at least, a much more thorough, detailed and representative account of it than ever before. What emerges above all is that classical Greek *tragôidia* was a fascinatingly rich, heterogeneous and, in many ways, unfamiliar type of drama. Certainly it possessed much more breadth and variety than we can appreciate if we only ever look at the tiny number of plays that survive.

The main justification for this book, then, is that it makes possible a more complete picture of a genre which is still very widely read, studied and performed. But it may also appeal to those who are fascinated by what we might call 'the aesthetics of loss' in a more general sense. It is clear that lost works of art possess an unusually powerful attraction for a certain type of individual. I myself am such a person: I have always been intrigued by lost books, stolen manuscripts, *variorum* editions of works that were rewritten, proofs of books that were withdrawn before publication, deleted scenes from films among the DVD extras, and so on. It is hard to say exactly why this should be so (maybe there is some subconscious psychological explanation that I would be happier not to discover), but the large pile of books on my desk proves that I am not alone. These works include, for example, Rick Gekoski's *Lost, Stolen, or Shredded: Stories of Missing Works of Art and Literature*; Christopher Woodward's *In Ruins*; Philip Mould's *Sleuth: The Amazing Quest for Lost Art Treasures*; Michael Bywater's *Lost Worlds*; Umberto Eco's *The Name of the Rose*; George Steiner's *My Unwritten Books*; Douglas Brode's *Lost Films of the Fifties*; Gavin Stamp's *Lost Cities: A Chronicle of Architectural Destruction*; Robert Harbison's *Ruins and Fragments*; and Bernard Richards' *The Greatest Books You'll Never Read*.

Such titles bear witness to a whole sub-genre of cultural studies that seems to have emerged or flourished during the last couple of decades; and it has been thought that this preoccupation reflects the peculiar anxieties of our own fragmented, postmodern twenty-first-century world.[3] On the other hand, one can point to other historical contexts dominated by the aesthetics of loss, such as

---

[2]   Kotlińska-Toma (2014); cf. Sens (2010).
[3]   Most (2009) 19.

the fascination with ruins and fragments in eighteenth- and nineteenth-century Romanticism.[4] But perhaps it could be said that all who have ever engaged in the study of antiquity have experienced a similar feeling to some degree – a vicarious nostalgia for a time and place in which we have never lived and which, until the invention of time-travel, will always remain impossible to access as fully as we would wish. Thinking about lost texts and reading fragments is very like being in a classical land and standing among the ruins of an ancient site: we can almost perceive what it used to be like in its original state, but *not quite.* Part of the appeal lies precisely in the mixture of closeness and distance, reality and imagination, longing and unattainability.

A genre in fragments

The ancient Greek world continues to hold an enormous fascination for many people, but this fascination sometimes seems to be inversely proportionate to the amount that is actually known about it. Essentially, we are dealing with a lost and vanished world, and we can scarcely remind ourselves often enough of its remoteness and obscurity. Every aspect of classical Greek civilization – its history, its religion, its politics, its culture, its art and its literature – is nowadays visible only in the tiniest of glimpses, via evidence which is drastically inadequate and hopelessly fragmentary.

This is no less true of Greek drama than of any other aspect of Greek culture. The Greeks of the archaic and classical period entertained themselves with many different types of poetry and performance, but these have almost entirely vanished – not just in the sense that hardly anything survives of them, but in the sense that they have had virtually no influence in shaping subsequent literature or performance traditions. What do dithyrambs, satyr-plays, or mimes signify to most twenty-first-century readers or theatregoers? What except the merest vestigial trace is left of paeans, of propemptika, of partheneia, of prosodia, of circular choruses, of citharodic nomes? These and many other Greek performance genres are barely known even to those few scholars and specialists who still pore over the exiguous scraps of evidence. They have to be regarded not simply as lost but as more or less extinct.

Greek tragedy, by contrast, can seem strangely – even miraculously – familiar to us. A number of fifth-century tragedies are still frequently performed, either

---

4   See (e.g.) Macaulay (1953), Harries (1994), Woodward (2002), Tanehisa (2009).

in 'authentic' original-language productions or in various modern versions and adaptations, more so than at any time since antiquity.[5] Certain plays – one thinks especially of *Agamemnon, Medea, Oedipus Tyrannus, Hippolytus* and *Antigone* – are well known to theatre audiences and the general public all over the world. People still go, in their thousands, to watch these plays, and (presumably) they see them not just as quirky historical curiosities but as accessible and enjoyable works of drama. Books with such titles as *The Living Art of Greek Tragedy, Greek Tragedy at the Dawn of the Third Millennium* and *How to Stage Greek Tragedy Today* pour from the presses.[6] More broadly speaking, the tragic genre, unlike the other genres just mentioned, appears to have survived into modern times by a process of direct linear descent – or, at least, plays identifying themselves as tragedies have been written and performed almost continually for the last two and a half millennia. One can argue, of course, over the exact degree to which any of these post-classical 'tragedies' actually resemble Greek *tragôidia*, but the fact remains that the genre and concept of tragedy still seem astonishingly recognizable. Tragedy is part of our modern culture.

Certainly tragedy has always been central to the academic study of the classics. Plays by Aeschylus, Sophocles and Euripides continue to be very widely read and studied, and they are invariably included as core texts in the curriculum. At this moment there are literally thousands of school, college and university courses devoted to Greek tragedy (though it is telling that I have not been able to track down a single course in which fragmentary plays appear on the list of prescribed texts). Meanwhile the production of books, articles, conference papers and doctoral dissertations on tragedy-related topics continues at a rapid rate. If one opens the latest volume of any classical journal or any publisher's catalogue, or if one searches for 'tragedy' in the bibliographic database of *L'Année Philologique*, it will be immediately obvious that tragedy remains one of the most popular areas within classical scholarship.

It would be easy to deceive ourselves that we know and understand Greek tragedy pretty well. But one of the main assumptions of this book is that we do not. Greek tragedy is, in a very real sense, a *lost* genre. It may not be quite as dead and buried as the dithyramb or the prosodion, but it is a much more obscure and shadowy art form than is generally thought.

---

[5]   See the database of Oxford University's Archive for the Performance of Greek and Roman Drama (http://www.apgrd.ox.ac.uk).
[6]   McDonald (2003); Hall, Macintosh and Wrigley (2004); Goldhill (2007).

'Minor' tragedians and the canon

To many people – including the majority of students in university classics departments – it may come as a surprise that there were any tragedians apart from Aeschylus, Sophocles and Euripides, and that many of these other tragedians enjoyed comparable fame and success in their own day. Even professional scholars tend to treat Greek tragedy as practically synonymous with this familiar triad of writers, while all the other poets are largely ignored or relegated to occasional references in footnotes or parentheses.

Classical Athens teemed with tragedians. Apart from the famous triad, there were many other playwrights who produced tragedies in Athens and elsewhere during the fifth and fourth centuries BCE. This book deals with over eighty poets whose names are known to us, but of course there will have been others. The loss of their work means that they have slipped from view, but there is a good deal that can still be said about these writers and their plays. Anyone with an interest in theatre history needs to know more about these neglected tragedians, including such figures as Phrynichus, Agathon, Neophron, Diogenes, Ion, Critias, Astydamas, Chaeremon and Theodectes (to name but a few). It is unfortunate that, if they are talked about at all, they are conventionally referred to as 'minor tragedians'.[7] Still more unfortunately, some of them – Xenocles, Sthenelus, Morsimus and Dionysius, in particular – have even become bywords for *bad* writing, a state of affairs for which Aristophanes and other comedians must be held largely responsible.[8]

It is perhaps inevitable that these shadowy figures should seem to be of minor importance in the history of the genre. After all, no one has been able to read their work properly for hundreds or even thousands of years, so they have not had a chance to shape the popular or critical reception of tragedy. But we do them a terrible injustice if we assume that in their own time they were all nonentities. Some of them were no doubt better than others, judged by some criterion or other, but there is no justification for lumping them all together as 'minor' figures and consigning them to the scrap-heap of history. During their own times many of these lost writers were prominent and successful figures. They were selected to compete in the major festivals and often won prizes;

---

[7] E.g. Snell's edition of the remains (*TrGF* 1) groups them together as *Tragici Minores*; cf. the surveys of the genre by Knox (1985), Sommerstein (2003), Scodel (2010) and others.

[8] See (e.g.) Kaimio and Nykopp (1997), where they are referred to as a 'Bad Poets Society' (*sic*). Comic mockery of tragedians is discussed in later chapters, poet by poet; note also that several ancient scholars (following the comedians) refer disparagingly to these poets, even when it is clear that they have not read their work: e.g. *TrGF* 1.25 T5b, 1.31 T1, 1.44 T1, 1.47 T1, T4.

they were famous enough to be the subject of topical jokes and parodies in contemporary comedy; they were important figures in contemporary cultural life; their plays were quoted, discussed, or adapted by other writers. In many cases we possess enough information about their work to be able to say that it was distinctive or original.

As for the evidence of comedy, it needs to be stressed that being mocked or parodied is not in fact a reliable sign of a poet's quality or status. It has been argued that these jokes are actually a sign of prestige, and that they often functioned as a means of popularizing the work of poets and establishing a fan-base for their work.[9] However that might be, we are not entitled to assume from the comedians' jokes that Xenocles, Dionysius and others were 'bad' poets, whatever that label might mean in any case. Just imagine that nothing remained of Aeschylus except the jokes made about him by Aristophanes: we would be in danger of dismissing him too as a bad poet, a pompous fool and a sesquipedalian windbag, of importance mainly as a footnote in the history of stylistic excess.[10] Whenever we read a comic text we have to ask ourselves very carefully what the jokes actually mean. It may not always be possible to answer this question definitively, but it is worth making an effort to understand just what is at stake, and to speculate as to what sort of social, critical or cultural attitudes are underpinning the joke. Often it turns out that the comedians' jokes are not simply equivalent to qualitative critical assessments; but even if some sort of judgement is being expressed, these jokes can sometimes be shown to contain some specific factual information about these poets or their work. It is this information – rather than banal or obfuscatory labels such as 'good', 'bad', 'frigid', 'bitter', or similar – that the historian of tragedy can put to use. It is also crucial to note that the comedians almost never express positive approval of *any* poet's work.

Let me be clear that I am not claiming that all of these neglected authors should be reclassified as 'major' poets; nor am I proposing to argue for their critical rehabilitation on the grounds that they were actually good rather than bad writers after all. (This is the sort of approach that Louis MacNeice ironically evoked in the verses quoted above as the epigraph.) In fact, I think it is safest to avoid making any sort of *qualitative* judgement on these poets, not (or not only)

---

[9]   Rosen (2006), Bakola (2008).

[10]   Jokes about Aeschylus include Aristophanes, *Clouds* 1366–7, *Frogs* (*passim*; but see esp. 814–29, 939–44, 1008–88, 1500–04); cf. Pherecrates F100 K-A and Chamaeleon F40 Wehrli (which is almost certainly based on a lost comedy). See also Chapter 3 (pp. 64–9) and Chapter 5 (pp. 130–43) on the interpretation of jokes about Agathon and Dionysius in particular. For different approaches to reading comic 'criticism' in general, see Wright (2012), Hanink (2014a) 159–90.

because such judgements are inherently questionable, but because there is insufficient material on which to base a judgement. What I am arguing is that a complete and representative history of classical tragedy must incorporate these so-called minor playwrights, and that it must attempt to take them seriously, treating the fragments of their work without prejudices or preconceptions.

Greek tragedy should not be treated as if it were coterminous with the work of Aeschylus, Sophocles and Euripides. These three writers were to become hugely celebrated and important as 'classic' or quasi-canonical authors, but that was not until much later on. Of course, it would be silly to deny that they are figures of major importance, but in their own lifetimes they did not possess the extraordinary status that they later came to acquire; they represented just three among many other successful dramatists. They each produced a large body of work, but others (including Philocles and Theodectes) were comparably prolific or even more so. They each won a large number of prizes (Euripides notably fewer than Aeschylus or Sophocles), but others are known to have been equally or more successful.

The most prolific and decorated tragedian known to us was Astydamas the Younger, to whom 240 plays and fifteen first prizes in major festivals are attributed.[11] In 340 BCE, Astydamas was also the first ever tragedian to be honoured by the Athenians with a bronze portrait statue in the Theatre of Dionysus. The statue base, with part of the poet's name visible – ΑΣΤΥ – can still be seen there today.[12] The significance of this honour lies partly in the fact that such statues had previously only been used to commemorate politicians, successful generals, athletes and other public benefactors: this was the first time that a tragedian had been memorialized in this way.[13] But it is also extremely significant that Astydamas was commemorated in his own lifetime *and* before Aeschylus, Sophocles or Euripides: these other writers did eventually receive statues of their own, but not till a decade or more later.[14] This is noted by Diogenes Laertius, who mentions it – along with the condemnation of Socrates – as a prime example of the misguided decisions that the Athenians were prone to make from time to time.[15] But Diogenes was writing six centuries later, at a time when all tragedians except the 'classic' triad were judged to be of lesser

---

[11]   *TrGF* 1.60: see Chapter 4 (pp. 101–5).
[12]   *IG* ii² 3772a.
[13]   This is pointed out by Scodel (2006) 147, comparing Andocides *On the Mysteries* 38 for a description of a general's bronze statue in the fifth-century theatre; cf. Hanink (2014a) 183–8.
[14]   See Krumeich (2002).
[15]   Diogenes Laertius 2.43 (*TrGF* 1.60 T8a).

importance: it is unsurprising that a writer with this sort of outlook should deem Astydamas' honour to be incongruous or inexplicable.

The second-century CE lexicographer Pausanias also records the story that Astydamas composed an epigram in which he expressed an ambition to be taken seriously alongside the 'canonical' writers, but that the Athenians judged it too vainglorious to be inscribed on the base of the statue:

> If only I had been born among them, or they had lived in our time,
>> those poets who are thought to bear the first prize with their speech,
> then I could have been judged on a true basis, starting level with my competitors;
>> but as it is they run ahead, taking the lead given by time, and no envy attaches to them.[16]

These verses have been interpreted as a genuine attempt on Astydamas' part to 'challenge the canon',[17] but their authenticity has been doubted.[18] It seems more likely to me that the epigram and accompanying anecdote were invented later in the tradition, in order to recast Astydamas in the role of latecomer or challenger. But why was this recasting thought to be necessary, and how was it that Aeschylus, Sophocles and Euripides came to be seen as the only tragedians worth taking seriously? These questions cannot be answered definitively, but if we want to search for an explanation we will have to begin by examining cultural currents at Athens in the fourth century BCE.

It is important to note that there was never an official canon of authors (as such) until the Christian era, and thus the concept of 'canonical' authors, though frequently encountered in modern classical scholarship, is somewhat problematic.[19] Nonetheless, it is clear that (from time to time, and in different contexts) certain writers were regarded as especially admirable or worthy of study. It has been shown that, from relatively early in the fourth century, theatre audiences and readers were starting to treat Aeschylus, Sophocles and Euripides as something akin to 'classics', in the sense that their plays were quite frequently revived on stage in Athens and elsewhere, as well as being discussed, quoted,

---

[16]   Pausanias Atticista Σ 6 (*TrGF* 1.59 T2a).
[17]   Scodel (2006) 147–9, followed by Hanink (2014a) 185: 'an early moment of conscious "epigonality" or belatedness in classical literature'.
[18]   Page (1981) 33–4. Cf. *Palatine Anthology* 7.410 (on Thespis) for a comparable case of a literary epigram posing as an inscription.
[19]   See Pfeiffer (1968) 206–7, who points out that *canon* is not an ancient term but 'a modern catachresis that originated in the eighteenth century': he traces its first use to David Runken's *Historia critica oratorum Graecorum* (1768). Alexandrians and later scholars in antiquity sometimes used οἱ ἐγκριθέντες ('the select') or *classici* ('first-class') in a similar but not identical sense. Cf. *Oxford Classical Dictionary*[3] (1996, p. 286) s.v. 'canon'.

parodied and evoked in pictorial art.[20] However, it seems to me that the later reception of tragedy was definitively shaped by a single event in the late fourth century: namely, the official selection and commemoration of Aeschylus, Sophocles and Euripides as the state tragedians of Athens.

The individual responsible for this process was Lycurgus, son of Lycophron, the eminent Athenian statesman who held various positions of power between *c.* 337 and 324 BCE, including control of the state treasury and oversight of the theatre.[21] During Lycurgus' time the Theatre of Dionysus was greatly expanded and rebuilt, and at some point during the 330s or 320s

> Lycurgus decreed that bronze statues of Aeschylus, Sophocles and Euripides should be erected at Athens, and that copies of their tragedies should be written out and preserved in the state archives (*en koinôi*), and that the city clerk should collate copies (*paragignôskein*) for the use of actors, and that it should be forbidden to perform versions that did not conform to these texts.[22]

This decree has been interpreted as a sign of an enormous change in the way that Athenians viewed, or made use of, their cultural heritage. Lycurgus himself is unlikely to have been single-handedly responsible for this change, but nonetheless he oversaw the formal establishment of the triad as a quasi-canonical group, as well as 'the institutionalization of tragedy as a unique cultural possession and the source of education for the Athenian state'.[23] One could no doubt argue about the reasons underlying Lycurgus' choice of precisely these three tragedians to represent the best that Athens could offer to the world. But it is obvious that the official creation of the triad was an event of cataclysmic importance in terms of subsequent literary history. From this time onwards, an enormous amount of prestige and cultural status became attached to the triad, and much less attention was given to the work of all the other playwrights.[24] An author such as Heraclides of Pontus, writing around this period, could now issue a book with the title *On The Three Tragedians,* as if there were *only* three.[25]

It cannot be emphasized strongly enough that modern views of tragedy are

---

[20] See Hanink (2010); cf. Nervegna (2013) on contexts for the reception of drama in the fourth century, and Taplin (2007) on the fourth-century spread of tragedy as evidenced by vase-painting.

[21] See Hanink (2014a), esp. 62–103, on all aspects of Lycurgus' career and his influence.

[22] [Plutarch], *Lives of the Ten Orators* 841f. The meaning of some key terms is disputed: *en koinôi* could mean 'in a collected edition', and *paragignôskein* could mean 'read out'. See Kovacs (2005) 382, Scodel (2006) 129.

[23] Scodel (2006) 130; cf. Hanink (2014a) 7–9, 65–7.

[24] Note, however, a handful of references suggesting that very occasionally writers later in antiquity treated other names apart from the triad (e.g. Phrynichus, Aristarchus, Ion or Achaeus) as quasi-canonical or 'classic' tragedians: *TrGF* 1 CAT A 2–3; 1.14 T4; 1.19 T7a; 1.20 T4, T6. Cf. the later 'Pleiad' of Hellenistic tragedians (*TrGF* 1 CAT A 5).

[25] Heraclides of Pontus F179 Wehrli (= Diogenes Laertius 5.87).

the product of historically contingent processes. The 'classic' tragic triad may reflect the cultural currents of Lycurgan Athens or the preoccupations of later classical scholarship, but it is not an objective marker of greatness or importance, and it is very far from being an accurate reflection of the whole tragic genre or audience tastes in the classical period.[26] The image of tragedy that emerged at the dawn of the Hellenistic period was one that had been radically pruned down and neatly packaged to meet the needs of a particular age, but it is a selective, partial, and in many ways misleading image. The challenge facing the modern scholar, then, is to unwrite literary history, in an attempt to see tragedy through the eyes of its original audiences in the period before the Lycurgan decree changed everything. The whole genre of tragedy is not synonymous with the triad; it did not come to an end with the deaths of Euripides and Sophocles in 406–405 BCE; it cannot be understood properly in terms of 'major' *versus* 'minor' or 'canonical' *versus* 'non-canonical' tragedians; it was not an exclusively Athenian or Athenocentric genre;[27] the period of its flourishing was not limited to a fifth-century golden age.

Lost tragedies can serve as a focal point for discussions about cultural memory, canon formation and the Greeks' preservation of their literary heritage. In this respect the history of the transmission of tragic texts from the classical period to the modern age raises important (and not entirely answerable) questions. The process seems to have involved a degree of deliberate selection along with a large element of accident and mystery.[28] Despite the efforts of Lycurgus and subsequent generations of librarians and scholars, nearly all the plays of Aeschylus, Sophocles and Euripides have disappeared, and the few complete plays that we possess – seven by Aeschylus, seven by Sophocles and eighteen by Euripides[29] – mostly seem to represent the remnants of selected editions made in the third century CE or thereabouts.[30] The only reason we have

---

[26] It is sometimes thought that Aristophanes' *Frogs* (405 BCE), which features all three members of the triad, reflects the fact that the 'canon' was already being formed as early as the fifth century: see Seidensticker (2002). But *Frogs* is far from unique, and many other tragedians are treated in a very similar way in fifth-century comedy: see Wright (2012).

[27] This point is forcefully made by a number of recent studies which point out the wide variety of the plays' content and the large number of festivals and performance venues apart from the Athenian Dionysia and Lenaea: see (e.g.) Deardon (1999), Heath (2009), Csapo (2010), Bosher (2012), Csapo et al. (2014).

[28] See Garland (2003) for an accessible account of the textual transmission and reception of tragedy from the fifth century to the modern age.

[29] Note, however, that the authorship of the Aeschylean *Prometheus Bound* and the Euripidean *Rhesus* are disputed.

[30] Wartelle (1971) is a good discussion of such matters (with specific reference to Aeschylus); cf. Zuntz (1965) on Euripides, and the contributors to Battezzato (2003) on various specific aspects of tragic textual history.

more plays by Euripides than the others is that a single volume survived from a complete edition organized alphabetically by title (including tragedies beginning with the letters eta and iota).[31] In other words, even quasi-canonization did not reliably ensure survival. And there is something curious and inexplicable about the fact that so little trace remains of all the others, given that tragedy was such an influential and widely read and performed genre throughout antiquity. Obviously the texts of the tragedians, 'classic' and 'non-classic' alike, remained available for many years, since the plays were quoted, discussed, adapted or reperformed by many others in the ancient world. But at some point between late antiquity and the Middle Ages, these texts vanished without trace, leaving us with just thirty-two complete tragedies out of a total that must have run into the hundreds or even thousands.

Types of evidence

That we have any information at all about the lost plays is thanks to a motley and random selection of sources, all of which present certain limitations or interpretative difficulties. Some readers, especially students and non-specialists, may find it helpful to have a brief summary of the different types of fragmentary evidence.

The word 'fragment' is potentially misleading, as it suggests literal fragmentation, as in the case of shards of pottery or glass. Sometimes literary 'fragments' are indeed torn or damaged scraps of papyrus or parchment, discovered in the course of archaeological excavations at sites such as Oxyrhynchus or Herculaneum. But more often fragments are simply quotations from lost works, preserved in the writings of other ancient authors who may well have had access to the complete texts. Quotations of this sort are usually referred to as book-fragments: they tend to be more satisfying to read than papyrus fragments, because the source texts often quote complete phrases or passages, and they do not have the frustrating gaps (*lacunae*) that mar papyrus texts. However, quotations can give a distorted impression of the lost work in question, since the author who quotes the words typically has some other purpose than giving his readers a representative flavour of the whole work.

For example, one of our main sources of dramatic fragments is Athenaeus, the

---

[31] This strand in the textual tradition is represented by the fourteenth-century *codex Laurentianus*. Herington (1985) 130 makes the significant point that these 'alphabetic' plays are considerably more diverse in nature and content than the ten 'selected' plays.

second-century CE author of a compendious work called *Deipnosophistae* ('The Scholars at Dinner'). This book is essentially a patchwork of quotations linked by the theme of banquets and symposia, which means that most of the material preserved there is concerned with food, drink or entertainment in some way. Athenaeus is keen to display his encyclopedic knowledge of the literary tradition, but this knowledge characteristically takes the form of incidental details, *obiter dicta,* arcane information or quirky trivia.[32] Thus he offers no more than an oblique and partial reflection of the content and themes of the authors quoted.

Ancient anthologies of quotations are another hugely important source of fragments. A name that crops up regularly in the footnotes is John of Stobi (usually referred to by his Latinized name Stobaeus), the fifth-century CE compiler of an enormous anthology of quotations from classical authors, arranged thematically in four books.[33] Almost all the fragments preserved here take the form of ethical maxims (*gnômai*) relating to topics such as human nature and relationships, the vicissitudes of fortune, the gods' behaviour towards people, the problems of wealth and poverty, and so on. Such maxims almost invariably possess a proverbial or traditional quality, which makes it very difficult to detect any individual differences between specific tragedians' treatment of the themes in question, though it is striking that certain authors (such as Agathon and Chaeremon) are quoted much more often than average.[34] The anthologist provides virtually no linking material or commentary, which means that it is impossible to identify the speaker or dramatic context in most cases.

Aristotle quite often quotes and discusses tragedy, not just in his *Poetics* (our most important single source for the ancient critical reception of tragedy) but also in his *Rhetoric, Ethics, Topics* and other works. Aristotle is a particularly valuable source because, as a fourth-century writer, he is very close in time to most of the tragedians whom he discusses. His idiosyncratic philosophical and literary views mean that he cannot be treated as a guide to mainstream literary tastes in the period, and by his own admission the *Poetics* is more concerned with providing analytical guidelines for 'the best type of tragedy' than with describing the whole genre in all its variety. Nevertheless, more than most

---

[32] See Collard (1969) on Athenaeus' tragic quotations, and more generally Braund and Wilkins (2000) on Athenaeus in his literary context.

[33] See Dickey (2007) 105–6 and Reydams-Schils (2011) on Stobaeus and his work; cf. Gill (2005) on some of his ethical quotations from tragedy.

[34] See Chapter 3 (pp. 73–7) and Chapter 5 (pp. 123–7) for further discussion of these poets' work in relation to ancient quotation culture.

writers Aristotle conveys a substantial sense of the characters and plots of the plays that he discusses. It is also important to note that Aristotle, who was probably writing before (or perhaps in opposition to) the Lycurgan establishment of the triad, discusses fourth- and fifth-century tragedians, or so-called 'major' and 'minor' writers, side by side, without any apparent sense of differentiation or hierarchical distinction; and he treats tragedy as a universal literary form rather than a specifically Athenian phenomenon.[35]

I have already mentioned some of the problems of using ancient comedians as evidence for the quality or standing of the tragedians at whom they poke fun. But comedy is also a source of fragments, albeit a highly problematic source. Verses from the lost plays might be quoted, either *verbatim* or in an altered form, for the purposes of parody or humour. Often it is difficult to make sense of this material, with its distortions and exaggerations, or to decide what proportion of the comic text represents the actual words of the tragic poet in question.[36] This can pose a particular problem if (as in some cases) comedy is our *only* source of information about a lost author. But whatever the shortcomings of comedy as evidence, its big advantage is that it is the only truly contemporary witness to the lost plays and their immediate reception at Athens.

Many other ancient critics, historians, scholars, biographers, grammarians and lexicographers talk about tragedians and their work, or use tragedy as a source of illustrative material. One such source is the *Suda* (its title means 'Stronghold'), an anonymous Byzantine encylopedia dating from the tenth century CE but largely consisting of a compilation of much earlier material.[37] As we shall see in the chapters that follow, the *Suda* is sometimes demonstrably unreliable or inaccurate, but it is often our best available source of biographical details about the lost tragedians, the titles of their plays, and their production histories.

A good deal of useful information has been handed down in the ancient manuscript tradition apart from the texts of the surviving plays. Apart from plot-summaries (*hypotheses*), which often contain information about the circumstances of a play's production and the dramatic competition in which it first appeared, the manuscripts of many classical works include marginal

---

[35] Admittedly, Aristotle cites Euripides and Sophocles much more than anyone else, but he also cites and discusses Theodectes, Aeschylus, Agathon, Astydamas, Carcinus, Dicaeogenes, Chaeremon, Cleophon and others. See Heath (2009); cf. Karamanou (2010), Hanink (2014a) 192–3 and (2014b) 202.

[36] See Rau (1967), with particular reference to Aristophanes.

[37] See Dickey (2007) 90–1, Wilson (1983) 145–7.

comments (*scholia*). Such material reflects the agglomerated results of centuries of ancient literary scholarship, and is often impossible to pin down to a particular author or date, but it incorporates a great deal of contextual information as well as quotations and critical discussions of lost plays.[38]

A couple of other writers whose names are often mentioned in relation to lost plays are Hyginus, the Roman mythographer of the first century CE, who compiled a collection of mythical narratives entitled *Fabulae* ('Stories'), and Apollodorus, a writer of uncertain identification and date, who made a similar compilation known as the *Bibliothêkê* ('Library'). These sources offer straightforward accounts of mythological and genealogical material, including many myths that were the subjects of lost tragedies. Hyginus and Apollodorus seldom explicitly refer to their source material, but it is generally accepted that tragedy, owing to its popularity and cultural influence, will have influenced their presentation of the myths.[39] It has become standard practice to use these two mythological handbooks, with due caution, as a rough guide to the contents of lost plays, though they can suggest little more than the approximate outlines of the plots, and (as we shall see) the tragedians often departed from the best-known versions of myths in major or minor details.

Epigraphic evidence tells us a certain amount about specific dramatic competitions and festivals. Of particular value are three groups of inscriptions normally referred to as the '*Fasti*', the '*Didascaliae*' and the 'Victors' Lists': these are the remains of monumental records of performances and prize-winners at the City Dionysia and Lenaea festivals, and they obviously derive from the official records of the Athenian state. Even though they are incomplete and mutilated, these inscriptions contain much information that cannot be obtained from literary sources, and they can (presumably) be relied upon as factually accurate.[40]

Finally there is Greek vase-painting, which is probably the most controversial category of evidence. Many red-figure vases from the late fifth and fourth centuries depict mythical scenes in a way that seems closely comparable to dramatic versions of those myths. But scholars have disagreed about the exact nature of the relationship between art and text. Some have been happy to refer to the vase-paintings as 'illustrations of Greek drama', while others argue that

[38]   Dickey (2007) is an invaluable guide to finding, reading and understanding scholia and related material.
[39]   See Cameron (2004) 33–51, 93–104.
[40]   *IG* ii² 2318; *IG* ii² 2319–24; *SEG* xxvi 203; *IG* ii² 2325. All these inscriptions are freshly edited and annotated in the excellent modern edition of Millis and Olson (2012).

pictorial art is an autonomous field of activity that does not need to be understood in relation to – or as subordinate to – literature.[41] Oliver Taplin, whose book *Pots and Plays* is the most recent as well as the most judicious treatment of the material, refers to these two scholarly positions as the 'philodramatic' and the 'iconocentric' schools; he positions himself somewhere in between the two extremes, preferring to talk about a variable series of 'interactions' between tragedy and vase-painting. Every individual case, says Taplin, must be judged on its own terms, comparing painting and text with careful attention to pro- and contra-indications. It is argued that certain paintings are informed or made more powerful by knowledge of specific plays: 'they mean more, and have more interest and depth, for someone who knows the play in question'.[42]

I think Taplin is right to say that vases often reveal the influence of tragedy on the artistic and popular imagination, and in cases where the plays survive in full we can study these interactions in detail. But it is not really possible to use vases as evidence for the content of lost plays, because here there is no interaction to observe. We have no way of knowing which elements in a painting were suggested by a lost play or by some other source altogether, nor is there any way of identifying pro- and contra-indications. Taplin tentatively identifies a number of vases that may relate in some way to lost plays (including Chaeremon's *Achilles, Killer of Thersites*, Carcinus' *Medea* and Astydamas' *Hector*),[43] and these will be mentioned in later chapters. However, it may be that they are completely unrelated, and it is probably best not to base too much speculation on such shaky foundations.

'Reading' lost works

'Reading' fragmentary texts – the inverted commas are important – is in some ways an inherently different sort of activity from reading complete texts, but the exact nature of the activity has often proved hard to pin down. Fragmentologists have often resorted to suggestive metaphors or analogies, describing themselves (or rival scholars) as salvaging the flotsam from shipwrecks, or solving crosswords or jigsaw-puzzles, or interpreting dreams, or practising divination, or

---

[41] The two poles are exemplified by Trendall and Webster (1971) and Small (2003). Cf. Oakley (2009) for a recent survey of the scholarship.

[42] Taplin (2007), esp. 2–37 (quotation from p. 25).

[43] Taplin (2007) no. 91, 94, 101.

writing private poetry, or ghost-hunting, or solving crimes in the manner of
Sherlock Holmes.[44] I have suggested above that perusing fragments is rather like
standing among architectural ruins, and it could be said that the techniques
involved in approaching fragmentary texts are methodologically closer to
archaeology or ancient history than to literary criticism as normally practised.
Like the archaeologist, the fragmentologist has to find some way of constructing
a plausible narrative out of scanty and intractable source-material. In a sense, the
fragments and testimonia are not *texts* to be read so much as *evidence* to be
weighed and sifted.

What would be really desirable is a branch of literary theory specifically
designed with fragmentary literature in mind. In the absence of such a theory,[45]
and bearing in mind that there is no generally agreed approach to fragments
among classical scholars, I offer below a series of observations about what I
think it means to 'read' tragedies that no longer exist. Some of these are general
reflections, and others are more practical or methodological suggestions about
the use of evidence. These observations are not intended to represent anything
so ambitious as a theory, which is why I prefer to present them in the form of
disjointed fragments. They simply reflect the principles and working assumptions
that I have adopted in this book and elsewhere.

(i) It is important to distinguish carefully between fragments (the exact words
of the lost work) and testimonia (all other relevant sources that do not actually
quote *verbatim* from the lost work), and to assess the relative value of each type
of evidence in each individual case. We might think that fragments themselves
are always more revealing than other testimonia, but this is not true.

(ii) In the case of book-fragments, the context of citation is often as revealing
as the fragment cited. The internal evidence of the fragment itself has to be
weighed against the external evidence of the surrounding source text, and the
two separate works have to be read together *in dialogue* with one another. We
cannot assume that the source text provides a straightforward or neutral frame
in which to interpret the fragment.

(iii) It is necessary to practise a sort of micro-reading, in an attempt to push
the fragments to their limits and squeeze out every drop of meaning and nuance.

---

[44] E.g. Meursius (1619) 1, Scaliger (1629) 9, Nauck (1856) viii, Schenkl (1863) 490–1, Page (1942) viii,
Bardel (2005) 83, Sommerstein (2010). The metaphorical and often emotional character of much
scholarly writing on the subject is highlighted by Kassel (1991) and Harvey (2005).

[45] See, however, Barthes (1975) 92–5 and 1977, and Bayard (2007), for a series of highly suggestive
remarks on the 'fragmentary' nature of the reading/writing process. Cf. Tronzo (2009) on the
aesthetics of the fragment, viewed from a number of theoretical and contextual perspectives.

Inevitably we end up reading fragments more attentively than other types of text, and we spend proportionally more time on each individual word and detail. (Individual readers will differ as to whether this is a good or bad thing.)

(iv) We should establish an explicit context or framework in which to place the fragments and make sense of them. One way of doing this is to attempt to make the maximum possible number of connections, comparisons and analogies with other literary works, either surviving or lost. Most of Greek literature is lost, which is a dismal state of affairs to contemplate; but this places us in an extraordinary position, because it means that it is easily possible to read *everything* that survives from the genre or period in which we are interested.

(v) At the same time, it needs to be acknowledged that connections and parallels, while suggestive and often illuminating, do not conclusively prove anything.

(vi) It is natural to interpret the lost tragedies in the light of the surviving tragedies, but there is no reason to privilege extant works or to assume that they represent the generic norm.

(vii) Every reading can also be seen as an act of writing; and the fragment as a literary form represents what Roland Barthes would have called the 'writable' (*scriptible*) text *par excellence*.[46] This will no doubt strike many readers as a controversial assertion, but whether or not we choose to adopt a theoretical perspective, and whatever our own individual approach to fragments may be, there is no escaping the fact that the 'reader' of fragments is also, in a very real sense, the author. This fact needs to be explicitly acknowledged and built into the argument, because it is inevitable that our discussion (or interpretation, or 'reconstruction') of the fragments will involve an element of creativity and imagination. Since (as I have already observed) an interest in lost works tends to go hand in hand with nostalgic fantasies of one kind or another, a measure of self-awareness is salutary. Even the most sober and restrained scholars are going to be using this material, essentially, to tell the stories that they want to tell, and so it is as well to clear the air by frankly admitting this.

(viii) Given that fragmentology entails an element of creative fiction (which is not a dirty word), we should nevertheless try to avoid getting carried away into the realm of complete fantasy. In other words, we should try to keep our discussions free from 'the absurd speculations that have damaged so many

---

[46] See Barthes (1970) for the distinction between *lisible* and *scriptible*.
[47] Wilkins (1991) 18 (to take an example at random; in fact the scholarly literature is full of strictures of this sort).

studies of the fragments'.[47] This does not mean that we should never indulge in speculation or hypothesis at all. It means that we should always proceed with caution, asking ourselves questions such as: What _might_ this mean? How _might_ the evidence fit together? What difference would it make if it were _not_ so? What is at stake? It is the precise _combination_ between imagination and caution that is crucial.

(ix) Wherever possible, we should try to come up with alternative or multiple interpretations of the fragments. The words 'perhaps', 'possibly' and 'probably', together with the subjunctive mood, will make frequent appearances. It is up to us how much credulity or scepticism to adopt with regard to the evidence, but we should avoid dogmatism or dogged adherence to any one particular interpretation, for the nature of the material is such that our conclusions can only ever be tentative or provisional. Rather, we need to be exploratory and open-minded to different possibilities.

(x) Above all, we should aim to be scrupulously accurate when presenting the evidence, and to be open and explicit about what we are trying to do with it. In this way, whatever the shortcomings of our own discussions, it will be easier for other readers to see what is going on and weigh up the evidence for themselves.

Note on the plan and structure of this volume

I have divided the material into six main chapters, adopting a broadly chronological approach in order to give some sense of how the tragic genre developed over time. Within each chapter the material is arranged on an author-by-author basis, partly because this seemed the least confusing way to present the remains, and partly because I assume that many readers will be consulting this book in search of information about specific individual poets. (Volume 2 will adopt a more thematic approach to the plays of Aeschylus, Sophocles and Euripides.)

Chapter 1 examines the early origins of tragedy and the work of the first attested tragic playwrights (Thespis, Choerilus, Pratinas and Phrynichus). Chapter 2 discusses some of the better-attested tragedians of the fifth century, including Ion, Achaeus, Critias and others. Chapter 3 is entirely devoted to Agathon, perhaps the most fascinating and original of all the lost tragedians, or (at any rate) the one about whom most can be said. In Chapter 4 I examine the surprisingly large number of tragedians who were members of the same families, and I speculate on the significance of these family connections when it comes to interpreting their plays. Chapter 5 deals with a selection of fourth-century tragedians (including Chaeremon, Theodectes, Dionysius, Diogenes and numerous other neglected figures), and it also discusses the ways in which continuities or discontinuities might be traced between the fifth and fourth centuries. Chapter 6 explores what can be said about 'the very lost', those unfortunate playwrights of whom not a single word survives. Finally a brief 'Epilogue' draws together some of the points that emerge from the discussions in this volume; a more considered and extensive set of conclusions will follow in Volume 2. A number of Appendices contain translations and other useful information (see next section).

Note on conventions and abbreviations

This book is designed to be as reader-friendly as possible, in contrast to most other works on the same topic, which, for all their merits, sometimes strike me as reader-*unfriendly* in the extreme. Even as an experienced fragmentologist I have often found myself staring at the pages in specialist publications, with their dense and complex apparatus of annotations and unusual conventions of presentation, and thinking: 'What *is* this stuff in front of me? How do I make sense of it?' Assuming that many of my readers may well have experienced the same difficulties, I have attempted in the pages that follow to compensate for the unfamiliarity of the material and to reduce bafflement as much as possible.

My aim has been to write in a lucid and readable style, in spite of the diffuse, itty-bitty nature of the material under discussion. In order to eliminate clutter, I have placed all sources and references in the footnotes rather than the main text, because they tend to be too long and complex to fit happily in parentheses. Many of the ancient works cited or discussed are relatively abstruse: for this reason my footnotes always refer to authors and titles in full, rather than by abbreviations that might mystify the average reader or slow down the reading process.

In the interests of absolute clarity, when quoting fragments and testimonia I always supply references in the same format: the relevant volume of the standard modern edition (*Tragicorum Graecorum Fragmenta*) is followed by the number assigned by the editor to the tragedian in question, followed by the number assigned to the fragment (F) or testimonium (T). Thus (for example) '*TrGF* 1.39

F1' denotes the first fragment of the thirty-ninth author (Agathon) in the first volume.

I have made liberal use of quotations from the various sources, because I believe that most readers will appreciate having all the relevant material collected and presented together in a single place. All these texts are quoted in (my own) English translations, because this is primarily a work of literary history rather than a linguistic or stylistic study. I have kept use of Greek to the absolute minimum, quoting in the original language only where the argument seemed to demand it.

This book makes all the fragments of these neglected tragedians available in English for the first time. As elsewhere, all translations are my own except where otherwise attributed. In the case of most authors, the remains are so scarce that it has been possible to insert these translated fragments into the text or footnotes of each chapter alongside the critical discussion. But in the interests of convenience and comprehensiveness, a complete collection of translated fragments is provided in Appendix 1 (where I also touch upon some of the problems inherent in translating fragments).

The list below explains a number of abbreviations – mostly referring to standard critical editions of fragments and inscriptions – which are used repeatedly in this book and elsewhere. However, the non-specialist reader will also find further guidance and basic orientation in Appendix 2 (Glossary), Appendix 3 (Chronology) and Appendix 4 (Guide to further reading and resources).

adesp.	*adespota* (texts that cannot be assigned to a particular author)
Davies	M. Davies (ed.), *Epicorum Graecorum Fragmenta* (Göttingen, 1988)
D-G	J. Dillon and T. Gergel (ed./tr.), *The Greek Sophists* (London, 2003)
D-K	H. Diels and W. Kranz (eds.), *Die Fragmente der Vorsokratiker*[6] (Berlin, 1951–2)
F	fragment (i.e. either a *verbatim* quotation from a lost text in the work of another ancient author or a portion of an ancient papyrus manuscript)
FGrHist	F. Jacoby et al. (eds.), *Die Fragmente der griechischen Historiker* (1923–)
IG	*Inscriptiones Graecae* (1873–)
K-A	R. Kassel and C. Austin (eds.), *Poetae Comici Graeci* (Berlin and New York, 1983–)

Pack	R. Pack (ed.), *The Greek and Latin Literary Texts from Greco-Roman Egypt*² (Ann Arbor, 1965)
P.Hib.	B. Grenfell, A. Hunt et al. (eds.), *The Hibeh Papyri* (London, 1906–55)
P.Oxy.	B. Grenfell, A. Hunt et al. (eds.), *The Oxyrhynchus Papyri* (London, 1898–)
PMG	D.L. Page (ed.), *Poetae Melici Graeci* (Oxford, 1962)
Rhet.Gr.	E.C. Walz (ed.), *Rhetores Graeci* (Tübingen, 1832–6)
SEG	*Supplementum Epigraphicum Graecum* (1923–)
T	testimonium (i.e. an ancient citation or discussion of a lost text that does not quote that text *verbatim*)
TrGF	R. Kannicht, B. Snell and S. Radt (eds.), *Tragicorum Graecorum Fragmenta* (Göttingen, 1971–2004)
Σ	an anonymous marginal comment (*scholion*) transmitted in an ancient manuscript

1

The Earliest Tragedies

Our earliest surviving tragedy, Aeschylus' *Persians*, was first performed in 472 BCE. Everything before that date is lost, but there has been considerable scholarly interest in what might be called the prehistory of the genre – including the very first playwrights, the content and character of those early tragedies that are recorded, and also the historical process by which tragedy as we know it came into being. In this chapter I give a very brief outline of what little is known about tragedy before 472.[1]

In all of what follows the central fact to be emphasized, even more than usual, is that our evidence is extremely poor. Several scholars have constructed ambitious theories about the early origins of tragedy, its relationship to Athenian politics or religious ritual, or its essential meaning and purpose. Many of these theories are ingenious, and often perfectly plausible, but they are essentially products of imaginative guesswork or fantasy. The truth is that we know almost nothing about these matters. Even those few authors within antiquity who wrote about the prehistory of the genre seem to have relied on guesswork as much as definite knowledge, and their accounts are extremely sketchy. Therefore it is advisable to keep an open mind when thinking about this material or the questions which it raises.

It is up to us whether to accept the evidence at its face value or to adopt a more cautious or mistrustful attitude. But perhaps the most important questions that we can ask are these: what does the evidence mean? How and why did it come to be written? What uses can be made of it, even if much of it is suspected to contain little or no factual truth? How far can we go in

---

[1] This is a deliberately cursory treatment of a topic that has attracted a good deal of attention: I do not attempt to convey more than the bare outlines. For further discussion of the subject, from a variety of very different viewpoints, see Burkert (1966), Else (1965), Leonhardt (1991), Lesky (1983), Patzer (1962), Pickard-Cambridge (1927) and (1962), Scullion (2002b), Seaford (1994), and the various contributors to Csapo and Miller (2007). I do not discuss the early twentieth-century 'ritualists' – e.g. Harrison, Cornford, Murray – whose work is refuted at length by Pickard-Cambridge (1927), because I regard their theories as pure fantasy.

interpreting the evidence, and how much scope should we allow to our imagination? Each reader will have his or her own answers to these questions. The discussion that follows is deliberately intended to provide an open-ended, exploratory introduction to the material, accompanied by a healthy dose of scepticism.

Submerged literature and the origins of tragedy

The search for *origins* – in literature, in science, in religion, or in any other area of life – is the sort of exercise that, inevitably, excites some people more than others. It is probably true to say that the subject of the origins of tragedy has occupied a disproportionate amount of scholars' attention, despite – or perhaps precisely because of – the lack of available evidence. There are several possible reasons why this topic has been so popular among ancient and modern scholars alike. Aside from the basic antiquarian instinct to discover and catalogue everything, one important consequence of the search for origins is that the results might seem to help us to understand the plays that survive from later on. If, for instance, tragedy originated in Dionysiac ritual, this might help to explain why it continued to be produced at festivals of Dionysus, or why it should be thought to have anything to do with Dionysus at all, despite the fact that Dionysiac themes or plots are not especially prominent in the plays known to us.[2] If tragedy, comedy, dithyramb and satyr-play all had their origins in a single source, this might help to explain certain similarities between these genres. If we want to understand how tragedy acquired the unusual set of formal features that it ended up with – its mixture of sung and spoken portions, its masks and costumes, the fact that it was performed by a company of three actors, a chorus and a coryphaeus, and so on – it may be that the answer lies in its origins. Or if we believe that the *essence* of a genre is to be found in its origins, this may help us to discover a play's underlying meaning, symbolism or purpose. Many readers, indeed, have been attracted by the idea that the meaning of individual plays depends on a sort of underlying generic master-narrative.

Whatever one's individual point of view on these matters, at the very outset it is vital to acknowledge that the task of trying to imagine or reconstruct these

---

[2] Dionysus is seen as absolutely central to (fully developed) tragedy by many scholars: see especially Bierl (1991) and Seaford (1981) and (1994); but cf. the counter-blast of Scullion (2002b).

pre-472 tragedies is a significantly different sort of task from (let us say) trying to reconstruct the lost plays of Euripides. Even though all these works can be lumped together as 'the lost plays of Greek tragedy', it is also accurate to say that some of these lost plays are *more lost* than others. I am not talking simply about the quantity of the remains, though it is quite true that many more lines survive from Euripides than from Thespis or Choerilus. What I mean is that the nature of the remains is different, and that the conditions of reception, preservation and transmission were fundamentally different in each case. The works of Euripides and other later fifth-century writers were preserved and commemorated, and official records of their performance were kept by the state; they remained well known for many years after their original performance; they were frequently reperformed; they were much talked about and quoted; they circulated widely as written texts; it was only much later on in history that they became lost, for reasons which are not altogether explicable. By contrast, however, the works of Thespis and some of the other earliest tragedians seem to have become lost almost immediately after their first performance. Even within the classical period – and certainly by the fourth century, when scholars such as Aristotle were first attempting to write comprehensive accounts of the genre – these early plays had *already* acquired the status of lost works.

In this case it is worth making a distinction between *lost* works and *submerged* works. The useful concept of 'submerged literature' (*la letteratura sommersa*) was formulated about twenty years ago by Luigi Enrico Rossi in relation to the performance culture of archaic Greece, and has more recently sparked off a series of lively discussions among Italian scholars of Greek cultural history.[3] 'Submerged' literature, as defined by Rossi, consists of:

> texts which were maltreated right from the very beginning of their transmission, or even texts which did not have any transmission at all. These texts did not have the benefit of any control or protection, perhaps because no community had any interest in preserving them, or perhaps because it was in the community's interest that they be concealed or suppressed: this last category is represented by literature that had to do with mystery-cult. But many of these texts – which from our point of view seem to be playing a game of hide-and-seek with us – have been enormously important in shaping the different stages of Greek culture as we know it; and clearly there would be a great deal to gain if we could seek

---

[3] Rossi (2000); cf. the recent collection edited by Colesanti and Giordano (2014), especially the contribution of Ercolani (2014) on questions of definition (see p. 17 for Ercolani's distinction between 'lost' and 'submerged' categories, which I adopt here).

to bring them back to light, even if, inevitably, such an attempt would be only partial.[4]

This definition seems to fit the earliest tragedies extremely well. The plays of Thespis, and other early practitioners whose names are not even preserved in the tradition, were apparently lost almost at the point of origin rather than at some much later date. The plays of Choerilus and Pratinas are perhaps less 'submerged' but almost as obscure. Little if any effort seems to have been made to write these plays down or preserve them in textual form; and indeed we are dealing with a period in which orality and performance culture were only slowly evolving into a world of literacy and book-reading.[5] Perhaps some of these performances were improvised or semi-improvised in any case (as Aristotle surmises),[6] which would naturally preclude the existence of any reliable text. Furthermore, if any records were kept of the details of these artists' performances, festivals or victories, they did not survive for long, since they do not seem to have been available to later writers.

In other words, then, it is practically impossible for modern scholars to produce a reliable account of the origins of tragedy – not only because this is, by its nature, the sort of subject for which there could never be any good evidence, but also because the ancient Greeks themselves had almost as little evidence as we do. These very early plays were nearly as remote to Aristotle as they are to us today.

Aristotle remains our earliest and best source, but to say this is (alas) to make no great claims for his evidence. What he says about the origins of tragedy is confined to a short section in Chapter 4 of his *Poetics*[7]:

> Coming into being from an improvisatory beginning – I mean both tragedy, which came about from the leaders of the dithyramb, and comedy, which came about from the leaders of the phallic songs, which even today are still customarily

---

4   Rossi (2000) 170: 'Con letteratura "sommersa" io intendo testo maltrattati fin dal primissimo inizio della trasmissione, o anche testi che non hanno avuto alcuna trasmissione affatto. Questi testi non hanno goduto di alcun controllo e di alcuna protezione sia perché le varie comunità non avevano alcun interesse a conservarli sia perché avevano, piuttosto, interesse a nasconderli o addirittura a sopprimerli: quest' ultima categoria è rappresentata da quanto era legato ai misteri. Ma molti di questo testi, che dal nostro punto di osservazione giocano a nascondino, hanno avuto grande importanza nel configurare i vari momenti della cultura greca così come ci si presentano, ed è ovviamente nostro interesse cercare di rimetterli in luce, sia pure di necessità parzialmente.'
5   See Wise (1998) for the interesting view that literacy (rather than, e.g., ritual) was the main catalyst for the invention of tragedy.
6   Aristotle, *Poetics* 1449a9–10 (see the first passage quoted below).
7   Aristotle, *Poetics* 1449a–b (with irrelevant passages omitted).

performed in many cities – it was gradually augmented, little by little, as the poets developed each successive stage that became visible. And after it had undergone many changes, tragedy stopped developing, since it now had its own nature. It was Aeschylus who first increased the number of actors from one to two, and decreased the amount of choral contributions, and gave the main role to spoken dialogue. Sophocles increased the number of actors to three and invented scene-painting. And then the size and scale of plays increased: because it changed from being satyric, its simple plots and ridiculous diction became serious only late in the process, and also its metre changed from trochaic tetrameter to iambic trimeter. At first they used the tetrameter because the poetry was satyric and rather dance-like, but when speech came in, nature found the appropriate metre; for the iambic is the metre most suited to normal speech.

And also the number of scenes [changed]; but as for how all these other elements are said to have been embellished, let us take the details as read – for it would probably be a big undertaking to go through them all one by one.

The changes that tragedy underwent and the identity of those responsible have not been forgotten, but comedy, on the other hand, was not taken very seriously at first, and the facts are not known.

One could argue – and scholars certainly have argued, at considerable length – about the exact interpretation and significance of this evidence, its value in terms of factual information, and the nature of the sources (if any) on which it was based.[8] There are certainly some serious difficulties and obscurities in the account, the most important of which is the fact that Aristotle seems to say that tragedy originated both in dithyrambic poetry *and* in satyric poetry. Some scholars have dealt with this apparent contradiction by assuming that there was a certain overlap between these two forms of poetry, both of which had Dionysiac connections, or by assuming that when Aristotle talks about 'the satyric' (*to saturikon*) he is not literally referring to satyr-play as it was known in the later classical period, but to a primitive sort of performance that *resembled* later satyr-play in some way.[9] This does not entirely remove the confusion; but in general it seems that Aristotle is imagining a sort of archaic 'proto-tragedy' which was simpler and cruder than classical tragedy and which shared some elements (somehow) with other broadly similar types of performance. As one recent scholar sums it up, on the basis of Aristotle 'it can be argued that all four of the theatrical genres of the City Dionysia at Athens in the classical period – that

---

[8]   See n. 1 above; on the details of the *Poetics* passage in particular cf. Lucas (1968) *ad loc.*
[9]   Seaford (1994) 268; cf. Depew (2007) 128–9.

is, tragedy, comedy, dithyramb, and satyr-drama – resulted from progressive differentiations of earlier and less differentiated forms of choral performances'.[10]

A further problem is that even if we accept Aristotle's teleological account of the tragic genre, he does not say that tragedy has any intrinsic connection with Dionysiac themes. In fact, he explicitly denies this, saying that the earliest poets chose 'any old myths' to adapt for the stage, in contrast with later tragedians who concentrated on a narrower range of myths involving conflicts within a few families.[11] If we believe that Aristotle had genuine knowledge of the earliest plays, this piece of information is hugely significant. Even if we take the view that Aristotle was inventing and hypothesizing on the basis of thin air, he obviously does not *believe* that early tragedy had anything to do with Dionysus, at least on the level of plot or theme; and this in itself is very significant.

Aristotle's explanation of how tragedy emerged progressively from earlier prototypes in ritual or choral performance has been very influential; but is it correct? Many scholars have accepted it as such, but it seems obvious that even if the bare bones of this account are broadly accurate, it is characterized on the whole by a fundamental vagueness and lack of detail. It is notable that Aristotle does not even mention the names of Thespis, Choerilus or any other pioneers of proto-tragedy, nor does he mention any specific features of their work; nor, indeed, does he mention religious ritual, Athenian politics or any of the other factors which scholars have from time to time regarded as inherent in the origins or essence of the genre. It has sometimes been thought that Aristotle's silence on all these matters reflects the fact that he treated these matters at greater length, and in more detail, in his other (now lost) works, such as *Performance Records* (*Didaskaliai*) or *On Poets*, but there is no basis for such a suggestion. The manner in which Aristotle discusses early tragedy and proto-tragedy in the *Poetics* strongly suggests that his vagueness is due not to reticence but to lack of knowledge.[12]

Aristotle's account gives the impression of having been formed by a logical process of deduction rather than observation of any evidence.[13] What he explicitly admits to describing in the passage above is a process of evolution. His

---

[10] Nagy (2007) 122; cf. Depew (2007), esp. 131 and fig. 42, for an Aristotelian 'genealogy of poetic genres'. Both Nagy and Depew accept the factual content of Aristotle as reliable (and cite a range of other like-minded scholars).

[11] Aristotle, *Poetics* 13.1453a17–22 ('any old myths' is *tous tuchontas muthous*).

[12] In this view, and in many other respects, I have been influenced by the hyper-sceptical account of Scullion (2002b); cf. Scullion (2005) for a summary of his earlier discussion and a critique of other (more traditional or literal) approaches to Aristotle.

[13] This was seen very clearly by Else (1957) 126.

repeated references to nature make it quite clear that he is talking about an exact analogy or equivalence between cultural and natural processes – which makes his approach seem rather like a bizarre precursor of literary Darwinism. His account is based on the assumption that in literature and drama, as in all other areas of life, simple forms develop into more complex forms according to a progressive linear process of development and the gradual accretion of more and more elements. A similar assumption has been shown to underpin several of Aristotle's other works on different topics.[14]

In other words, what Aristotle seems to have done in the *Poetics* is to apply *a posteriori* reasoning to the problem, based on observation of the features of the 'final' or 'perfect' form of tragedy that he knew. He could see that fully developed classical tragedy had three actors, a chorus and a separate chorus-leader, a mixture of spoken dialogue, singing and dancing, masks, scenery, and so on; and so he could work backwards from this basis to deduce what each earlier stage in the process might have looked like. On the assumption that through the passage of time everything becomes progressively more complex (i.e. 'embellished'),[15] he was able to conclude that each immediately preceding form must have been less and less complex. Thus the stage before fully-developed tragedy must have had only two actors; and the form before that must have had a single actor (perhaps identified with the chorus leader or *exarchôn*, unless this is seen as a yet earlier stage); and the form before that must have been a primitive sort of song-and-dance performance without spoken dialogue – and so on.

Apart from Aristotle, our main source is the Byzantine encyclopaedia known as the *Suda*, a miscellaneous and not entirely trustworthy collection of facts, inventions, anecdotes and other material, much of it dating back many centuries without being directly attributable to any particular source. The information contained in the *Suda*'s entries for Thespis, Choerilus, Pratinas and Phrynichus has for many years been taken at its word – no doubt owing to the depressing reason that if we reject it we are left with almost no hard facts at all. However, quite recently it has been pointed out, in an important article by Martin West, that the 'facts' provided by the *Suda* are suspiciously neat and schematic.[16] In fact,

---

[14] E.g. *Athenian Constitution* 3.3.11, *Politics* 1274a9–11: see Scullion (2002a) 106, who also compares Diogenes Laertius 3.56 for a more pronounced version of the same schematic outlook on history and culture. Cf. Dale (1967) for the analogies between Aristotle's approach to literature and his approach to natural and scientific phenomena.

[15] Cf. *Poetics* 1449a29 (quoted above, p. 5).

[16] West (1989). Scullion (2002a) goes even further than West, dismissing most of the literary evidence and mistrusting even some of the epigraphic evidence.

rather like Aristotle's theory of the origins of tragedy, they seem to have been invented to fit a pre-determined pattern. In the first place, as West observes, there was no reliable epigraphic or archival evidence for the period before the fifth century, and the writer of the *Suda* (or his source) seems to have come up with dates for the first productions of all the tragedians before Aeschylus on the basis of calculating several 'generations' of poets, each separated by an identical period of three Olympiads (i.e. twelve years).[17] This means that we can no longer be quite confident about the traditional dates for any of the earliest tragedians, and it also makes us doubt whether anyone in antiquity had access to any sort of reliable written or epigraphic evidence for drama prior to 499 BCE or thereabouts.

It is not just the chronology that is suspicious, but also the list of supposed inventions or innovations attributed to Thespis and the others by the *Suda* and Aristotle. As we shall see in the sections that follow, each of the early tragedians in turn is said to have 'invented' one or more of the key features that defined fully developed classical tragedy: the use of masks, the separation of chorus from speaking parts, the addition of extra actors one-by-one, and so on. Perhaps there are one or two grains of truth buried somewhere in all of this, but on the whole it does look rather like 'schematic pseudo-history' (as Scott Scullion puts it, in a valuable recent discussion).[18]

Because we are dealing here with literature at different levels of 'submersion', we will never get very close to the truth about the origins of tragedy. But it is probably better to abandon any straightforwardly teleological or evolutionary narratives. As a cautionary tale, let us consider just one example of the dangers of imposing schematic patterns upon the evidence. It used to be more or less universally accepted that Aeschylus' *Suppliant Women* was the most 'primitive', and therefore earliest, surviving example of tragedy. This was because it does not require three actors (and in fact, only a couple of short sections even require the presence of a second actor), it treats the chorus almost as the central character, and it contains a higher proportion of choral song than any other play, combined with relatively little spoken dialogue or action. In other words,

---

[17] West (1989) 251: 'This looks very much like a schematic construction designed to place the three known seniors of Aeschylus and Pratinas in their right order at suitable intervals'.

[18] Scullion (2002b) 105. Scullion also rejects the notion that an individual playwright could have been responsible for an innovation such as the addition of an actor, because (he says) such changes would have been made by the state, not by individuals. But this does not seem a very persuasive objection, especially given that we know so little about the competition rules and regulations, or about the role of the state in determining the form and content of drama.

it looks like the sort of production that Aristotle might have placed at an intermediate stage in the evolution of the genre. Consequently, a very early date was ascribed to that play, and most scholars tended to place it right at the beginning of the fifth century. But in 1952 papyrus evidence came to light which showed that *Suppliant Women* was actually one of its author's later works, produced *c.* 463.[19] Now one could respond to this fact, perhaps, by saying that Aeschylus towards the end of his career decided to write a deliberately 'archaizing' sort of tragedy, but this would be an odd way of twisting the evidence. A more obvious response would be to say that dramatic forms do not really evolve in the neat, linear way that Aristotle and others describe, and that literary history is a much messier and unsystematic affair that cannot be reduced to banal schemata.[20]

Furthermore, there are other odd bits of evidence that do not fit the pattern – such as Herodotus' discussion of what he calls 'tragic choruses' in sixth-century Sicyon, or indeed Aristotle's own statement, earlier in the *Poetics,* that the Dorians claim to have invented tragedy.[21] This raises further (unanswerable) questions about how distinctive or unique Athenian tragedy was, and how it may have related to other dramatic traditions elsewhere in the Greek world. But once again there is almost no evidence to go on, and we can only conclude that there was probably *some sort of* similarity between what went on in other cities and what went on at Athens. But this is very far from being able to trace a specific relationship, or any sort of developmental link, between the different traditions. Yet another question worth asking is why forms such as dithyramb or satyr-play should have a privileged place in literary genealogies, given that tragedy has so many demonstrable connections and continuities with other genres – including, above all, epic (which Aristotle himself treats as an important *comparandum*) and the archaic lyric tradition more generally.[22]

What I have provided in this section is, admittedly, a highly reductive and simplified account of some very complicated problems. As I have said, the reader

---

[19] *P. Oxy.* 2256 fr. 3.

[20] Cf. Lloyd-Jones (1964), esp. 373: 'the danger involved in the attempt to confine within the straitjacket of Platonic or Aristotelian idealism the untidy, wasteful, infinite pullulation of the forms of life is particularly well illustrated by the result of treating Aeschylean tragedy as a mere imperfect stage on the way to Sophoclean perfection'. Cf. Garvie (1969) on the issues surrounding *Suppliant Women* and its reception.

[21] Herodotus 5.67: see Pickard-Cambridge (1962) 102–5; cf. Aristotle, *Poetics* 3.1448a29–30.

[22] Herington (1985) is an excellent treatment of the ways in which tragedy relates to the pre-existing poetic tradition in general.

is invited to make up his or her own mind on such matters.[23] The main point to be stressed is that a lot of theories have been built on very little foundation. I myself am happy to keep an open mind on such questions because I do not really believe that tragedy's 'essence' is to be found in its origins.

What is by far the most revealing feature of these fragments and testimonia (I suggest) is that they show that the *idea* of lost works was already starting to exert a considerable imaginative appeal on certain literary-minded people, even within the classical period. During the fifth century BCE, it already seems that no one could remember very much, if anything, about the origins of the genre or its first practitioners. At this period there was little interest in trying to commemorate or preserve the early plays or to keep an accurate record (though we might also give serious consideration to Scott Scullion's suggestion that the earliest official records and archives were destroyed in 479 BCE, when Athens was ransacked and burnt by the invading Persians).[24] By the fourth century, however, enthusiasts of tragedy were attempting to retrieve or recreate what was already tantalizingly out of reach. Some, such as Heraclides of Pontus, were recreating specific lost works (see below, pp. 11–12); others were making up biographical anecdotes; others, such as Aristotle and other literary historians, were trying to write (or rewrite, or invent) the whole early history of tragedy. What is so fascinating is not what these writers say about their 'submerged' subject-matter, but *how* they go about approaching it – the methods that they apply, the assumptions that they bring to their study of the past, and the transformation of their lost literary heritage into the realm of the imagination.

Thespis

This murky and distant figure was supposedly the 'inventor' of tragedy – that is, presumably, the first author of *tragôidia* in a form that would have been recognizable as such to later Greeks.[25] Nevertheless, he has left behind few traces,

---

[23] A useful way of proceeding, from the beginner's perspective, would be to compare and contrast the very different accounts of Scullion (2002b) and the various contributors to Csapo and Miller (2007). One might also look (very carefully) at T.B.L. Webster's revision (1962) of Pickard-Cambridge's (1927) book, which does not quite reconcile the two authors' viewpoints (and thus provides a somewhat 'schizophrenic' treatment of the topic).

[24] Scullion (2002a) 82.

[25] *TrGF* 1.1 T9–14. Other, earlier names are occasionally recorded (such as Epigenes, Arion, etc.), but these are probably best seen as writers of 'proto-tragedy' (see the discussion above, pp. 4–5): *TrGF* 1.1 T1 (*Suda*); cf. Lesky (1983) 27, Pickard-Cambridge (1962) 85–9.

and indeed, as Arthur Pickard-Cambridge pointed out in his careful survey of the evidence, almost every single point in the testimonia is subject to doubt or controversy.[26] Even the name Thespis, which in Greek means 'inspired' or 'prophetic', has been thought to be fictional.[27] It may be that Thespis – rather like Homer – is to be seen as a legendary or semi-legendary figure, whose name functioned, in effect, as a shorthand way of denoting a long and complicated stage in the early development of drama.[28] However, whereas Homer (or 'Homer') is a person of great antiquity and disputed date, Thespis is a much more recent figure, whose dates seem to be quite precisely recorded. The *Suda* informs us that his first victory, coinciding with the first official production of tragedy at the City Dionysia, occurred *c.* 534 BCE.[29] This information, *if* accepted at face value, would make Thespis appear more real and pin him down to a particular time and place. Unfortunately, as I have said, on closer examination the information turns out to be (almost certainly) bogus.

Other supposedly factual details about Thespis are provided by various sources: he is said to have belonged to the Athenian deme of Icaria; he apparently acted in his own plays; he was supposedly the first playwright to adopt masks, following earlier experiments with face-paint or make-up; he is said to have initiated the use of a speaking actor, separate from the chorus, and to have introduced prologues and monologues into what was previously a mixture of singing and dancing; and the titles of some of his plays are recorded (*Games of Pelias*, also known as *Phorbas; Priests; Young Men; Pentheus*).[30] None of these details can be trusted. They are found only in very late sources whose value has often been disputed, and many of them are clearly the product of the sort of 'schematic pseudo-history' discussed in the last section. There also exist a few biographical anecdotes of even more dubious historicity.[31]

On this basis it seems reasonable to conclude that within antiquity almost nothing was known for certain about Thespis. Furthermore, it is clear that, as early as the fourth century BCE, some or all of the plays that were in circulation as 'the works of Thespis' were forgeries attributed to Heraclides of Pontus (the literary scholar whose *Compendium of Famous Poets and Musicians* is seen as

---

[26] Pickard-Cambridge (1962) 72: this was written *before* the crucial observations of West (1989).

[27] The word *thespis* is found in association with poets or poetry in Homer (*Odyssey* 8.498, 17.385; cf. *Homeric Hymn to Hermes* 442): see Lesky (1983) 25.

[28] Aristophanes, for example, treats Thespis, like Kronos, as a byword for antiquity: see *Wasps* 1476–81 (= *TrGF* 1.1 T5).

[29] *Suda* Θ 282 (*TrGF* 1.1 T1).

[30] *TrGF* 1.1 T1, T6–7.

[31] *TrGF* 1.1 T11–18, T22; see Pickard-Cambridge (1962) 72–4.

having 'filled out literary history with crowds of legendary and semi-legendary poets and singers').[32] Consequently, the few fragments traditionally attributed to Thespis are all considered spurious.[33]

Choerilus

The evidence – *if* we accept it as accurate – might suggest that this early tragedian enjoyed an unusually long life and career. Choerilus' first production in an Athenian festival is dated by the *Suda* to the sixty-fourth Olympiad (*c.* 523–520 BCE),[34] but according to the ancient *Life of Sophocles* he also competed against Sophocles, at some point after 469; in between these dates (*c.* 499–496) there is also evidence for a festival in which Choerilus exhibited plays alongside Pratinas and Aeschylus.[35] These details, like much in the *Suda*, cannot be accepted with any confidence, but it is nonetheless possible that Choerilus had a career lasting fifty-four years or more. The surprisingly large number of plays (one hundred and sixty) and first prizes (thirteen) attributed to Choerilus in the *Suda* also seems to suggest a long period of creative activity, even if the exact numbers are open to doubt. In this case, it would be natural to suppose that the nature and style of Choerilus' plays must have undergone considerable change and development during this time, for the sort of performance that won prizes in the sixth century would (surely) have seemed unacceptably old-fashioned to audiences in the 460s.

However, all too predictably, there is little evidence to suggest what Choerilus' work was like. The *Suda* goes on to say that Choerilus used masks and costumes in a novel way (without giving any details), and one ancient writer on poetic metre adds the information that Choerilus had a metrical unit or foot named after him (but this evidence is somewhat hard to interpret).[36] It may be that Choerilus' use of language and poetic imagery was judged obscure by some

---

[32] Diogenes Laertius 5.92, quoting Aristoxenus F114 Wehrli (= *TrGF* 1.1 T24), says that Heraclides of Pontus wrote tragedies which he passed off as the work of Thespis. Cf. West (1989) 252 on Heraclides' *Synagôgê tôn en mousikê eudokimêsantôn* (F157–9 Werhli).

[33] See Snell, *TrGF* 1, pp. 65–6, following the practice of earlier editors; cf. Lloyd-Jones (1966) 11–13 for further discussion of the (in-)authenticity of the fragments (with a focus on language and content).

[34] *Suda* X 594 (*TrGF* 1.2 T1).

[35] *TrGF* 1.2 T5 (*Life of Sophocles* 19; cf. T7), T2 (*Suda* Π 2230). Lesky (1983) 31–2 treats Choerilus as a 'shadowy' figure; Pickard-Cambridge (1962) 68, West (1989) and Scullion (2002a) also take a sceptical view of the evidence.

[36] *TrGF* 1.2 T6: see Pickard-Cambridge (1962) 68–9.

readers. Aristotle, in a discussion of the use of examples and comparisons by rhetoricians, makes passing reference to the tragedian, saying[37]:

> For the sake of clarity, one should adduce illustrative examples (*paradeigmata*) and comparisons (*parabolai*); but these examples should be relevant, and taken from things that are familiar to us, as in Homer, but not as in Choerilus.

It is hard to be certain from this brief mention exactly what Aristotle means, but it seems that in the fourth century Choerilus had acquired a reputation for obscurity. Note also that if Aristotle could quote from his work, we can assume that at least some of Choerilus' plays, in contrast to those of Thespis, had escaped total 'submersion'. Only two tiny fragments of his work survive, making a definitive judgement impossible. These fragments are not really obscure; they do, however, exhibit what is sometimes called 'frigidity', i.e. strained use of metaphor or circumlocution. Stones are described by Choerilus as 'the earth's bones', while rivers are 'the veins of the earth'.[38] One may or may not find this sort of thing attractive; but it would be unfair to accuse Choerilus of bad writing on the basis of such a small sample, and in any case other tragedians (and especially Aeschylus) frequently use expressions of this sort.[39]

Even though Choerilus wrote so many plays, we know the title of only one: *Alope*. This tragedy is mentioned by Pausanias in his *History of Greece* at the point when he is discussing the genealogy of Triptolemus:

> The Athenian Choerilus wrote a play called *Alope* in which is said that Cercyon and Triptolemus were brothers, and that Amphictyon's daughter was their mother, but Rharus was Triptolemus' father, whereas Poseidon was Cercyon's father.

The manner of citation suggests that *Alope* was actually known to Pausanias or his source: that is, it provides a further piece of evidence that at least some of Choerilus' works survived and were transmitted in textual form beyond his own lifetime. No more details are supplied about this play, but its title suggests a story-pattern very similar to other tragedies on the theme of incest, rape and abandoned children; and indeed Euripides and Carcinus the Younger also wrote later tragedies on the same subject. Alope was the daughter of Cercyon, who was raped by her grandfather Poseidon and subsequently gave birth to a son,

---

[37] Aristotle, *Topics* 8.1.157a14–15 (*TrGF* 1.2 T9). However, it may be that the epic poet Choerilus is meant rather than the tragedian.
[38] *TrGF* 1.2 F2–3.
[39] See Rutherford (2012) 403.

Hippothoon, whom she exposed. The baby was rescued by shepherds and brought before Cercyon, who ordered Alope to be slain; but in the end Poseidon transformed Alope into a spring of water which bore her name.[40] We cannot be sure whether all or part of this story found its way into Choerilus' version, but the title seems to indicate that Alope herself appeared as the main character. Bruno Snell pointed out that in this case *Alope* cannot have been one of Choerilus' earliest plays, because the *Suda* tells us that female characters were not seen in drama before Phrynichus, whose first production was not until *c.* 511–508 BCE.[41] But if we assume that the *Suda* is an unreliable source, this argument falls away.

Pratinas

It is recorded in the *Suda* that Pratinas wrote fifty plays, of which only eighteen were tragic and the other thirty-two satyric.[42] If these figures are correct, and if they represent his total output, it is clear that Pratinas' entries in the dramatic festivals did not usually follow what has come to be seen as the customary pattern – that is, tetralogies consisting of three tragedies plus a satyr-play. We might well conclude from this that the 'customary' arrangement (for which we have no direct evidence) was not customary at all, and that there was always a certain flexibility in the regulations at the City Dionysia; or we might conclude that the tetralogy rule was a late addition to this festival but did not yet exist when Pratinas began his career;[43] or that Pratinas exhibited some or all of his plays in other festivals or other settings where tetralogies were not expected. Alternatively, it may be that the *Suda* is unreliable, as in many other respects. Its statement that Pratinas was the *first* to write satyr-plays is surely wrong – unless, that is, Pratinas was the first to revive or update this ancient form of drama in the new setting of the Athenian Dionysia. But it is clear that in general (in later antiquity, at least) Pratinas was more celebrated for his satyr-plays than for anything else,[44] which makes it easy to imagine how a disproportionately large

---

[40] The myth is recounted by Hyginus, *Fabulae* 187; cf. Aelian, *Historical Miscellany* 12.42, Pausanias 1.5.2. Cf. also Fowler (2013) 484–5 on the development of the myth, and see Chapter 4 (pp. 111–12) on Carcinus' version.

[41] *TrGF* 1.2 F1, p. 67.

[42] *Suda* Π 2230 (*TrGF* 1.4 T1).

[43] The view of Pickard-Cambridge (1962) 66. See now Sansone (2015) for a reminder of how little we really know about the structure and ordering of competition entries.

[44] *TrGF* 1.4 T1, T5, T6, T7.

number of his satyric works might have remained familiar while his tragedies faded into obscurity.

A few other details are included in the *Suda* entry (to which the usual caveats apply): Pratinas competed against Aeschylus and Choerilus on one occasion (*c.* 499–496 BCE); he won only one prize during his career; and he must have been dead by 467 BCE, when his son Aristias won a competition by staging a production that included his father's posthumous work (*Perseus, Tantalus* and the satyr-play *Wrestlers*).[45] It is also said that an accident during one of his performances – the sudden collapse of the temporary wooden benches on which the spectators were sitting – led to the construction of a permanent theatre at Athens, though it is not clear how much truth is contained in this anecdote, or what sort of theatre building is being imagined here.

A number of other sources refer to Pratinas' special interest in music and choreography,[46] and it is suggestive to note that all the surviving fragments of his plays are composed in a variety of lyric metres rather than the iambics or trochaics of spoken dialogue; but Lesky's suggestion that Pratinas was a choral lyricist *rather than* a dramatic poet perhaps overstates the case.[47] If only a few more remnants survived, we might be able to appreciate the character of Pratinas' work more clearly. As it is, our main evidence consists of a curious seventeen-line fragment featuring a chorus of followers of Dionysus:

> What is this noise? What is all this dancing? What is this excessive behaviour that has come to the much-resounding altar of Dionysus? Bromios is mine, he is mine! It is my duty to cry out, my duty to make a loud noise as I rush about all over the mountains with the Naiads, like a swan leading the subtle, winged song. The Pierian Muse established song to rule over us, so let the *aulos* dance in second place – for it is but a servant. Would that the *aulos* might restrict its martial ambitions to the revel and the fisticuffs of young drunkards fighting at their lovers' front doors!
>
> Strike the man who makes a breathy noise like a spotted toad! Burn the reed that squanders saliva as it chatters away with its deep voice, discordant and arhythmical, its shape fashioned by the bore!
>
> Look here! See, I fling my right hand and foot in your honour, o thriambodithyrambic one, lord of the ivy wreath! Listen to my Dorian song and dance!

---

[45] One of our sources, the *Hypothesis* to Aeschylus' *Seven Against Thebes* (*TrGF* 1 DID C 4b), might be taken as indicating that only *Wrestlers* was the work of Pratinas.

[46] *TrGF* 1.4 T3–4, F7–9.

[47] Lesky (1983) 36.

Athenaeus, who quotes this passage,[48] refers to it as a *hyporchêma*, a word which often denotes a non-dramatic choral dance accompanied by music; but most modern scholars have tended to treat it as a choral song from one of Pratinas' satyr-plays or an extract from one of his dithyrambs. This vivid and colourful fragment has been frequently discussed on account of its Dionysiac content, imagery, musical description and self-referentiality; however, scholars have not been able to reach any clear conclusions regarding its date, genre or interpretation.[49] As far as I can tell, no one has ever tried to claim that this song belongs either to a tragedy or to the shady genre of 'proto-tragedy' – but such a claim would be impossible to rule out.

Apart from this *hyporchêma* fragment, all we have are a few titles and very short quotations, and again it is unclear whether these are the remains of tragic, proto-tragic, dithyrambic or satyric works. The title *Women of Dyme* (or *Caryatids*) gives nothing away about the subject-matter of that work, and its single surviving fragment, a reference to the 'sweet-voiced quail', is similarly unrevealing.[50] A few further fragments, from unknown works, all concern music and dancing in some way: they not only describe the sound of music, using vivid imagery from agriculture and the natural world, but they also show an awareness of distinctive musical traditions (or modes) from different parts of the Greek world.[51] In one fragment a chorus sings about 'the Laconian cicada, well-suited to dancing',[52] while in another passage a chorus or poet-figure makes what looks like a conventional rhetorical claim of poetic novelty, in contrast or competition with other poetry:

> . . . Not going over land that has already been ploughed,
> but in search of untouched soil . . .[53]

The metaphorical comparison of poetry to ploughing, familiar from other archaic poetry,[54] is also seen in another similar fragment:

> Pursue neither the tense nor the relaxed Muse,
> but as you are ploughing the middle of your field,

---

[48]   Athenaeus 14.617b–c (= *TrGF* 1.2 F3).
[49]   See Collard (2013) 242–7 for the most recent treatment, helpfully listing and summarizing previous discussions, and cf. Pickard-Cambridge (1962) 17–20.
[50]   *TrGF* 1.2 F1.
[51]   Athenaeus (9.392f, 14.632f, 11.461e, 14.624f) is the source of all these fragments as well as the *hyporchêma* fragment above.
[52]   *TrGF* 1.2 F4.
[53]   *TrGF* 1.2 F5.
[54]   E.g. Pindar, *Olympian* 9.25–6, 11.89; *Pythian* 6.1–3; *Nemean* 1.13; cf. *adesp.* F923, 947 *PMG*; discussed (with further examples) by Nünlist (1998) 135–41.

make an Aeolian sound with your song . . .
Indeed, an Aeolian harmony is fitting
for all those who are greedy for poetry.[55]

Athenaeus quotes this fragment apropos of a discussion of musical modes in general and the 'haughty, pompous and conceited' Aeolian mode in particular. He says nothing about its original context, but the fact that he quotes the Pratinas fragment alongside dithyrambic fragments by Lasus of Hermione and others may give a clue as to its genre. *If* any of these fragments are tragic (and it is a big 'if'), we may conclude that tragedy in Pratinas' time exhibited a degree of poetic self-consciousness that was commonly seen in earlier lyric poetry but had almost disappeared from tragedy by the later fifth century.[56]

Phrynichus

The best attested, least 'submerged' and most interesting of these early authors, Phrynichus was said to have been a pupil of Thespis; he was also the father of the tragedian Polyphrasmon (who is discussed in Chapter 4, apropos of tragic 'family trees'). According to the *Suda*, Phrynichus won first prize, probably at the City Dionysia, some time around 511–508 BCE.[57] If this information is accurate, Phrynichus seems to have enjoyed a reasonably long career, for he was still active in 476, when Themistocles acted as *choregos* for one of his productions.[58] After this date no further mention of Phrynichus is found, and it has been suggested that he died shortly before 472, when Aeschylus quoted Phrynichus in the opening scene of his *Persians* – a gesture which has been seen as an act of homage.[59] One late source records that Phrynichus died in Sicily[60]: this evidence, if true, may suggest that Phrynichus was one of several highly successful Athenian playwrights, including Aeschylus, Agathon, Euripides and Carcinus the Younger, who were induced by money or cultural prestige to take their work out to an international audience.

---

[55]   *TrGF* 1.2 F6.
[56]   On the reluctance of fifth-century tragedy to 'break the illusion' and comment upon itself, in contrast with comedy, see Taplin (1986); but cf. also Torrance (2013) on the limited use of metapoetic gestures in Euripidean tragedy towards the end of the century.
[57]   *Suda* Φ762 (*TrGF* 1.3 T1); but cf. West (1989) and Scullion (2002a), discussed above, for the view that this date is inaccurate.
[58]   Plutarch, *Themistocles* 5.5 (*TrGF* 1.3 T4): see discussion below, pp. 26–7.
[59]   Sommerstein (2008) 2: 'it is unlikely that Aeschylus would have chosen to pay such a compliment to a living rival.'
[60]   [Anon.] *On Comedy* 8.36 (*TrGF* 1.3 T6).

The *Suda* credits Phrynichus with a couple of important formal innovations: he is called the 'inventor' of trochaic tetrameter, a statement which is obviously untrue but which perhaps signals an interest in the presentation of verse dialogue and the effects of changes in rhythm; and he is also said to have been the first playwright to bring female characters on stage.[61] This latter innovation is of enormous importance, because it will have hugely expanded the dramaturgical, thematic and emotional possibilities of the genre. As usual, we have to treat everything the *Suda* tells us with a pinch of salt; but whether or not Phrynichus was actually the first to come up with the idea of women on stage, it seems reasonable to infer, at least, that he was known for writing powerful or memorable female characters.

It is hard to imagine the effect of Phrynichus' plays in performance, but nearly all of the testimonia mention how attractive his work was perceived to be, with special reference to his music, lyrics and choreography. In particular, we are told that he deliberately avoided chromatic embellishment or ornamentation in his music, and that he invented several dance moves (*schêmata*).[62] One anecdote recounted by Aelian records that one of Phrynichus' tragedies featured a dance routine based on the military-style *pyrrichê*, and that the music and choreography on this occasion so impressed the Athenians that they elected Phrynichus general.[63] Even though the anecdote is obviously fictional, it shows that Phrynichus' name was particularly associated with music and dance in the later critical tradition, and it also underlines the fact that success in the tragic competition was a form of official recognition by the state.

Aristophanes, in his comedy *Wasps* of 422 BCE, makes Phrynichus the favourite poet of the character Philocleon and the chorus of elderly jurors; and even though the joke lies in the fact that Phrynichus is now regarded as utterly unfashionable and out-of-date, the comedian still refers several times to the 'sweetness' or 'loveliness' of the older dramatist's lyric poetry.[64] An anonymous ancient commentator on *Wasps* quotes a couple of snippets from Phrynichus' *Phoenician Women* as examples of this 'sweetness', which shows that these plays were still familiar – as texts – to readers many years later.[65] But it is also striking

---

[61]   *TrGF* 1.3 T1.
[62]   *TrGF* 1.3 T15, T8.
[63]   Aelian, *Historical Miscellany* 3.8 (*TrGF* 1.3 T16).
[64]   Aristophanes, *Wasps* 219–20, 269–70; cf. *Women Celebrating the Thesmophoria* 164–7, *Frogs* 1298–1300 with Σ *ad loc.* (*TrGF* 1.3 T10a–e). *Wasps* 220 describes Phrynichus' lyrics as *archaia melisidônophrynichêrata* ('old honey-Sidon-Phrynichus-lovely'). For more discussion of Aristophanes' treatment of Phrynichus see Wright (2013a).
[65]   Σ Ar. *Wasps* 219–20, quoting Phrynichus F9–10 (*TrGF* 1.3 T10d).

that Aristophanes was able to introduce a parody of Phrynichus' distinctive style of choreography into the final scene of *Wasps*.[66] Philocleon's dancing seems to be deliberately mimicking Phrynichean dance-moves: he is described as performing high leg-kicks and crouching like a cock (perhaps an allusion to Phrynichus F17, 'the cock crouched, bending his wing as if in servile fashion').[67] The way in which this scene incorporates musical and visual jokes as well as verbal echoes strongly suggests that Phrynichus' work was still well known *through performance* to Aristophanes' audience; for how else would the parodic humour have worked? So perhaps we have to imagine that Phrynichus' plays – or parts of them – were still being performed, in some setting or other, as late as the 420s: this might also help to explain why Phrynichus should have retained such a long-lasting reputation for his choreography more generally.[68]

The *Suda* records the names of the following tragedies by Phrynichus: *Women of Pleuron, Egyptians, Actaeon, Alcestis, Antaeus* (or *Libyans*), *Just Men* (or *Persians* or *Men in Council*), and *Daughters of Danaus*. This probably represents only a fraction of his total output, but at any rate it is obviously not a complete list: it mostly consists of titles beginning with the first letters of the alphabet, and it omits Phrynichus' most famous tragedies, *The Sack of Miletus* and *Phoenician Women*, as well as other attested titles such as *Tantalus*. It has been suggested that *Phoenician Women* may have been an alternative name for the play denoted as *Just Men, Persians* or *Men in Council*; or it may be that these titles were all connected (perhaps as a trilogy or tetralogy on the same theme?);[69] but there is no way of knowing the truth. However, it seems that in later antiquity there was a certain amount of confusion about Phrynichus' titles and the relationship between his plays.

Very little survives of any of these works: their titles tell us the sort of story that Phrynichus put on stage, but the fragments do not reveal much about the precise details of their plots. (See Appendix 1 for a complete English translation

---

[66] Ar. *Wasps* 1476–1537. On the details of the parody and the specific choreography involved (in so far as this can be constructed), see Roos (1951) 76–88; Borthwick (1968). Cf. Parker (1997, 256–61), who points out that the prevailing metre of the final portion of *Wasps* (archilochean) is apparently paralleled in Phrynichus F13.

[67] *TrGF* 1.3 F17 (though the attribution of this line to Phrynichus has been doubted: see Snell *ad loc.*); cf. *Wasps* 1490. Note, however, that the scholiast *ad loc.* reads 'crouching', oddly, as a reference not to a dance move but to Phrynichus' failure with *The Sack of Miletus* in 492, when the Athenians threw the author off the stage 'crouching and fearful'.

[68] Cf. Plutarch, *Table-Talk* 8.9.3 (*Moralia* 732f = *TrGF* 1.3 T13) for the continuing association of Phrynichus with dancing.

[69] For different attempts to untangle the uncertain relationship between these plays, see Lloyd-Jones (1966) 24, Lesky (1983) 33–4, Sommerstein (2008) 3–6, Garvie (2009) ix–x.

of the fragments.) One of the tragedies, *Tantalus*, was concerned with the myth of the doomed house of Atreus, one of the most popular tragic myths of all time. Its title character, the father of Pelops and thus the ancestor of the whole awful family, earned eternal punishment for – among other crimes – killing his son and boiling him up as a meal for the gods.[70] *Egyptians* and *Daughters of Danaus* were evidently concerned with the fifty daughters of Danaus and their attempts to resist an enforced marriage to their cousins, the sons of Aegyptus: this myth is better known as the basis of the Aeschylean trilogy that included *Suppliant Women*. The play *Antaeus* (also known as *Libyans*) was about the Libyan giant who wrestled all passers-by to their death and used their skulls to build a temple to Poseidon: not a word of Phrynichus' version survives, but we know from an ancient commentator on Aristophanes that it included a description of Antaeus' final wrestling-match with Heracles that led to his defeat.[71] *Actaeon* dealt with the Theban hunter who was transformed into a deer by Artemis before being torn apart by his own hunting-dogs – a myth that was to become very popular in later literature and art, but does not seem to have been a normal theme of tragedy (though note that Aeschylus and Cleophon also treated the same story).[72]

Something of the background to *Women of Pleuron* is conveyed by Pausanias, who mentions Phrynichus' play in the course of a description of a painting at Delphi, by Polygnotus, of the Aetolian hero Meleager. When Meleager was born, the Fates decreed that he would live only as long as a firebrand in his parents' hearth remained unburnt. His mother, Althaea, hid the brand; but in later life Meleager killed two of his brothers while taking part in the famous Calydonian boar-hunt, and thus earned his mother's wrath[73]:

> The myth about the brand – how it was given to Althaea by the Fates, how Meleager was not destined to die until such time as the brand was consumed by fire, and how Althaea burnt it in her rage – this myth was first dramatized by Phrynichus, son of Polyphrasmon, in his *Women of Pleuron*:
>
>> [Meleager] did not escape his chill fate;
>> but as the wooden brand was destroyed by his terrible mother,
>> contriver of evil, the flame swiftly consumed him.

---

[70]   Apollodorus, *Epitome* 2.1-3.
[71]   Σ Aristophanes, *Frogs* 689 (= *TrGF* 1.3 F3a). Cf. Apollodorus 2.5.11 for the myth.
[72]   Aeschylus, *TrGF* 3 F241–4; Cleophon, *TrGF* 1.77 T1. Cf. Diodorus Siculus 4.81.3–5; Euripides, *Bacchae* 337–40 also briefly alludes to the myth.
[73]   Pausanias 10.31.4–5 = *TrGF* 1.3 F6.

And yet it seems that Phrynichus did not develop the story at length, in the way that a poet would treat his own invention, but merely touched upon it in passing (*prosapsamenos*), since it was already well known throughout the whole Greek world.

This well-known story frequently appears in Greek literature, but it is not quite clear what portion of the myth found its way into Phrynichus' tragedy. Pausanias' summary implies that Meleager and the firebrand were not a central feature of the play, as they are in other accounts. It has been suggested that Phrynichus' main subject was the wooing of Meleager's sister Deianeira by Achelous and her subsequent marriage to Heracles, events that form the background to Sophocles' *Women of Trachis*.[74] Another fragment from the play survives, but it gives us no further assistance in reconstructing the plot, and indeed its reference to an invasion and widespread destruction by fire is hard to match up with the rest of the myth:

> Once upon a time a body of men made their way to this land, an ancient people, who inhabited the land of Hyas; and rapid fire consumed in its wild jaws the whole of the open country and the coastal plain.[75]

These lines seem to describe an invasion of Aetolia by the Hyantians, who were early inhabitants of Boeotia; or perhaps (if the text is slightly emended) what is being described is an invasion of Boeotia which drove the Hyantians to resettle in Aetolia.[76] Either way, the events narrated here must either precede or follow the story of Meleager, if they have anything to do with that myth at all. (Perhaps they belong to a narrative-style prologue recounting earlier events, but it is impossible to say.)

Phrynichus' *Alcestis*, like that of Euripides, dramatized the myth of Admetus, king of Pherae, who managed to avert his fated death by persuading his noble wife Alcestis to die in his place. Not much can be said about Phrynichus' handling of the plot, but one of the fragments apparently features Heracles wrestling with Death and overcoming him ('... [he] exhausts his fearless body, limb-shaken ...').[77] At least one other striking detail from Phrynichus' version –

---

[74] Sourvinou-Inwood (2003) 270–1.
[75] *TrGF* 1.3 F5.
[76] See Huxley (1986) for this alternative version of the text, as well as general discussion of the fragment.
[77] This is Snell's interpretation (*TrGF* 1.3 F2 *ad loc.*); the source (Hesychius A 1529) gives no context or clue. Parker (2007) xv–xvi assumes that not just Heracles and Death but the whole plot of Euripides' *Alcestis* was taken from Phrynichus, and that the rescue of Alcestis from the dead was entirely Phrynichus' invention; she also suggests that Phrynichus' play included the story of Apollo's making the Fates drunk in order that they might grant immortality to humans (as in Aeschylus, *Eumenides* 723–8).

the entrance of Death carrying a sword, with which he proceeded to cut off a
lock of Alcestis' hair – was borrowed by Euripides and reused in his own *Alcestis*;
and it may be that other elements in Euripides' play also recall or adapt the earlier
poet's work.[78] The most recent commentator on the Euripidean version assumes
that this later play would have presented itself as 'an "improved" version of the
work of the earlier dramatist: more subtle, more morally sensitive, above all,
more tragic'; she also suggests that Phrynichus' play was not a tragedy as such,
but rather an example of the primitive, 'undignified' sort of proto-tragedy or
tragi-satyric hybrid implied by Aristotle's evolutionary history of the genre (see
above, pp. 4–7).[79] Such a suggestion is not unattractive – apart from anything
else, it may offer a clue as to why Euripides in 438 chose to exhibit his own *Alcestis*
as the fourth play in a tetralogy, i.e. the position often filled by a satyr-play – but
it is perhaps a little unfair to dismiss Phrynichus' play as primitive or lacking in
subtlety when we are not in a position to judge it properly. Furthermore, we are
not obliged to regard all intertextual activity as inherently emulous in spirit. It
may be that Euripides was not aiming to 'improve' his predecessor's work so
much as to engage in an artistically fruitful dialogue with it, or to demonstrate
awareness of the dramatic tradition, or to pay homage to a famous literary
ancestor.

Even if some Athenians in the later decades of the fifth century did perceive
Phrynichus to be an unsophisticated or antediluvian figure,[80] it is clear that his
work continued to exert an influence on the imagination of later poets. Euripides'
Alcestis is not the only work in which we can tentatively perceive echoes of
Phrynichus. Aeschylus also paid tribute to the older poet's *Phoenician Women* in
his *Persians* (discussed later in this section), and it is possible that his *Egyptians,
Daughters of Danaus, Suppliant Women*, and *Female Archers* owed some debt to
Phrynichus' tragedies on the same themes. Some form of intertextual relationship
has been hypothesized between Phrynichus' *Women of Pleuron* and Sophocles'
Women of Trachis;[81] and it may be that this tragedy in some way influenced
the *Meleager* plays by Sophocles and Euripides, or Bacchylides' fifth ode (which
was composed in 476 BCE, presumably quite close in date to Phrynichus'
tragedy). There are even indications that Phrynichus himself was a cultured and

[78]   Euripides, *Alcestis* 74; cf. Phrynichus *TrGF* 1.3 F3.
[79]   Parker (2007) xvi; the play's genre is also questioned by Pickard-Cambridge (1962) 64.
[80]   The character Euripides in Aristophanes' *Frogs* 909–10 (= *TrGF* 1.3 T10b) says that Phrynichus had
       reared an audience of 'morons' for Aeschylus to inherit, but this is not exactly straightforward
       evidence for the nature or quality of Phrynichus' work.
[81]   Sourvinou-Inwood (2003) 270–1.

self-aware poet, fully conscious of his place in a long poetic tradition. Aristophanes, in a choral ode which may derive from a genuine passage of Phrynichus, describes the tragedian as resembling a bee, gathering his ambrosial songs from flowers. This is a striking image of poetic activity which (as used elsewhere by Pindar, Horace and others) seems to denote painstakingly elaborate work characterized by its allusiveness, its attention to detail, and its borrowing from other sources.[82]

Phrynichus' *Phoenician Women*, like Aeschylus' *Persians*, was an imaginative attempt to depict the Persians' response to their defeat by the Greeks at the Battle of Salamis. Aeschylus' play begins by paraphrasing the opening line of Phrynichus' tragedy, a striking gesture which would have drawn attention to the similarity between these works: no other tragedy is known to have alluded to another specific play in its very first line. Whether this is to be seen as an act of homage on the part of the younger poet, or as implying a more defiant or agonistic sort of attitude, is unclear. This is because we cannot know exactly what use Aeschylus made of the Phrynichean original, or to what extent his *Persians* represented an adaptation of Phrynichus rather than an original treatment of events that were widely known.[83] The fragments of *Phoenician Women* include some sort of reference to the defeat and death of the fighting men (F10a) and an evocation of songs or laments sung in response to the sound of harps (F11), but its plot and narrative remain unclear. It seems that lamentation played a major part in both plays, but one important difference is seen in the identity of the singers who perform these laments: Phrynichus' chorus (as is clear from the title and F9–10) consisted of women from Sidon, who were presumably the widows of dead Phoenician sailors; but in Aeschylus it is Persian men, accompanied by Xerxes himself, who sing the laments and thus take on a function more normally performed (in tragedy or ritual alike) by women. This 'feminization' of the enemy has been seen as a defining feature of Aeschylus' presentation of barbarians as well as an important strand in tragedy's construction of Greek identity more generally.[84]

---

[82] Aristophanes, *Birds* 743–51 (= *TrGF* 1.3 F19): Snell (*ad loc.*) judges this to be a parody or pastiche of a lost Phrynichean original. For the image of poet as bee, cf. Simonides F593 *PMG*, Pindar, *Pythian* 10. 53–4, Horace, *Odes* 4.2.27–32, etc.; cf. Wimmel (1960) 271 for the view that this is a 'Callimachean' trope. Herington (1985) 108 interprets F19 as a reference to Phrynichus' *musical* borrowing (from pre-dramatic and ritual choral forms).

[83] For speculative discussions of the relationship between the two plays, see Stoessl (1945), Sommerstein (2008) 2–6. Glaucus of Rhegium (= *TrGF* 1.3 F8, quoted below) uses the word *parapepoiêsthai* to describe Aeschylus' use of Phrynichus, but this word need not necessarily imply a thoroughgoing 'adaptation' as such.

[84] See esp. Hall (1989) 209–10, Garvie (2009) 62–3.

Another important difference between the two plays lies in the way that the Persians' defeat was presented: in *Persians* the news arrives half-way through the play, allowing a significant build-up of tension beforehand, whereas in *Phoenician Women* it was announced right at the start. This information is given by the writer of the ancient *Hypothesis* to *Persians*, who names as his source the fifth-century scholar Glaucus of Rhegium:

> Glaucus, in his book *On Aeschylus' Plots*, says that *Persians* was adapted from Phrynichus' *Phoenician Women*, and he quotes this opening line of the play:
>
> 'All this belongs to the Persians, who have gone long ago . . .'[85]
>
> However, at the beginning of that play a eunuch is announcing the defeat of Xerxes, but in Aeschylus' play it is a chorus of elders who sing the prologue.

The opening scene of Phrynichus' play is said to show a eunuch arranging the seats for the speakers in the Persian Council, a scenario which is interestingly vivid and naturalistic in comparison with Aeschylus' elaborate choral opening. As one critic memorably comments, 'it seems a curiously cosy opening for a tragedy: one recalls the openings of so many English light comedies of the years around 1900, where the curtain rises on a butler or a parlourmaid tidying the drawing-room before the arrival of the main characters'.[86] Perhaps this is a somewhat anachronistic description – after all, several other Greek tragedies feature servants or homely domestic scenes at the beginning[87] – but it is undoubtedly surprising to discover such a scene in the work of a playwright who is often seen as primitive or lacking in dramatic action. Even if, as seems likely, there was more chorus than dialogue or action in Phrynichus' work,[88] it is clear that he was capable of constructing dramatic scenes with some visual detail and a degree of verisimilitude.

These two plays are particularly interesting to the historian of theatre because they were based on real-life subject-matter rather than myth. They are often referred to as 'historical tragedy', but that label is perhaps slightly misleading. The Greeks of the early fifth century did not make a strong distinction between 'myth' and 'history', both of which categories refer to similar ways of conceptualizing the past. But more importantly, the really striking feature of *Phoenician Women* and

---

[85]   *TrGF* 1.3 F8 (τάδ' ἐστὶ Περσῶν τῶν πάλαι βεβηκότων). Another possible translation would be 'These are the [ ] of the Persians, who have gone long ago' (or 'This is the [ ] of the Persians . . .').

[86]   Herington (1985) 271.

[87]   E.g. Euripides' *Electra* and *Ion*; cf. the nurse Cilissa who begins an important scene in Aeschylus' *Libation-Bearers,* or (perhaps) the Guard at the start of *Agamemnon.*

[88]   This is the view of Pickard-Cambridge (1962) 63–5, Lesky (1983) 33, etc.

Persians is that they are not concerned with the distant past but with events from living memory. The Persian invasion of Greece was a very recent occurrence, which these playwrights and their audiences had witnessed at first hand. *Phoenician Women* is normally dated to 476 BCE, the year in which Themistocles acted as Phrynichus' producer,[89] and *Persians* was produced in 472; but the events described in these plays had only occurred in 480–479. It may be thought that the Greeks' victory over the Persians was so extraordinary that it instantaneously assumed mythical or quasi-mythical status;[90] but even if this is true, it is obvious that we are dealing with not historical tragedy but *contemporary* tragedy.

It is curious that no other fifth-century tragedian seems to have written plays on contemporary or real-life subjects. Everybody else, with a few exceptions, stuck to the world of myth.[91] Whether this was due to the official regulations of the dramatic competition, or to a generally accepted convention, or to audience tastes, or to a wish to keep tragedy as separate as possible from comedy, is not known. However, another possible explanation is suggested by the disastrous reception of the only other known fifth-century example of contemporary tragedy – *The Sack of Miletus*, also by Phrynichus. This play, which had its première in 492 BCE, dramatized the revolt of the Ionian Greeks against Persian domination and the events leading to the siege and destruction of Miletus in the autumn of 494. Herodotus, who describes this period and the terrible suffering of the Milesians, also mentions Phrynichus' play in passing:[92]

> The Athenians demonstrated their deep grief for the capture of Miletus in many ways, but especially in this: when Phrynichus wrote his *Sack of Miletus* and put it on stage, the whole theatre burst into lamentation. The Athenians fined Phrynichus one thousand drachmas for reminding them of their own misfortunes, and they banned all future use of the play.

This notorious episode is well known to literary historians because it is the earliest attested case of censorship in literature or drama, and indeed the only

---

[89] Suggested by Plutarch, *Themistocles* 5.5 (*TrGF* 1.3 T4 = DID B1): see Pickard-Cambridge (1962) 64, Lloyd-Jones (1966) 23, Lesky (1983) 33–4.

[90] This is the view of Herington (1985) 129; cf. Garvie (2009) xi.

[91] Agathon's 'fictional' tragedy *Anth*[ ]*s* furnishes a notable exception (see Chapter 3). A few other tragedians in the fourth century and later are known to have written tragedies on historical or real-life topics, e.g. Dionysius of Syracuse (who wrote plays about himself), Theodectes, *Mausolus*, etc. (see Chapters 4 and 5); cf. also Moschion, *Themistocles* and Ezechiel, *Exagoge* from the Hellenistic period (*TrGF* 1.97 F1, 1.128 F1). Fragments of a *Gyges* tragedy (*TrGF* 2 adespota F664), tentatively attributed to Phrynichus by Lloyd-Jones (1966, 24), are probably of much later date: see Lesky (1983) 34–5.

[92] Herodotus 6.21.2–3 (*TrGF* 1.3 T2).

example of censorship relating to Greek tragedy from any period.[93] It is also an important sign that, despite what is often thought and written, the life of a tragedy was *not* normally confined to a single performance. Herodotus explicitly says that the author was not just fined but banned from 'using' (*chrâsthai*) the play again. In other words, the Athenians envisaged the likelihood of repeat performances, even of an unpopular play, in other festivals or other types of setting. It may be that even as early as 492 there was also a small but significant reading audience for texts of tragedy, and if so, a general ban on all 'uses' of the play would have prohibited the making of further copies – and even, presumably, necessitated the destruction of existing ones. Consequently, not a single quotation survives, and the play is never mentioned by anybody again.

But what had Phrynichus done wrong, and what laws or standards of taste had he broken? These questions are hard to answer. It is obvious that this play was unusually effective at arousing powerful or empathetic feelings in the spectators, to such an extent that they joined in with the characters and chorus in their own lamentation. This would no doubt have been an emotionally draining or unsettling experience; but after all, tragedy was *supposed* to arouse strong emotions: if Phrynichus made people cry, this was surely a sign of artistic success, not a reason to prosecute him. It cannot be that there was a law or festival regulation prohibiting the dramatization of real-life events, or else Phrynichus and Aeschylus would not have returned to real-life subjects a few years later. Most commonly it has been suggested that the subject-matter in this case was simply too sensitive, given that the fall of Miletus was so recent, and that the Persian threat to the Athenians themselves remained all too real. This explanation is quite attractive, but it still does not explain exactly what convention or law Phrynichus had violated: was it, perhaps, illegal at this period to put on a play which showed Greeks being defeated?

An alternative explanation is suggested by Hugh Lloyd-Jones, who suspects that personal politics rather than general principles lay behind Phrynichus' prosecution.[94] It is clear that the politician Themistocles was an associate of Phrynichus – he acted as producer for the tragedian on at least one occasion – and it is interesting to note that he was archon in the year that *Sack of Miletus* was produced. Perhaps Themistocles is to be seen as having directly influenced Phrynichus' choice and treatment of subject-matter, and perhaps the play's fate

---

[93]   I discount the tradition that Euripides was prosecuted for the theological content of his plays: see
        Dover (1988) for more discussion of 'the freedom of the intellectual' in classical Greece.
[94]   Lloyd-Jones (1966) 22–3; cf. Lesky (1983) 33–4.

reflects an attack on Themistocles by his rivals, rather than a judgement on the play itself.

It seems unlikely that we will ever get to the bottom of the matter.[95] For some reason or other, the Athenians decided at an early date that tragedy should centre exclusively on mythical subjects, but it is impossible to know for certain whether Phrynichus had any influence on this decision. At the same time, it is hard to explain why (apparently) no other tragedian attempted to test out the boundaries of the genre by experimenting with other types of plot.

See Appendix 1 for an English translation of the fragments of Phrynichus. The incomplete nature of these utterances and the lack of context mean that any attempt at a translation must be treated as provisional rather than definitive, but I have tried to convey a reasonably clear sense of what I think Phrynichus meant. It must be admitted that none of the fragments is particularly revealing, though here and there we can glimpse a few interesting features, such as a chorus' self-referential description of the harp music which accompanies their song (F11); a description of a Phrynichean dance-move (F17); a reference to the way in which erotic love can transform one's appearance (F13); a portion of a narrative in which someone violates the law of *xenia* by decapitating a dinner-guest (F14); and a hint that Phrynichus' tragedies included messenger-speeches (F16a).

---

[95]   See Rosenbloom (1993) for further discussion of the play (in relation to the emotions of the theatre audience).

2

Some Fifth-Century Tragedians

In this chapter I examine the surviving evidence for a number of neglected fifth-century tragedians, in an attempt to show exactly what can still be said, with reasonable confidence, about the nature and character of each poet's work. These poets were contemporaries of Aeschylus, Sophocles and Euripides, the three playwrights who were to become quasi-canonical, and there are signs of similarities as well as differences between the individual writers' work; but it is hard to find any compelling explanations why it came about in later times that almost everyone apart from the triad was relegated to the status of 'minor' poets. Was there really something so very different, or significantly less attractive, about their plays? It is impossible to say. However, all the indications suggest that in their day, and for some years afterwards, these writers were celebrated and considered worthy of serious attention; and the remnants of their work, though pitifully thin, are full of interest and signs of originality. No overall patterns or tendencies seem to suggest themselves – instead, one is struck (as ever) by the considerable variety of subject-matter and themes on view – but it is noticeable that there is much more evidence for tragedy from the latter part of the century than from the first few decades.[1] This uneven distribution could be purely the result of accidental survival or loss, but it may also reflect a gradual expansion or 'boom' in the Athenian theatre during the height of the Athenian empire.

Ion and Achaeus

These two poets present us with an odd sort of paradox. They are by far the best preserved of all the lost tragedians, in terms of the number of quotations made

---

[1] Other fifth-century tragedians are discussed in chapters 3, 4 and 6, but there too the evidence is weighted towards the last few decades of the century.

from their work during antiquity: we possess fifty-six fragments from Achaeus and sixty-eight from Ion. Nevertheless, in spite of their disproportionately large number these fragments are curiously unrevealing, and many are from satyr-plays rather than tragedies. Neither the testimonia (which are surprisingly few in number) nor the fragments themselves seem to tell us much about the flavour of each poet's work: we can say a certain amount about their choice of subject-matter, but very little about their style, themes, preoccupations, or any other distinctive qualities of their plays. This is a gravely disappointing situation, but it makes us reflect once again on the extraordinary nature of our evidence, and the high degree of randomness and inexplicability that inheres in the process of transmission. In other words, having more fragments is *not* necessarily a good thing.

It is also remarkable that there are almost no surviving references in comedy to either poet.[2] This fact may well make us wonder just how prominent Ion and Achaeus really were, in comparison with the other so-called 'minor' tragedians. Does the large number of fragments correlate to their perceived status during the fifth century, or is comic mockery or parody a more reliable indication of which dramatists were considered by their contemporaries to be more important?[3] As usual, it is impossible to reach confident conclusions on these matters because of the gaps in our evidence: it may be that the lost comedies were crammed full of jokes about Ion and Achaeus. Nevertheless, the apparent silence of comedy does seem a little suspicious. It also raises a further question, *viz.* why Ion and Achaeus in particular should have *become* disproportionately popular or widely quoted in the centuries after their death.

In the case of Ion, at least, his prominence in the indirect tradition is probably due to his famous versatility as a writer in a number of different genres, including lyric and elegiac poetry, dithyramb, history and philosophy as well as tragedy.[4] Ion seems to have been perceived generally as an important writer, the sort of author whom one might well read and quote for a variety of purposes, and he was important enough to have commentaries written on several of his plays (by

---

[2] Aristophanes, *Peace* 832–7 (*TrGF* 1.19 T2a) makes an oblique reference to a non-dramatic poem about the Dawn Star by Ion (*PMG* F745 Page, quoted by the scholiast *ad loc.* = *TrGF* 1.19 T2b), and jokes that Ion himself has been transformed into a star. This joke implies that Ion had died by 421 BCE (when *Peace* was produced). Aristophanes also quotes a tiny snippet from Achaeus (which may be a proverbial phrase) at *Wasps* 1081.

[3] Cf. Rosen (2006) for the plausible suggestion that comedians were largely responsible for creating a 'fan-base' for tragedians.

[4] Generic versatility (*polyeideia*) is seen as Ion's defining characteristic by several authors, ancient and modern: see *TrGF* 1.19 T8-15 Leurini and the recent discussion by Henderson (2007).

Aristarchus and Didymus),[5] but this status was perhaps not earned by his tragedies alone. Indeed, it appears that his prose works were notably more successful and influential than his poems or plays. Longinus, the author of *On the Sublime*, delivered the following nastily memorable verdict on Ion, in the course of his discussion of literary genius *versus* mediocrity[6]:

> It is necessary to pose the general question, in relation to prose or poetry, whether genius accompanied by certain flaws of execution should be valued above flawless mediocrity.... My own view is that the greater merits, even if they are not consistently maintained, are always more likely to achieve success, precisely because of the greatness of spirit that they exhibit.... In lyric poetry, would anyone choose to be Bacchylides rather than Pindar? In tragedy, would anyone rather be Ion of Chios than Sophocles? Ion and Bacchylides are flawless, uniformly attractive writers with a polished style, but Pindar and Sophocles are the writers who sometimes set the world ablaze with the force of their poetry, even though their flame often goes out and they fall to pieces completely. But for all that, no sane person would rate all of Ion's plays together as being worth as much as just one play – *Oedipus* – by Sophocles.

In some respects this passage reflects the idiosyncratic views of its author – in its polarizing outlook, its contrast of canonical *versus* non-canonical authors, its use of bold metaphors, and its lack of explicit definition or illustration of key terms – but in general it seems likely that Longinus is encapsulating the sort of critical assessment of Ion's poetic talent that persisted throughout antiquity.[7]

That is not to deny that Ion had some success as a dramatist. He wrote at least twelve and maybe as many as forty plays,[8] and he competed at the major Athenian festivals on several occasions from *c.* 451–448 BCE onwards, winning at least one first prize.[9] It is said that in celebration of this victory Ion presented every one of the Athenians with a small jar of wine from his homeland, Chios: this was ostensibly an expression of gratitude and goodwill, but also a conspicuous display of magnificence and a political gesture symbolizing the cultural prestige of the Chians.[10] One recent discussion of this episode interprets Ion's gift of wine as a form of cultural exchange directly analogous to his dramatic offering at the

---

[5]   *TrGF* 1.19 T7b.

[6]   Longinus, *On the Sublime* 33.1-5.

[7]   Cf. Dover (1986) 27, who sees the fourth-century establishment of the tragic 'canon' as the key factor in Ion's subsequent reception.

[8]   The *Suda* (I 487 = *TrGF* 1.19 T1) reports that the number is given differently in different sources.

[9]   However, Ion's only securely attested competition is the 428 Dionysia, where he was defeated by Euripides and Iophon (*TrGF* 1.19 T5 = DID C13).

[10] Athenaeus 1.3f; cf. *Suda* A 731 and Σ Aristophanes, *Peace* 835 (*TrGF* 1.19 T3).

festival, since both wine and tragedy can be seen as high-value commodities for export: Ion's gesture is interpreted as an announcement to the world that his victory at Athens is specifically the victory of Ion *of Chios*.[11]

This is a significant fact in terms of the politics of tragedy, because Ion was one of a minority of non-Athenian poets who produced tragedies at Athens during the fifth century. The Athenian tragic festivals have been widely seen as inherently political occasions.[12] The Greater Dionysia, in particular, is normally viewed by scholars as a prominent display of Athens' magnificence as well as an occasion for the exploration of Athenian values. Political and civic meanings have been found both in the ceremonies and framing devices of the festival and in the content of the plays themselves. If this sort of interpretation really reflects the reality of the situation, Ion's behaviour could have been viewed as provocative and potentially challenging, an obtrusion of non-Athenian values into a quintessentially Athenian event. Alternatively, it could have been viewed as a statement of the Chian elite's identification with Athenian values (since Chios was generally a close ally of Athens). It would be natural, perhaps, to assume that Ion's plays themselves, in their handling of myth or their ideological content, represented a political or local perspective that somehow contrasted with, or complemented, the normal Athenocentric viewpoint of tragedy. Unfortunately, however, there is nothing in the content of the fragments to tell us whether or not this was the case. It has been pointed out that some of the fragments exhibit Homeric vocabulary, which may possibly hint at some sort of attempt on Ion's part to present himself as the heir to the most famous Chian poet of all.[13] But the remains of Ion's work do not allow us to pursue this line of argument any further; and indeed it appears that when Ion engages with the epic tradition it is not Homer but rather the Epic Cycle that he draws on for material (though in antiquity Homer was often treated as the author of the cyclic epics).

Ion's tragedy *Guards* (*Phrouroi*) seems to have been based on a scenario from the *Little Iliad* in which Odysseus, in disguise, came to Troy by night on an espionage mission; he was eventually recognized by Helen, and the two Greeks between them plotted the capture of the city.[14] Some of the fragments could

---

[11]   Stevens (2007), esp. 243–5.

[12]   See especially Goldhill (1990) and, more recently, Carter (2007) and (2011); but contrast the apolitical perspective of Griffin (1998).

[13]   Webster (1936) 270; cf. Maitland (2007) 269–70, with reference to *TrGF* 1.19 F10 (ὑπερφίαλον, κελαρύζετε), F13 (κυδρός), F30 (τριστοίχους), F41b (ἀμφαδόν).

[14]   See *TrGF* 1.19 F43a, referring to a suggestion made by Welcker; cf. *Little Iliad* (as summarized by Proclus, *Chrestomathia* = F53 Davies, lines 19–22); see also Stevens (2007) 249–51 for speculative reconstruction of the plot (and possible similarities with Euripides' *Hecuba*).

plausibly fit into such a scenario – they include references to 'snow-white Helen', a stranger's mysterious arrival at [Helen's?] bedchamber, and an odd cock-crow which sounded like a pan-pipe from Mount Ida – but they give little clue as to how the myth was handled by Ion.[15] The fact that the chorus was composed of soldiers or watchmen guarding the city suggests that they had a more active, involved role in the plot than other typical tragic choruses. It may even be that they were killed by Odysseus: other versions of the story narrate Odysseus' slaughter of the guards on his way out of the gates of Troy,[16] but it would have been an extraordinary *coup de théâtre* for a tragedian to kill off his chorus on stage. One line from *Guards* was striking enough for it to be parodied by Aristophanes: 'It's silent, but rancorous; yet, at any rate, it wants him.'[17] Aristophanes re-imagines the line as a description of the city of Athens in 405 BCE, yearning to have the politician Alcibiades back from Sparta in spite of his unpredictable nature; but in Ion's original version the line was spoken by Helen to Odysseus, and probably referred to the city of Troy yearning for the return from war of its problematic prince Paris.

Ion's other tragedies included *Agamemnon, Alcmene, Men of Argos, Children of Eurytus, Laertes, Teucer,* and *Phoenix* (this last title is sometimes recorded as *Caineus* or *Oineus*). The fragments are extremely unrevealing, but the titles indicate that Ion treated much the same range of mythical subject-matter as his rivals. Perhaps one can tentatively detect a slight preference for plays dealing with the Trojan War (and its aftermath) and the myth of Heracles, but the other lost titles may have told a different story. The bizarre and apparently unique title *Mega Drama*, attributed to Ion by several sources, tells us nothing at all about the subject or indeed the genre of the play in question: one of its fragments mentions a fennel stalk, which might (just conceivably) indicate that this 'big play' had something to do with Dionysus (or Prometheus?), but further evidence is lacking. Ion also wrote a satyr-play on the subject of Heracles' subjection to Omphale: this play falls outside the scope of the present volume,[18] but it has been

---

[15] *TrGF* 1.19 F46, F43b, F45.

[16] This is suggested by Stevens (2007) 253–4, comparing Proclus' summary of the *Little Iliad* (as in previous note) and also Euripides' *Rhesus* 506–7 for the same detail.

[17] *TrGF* 1.19 F44 (σιγᾶι μέν, ἐχθαίρει δέ, βούλεταί γε μην); cf. Aristophanes, *Frogs* 1425: the original speaker and addressee are mentioned by Σ *ad loc*. However, the subject and the object of the utterance are both unclear, and the reading offered here is only a guess: see Stevens (2007) 251. Moorton (1988) interprets the line as an erotic metaphor, comparing Catullus' *odi et amo*. Note that *Frogs* 1431–2 (a reworking of an Aeschylean simile) implicitly compares Alcibiades to Paris but also to Helen.

[18] For further discussion see Krumeich et al. (1999) 480–90; cf. Easterling (2007), Webster (1936). Note that *Omphale* is Ion's most quoted play, with eighteen surviving fragments.

suggested that *Alcmena, Children of Eurytus,* and *Omphale,* together with one other tragedy, formed a connected tetralogy on the subject of Heracles and his exploits in Oechalia.[19]

The fragments of these and other lost tragedies by Ion are translated in Appendix 1 at the end of this book, but (as already stated) they are disappointingly thin. A large number of them consist of just one or two words which were quoted by ancient scholars on account of their lexicographical interest. Some of them take the form of maxims preserved by writers who treated them, along with many similar gobbets excerpted from tragedy, as a source of quotable wisdom, though in the absence of any context in which to situate them, their content tends to strike us as extremely conventional or banal.[20] A few curious fragments show an interest in natural history, especially the habits of hedgehogs, octopuses and dolphins,[21] or describe the sound made by different musical instruments.[22] But most of these lines, quoted by Athenaeus for specific purposes of his own, can scarcely be treated as indicative of Ion's thematic range. Perhaps one day further literary finds will help us to make more of these fugitive remains, or to rehabilitate Ion's reputation to some extent, but in the meantime Sophocles' position in the tragic league table looks fairly safe.

Achaeus' reputation in antiquity seems to have been more secure; at least, he did not suffer the indignity of being dubbed a second-rater by Longinus or others. In fact, the few references to him in antiquity are extremely flattering: Athenaeus praises him for the smoothness of his style and the fluency of his composition; Didymus seems to have written commentaries on his plays; and Diogenes Laertius reports that Achaeus was thought by some to be superior to Sophocles and second only to Aeschylus (in the writing of satyric drama, at least).[23] What little we know about his life and career comes from his entry in the *Suda.* The son of Pythodorus (or Pythodorides), Achaeus was born *c.* 484–480 BCE, making him a rough contemporary of Sophocles and Euripides. He competed at the Athenian festivals with up to forty-four plays (though the number was sometimes given as thirty or twenty-four), and won one victory.[24]

We know the titles of nineteen plays by Achaeus. At least six of these are definitely attested as satyr-dramas (*Aethon, Alcmeon, Hephaestus, Iris, Linus,* and

---

[19]   Schmid and Stählin (1929) 517, followed by Webster (1936) 267 and Easterling (2007) 284.
[20]   *TrGF* 1.19 F5a, F8a, F55, F58, F63.
[21]   *TrGF* 1.19 F36, F38, F58.
[22]   *TrGF* 1.19 F39, F42, F45.
[23]   Athenaeus 10.451c, 15.689b; Diogenes Laertius 2.133 (*TrGF* 1.20 T6–8).
[24]   *TrGF* 1.20 T1 (*Suda* A 4683).

Omphale), and perhaps others were also satyric: the fragments of *Contests* (*Athla*) are concerned with athletics and food, which may be seen as satyric rather than tragic themes, and the fragments of *Fates* (*Moirai*) contain brief snippets of erotic subject-matter and colloquial language.[25] Other titles hint at characters or subject-matter which might seem unusual in comparison with other tragedies – such as *Mômus* (the personification of blame, known from brief references in Hesiod and the Epic Cycle[26] but otherwise an obscure figure, hardly typical of tragic myth), or *Cycnus* (perhaps dealing with the same character as Stesichorus' *Cycnus*, a monstrous son of Ares who robbed and killed visitors to Delphi until he was defeated by Heracles[27]) – or which are completely obscure, such as *The Attack* (*Katapeira*), a title which might conceivably relate to almost any myth.

The remaining titles give us a broad idea about Achaeus' choice of tragic myths, but there are few specific clues to suggest just what he did with these myths. *Adrastus* must have had something to do with the legend of the Seven against Thebes, as narrated in the lost *Thebaid* and frequently dramatized or alluded to in tragedy, for its title-character was the leader of the first Argive expedition against Thebes. The subject-matter of *Azanians* (another name for the Arcadians) is more difficult to imagine: its sole fragment takes the form of a suppliant plea that a sacrifice to Zeus be averted, but this tells us nothing about the characters or their situation. The play *Alphesiboea* may have been related (somehow) to the satyric *Alcmeon*, since its title-character was Alcmeon's wife, but its surviving fragment (an oblique allusion to the Hyades, quoted for its astrological interest) is altogether unrevealing.

Several plays – *Oedipus, Philoctetes, Peirithous, Theseus* and *Phrixus* – were treatments of popular subjects that were also dramatized by many other playwrights. Occasionally there are signs of similarities or differences between Achaeus' tragedies and other versions. The fragments of Achaeus' *Theseus*, which contain references to the Saronic Bay at Troezen and the terrifying bull from the sea, may suggest that the plot of this work resembled that of Euripides' *Hippolytus*;[28] whereas the remains of Achaeus' *Philoctetes*, in which Agamemnon is seen rousing up the Achaeans for battle with a loud war cry, seem to indicate that this play dealt with a later stage of the myth than in other dramatic versions.[29] This tragedy evidently dramatized the Greeks' attack on Troy, which implies that

[25] Snell tentatively identifies both these plays as satyric: see *TrGF* 1.20 *ad loc.*
[26] Hesiod, *Theogony* 214; cf. *Cypria* F1 Davies.
[27] However, there were other Cycnuses in myth, including a son of Poseidon killed by Achilles (*Cypria*, Proclus *Chrestomathia* 10 Davies).
[28] *TrGF* 1.20 F18–18a.
[29] *TrGF* 1.20 F37. Cf. Sophocles' *Philoctetes at Troy* (following Radt, *TrGF* 4, p. 483).

Philoctetes had already been rescued and rehabilitated, but we know that the *Philoctetes* plays by Aeschylus, Sophocles and Euripides, by contrast, all took place on Lemnos and dealt with Odysseus' attempts to obtain Philoctetes' bow before the capture of Troy could take place.[30]

As in the case of Ion, almost all of the fragments, from named or unidentified plays alike, take the form of single words or the briefest of phrases, quoted by lexicographers or historians without regard for their dramatic context or any intrinsic interest. I provide an English translation of Achaeus' tragic fragments in Appendix 1: perhaps my readers will be able to read more significance into these fragments than I have been able to do, but they will be hard pressed to rescue Achaeus from obscurity.

Neophron

Neophron (or Neophon – the alternative spelling is also attested) was obviously a successful and popular playwright. If the figure quoted in the *Suda* is correct, he produced 120 tragedies (considerably more than Aeschylus, Sophocles or Euripides), which makes him one of the most prolific dramatists known to us.[31] Nevertheless, he has left behind surprisingly few traces of his existence, and some have even doubted that he was a fifth-century poet. There are signs that he was something of an innovator in terms of plot and character, for he is said to have been the first to bring on stage the tutors of children (*paidagôgoi*) and to depict the torture of slaves.[32] In other words, if this evidence can be trusted, Neophron seems to have had an interest in expanding the social range of character types in tragedy and exploring the life and situation not just of kings and heroes but also of low-status individuals.[33]

Of all those 120 plays the only one known to us is his *Medea*. This play seems to have had a storyline very similar to Euripides' play of the same name. It dramatized the final portion of the myth of Medea and Jason, long after their experiences in Colchis and their journey on the *Argo*: they are now living as exiles in Corinth, but Jason has abandoned Medea in favour of a new wife; and

---

[30] This is shown by Dio Chrysostom's discussion of all three plays (*Oration* 52); see Russell and Winterbottom (1972) 504–7.

[31] *Suda* N 218 (*TrGF* 1.15 T1). It is suspicious that no satyr-dramas are mentioned in this total (unless the *Suda*'s τραγωιδίας is a slip for δράματα).

[32] See note 31. In the light of the discussion that follows, it may be relevant to note that the first securely attested *paidagôgos* in tragedy is found in Euripides' *Medea*.

[33] On the 'sociology' of Greek tragedy in general see Hall (1997).

eventually Medea, in great distress, murders her own children, a deed which may stem from terrible desperation or a wish to exact a sort of revenge.

The ending of Neophron's play incorporated a radical innovation, as we are informed by one ancient scholar[34]:

> Some say that, as a result of Medea's fury or at her command, Jason fell asleep beneath the prow of the *Argo* and died when a bit of wood fell on him; but Neophron, rather more outlandishly, says that he died by hanging himself, and he brings his Medea on stage addressing Jason's body thus:
>
> > In the end you will kill yourself and meet a most shameful fate, tying a knotted noose around your neck – this is the sort of destiny that awaits you in return for your evil deeds, and acts as a lesson to others for countless days to come: that mortals should never try to raise themselves above gods.[35]

This version of the end of the myth is not seen elsewhere, and it significantly alters our view of Jason's character and situation. Rather than being left to suffer for a prolonged period without relief, as in Euripides or Seneca, Jason is made to destroy himself, in grief or in remorse as it might be, while Medea lives on. The manner of Jason's death is clearly meant to diminish him, since hanging was regarded as a distinctly female method of suicide.[36] Medea emphasizes the grotesque and sordid nature of his death by lingering pleonastically on the gruesome details; and by her stress on 'fate' or 'destiny' (using two different but related words, *moros* and *moira*) she makes it seem as if superhuman powers are responsible for Jason's end, as well as implying that there is a sort of grim inevitability about this outcome. Medea – though a murderess – wants to present herself as in the right, on the side of the gods and fate, while Jason is seen as being firmly in the wrong. These lines obviously come from the very end of the play, and it may be that Medea delivered them *ex machina,* as in Euripides' version. At any rate, there is a quasi-divine tone to Medea's words – in their apparent omniscience, their ability to foretell the future, their lofty pronouncements about 'mortals' in relation to the gods, and their identification of a moral lesson or message underlying the action.

---

[34] Σ Euripides, *Medea* 1386 = *TrGF* 1.15 F3; the alternative version mentioned here is attributed to Staphylus (*FGrHist* 269 F11).

[35] τέλος φθερεῖς γὰρ αὐτὸν αἰσχίστωι μόρωι
δέρηι βροχωτὸν ἀγχόνην ἐπισπάσας.
τοία σε μοῖρα σῶν κακῶν ἔργων μένει,
δίδαξις ἄλλοις μυρίας ἐφ' ἡμέρας
θεῶν ὕπερθε μήποτ' αἴρεσθαι βροτούς.

[36] See Loraux (1987), especially 7–17 (on 'The Rope and the Sword').

As in other versions of the myth, Medea was depicted by Neophron as an unusually clever and resourceful woman. It is unclear whether (as elsewhere) she was an expert in witchcraft or magical potions, but her special skills here did include an ability to decipher riddling oracles. At one point in the play the Athenian king Aegeus deliberately came to visit Medea in Corinth in order to find out the meaning of an oracle that he had received[37]:

> Indeed I came here in person to find out some solution from you, for I have no means of interpreting the prophetic voice which Apollo's priestess revealed to me. By coming to speak to you I hoped that I might learn.

It is because Medea is naturally such a strong, capable woman that her eventual mental unravelling would have been all the more painful and distressing to watch.

This process of unravelling, culminating in her decision to murder her sons, was articulated in a long monologue, fifteen lines of which survive (and which constitute one of the most substantial and revealing of all tragic fragments).[38] They were quoted by John of Stobi in the section of his literary anthology entitled 'On Anger', though in fact the emotions that Medea experiences here are considerably more varied than anger alone, and more difficult to comprehend fully.

εἶέν· τί δράσεις, θυμέ; βούλευσαι καλῶς
πρὶν ἐξαμαρτεῖν καὶ τὰ προσφιλέστατα
ἔχθιστα θέσθαι. ποῖ ποτ᾽ ἐξῆιξας τάλας;
κάτισχε λῆμα καὶ σθένος θεοστυγές.
καὶ πρὸς τί ταῦτα δύρομαι, ψυχὴν ἐμὴν
ὁρῶσ᾽ ἔρημον καὶ παρημελημένην
πρὸς ὧν ἐχρῆν ἥκιστα; μαλθακοὶ δὲ δή
τοιαῦτα γιγνόμεσθα πάσχοντες κακά;
οὐ μὴ προδώσεις, θυμέ, σαυτὸν ἐν κακοῖς;
οἴμοι, δέδοκται· παῖδες, ἐκτὸς ὀμμάτων
ἀπέλθετ᾽· ἤδη γάρ με φοινία μέγαν
δέδυκε λύσσα θυμόν. ὦ χέρες,
πρὸς οἷον ἔργον ἐξοπλιζόμεσθα. φεῦ,
τάλαινα τόλμης, ἣ πολὺν πόνον βραχεῖ
διαφθεροῦσα τὸν ἐμὸν ἔρχομαι χρόνωι.

---

[37] *TrGF* 1.15 F1 (quotation and context supplied by Σ Euripides, *Medea* 666). In Euripides' version, by contrast, Aegeus encounters Medea by chance en route from Delphi to Troezen.
[38] *TrGF* 1.15 F2 (Stobaeus 3.20.33).

Well, then – what will you do, my heart? Think hard before you slip up and turn your dearest friends into bitterest enemies. Wretched heart, whither have you rushed forth? Restrain your impulse and your terrible strength that is hateful to the gods.

And why is it that I am crying about all this, when I can see my soul desolate and forsaken by those who least of all ought to have abandoned me? Am I, then, to become weak, indeed, as I undergo such awful sufferings? My heart! Do not betray yourself, even among such evils!

[*She sighs.*] Alas! My mind is made up.

[*Speaking to her children*] Out of my sight, boys! Get away from here! For by now a murderous madness has already sunk deep within my heart.

Oh, hands! My hands! What sort of deed is this to which we are steeling ourselves! Ah! I am wretched even in my daring, I who now set out to destroy my long travail in a short moment.

To a modern reader the writing may appear artless or stilted, but in a fifth-century context this passage would have struck its audience as extraordinarily powerful. Neophron is attempting to convey a complex psychological state in what, for his time, seems unusually vivid and explicit language. Perhaps one might detect a certain clumsiness in Medea's diction or turn of phrase, but no doubt this is meant to be indicative of the extreme distress and desperation in which she finds herself; or perhaps all these inchoate sentences, internal contradictions and abrupt changes of direction are to be seen as signs of a disordered mentality.

Two features of Medea's language are of particular interest. First of all, Medea explicitly – and, to all appearances, rationally – informs us that madness (*lussa*) has entered her heart. This seems to create a troubling sense of paradox, or, at least, it establishes an implicit tension between passionate emotion and rational thought, and it makes us wonder just how far Medea is in control of her own words or actions. Secondly, and even more significantly, it is not altogether clear whom Medea is addressing here. At times she seems to be talking to an imaginary third party (which, as in all tragic monologues, may conventionally be represented by the audience); at times she seems to be talking to her sons (who may or may not be present on stage to hear these terrifying words);[39] but at other times she is apostrophizing herself (either in a general sense, or in terms of specific individual parts such as her heart or hands). Medea blurs together these different imaginary addressees in an ambiguous and confusing manner. Sometimes the grammar

---

[39] Cf. Euripides' *Medea* 1019–55, where the children *are* present during a similar monologue.

adds to the sense of confusion, as Medea jumbles together nominative and vocative forms, or first-person singular and plural verbs, when referring to herself. But it is clear that Neophron's aim is (among other things) to represent a sense of a *divided* self, as if Medea conceives of her own personality or identity as a fragmented entity, separable into distinct parts.

These lines tell us a lot about the way in which Neophron portrayed his heroine, but they also provide an important source of evidence for anyone interested in ancient Greek concepts of psychology or emotions more generally. How unusual was the concept of the divided self, and how original was Neophron's version of the concept? Our fragment has been discussed in relation to these questions by Bruno Snell, who concludes that Neophron was probably not offering a particularly novel interpretation of human psychology: he compares Medea's monologue to passages in Homer and archaic poetry where characters apostrophize their own heart or soul (*thumos*, *kradiê*, or similar expressions) or where emotions are seen as external forces acting on the individual.[40] Nevertheless, he concedes that this remains an unusually forceful portrayal of a person's emotional state, which is more detailed and nuanced than anything found in earlier poetry; and he does regard Neophron's outlook as characteristically fifth-century or modern in one sense, in that he believes that the contrast between reason and passion is the key to understanding the impact of the scene.[41]

It is important to note that Snell's position is an elaboration of a larger argument running through several of his earlier works (notably, *The Discovery of the Mind*), in which the development of Greek psychology from the archaic period onwards is seen as an evolutionary process culminating in the notion of a unitary, autonomous self. In fact it is Euripides' *Medea*, in particular, that Snell identifies as the first text in which the concept of self-division is seen specifically in terms of division *within* a single self.[42] Euripides' play, as is well known, also features a monologue of self-division, including the heroine's apostrophe of her own *thumos*; but in that play Medea actually says that her heart (*thumos*) is more powerful than her intellect (*bouleumata*),[43] which Snell takes to be an explicit sign of a new conception of the human personality (i.e. autonomous and self-contained but internally divided, with one element mastering another). Snell

---

[40]   Homer, *Iliad* 2.195–6, 9.239, 9.553–4; Hesiod, *Shield* 149; Archilochus F78, 88, 112 West, etc.
[41]   Snell (1971) 199–205.
[42]   See Snell (1953) and (1964).
[43]   Euripides, *Medea* 1021–80; the crucial passage for Snell is 1078–9.

adopts the traditional view that Neophron was writing earlier than Euripides, which means that he has to view him as merely a forerunner.

A different perspective on self-division has been given more recently by Christopher Gill (although, curiously, Gill does not mention Neophron at all).[44] Rejecting Snell's ('subjective-individualist') conception of the unitary, autonomous 'I', which he regards as anachronistically modern, Gill tends to see Greek texts as based on an 'objective-participant' conception of personality, in which the self is seen as a participant in a dialogue, either between different parts of the psyche or between different people in different ethical situations. On Gill's reading, Euripides is not doing anything original in comparison with Homer: rather, both are articulating, in their different ways, essentially the same sort of outlook. What is unusual about Euripides' Medea, according to Gill, is the extreme situation in which she finds herself: the particular form of self-division seen in Euripides' tragedy reflects the fact that Medea is especially isolated, and so she speaks to herself in the absence of opportunities for other types of dialogue – 'a mode of articulating ideas which stem from (and could be expressed appropriately within) an interpersonal relationship, were it not for the figure's exceptional isolation'.[45] In other words, it is the internalization of dialogue that marks out Medea's speech in Euripides as something unusual, rather than any fundamental shift in the way that the self is conceived. I think Gill is absolutely convincing in his analysis – but one could go further and add that more or less everything he says about Euripides could also be said about Neophron. So perhaps Neophron can be seen as doing something novel after all. Even if (unlike Euripides) he does not explicitly describe the struggle of one part of Medea's self with another, he does certainly dramatize 'the internalization of dialogue' in a more extended and sustained manner than any previous poet known to us.

Neophron's *Medea* has been discussed (if at all) largely in relation to Euripides' *Medea*.[46] Several ancient scholars, observing certain similarities between these two tragedies, came to the conclusion that Euripides was influenced by Neophron – or even that he had plagiarized or stolen the work of his rival. The writer of the *Hypothesis* to Euripides' *Medea*, who names Dicaearchus and Aristotle as his sources, reports that 'Euripides appears to have taken the play from Neophron, revised it, and passed it off as his own work'.[47] The entry under 'Neophron' in the

---

[44] Gill (1996), esp. 10–12, 154–83, 216–26.
[45] Gill (1996) 183.
[46] Apart from the works already mentioned, see especially Page (1938) xxx–xxxvi; Thompson (1944); Manuwald (1983); Michelini (1989); Mastronarde (2002) 57–64; Diggle (2008).
[47] *TrGF* 1.15 T2.

Suda gives the same information, introducing Neophron as 'the tragedian whose work they say Euripides' *Medea* is'.[48] Diogenes Laertius too reports that Euripides' play is the work of Neophron, 'according to some people' – a detail showing that opinion was divided, and also suggesting that Diogenes was not any longer in a position to check the facts (though surely the same cannot be said of Aristotle).[49] Of course these accounts may contain a degree of exaggeration – surely Euripides did not surreptitiously steal an *entire* play from Neophron? – but nonetheless it is obvious that Medea's agonized internal dialogue was presented in an extremely similar way by both poets, and it may be that Euripides took many other big or small details from Neophron, including the bare bones of his plot.[50]

The majority of modern critics have tried to defend Euripides from this charge, most commonly (and yet radically) by reversing the order of these two plays and suggesting that Neophron, not Euripides, was the plagiarist. Denys Page, for instance, re-dated Neophron to the fourth century,[51] while more recently Donald Mastronarde has suggested that the fragments we possess are not from Neophron's *Medea* but some other, post-Euripidean *Medea* that was later misattributed to Neophron by scholars who knew that he had written a play of this title.[52] There is no way of disproving this sort of scenario, but it seems to be based on certain questionable preconceptions about literary quality: not just the relative merits of Euripides and Neophron but the assumption that the label 'fourth-century' is synonymous with 'inferior'.[53]

Indeed, a surprisingly large proportion of the scholarship centres (as so often) on the question of the poetic quality or aesthetic value of each poet's work, as if that were somehow a decisive factor in the argument. Could it really be that a 'great' poet such as Euripides would stoop to plagiarism? Could it really be that Euripides copied, or was substantially influenced by, a *bad* playwright? James Diggle, in the most recent treatment of the problem, thinks not; and he even goes out of his way to remind us (six times in a seven-page-long article) that Neophron was a 'bad' or 'very bad' poet. Diggle lists several striking verbal similarities between Neophron's fragments and Euripides' *Medea,* not just within Medea's

---

[48]   *Suda* N 218 (*TrGF* 1.15 T1).
[49]   Diogenes Laertius 3.134 (*TrGF* 1.15 T3).
[50]   Michelini (1989) suggests various ways in which Euripides' play may owe a debt to Neophron, including various illogical or seemingly unmotivated plot developments (such as the inclusion of Aegeus and the *ex machina* ending). It has also been pointed out that Euripides' *Medea* requires only two actors, which may suggest its derivation from an earlier (two-actor) type of tragedy: see Thompson (1944) 11.
[51]   Page (1938) xxx–xxxi.
[52]   Mastronarde (2002) 57–64.
[53]   See Chapter 5 for further discussion of this problematic assumption.

monologue but also in other portions of the play.[54] 'It is not believable,' he writes, 'that Euripides would remember such bad poetry so well that he would allow the memory of it to creep into other parts of his play too'. But is it really unbelievable? Leaving aside the knotty and subjective question of what constitutes literary quality in the first place, it must surely be admitted that certain lines of verse do have an odd tendency to stick in the mind, despite (or even precisely because of) their perceived badness.[55] Even if we concede that Neophron's poetry was really so very bad (and I do not think this is self-evident) might there not have been some quality about it – even its very badness – which was sufficient for a few verses or phrases to etch themselves on Euripides' memory?

Nevertheless, all these qualitative evaluations constitute something of a red herring.[56] In the first place, it seems perfectly possible that a 'great' poet might be influenced, in some sense or another, by a 'lesser' one. Perhaps we might imagine Euripides' motive as having been not to steal someone else's original work and secretly pass it off as his own, but rather to identify some promising feature or brilliant conceit that didn't quite seem to come off in Neophron's work, and transform it into something even better. Even if we sneer at Neophron's poetic abilities, we have to admit that his unusual attempt to depict Medea's divided state of mind is extremely bold and striking. Perhaps Euripides saw this as an idea which was too good to let drop.

But in any case, I suggest that scholars have been wrong to frame the discussion in terms of originality *versus* plagiarism. This is how ancient critics – often demonstrably malicious or misinformed – tend to talk about any sort of allusion or intertextual relationship; but it usually turns out to be an oversimplification or distortion of the evidence. One might well compare the way in which fifth-century comedians routinely accuse one another of 'plagiarism' when they are really referring to a complex and clever series of deliberate echoes, allusions and running gags.[57] They are not literally plagiarizing one another's work in the hope that no one will notice; rather, they are openly reusing each other's material and

---

[54] Diggle (2008) 411, citing Euripides, *Medea* 16 and 572–3 (cf. Neophron F2.2-3), 1236 (cf. F2.10), 1242 (cf. F2.13).

[55] Who is there alive that cannot quote a few verses of William Topaz McGonagall? Why is it that every classicist of my acquaintance seems to remember that abysmal line of Cicero's: *o fortunatam Romam me consule natam* (F8 Courtney)? These matters are perpetually mysterious; but see D.B. Wyndham Lewis and C. Lee, *The Stuffed Owl: An Anthology of Bad Verse* (London, 1930), esp. vii–xxiv.

[56] This was seen by Michelini (1989) 115–16.

[57] E.g. Aristophanes, *Clouds* 545–59, Hermippus F64 K-A, Lysippus F4 K-A, Eupolis, *Baptai* F89 K-A, Platon, *Perialges* F115 K-A, etc. See Ruffell (2002) for a more sophisticated analysis of comic 'plagiarism' as calculated intertextuality.

creatively transforming it. The literary effect, and the humour, depends precisely on their negotiation of the relationship between the new text and the source text. In just the same way, when we detect some similarity between Euripides and Neophron we do not need to see it as a furtive act of misappropriation; rather, it could be a markedly intertextual act. Euripides can be seen as reworking and responding to Neophron, creating a deliberate and obvious tension between his predecessor and his own new version of the story. This is a technique for which Euripides is already very well known: several of his tragedies (including, above all, *Orestes, Helen, Phoenician Women* and *Heracles*) self-consciously respond to earlier plays by rival tragedians or by Euripides himself.[58] The most famous intertextual reworking of this sort is the recognition scene in Euripides' *Electra*, which is a creative and critical response to Aeschylus' *Libation-Bearers*. This fact is well known and has been much discussed. Now it may be that an ancient scholar, noting the similarities between these two texts, would have accused Euripides (or even Aeschylus!) of 'plagiarism'. But clearly this would be a crude and misguided accusation.

I prefer to read Euripides' *Medea*, and especially its heroine's great monologue, as an intertextual response to Neophron's *Medea*. It is hard to judge whether Euripides' version should be seen as a critique of Neophron, or as an implicit judgement on some aspect of his dramatic technique or handling of myth. Could Euripides be read as implying that the division of an individual person into separate parts is impossible, or that the apostrophe of one's own body parts is ludicrous? Might his intention, perhaps, be almost satirical or parodic? (That is precisely how some have interpreted the recognition scene in *Electra*.[59]) This is not the place to discuss Euripides' play, which, for all its difficulties of interpretation, at least has the advantage of surviving intact.[60] Nevertheless, it is fair to say that Euripides' *Medea* looks rather different if we interpret it not as an example of plagiarism but as a play openly and self-consciously written in dialogue with another well-known tragedian's work. This would be equally true even if it could be proved that Neophron's *Medea* came second: the important

---

[58] Mastronarde (2002) alludes to Euripides' reputation (in antiquity and in the modern world) as an innovator, pointing out that this fact has been adduced in support of the view that Euripides could *not* be a plagiarist. But in fact Euripides' innovation often resides precisely in intertextual games and significant allusions: see (e.g.) Zeitlin (1980), Torrance (2013).

[59] For discussion see (most recently) Davies (1998), Torrance (2013) 13–33.

[60] Or *more or less* intact, depending whether one shares the view of Diggle, Kovacs and others that various portions of Euripides' *Medea* are in fact spurious. It should be noted that the question of the relationship between Neophron and Euripides is complicated further by the possibility that some of Medea's great monologue at Euripides, *Medea* 1021–80 is the work of later interpolators. See Diggle (2008), cf. Kovacs (1986).

fact is that these are two tragedies in dialogue with one another. Perhaps more work remains to be done on the exact nature of this dialogue and its implications for our knowledge of textual relations and literary self-reflexivity at the end of the fifth century.

Aristarchus

Even though Aristarchus is scarcely a familiar name to many people today, there are signs that he remained widely known for several centuries after his death, perhaps more so than many of his contemporaries. He is mentioned in the *Suda* as being active at around the same time as Euripides, as the author of seventy plays and winner of two first prizes, and as being the first to compose tragedies 'of the same length as those of the current day'.[61] This last piece of information is slightly ambiguous, partly because we do not know what period is being referred to as 'current'. However, the thirty-two complete tragedies that survive indicate that the average length of plays did increase over time – the longest examples, all from the very late fifth century, are Sophocles' *Oedipus at Colonus* (1779 lines) and Euripides' *Phoenician Women* (1763) and *Helen* (1692), compared with Aeschylus' earlier *Persians* (1077) or *Seven against Thebes* (1078) – so it is quite reasonable to assume that Aristarchus' plays were longer than average, though it is impossible to know whether he consciously set out to write very long plays, and, if so, what effect he was hoping to create.[62]

Aristarchus' name and reputation were known to the ninth-century Byzantine chronicler Georgius Monachus, who included Aristarchus in a roll-call of what he saw as especially prominent writers active in the last decades of the fifth century (alongside other luminaries such as Sophocles, Euripides, Thucydides, Hippocrates, Pherecydes and others).[63] He was also familiar to Roman audiences through the work of Ennius, who is said to have produced Latin versions of many tragedies by both Aristarchus and Euripides.[64] Plautus too expected his audience to have knowledge of Aristarchus, since the start of his comedy *Poenulus* explicitly announces itself as a self-conscious reworking of Aristarchus' tragedy *Achilles*:

---

[61] *Suda* A 3893 = *TrGF* 1.14 T1.
[62] Cf. my discussion of Agathon, whose experimental attempt to fit an entire epic into a tragedy may have resulted in an unusually long play (see Chapter 3, pp. 80–1).
[63] Georgius Monachus, *Chronicon* 6.10 (1.284 de Boor) = *TrGF* 1.14 T3.
[64] *TrGF* 1.14 T4.

I wish to declaim the *Achilles* of Aristarchus, whence, from that very tragedy, I shall take my own beginning: **'Be silent and keep quiet and pay attention! Your commander orders you to listen!'** – the commander of this company of actors, I mean to say – and people should all settle down in their seats in a good frame of mind, both those who are hungry and those who ate before they came out. Those of you who have eaten have done the most sensible thing by far; but those of you who haven't, fill yourselves up with what's on offer in this play. If a person's got something to eat right in front of him, as far as we're concerned it's just plain silly for him to sit there unfed. **'Rise up, herald! Make sure that the people hear!'** I've been waiting for ages now to find out if you know your duty.[65]

The phrases highlighted in bold are apparently direct quotations from Aristarchus (duly Latinized by Plautus), and Snell prints them as part of his 'Aristarchus F1a'.[66] If this is correct, it appears that Aristarchus' *Achilles* had an arresting opening scene, in which an army commander – such as Agamemnon, or Achilles himself? – addressed his troops. But the situation is complicated by the fact that Plautus' play is not simply based on Aristarchus. As becomes clear later in the prologue, *Poenulus* is substantially derived from a lost Greek comedy called *Carchêdonios* (probably the work of the fourth-century playwright Alexis), and it may well be that Plautus was using not just Aristarchus' tragedy but also Ennius' Latin version of the same play.[67] In effect what we have here is a palimpsestic text consisting of four different layers, which means that any attempt to identify an individual author's hand, or to trace the ultimate source of any feature in the text, must be regarded as provisional.

Nevertheless, if we assume that this Plautine opening does indeed reflect the opening of Aristarchus' *Achilles*, it seems that this tragedy had an unusually abrupt opening scene, immediately placing the audience *in medias res*. Indeed, Plautus is drawing our attention to the fact that this apparently naturalistic opening device fulfilled a dual function in the theatre. The speaker is simultaneously a character in the world of the play, using his opening lines to get the attention of his men, and also an actor, using the same lines to alert the spectators to the fact that the play has now begun and encourage them to be quiet. This piece of evidence is highly suggestive in terms of Aristarchus' stagecraft. As is well known, the classical Greek theatre had no curtain, which means that we always have to think carefully about the exact point at which any play can be said to begin, and about the different ways in which a boundary is

---

[65] Plautus, *Poenulus* 1–12. The portions highlighted in bold type are printed by Snell as *TrGF* 1.14 F1a.
[66] Jocelyn (1969) 164–5 is more sceptical about their attribution to Aristarchus.
[67] See Arnott (1959).

established between the real world and the fictional or mimetic world of the drama. Aristarchus in this case is 'raising the curtain' in an unexpected manner which finds no exact parallel in any other play known to us. It might be thought that this technique resembles something from a comedy rather than a tragedy; and even though Aristarchus is very unlikely to have addressed the audience explicitly, as Plautus does, his opening lines are quasi-metatheatrical, in that they draw our attention to a dramatic convention and stimulate us to think about the nature of the theatrical 'illusion'.

Aristarchus' other plays included an *Asclepius*, which apparently combined the themes of medicine and religion. No fragment of this tragedy survives, but it seems that the plot was concerned in some way with the healing of disease in the real-life sanctuary of Asclepius at Epidauros. Perhaps it was based on the myth of Asclepius' death and deification, with an aetiological description of the foundation of his healing-cult. The ancient biographical tradition recorded that Aristarchus wrote the play as a thank-offering in return for his own treatment at the hands of the healing god.[68] Though many tragedies engaged in some way with the developing science of fifth-century medicine or the linguistic discourse of disease and healing,[69] it is rare to see a play that is centrally concerned with the myth of Asclepius. Our main literary source for both the myth and the cult is Pindar' third *Pythian Ode*, but Aristophanes' *Wealth* (388 BCE) is the earliest surviving dramatic work to take a major interest in Asclepius and his sanctuary.

Aristarchus was also one of many tragedians to dramatize the awful myth of the family of Tantalus and Pelops: his *Tantalus* must have dealt with a relatively early part of the myth. It is possible to imagine the broad outlines of its plot on the basis of other poetic treatments of the story, but the only surviving fragment is a five-line piece of gnomic generalization on the topic of rhetoric, which might belong to almost any dramatic context[70]:

> In this matter it makes no difference whether you speak well or whether you don't. Whether you try to find things out or fail to find out anything at all, it's all the same. Wise men do not understand any more about these matters than those who are not wise. If anyone claims to be better than anyone else, he is an excellent speaker [but]

It is hard to see any wider significance to this pessimistic-sounding quotation in terms of its original context, but its inclusion in John of Stobi's anthology shows

---

[68] *TrGF* 1.14 F1: not technically a fragment but rather a testimonium in the *Suda* (A 3893), based on an anecdote told by Aelian (F101).

[69] See Craik (2001), Clarke Kosak (2005), Allan (2014) etc. (but no reference is made to Aristarchus).

[70] *TrGF* 1.14 F1b (Stobaeus 2.1.1).

that Aristarchus was still being used as a source of wisdom or solace many hundreds of years after his death (though Stobaeus may have relied on earlier anthologies rather than first-hand acquaintance with the tragedies). The same anthology also preserves another couple of gnomic fragments from unknown plays.[71] One of these fragments – 'O death, the restoration of good sense to those who lack judgement' – is a slightly unusual variation on the conventional theme of death the 'leveller', and the other is a more substantial soundbite concerning the inescapable nature of erotic love, along with its miraculous benefits for mankind:

> Among human beings whoever has no experience of love is ignorant of the law
> of necessity – in obedience to which I am overwhelmed to such an extent that I
> make this journey here. For the god of love has the power to make sick people
> healthy, and to make the helpless man find a way . . .

Once again one notes the medical imagery, which (to judge by that biographical anecdote mentioned above) may have been a recurrent strand in Aristarchus' work; and one is also struck by the speaker's wholly positive view of love and its effects, a view that contrasts with the problematic or destructive status of *erôs* as often seen elsewhere in tragedy.[72]

Theognis

Nowadays a very obscure figure, Theognis is, unfortunately, remembered for just one thing: his perceived 'frigidity' as a writer. This quality of Theognis' poetry, which is emphasized on several occasions by Aristophanes, is normally taken to be a stylistic trait (or defect),[73] since this is how the metaphor is used by several rhetorical theorists in antiquity. For instance, Demetrius in his treatise *On Style* defines frigidity (*psychrotês*) as excessive or hyperbolic use of language 'which transcends the expression appropriate to the thought', typically involving odd vocabulary, ill-judged epithets, over-use of compound adjectives, or strained

---

[71] *TrGF* 1.14 F2-3 (Stobaeus 4.20.9, 4.52.21). The remaining fragments of Aristarchus are unrevealing: F4 is a banal conversational tag quoted by Athenaeus to lend a vaguely 'literary' flavour to his own work; F5 is a mere reference to Parthenopaeus' father Talaos (or Kalaos); and F6 is a single word quoted by Photius for its lexicographic interest. See Appendix 1 for translations.

[72] See Thumiger (2013) on the morbid or terrible effects of *erôs* in tragedy. Contrast Wright (forthcoming a) for more nuanced discussion of tragic *erôs*, and cf. my discussion of Gnesippus, pp. 193–5.

[73] Aristophanes, *Acharnians* 9, 138–9; *Women Celebrating the Thesmophoria* 170 (= *TrGF* 1.28 T1–3).

metaphors.[74] The sole surviving fragment of Theognis' work is a two-word description of a bow as 'a lyre that plays no tune' (*phorminx achordos*). This phrase is quoted specifically as an illustration of the dangers of frigidity by both Demetrius and Aristotle: it is cited in a discussion of 'risky' metaphors which poets try to make 'safe' by adding explanatory epithets.[75]

Diogenes of Athens

This writer is also rather obscure: it is said in the *Suda* that he flourished around the very end of the fifth century, but the various tragedies listed under his name (*Achilles, Helen, Heracles, Thyestes, Medea, Oedipus* and *Chrysippus*) may be wrongly attributed: Snell reassigns them to the fourth-century tragedian Diogenes of Sinope.[76] There was also a tragic actor by the name of Diogenes, who may or may not have been the same man as the poet.[77]

A single fragment survives, from Diogenes' tragedy *Semele*. The title indicates a Dionysiac theme,[78] but this intriguing eleven-line passage is concerned not with the worship of Dionysus but with the rituals associated with the Phrygian Mother goddess Cybele. It is quoted by Athenaeus in the course of a discussion of exotic stringed instruments. He reports that, according to Diogenes, a *pêktis* is distinct from a *magadis*, and he illustrates this distinction with the following verses[79]:

> And indeed I hear the female followers of Asian Cybele, wearing their headbands, the children of wealthy Phrygians, making a loud noise with their drums and rattles and the clashing of bronze cymbals that they hold in both hands <...> the gods' wise songstress and healer. And I hear the Lydian and Bactrian maidens who dwell beside the River Halys worship the Tmolian goddess Artemis in her sacred grove in the shadow of laurel trees, entertaining her with notes played in counterpoint[80] on the triangular *pêktides*, plucking the strings of the *magadis*, where the *aulos*, entertained as a guest, joins in with the choruses in a Persian tune.

---

[74] Demetrius, *On Style* 115–127; cf. Aristotle, *Rhetoric* 3.3.2–6, 1405b–1406c. For discussion of frigidity in rhetorical theory and its meaning in terms of comic poetics see Wright (2012) 108–10.

[75] *TrGF* 1.28 F1 (Demetrius *On Style* 85; Aristotle, *Rhetoric* 3.11.1413a1).

[76] *TrGF* 1.45 T1 (*Suda* Δ 1142; Diogenes Laertius 6.73; cf. Diogenes Sinopensis (*TrGF* 1.88): see Chapter 5, pp. 153–63.

[77] Aelian *Historical Miscellany* 3.30, *History of Animals* 6.1 (*TrGF* 1.45 T3).

[78] Cf. Spintharus' *Semele Struck By Lightning* (*TrGF* 1.40): see discussion below, p. 183.

[79] *TrGF* 1.45 F1 (Athenaeus 14.636a).

[80] The word which I tentatively translate here as 'in counterpoint' is ἀντιζύγοις, which might alternatively refer to harmony, balance, contrast (or perhaps even 'unison'): without hearing the music it is impossible to say precisely what effect is denoted.

This text can be situated within a context of late fifth-century religious syncretism, in which the worship of traditional gods at Athens was transformed and revitalized by the introduction of new gods from elsewhere.[81] Tragedy has been seen not just as a reflection of changing ritual practices but as a dynamic force within society, bringing about changes in people's perception of religious matters, or assimilating new customs and beliefs into the mainstream.[82] Diogenes' play looks like an attempt to represent or explore the syncretism of the cults of Cybele and Dionysus,[83] and it is interesting to imagine the religious and dramatic possibilities presented by a chorus of devotees of Cybele, as apparently described in this passage, within a Dionysiac-themed tragedy; the same passage also makes a further connection of some sort with the goddess Artemis.

The highly self-referential language of the passage above makes it very likely that Diogenes was also experimenting with various contrasting musical styles in this performance. It is an unusual mixture of old and new elements, Greek and oriental; and the musical accompaniment incorporates an array of stringed, woodwind and percussion instruments from different traditions (this is emphasized on a verbal level, as the Greek *aulos* is explicitly described as a 'guest' or 'visitor' being entertained and included in the mixture). The overall impression given by this passage might make us think of the 'New Musical' revolution (an innovative approach to sound exemplified by other tragedians such as Agathon, Euripides or Gnesippus),[84] but the broader importance of this musical culture-clash is that it exactly reflects the collision of religious and ritual influences that is being explored in the plot. In other words, what we have here is a remarkable balance of form, performance, content and theme. It is a great pity that so little remains of what was obviously a fascinating and unusual play; but even this small fragment constitutes an important piece of evidence for the historian of Greek theatre and religion.

Critias

This man is better known for his political activities than for his literary pursuits: he was one of the so-called 'Thirty Tyrants', the oligarchic committee installed by

---

[81]　See Parker (1996) 188–98.

[82]　On all such matters see the excellent and wide-ranging discussion by Allan (2004), esp. 131–3 (on *Semele*).

[83]　A similar syncretism is suggested by the end of the 'Magna Mater' ode in Euripides' *Helen* (1301–7). See Parker (1996) 188–94 for discussion of the cult of Cybele (or 'the Mother') at Athens in the late fifth century.

[84]　See West (1992) 356–72.

the Spartans to govern Athens at the end of the Peloponnesian War in 404 BCE, and he was killed by democratic forces during the following year.[85] Previously Critias had also been linked with the sophistic movement: he is included among the group of other sophists and associates of Socrates in Plato's *Protagoras*, though he does not seem to have taught students or written any philosophical works himself.[86]

Critias' works included a number of poems in elegiacs and hexameters, as well as prose works on political and rhetorical themes.[87] We also possess fragments of four tragedies that have conventionally been attributed to him – *Tennes*, *Rhadamanthys*, *Peirithous* and *Sisyphus* – though there has always been considerable doubt about the authorship of these works. In our various sources we find that fragments or citations are attributed to Critias, or to Euripides, or to 'Critias or Euripides'.[88] It is easy to see why this uncertainty might have arisen, since both of these authors were sometimes associated with similar subject-matter and intellectual preoccupations (and, especially, with heterodox theological views, a consideration which is relevant to the study of *Sisyphus*).[89] But there is nothing about the linguistic style or the content of the fragments to mark them out as definitively Euripidean or non-Euripidean, which means that until more evidence should emerge, it is simply impossible to decide who wrote these works. In what follows I adhere to the conventional attribution, though the name Critias should be imagined as having a large question-mark over it each time it occurs. But in any case, it may be thought that the question of authorship has attracted a disproportionate amount of scholarly activity, distracting from the more interesting question of what these plays were actually about.

The myth of Tennes, not apparently treated in any other tragedy, has striking similarities to the story-patterns of Hippolytus, Bellerophon, Danae and others.[90] Tennes was said to be the son either of Cycnus, king of Colonae, or of the god Apollo; after he was falsely accused of rape by his stepmother, he was locked inside a chest by Cycnus and thrown, together with his sister Hemithea, into the

---

[85] See (e.g.) [Aristotle] *Athenian Constitution* 34–40, Xenophon, *Hellenica* 2. 3–4. Modern discussions of Critias' political career include Centanni (1997) 9–32, who attempts to link Critias' politics to his poetry and its reception, cf. Krentz (1982) and Ostwald (1986) 160–96 on Critias' career in relation to Athenian politics more generally.

[86] See Kerferd (1981) 52–3 and de Romilly (1992) 108–11 on Critias' place within the sophistic movement (both these authors consider him to be a marginal figure). Cf. Plato's *Critias*, in which he is the title character.

[87] See D-K 88 for fragments of non-dramatic works by Critias (cf. *TrGF* 1.43 T4).

[88] The various ancient and modern opinions on the attribution of Critias' works are summarized with admirable clarity and concision by Collard (2007a) 164–7; cf. Collard and Cropp (2008) II.630–5.

[89] See Dillon and Gergel (2003) 239–40 on some of the main similarities between the two men.

[90] See Apollodorus 4.3.24–5; Plutarch, *Moralia* 297d–f. Cf. Gantz (1993) 590–2.

sea; the chest eventually drifted ashore at Tenedos. Later on Cycnus realized the truth and sailed to Tenedos to put matters right, but Tennes refused to let him land. Eventually Tennes went to fight in the Trojan War, and was later killed by Achilles on Tenedos. It is not absolutely clear how much of this story made its way into Critias' *Tennes*, but at least some of these events seem to be referred to in the remains of an ancient plot-summary[91]:

> ... shutting ... witness of ... repented ... when he heard that Tennes had safely reached the island opposite. At Apollo's instruction he named the island Tenedos and killed the woman who had deceived him.

It is likely that Apollo appeared *ex machina* at the end of the play, and that this ending, like that of many other tragedies, incorporated an aetiological element, explaining the origins of the eponymous hero-cult of Tennes that still existed at Tenedos in the late fifth century. Otherwise little more can be said about this tragedy. Only a single line survives, which is a conventionally pessimistic soundbite preserved as a gnomic quotation by John of Stobi: 'Ah! There is no justice at all in the present generation'.[92]

The contents of Critias' *Rhadamanthys* are also uncertain. A very small portion of its plot seems to be preserved in a papyrus hypothesis, which indicates that the playwright made some sort of connection between the Cretan king Rhadamanthys, brother of Minos, and the myth of Helen and her brothers:

> After Polydeuces' death, Castor was killed when fighting alone. While Rhadamanthys was rejoicing at the victory but also grieving for his daughters, Artemis appeared and commanded Helen to establish rituals honouring her two dead brothers; and she announced that his daughters would become goddesses.

Whose daughters are being referred to here? It is hard to see what Rhadamanthys' own daughters have to do with the story of the Dioscuri, or why they should have been deified.[93] But it may be that this play dramatized events that are not mentioned in the surviving portion of the hypothesis but are described in detail elsewhere. Pindar, Theocritus and others[94] tell of a quarrel that arose when Castor and Polydeuces abducted Leucippus' daughters Phoebe and Hilaeira, who were already betrothed to Idas and Lynceus, the sons of the Messenian king Aphareus. Idas and Lynceus responded by attacking the Dioscuri, and a larger-scale conflict

[91] *TrGF* 1.43 F20 = *P.Oxy.* 2455.14.
[92] *TrGF* 1.43 F21.
[93] So Collard and Cropp (2008) II.658–9.
[94] Pindar, *Nemean* 10. 49–90; Theocritus, *Idyll* 22; cf. Apollodorus 3.10.3, 3.12.2.

subsequently arose between the Spartans and the Messenians. Thus it may be that Critias' play had something to do with political and ethnic differences in the Peloponnese, as well as another aetiological explanation of cult practice and an example of the familiar tragic theme of perverted or disrupted wedding ritual.[95] But, in that case, where does Rhadamanthys fit in? He does not figure in the other accounts of this myth. He is usually characterized as a wise man or judge, so perhaps he was called upon to arbitrate between the disputants. However, in several Greek and Roman texts Rhadamanthys appears in a more specific role as judge of the dead,[96] which opens up the possibility that this tragedy, like *Peirithous*, was somehow concerned with the Underworld: did some of the action take place in the world below?

The few surviving fragments do not enable us to answer this question, but they are not without interest. A reference to 'those who possess the land of Euboea, the neighbouring state' (F16) may give a further sign that *Rhadamanthys* was preoccupied with the mythical background to political power-struggles during the fifth century. The longest fragment is a ten-line passage quoted (once again) by John of Stobi for its moralizing content and general applicability to life[97]:

> In life all sorts of desires come upon us: one man yearns to gain nobility, while another cares nothing for rank but longs to be called the father of many possessions in his house; it pleases another to persuade those around him to embark on daring crimes, but his words contain no decent sentiment; meanwhile others among mortals seek shameful gain rather than good. Such are the ways in which human life is fallible. But for myself I desire none of these things; rather, I should wish to have the renown of a good reputation.

The speaker, who is not identified, is presumably Rhadamanthys himself or some other admirable character of moderate views. It has been suggested, by the most recent editors of the fragment,[98] that these were the opening lines of the play – a suggestion which is (as usual) unprovable, though one can point to several other tragedies which begin with a similar 'priamel' device, consisting of a general maxim followed by a specific application of the maxim to a character's situation.[99]

---

[95] On this last theme see Seaford (1987), Rehm (1994).
[96] Apollodorus 3.1.2; cf. Pindar, *Olympian* 2.75; Plato, *Apology* 41a, *Gorgias* 524a; Vergil, *Aeneid* 6.566.
[97] *TrGF* 1.43 F17.
[98] Collard and Cropp (2008) 2. 663.
[99] Sophocles' *Women of Trachis* and Euripides' *Orestes*, *Stheneboea*, *Aeolus* and *Children of Heracles* all began in precisely this way.

It may be that we also have the opening lines of *Peirithous*,[100] but what is even more valuable is that the author who quotes these lines (the Byzantine commentator Ioannes Logothetes) also supplies a narrative summary of their dramatic context and the plot of the tragedy, as follows[101]:

> Peirithous descended into Hades, accompanied by Theseus, in order to woo Persephone – and he met with a fitting punishment. Shackled to a seat of rock that was impossible to move, he was guarded by snakes with gaping mouths. Meanwhile Theseus too chose to live down in Hades, since he considered it shameful to abandon a friend. But when Heracles was sent by Eurystheus to abduct Cerberus, he defeated the creature by force and released Theseus and his entourage from their constraints, thanks to the support of the gods of the Underworld. Thus with a simple act he defeated his opponent and showed pity to his friends in their unfortunate circumstances, and he also won the god's favour. At any rate, Aeacus is brought on stage, speaking to Heracles as follows:

> *Aeacus:*
> Hey! What is happening here? I spy someone making his way here in haste and with an exceedingly bold demeanour. Stranger, you who approach this region, it is right that you should tell me who you are and what is the purpose of your journey.

> *Heracles:*
> I shall reveal the whole story to you without any hesitation: my native land is Argos, my name is Heracles, and I am sprung from Zeus, father of all the gods – for Zeus came to my mother's noble bed, as it is told to us by a true account. I have come here under compulsion, obedient to the command of Eurystheus, who sent me with instructions to bring back alive the hound of Hades to the gates of Mycenae. Eurystheus did not actually wish to see Cerberus, but he imagined that he had come up with this task as an impossible challenge for me. In pursuit of such a task I have travelled all around Europe and into the secret places of the whole of Asia.

Thus it is clear that some of the action of this play – unusually for tragedy – did take place down in Hades. It has been suggested that *Peirithous* was a significant model for Aristophanes' *Frogs*, which is also based on a similar story pattern involving two companions undertaking a journey to the lower world

---

[100] *TrGF* 1.43 F1. See, however, Collard and Cropp (2008) II.637–8, who think that a dialogue-style opening is unlikely and re-number the fragment as part of F4 in their Loeb edition (pp. 644–6).
[101] Ioannes Logothetes, *Commentary on [Hermogenes]*, Means of Rhetorical Effectiveness 28; some lines are also quoted by Gregory of Corinth, *Rhet. Gr.* 7.1312.

(*katabasis*).[102] This is a perfectly plausible suggestion, though impossible to prove; and it must be admitted that the case is weakened by the absence of any definite verbal similarities between *Frogs* and the remains of *Peirithous*. Whether or not there was a specific intertextual relationship between these two plays, it remains obvious that they both relied on the same basic structural pattern, consisting of a *katabasis*, followed by some sort of ordeal or challenge to be overcome, followed by an eventual return to the upper world. This story pattern may be seen as reflecting structures from religious rituals, particularly rites of passage or initiation into mystery cult.[103]

In fact one of the fragments of *Peirithous* does make explicit reference to mystery cult: '. . . so that in silence we may pour these *plêmochoai* into the chasm in the earth'. This is a direct allusion to the ceremony of Plemochoai that took place during the final day of the initiation into the Eleusinian Mysteries.[104] Pollux, who quotes the fragment, adds the information that the *plêmochoê* was a ceramic vessel (also called *kotyliskos*) resembling a spinning-top, and says that on the day of Plemochoai the initiates fill two such vessels and then turn them upside-down onto the ground while reciting a mystic formula. These words were sung by the chorus, who therefore are likely to have been a chorus of mystic initiates or *epoptai*;[105] and the choral odes in the tragedy may have taken the form of cult hymns or incorporated other ritual formulas. We are also told by other sources that Heracles underwent initiation into the Mysteries before making his descent into Hades,[106] so it would be reasonable to assume that *Peirithous* dramatized this process or perhaps even acted out Heracles' (and the chorus members') initiation on stage.

There are fourteen fragments of *Peirithous* in all (see Appendix 1 for an English translation), and some of them are comparatively substantial, allowing us a reasonable glimpse of how the plot developed and how the characters were portrayed. As we have seen, there were two connected strands to the plot – the labour of Heracles and the ordeal of Peirithous and Theseus. Peirithous' present

---

[102] Centanni (1997) 184–212 (including, on p. 182, a useful table summarizing the structural and thematic parallels between the two plays): she sees Aristophanes as using Critias' own tragedy as an oblique way of criticizing his politics. Cf. Dobrov (2002) 133–56, developing earlier hypothetical discussions by Wilamowitz and others (though he sees Euripidean authorship as crucial to Aristophanes' 'reworking' of *Peirithous*). But contrast Lloyd-Jones (1966) for the idea that 'a standard account of the descent of Heracles', originating in the epic tradition, underlies both plays.

[103] On structural approaches to rites of passage see Van Gennep (1909); cf. Lada-Richards (1999) for a reading of *Frogs* in this light.

[104] *TrGF* 1.43 F2. See Athenaeus 11.496a–b; cf. Parker (2005) 350.

[105] Collard and Cropp (2008) 2.643 infer that they are *dead* initiates, repeating the rituals that they had learnt at Eleusis.

[106] Apollodorus 2.5.12; Diodorus Siculus 4.25.1.

situation was also viewed in the context of his family's earlier history, including his father Ixion's seduction of Hera and his subsequent punishment (F5). Much was made of the admirable qualities of Theseus, chiefly his steadfast loyalty and his willingness to help those in trouble (F6, F7); and it may be that the play more generally set out to explore the nature of friendship or the importance of good behaviour to one's fellow human beings, since several moral maxims are devoted to this topic (F7, F10-12).[107] In the light of Critias' (or Euripides') reputation for fashionable intellectual speculation, it is also interesting to see that two of the fragments allude to cosmological science. One of the choral odes (F3) describes time as being in endless, self-regenerative flux (an image which may relate to the theories of Heraclitus), and also alludes to the 'twin Bears', Ursa Major and Ursa Minor, and their spatial relation to the celestial poles; while another ode (F4) is addressed to Mind (*Nous*) as creator and sustainer of the universe, an idea which surely reflects the influence of Anaxagoras.[108]

It is striking that three of the four plays attributed to Critias were concerned in some way with the Underworld. *Sisyphus*, like *Peirithous*, seems to have been based on a story pattern involving *katabasis* and *anabasis*. Its main character, Sisphyus, son of Aeolus (and in some accounts the father of Odysseus), features in Greek myth as an archetype of wily cunning.[109] He angered Zeus by revealing one of his secret love affairs, and was punished in Hades by being forced to roll a boulder endlessly uphill. Nevertheless, Sisyphus managed to persuade the Underworld deities to allow him to return to the upper world for a short time, and once he had made his ascent he escaped for good. It is not clear how this myth was treated by Critias or how the action of *Sisyphus* developed, since in this case we do not possess a hypothesis or any other testimonia; all that we have is a single fragment, which gives no help at all in reconstructing the plot.[110]

However, this fragment is an extraordinary and fascinating text, which has been much discussed on account of its unusual theological content. It is part of a sophistic-style description of the evolution of human culture, with distinct similarities to the 'civilization myths' narrated in Plato's *Protagoras* and Aeschylus'

---

[107] Note that Plutarch quotes F6 several times in a quasi-proverbial sense (*Moralia* 96c, 482a, 533a, 763f), apparently treating Theseus and Peirithous in this play as a paradigm of friendship. Cf. the relationship between Theseus and Heracles in Euripides' *Heracles*.

[108] Clement of Alexandria (*Miscellanies* 5.115) clearly names Nous as the addressee (though Collard and Cropp (2008) II.645 suggest Zeus or Time as possibilities). Centanni (1997) 141–2 sees a political as well as a philosophical significance in this reference to *nous*, linking the fragment to Critias' other writings (e.g. his discussion of *euxunesia*, 'intelligence', in B73 D-K).

[109] See Apollodorus 1.9.3; Homer, *Iliad* 11.593-600; Pherecydes *FGrHist* 3 F119.

[110] *TrGF* 1.43 F19.

Prometheus Bound. It also shows signs of engagement with contemporary discussions of human nature (*physis*) *versus* social convention (*nomos*), as reflected in the remains of Antiphon, Democritus and others.[111] Its speaker, who is identified in one source as Sisyphus himself,[112] explicitly states that religion and the gods were a human invention designed to maintain social order and prevent crime.

> Once upon a time human life lacked order: it was bestial and subservient to physical force, and there was no reward at that time for good behaviour, neither was there any punishment for the wicked. But then, so it seems to me, humans established laws, so that justice might be their ruler <...> and reduce wilful aggression to servitude. If anyone still did wrong, he was punished. Then, when laws prevented them from committing violent crimes out in the open, they began to commit them in secret; then at last (so it seems to me) some ingenious and clever man invented the fear of the gods for the benefit of mortals, so that terror might be implanted in the hearts of the wicked, even if they were doing or saying or thinking anything in secret. And thus it came about that he introduced religion (*to theion*) – the belief that there exists a deity, flourishing in eternal life, who hears and sees in his mind, who considers and pays attention to these things, who has a divine nature, who will listen to everything that is said among humans and will be able to see everything that is being done; and that if you silently concoct some wicked plan, it will not go unnoticed by the gods, for they have the power of thought. By telling such tales as these, he introduced the pleasantest of teachings, concealing the truth with his lying speech . . . .[113]

These words have been interpreted in very different ways – as a statement of radical atheism, as a criticism of the gods, as a denunciation of traditional religion, as a celebration of the positive benefits of religion despite its fictional basis, as a provocative challenge to orthodox religious opinion, as the author's own personal creed, or even as a self-conscious meditation on the role of poetry and drama in the creation and dissemination of religious myths and ideas.[114] Perhaps it is possible to overstate the originality or shock value of Critias' verses, since there had always existed a considerable variety of religious views in Greece,

---

[111] See O'Sullivan (2012), who cites a range of similar texts including Plato, *Protagoras* 320d–323e, 338c–d; Antiphon B44 D-K; Democritus B181 D-K; Protagoras B4 D-K; Isocrates, *Busiris* 24–5, etc.; cf. Centanni (1997) 141–61. Note that the contrast of *nomos* and *physis* is also central to Critias F11.

[112] Aetius, *Opinions* 1.7.

[113] *TrGF* 1.43 F.19, lines 1–26. The fragment is translated in full in Appendix 1.

[114] See (in particular) Sutton (1981), Davies (1989a), Centanni (1997), O'Sullivan (2012), Whitmarsh (2014).

as well as a fairly robust tradition of intellectual freedom.[115] Nevertheless, the *Sisyphus* fragment remains the most extreme statement of atheism (as such) that we possess from the fifth century, and it represents a religious world-view that is quite distinct from anything else seen in tragedy, even including the quasi-atheistic or questioning viewpoint expressed by certain Euripidean characters.[116] Of course, it must be noted that this statement appeared in the mouth of a character whose eventual fate was to endure eternal punishment in Hades, which means that (as in Euripides' case) it can hardly be said that this play straightforwardly endorsed atheism.

Not only the authorship but also the genre of *Sisyphus* has sometimes been called into question. The prominence of Underworld-related myths in the plays attributed to Critias led Wilamowitz to suggest that all four of these plays formed a tetralogy, with *Sisyphus* as the concluding satyr-play.[117] This suggestion has been taken seriously by several scholars, but there is no evidence in its support. In fact, the *Sisyphus* fragment does not seem at all satyric or humorous in either its tone or its language.[118] It might be thought that its preoccupation with the invention of religion and the figure of the inventor is a significant clue about its genre, since 'marvellous inventions or creations' have been identified as a characteristic theme of satyr-play.[119] However, it should be pointed out that an interest in inventions and origins is more generally a characteristic of sophistic thought.[120] Furthermore, it is obvious that Critias had a personal interest in this topic which transcended literary genre: one of his long elegiac fragments is entirely devoted to the theme of first inventions, and there are a couple of further references to the same theme in his other works, including the *Constitution of the Spartans*.[121] On balance there does not seem to be any good reason to question the normal view that *Sisyphus* was a tragedy.

---

[115] Kerferd (1981) 163–72 offers a balanced assessment of the intellectual context, citing a large variety of 'heterodox' texts; cf. Dover (1988) on intellectual freedom and the (often dubious) tradition of prosecutions for atheism.

[116] The closest parallels are Euripides, *Bellerophon* F286, *Helen* 1137–50 *Heracles* 1340–1; but on Euripidean 'atheism' cf. Michelini (1987) 11–27; Lefkowitz (1987) and (1989); Wright (2005) 339–52.

[117] Wilamowitz (1875) 161–72; cf. more recent discussions by Dihle (1977), Sutton (1981), Davies (1989a). Note that the *Sisyphus* of Euripides *was* satyric.

[118] The presence of a diminutive form, χωρίωι (line 39), has been thought out of place in tragic diction, but this is not conclusive evidence. Whitmarsh (2014) 4 calls this feature 'prosaic' and believes that it is in keeping with the generally prosaic, down-to-earth language of the passage.

[119] Cf. Davies (1989a) 29, quoting Seaford (1984) 33, 164 on satyr-play. Davies concludes on balance that *Sisyphus* is too serious to be satyric, though it is hard to judge the tone of an entire play from a single fragment.

[120] As noted by (e.g.) Collard (2007a), Kerferd (1981).

[121] Athenaeus 1.28b, 15.666b (= Critias F22 D-G); Mallius Theodorus, *On Metres* 6.589, 220 Keil (= Critias F23 D-G); Athenaeus 10.432d (= Critias F25 D-G).

3

Agathon

Of all the tragedians apart from the triad, Agathon is nowadays the best known.[1] He is the only one, indeed, that most students of the classics would be able to name if pressed. When we consider the paucity of his remains (a mere thirty-four fragments, the longest of which constitutes six verses), it seems all the more remarkable that Agathon should still somehow stand out as a familiar figure about whom significant things can be said. This is due in part to his extraordinarily vivid portrayal in Plato's *Symposium* and Aristophanes' *Women Celebrating the Thesmophoria*, two of the texts most frequently found on the syllabus in schools and universities. From these sources, and from a motley assortment of other evidence, scholars have been able to construct an image of Agathon as a distinctive personality whose work was characterized by a high degree of inventiveness and idiosyncrasy in terms of its content and its style.

In this chapter I attempt to give an outline of the main aspects of Agathon's life and work, as far as they can be known. Along the way I also examine some of the uses, and some of the limitations, of the biographical and critical testimonia. These testimonia are normally treated as *evidence*, as providing factual data or a context for interpretation, but they are rather more than just evidence, and of course (for the most part) they were not written with the purpose of simply conveying information to literary historians of the future. It is important to treat such texts not just as source material but as independent literary works with their own – often complicated or eccentric – rhetorical agenda. This is particularly true of Aristophanic comedy, but also of other texts to a greater or lesser degree.

---

[1]   However, he has not been much studied: the only substantial treatment is that of Lévêque (1955), and the most recent discussions (which discuss only selected aspects of Agathon's work) are Muecke (1982), Knox (1985).

Life and career

Agathon's *floruit* was fairly short by the standards of other fifth-century dramatists. His first production seems to have been staged in or around 416 BCE,[2] and he had evidently already quitted Athens by the time that Aristophanes' *Frogs* was performed ten or eleven years later, since in that play the comedian laments Agathon's departure, referring to him as 'a fine poet, much missed by his friends'. Now that Agathon has gone, it is said that there are no longer any tragedians of distinction left in Athens, but only feeble and picayune poetasters. What happened to Agathon? Aristophanes says that he has gone off 'to the banquet of the blest', which might be taken as implying that he is dead, but the ancient commentator on this line explains that Agathon had in fact departed for Macedon, a fact also confirmed by other sources.[3] In other words, it appears that Agathon, like Euripides and other well-respected tragedians, was lured away from Athens and the world of democratic state-sponsored festivals by the royal court of Archelaus, which, presumably, offered favourable working conditions and better pay. Whether or not one can infer anything from this about Agathon's political views is a matter for debate.[4]

It is clear that Agathon emerged more or less overnight at Athens as a figure of great fame and distinction. His first victory at the Lenaea festival, which was commemorated in the lavish celebratory party that forms the backdrop for Plato's *Symposium*, was achieved at a precociously early age; but unlike Aristophanes, that other theatrical *Wunderkind* of the same period, Agathon seems to have produced his plays under his own name right from the start.[5] A few years later, 'the famous Agathon' (as Aristophanes calls him) was the subject of a large-scale parody in *Women Celebrating the Thesmophoria*, indicating that the theatre audience in 411 BCE had a quite detailed knowledge of his work and its characteristics.[6] Jokes about Agathon also continued to feature in other comedies during the following decades, including Aristophanes'

---

[2] Athenaeus 5.216f-217a; cf. Σ Aristophanes, *Women Celebrating the Thesmophoria* 32 (*TrGF* 1.39 T1, 4).

[3] *Frogs* 83–6 (with Σ *ad loc.*); cf. *Suda* A 124, [Euripides] *Epistle* 5.2, Aelian, *Historical Miscellany* 13.4, Plutarch, *Moralia* 177a (*TrGF* 1.39 T 7a–b, 9, 22a–b).

[4] But for Plato (*Republic* 8.568b) Agathon and Euripides were apologists of tyranny who should be excluded from the ideal state.

[5] This is implied by Plato, *Symposium* 194a (*TrGF* 1.39 T2), who says that Agathon was not intimidated by the competition.

[6] Rau (1967) 114 notes that in order to have been parodied at such length Agathon must have been a figure of major importance; he even takes it as implying that Agathon must have been next in importance to Aeschylus, Sophocles and Euripides.

Gerytades, Frogs and the later (revised) version of *Women Celebrating the Thesmophoria.*[7]

The period in which Agathon enjoyed his fame and success coincided with the last decade or so of the Peloponnesian War and the closing years of the fifth century. This was a period of considerable intellectual excitement at Athens, owing in part to the prominence of avant-garde thinkers such as Socrates and the sophists – one of whom in particular, Gorgias, exerted a big influence on Agathon's work (see 'Agathon's style' below). But this same period is often presented, by ancient and modern historians alike, as a time of marked political and social crisis; and writers of literary history have sometimes extended this narrative to include literary and cultural decline.[8] Could Agathon, like Euripides, be seen as the embodiment of *fin-de-siècle* decadence? Perhaps so.[9] Several ancient sources, at any rate, associate Agathon with aesthetic and moral degeneracy, or with the 'destruction' of music and verbal style.[10] Nevertheless, it is obvious that Agathon was a technically innovative poet who challenged the expectations of his audience, and arguably it was these traits that led to his being perceived as controversial or problematic in certain quarters. It is also telling that Aristophanes – who seems to be largely responsible for this idea of literary decline in the first place – seems to place Agathon *before* the decline: in *Frogs*, Agathon is seen as the last good tragic poet before everything went wrong. Agathon is treated with apparent respect or admiration by other later writers as well, and his work was still being quoted and anthologized several centuries after his death, by which time the work of nearly all the other tragedians had been forgotten.[11]

About Agathon's life and character relatively little is known. Our best source is Plato's *Symposium*, which cannot be trusted absolutely as a factual record. Dating from several decades after the poet's death, it is a philosophical dialogue

---

[7] Aristophanes, *Frogs* 83–6; F169, 326 K-A; another source refers to Agathon's treatment by 'comic poets' (Diogenes, *On Music* F76 = *TrGF* 1.39 T 19).

[8] Euripides, in particular, has been seen as the 'destroyer' of tragedy in this period: see Nietzsche (1872), Nestle (1901), Reinhardt (1957) etc. Conventional narratives of literary history have tended to see a decline in the quality of tragedy and comedy after the end of the fifth century: see Chapter 5.

[9] Cf. Rachet (1973) 238: 'Les innovations d'Agathon . . . représentent des signes évidents de decadence et annoncent la fin de la tragédie'.

[10] Apart from *Women Celebrating the Thesmophoria* (which presents special interpretative problems: see the following section), see Diogenes, *On Music* F76; Hesychius A 281; Photius A 83; *Suda* A 125 (*TrGF* 1.39 T19-20); cf. Aristotle, *Poetics* 18.1456a25–30.

[11] Admittedly, Agathon is cited much less often than Aeschylus, Sophocles or Euripides. But apart from the triad, as Lévêque (1955) 13–15 points out, the only other tragedians whose work is 'honourably represented' in the fragmentary tradition are Agathon (32 fragments), Chaeremon (41), Achaeus (56), and Ion (68).

which in some respects reads like a work of drama or fiction, and the portrait of Agathon that it gives us must be seen as selective and stylized. All the same, Agathon was such a well-known figure that an out-and-out biographical invention would have been easily detectable (and what would have been the point of such an invention?). If we assume, then, that Plato's portrayal gives a reasonably faithful outline of the basic facts, the tragedian emerges as a rich and successful public figure, whose house was the haunt of many other famous and talented men; as a charming and hospitable person, who entertained his guests in some style; and as a sparkling raconteur and wit.[12] He was also famous for his stunning good looks: not just Plato but many other writers too describe him as 'the beautiful (*kalos*) Agathon'.[13]

It seems that many people, including Socrates, were captivated by Agathon's beauty and charm. For instance, it was said that Euripides was in love with Agathon, and wrote his *Chrysippus* (a tragedy on an erotic theme, concerning Laius and his infatuation with Pelops' son Chrysippus) specifically in order to please him.[14] Admittedly, our source for the story is Aelian, writing several centuries later; but this relationship between the two tragedians, real or alleged as it may be, may lie behind an Aristophanic scene in which the character Euripides bitchily implies that Agathon has been to bed with everyone in Athens: the joke has more force if we see Euripides in the role of jealous lover.[15] But however many admirers Agathon may have had, his regular lover was Pausanias, with whom, apparently, he lived for many years.[16] Our (imperfect) knowledge of fifth-century sexual morality suggests that this relationship may have been seen as unusual. Many Athenian men had boyfriends at one time or another, but for Agathon to have remained in a stable, long-term relationship with another man, even in his maturity, seems to have been remarkable.[17]

---

[12] Cf. also Σ Aristophanes, *Frogs* 83–4 and *Suda* A 24 (*TrGF* 1.39 T3, T12), which probably derive from Plato.

[13] Plato, *Symposium* 174a, 212e, 213c, *Protagoras* 315d; cf. Aristophanes, *Women Celebrating the Thesmophoria* 192, Plutarch, *Table-Talk* 3.1 (*Moralia* 645d); Lucian, *Advice to the Rhetor* 11; Maximus of Tyre 18.4b (see *TrGF* 1.39 T2, T14). Of course *kalos* does not refer exclusively to physical beauty; and part of the force of the epithet lies in its similarity to the common formulation *kalos kagathos*.

[14] Aelian, *History of Animals* 6.15, *Historical Miscellany* 2.21; Cicero, *Tusculan Disputations* 4.71 (= Euripides, *Chrysippus*, *TrGF* 5 test. iv.a–c). Cf. Aelian, *Historical Miscellany* 13.4 and Plutarch, *Moralia* 177a, 770c (= *TrGF* 1.39 T22a) for another anecdote concerning Euripides and Agathon.

[15] *Women Celebrating the Thesmophoria* 29–35. For Sommerstein (1994, 160) the joke implies that Agathon is a male prostitute (or generally 'easy'), but it is significant that it is Euripides and not someone else who is making the implication.

[16] Plato, *Symposium* 177d, 193b–c; Xenophon, *Symposium* 8.32; Maximus of Tyre 20.7a (*TrGF* 1.39 T15).

[17] 'Boyfriends' (*paidika, neoi, neaniskoi, erômenoi* or similar terms in Greek) were typically young men or boys, and such relationships would normally end before the boyfriend reached adulthood: see

It has been seen as particularly appropriate that the *Symposium*, a work all about erotic love, should have featured Agathon in such a prominent role, and that Plato should have put into his mouth an entire speech on the subject of love. In the ancient biographical tradition more broadly Agathon seems to have acquired a special association with love and sex. For instance, one story (preserved by Aelian and Plutarch) finds Agathon and Euripides reclining in one another's arms at the royal court in Macedon.[18] When King Archelaus asks Agathon, who by this time is forty years old, whether he still considers it right to be someone's boyfriend (*erômenos*) at his age, Agathon (or Euripides) replies: 'Yes, by Zeus, for it isn't just springtime that is the most beautiful season, but also autumn' – a *bon mot* that evidently became well known as a proverb. In another anecdote Archelaus, observing how frequently Agathon and Pausanias seem to quarrel, asks Agathon why he is so intent on causing offence to the man who loved him. 'Well,' he replies, 'if I know anything about character from any source, including poetry, I find that the pleasantest thing for lovers is making up after a fight, and I am convinced that nothing else gives them so much pleasure. And so I often provide Pausanias with this pleasure, by falling out with him constantly.'[19] This reply, whether or not it is authentic, fits neatly into the mouth of an author who was famous not just for his love-life but for his paradoxical wit.

These testimonia prompt a question which is difficult to answer, *viz.* how much biographical fact do they contain? As several scholarly studies have shown, many of the supposedly factual details in the ancient *Lives* of poets were actually invented using a hotchpotch of details from other sources, including the poets' own works as well as satirical caricatures by comedians.[20] This is demonstrably true in the case of other tragedians such as Aeschylus, Sophocles and Euripides, where we are able to read the 'biographical' material alongside the plays and identify suspicious similarities. (For example, the ancient story about Euripides' being attacked and torn to death by dogs or women is clearly a fabrication based on his own *Bacchae* and Aristophanes' *Women Celebrating the Thesmophoria*.[21]) In the case of Agathon, however, we do not possess enough of his original work to compare it with the Aristophanic and other biographical

---

Dover (1978), esp. 62, 84–7, 144. Levêque (1955, 48–53) devotes some considerable space to this (as he sees it) extraordinary aspect of Agathon's personal life: he suggests that Agathon and Pausanias represented a model of perfect love (and inspired the discussion in Plato's *Symposium* for that very reason).

[18] Aelian, *Historical Miscellany* 13.4; cf. Plutarch, *Moralia* 177a, 770c (*TrGF* 1.39 T22a).
[19] Aelian, *Historical Miscellany* 2.21 (*TrGF* 1.39 T 25).
[20] See esp. Lefkowitz (1981).
[21] [Anon.] *Life of Euripides* §§29–32; cf. *Suda* E 3695. See Lefkowitz (1981) 88–104.

material – which rules out any firm conclusions. Nevertheless, it seems quite likely that these stories about Agathon's love-life came into being precisely because of the content of his tragedies.[22] Was Agathon perceived as dwelling on love affairs more than other tragedians did, or as deliberately choosing myths with erotic themes, or as offering unusually poignant dramatizations of love's effects? A couple of his fragments do indeed contain memorable remarks on the subject of love,[23] though they scarcely constitute conclusive evidence. All the same, it is easy to see how a poet who wrote about love might be imagined to be a notable lover.

Art and Life: The evidence of Aristophanic comedy

The idea that a poet's work directly reflects his life, personality and opinions, and, conversely, that knowledge of a poet's life can help us to understand his work, is encountered throughout most ancient (and much modern) criticism. Now this may or may not be a valid critical assumption; but even in cases where we possess very full and accurate biographical information, the relationship between real life and art is difficult to assess. In the case of a writer such as Agathon, where both the work and the external evidence are largely missing, and where any 'biographical' information may be derived from the plays anyway, the critic's task becomes nearly impossible.

Apart from Plato, our most extensive 'biographical' source – the inverted commas are very important – is the comedian Aristophanes. As a direct contemporary of Agathon, Aristophanes must be regarded as a hugely significant and valuable witness, but he does not provide a straightforward frame of reference. Perhaps the most striking feature of Aristophanes' portrait of Agathon is the fact that it comes precisely at the point at which the perceived connection between Art and Life is being exploited for its comic potential. Aristophanes actually makes Agathon the mouthpiece for the theory that poetry inevitably reflects the character (*physis*) of its writer.[24]

---

[22] Cf. (again) Euripides, who was assumed to have had a complex love-life on the basis of his own tragedies or Aristophanic comedies: see *TrGF* 5.1 T106–7 (pp. 97–9).

[23] F31, which became a famous quasi-proverbial line quoted by many other authors (see *TrGF ad loc.*), links erotic love to the power of appearances; and F29 wittily juxtaposes the name of the love-goddess (*Kupris*) with the Greek word *hubris*, implying that love is cruel or unjust. On the problematic poetics of *erôs* in Greek tragedy more generally, see Thumiger (2013) and Wright (forthcoming a).

[24] *Women Celebrating the Thesmophoria* 29–265. See Austin and Olson (2005) 105–21; cf. Muecke (1982), Wright (2012) 123–5.

AGATHON: A poet must adopt habits (*tropoi*) that correspond to the plays that he has to write . . .[25]

The meaning and effect of the character Agathon's words is complicated by the fact that as he speaks them he is dressed up as a woman. Indeed, it transpires that his interpretation of the principle Art = Life is based on clothing rather than psychology or the writer's inner nature. This comical Agathon seems to believe that it is important for a poet to dress up as the sort of character whose part he happens to be writing: 'For example, if one is writing plays about women, one must adopt their habits'.[26] Agathon goes on to add: 'Look at Phrynichus – you must have heard of him – he was a beautiful man and dressed beautifully, and for that reason his plays were beautiful. We needs must compose poetry according to our nature (*physis*)'.[27]

Having thus introduced the figure of Agathon into the play, Aristophanes proceeds to give us an entire song – a hymn or paean in honour of Apollo, Artemis and Leto – which is performed by Agathon in female guise, taking the alternate roles of chorus-leader and chorus.[28]

— Maidens, receive the holy torch of the twain chthonic goddesses, and dance freely with the loud cry of your homeland.
— To which of the gods shall I address my song? Tell me now. My spirit is easily persuaded to worship the immortal powers.
— Come now, and with music bless him who draws back the golden bow, Apollo, who established the sacred enclosure of the region in the land of the Simois.
— Hail, Apollo! Rejoice in our most beautiful song, being first to receive this holy privilege in our fine, honorific music . . .
— Also sing praises to Artemis of the wild, the maiden goddess in the mountains where oak-trees grow.
— I follow you, celebrating the holy and blessed offspring of Leto, the virgin Artemis.
— And also Leto, and the Asian lyre's music, which is out of time and in time to our step, at the behest of the Phrygian Graces.
— I worship Leto, our sovereign goddess, and also the lyre, mother of songs, known for its masculine sound.

---

[25] *Women Celebrating the Thesmophoria* 149–50.
[26] *Women Celebrating the Thesmophoria* 151–2, playing on the double meaning of Greek *tropoi* (which, like the English 'habit', can refer to either character or costume).
[27] *Women Celebrating the Thesmophoria* 164–7.
[28] *Women Celebrating the Thesmophoria* 101–29. See Austin and Olson (2005) and Sommerstein (1994) *ad loc.* for detailed discussion; cf. Rau (1967) 99–114, who provides a list of tragic parallels for specific words and phrases in the song.

— With its music the light streams forth from the eyes of the god, and through your rapid song as well; give thanks for all this to Lord Apollo. Hail, blest son of Leto!

This is clearly a comic parody or pastiche of the type of song that the audience would have recalled from Agathon's tragedies, but interpreters differ in their assessment of how much of its content (if any) is authentic Agathon.[29] It may be thought significant that this song is dramatically irrelevant within the scene in terms of its content, as well as lacking in any obvious humour: both of these considerations could suggest that it is based on a genuine tragic model. Certain specific aspects correspond to what we know of Agathon's work, including the 'eccentric medley' of its musical structure,[30] as well as some characteristically paradoxical verbal formulations – as when a dance-step is described as simultaneously both in time and out of time, or a lyre is described as 'the mother of hymns' but also as the possessor of a 'masculine' voice.[31]

Aristophanic comedy constitutes evidence – of a sort – for Agathon's immediate popular and critical reception at Athens, but it is scarcely to be treated as documentary realism. Rather, it is a ludicrous caricature which contains elements of fiction and fantasy. It might also be seen as a sort of critical 'reading' of Agathon's work, but it is obviously an eccentric and oblique reading. It is important to take the utmost care when assessing the evidence of comedy, and, above all, to beware of taking Aristophanes too literally. It seems to me that many scholars, while duly acknowledging that Aristophanes was trying to be funny, have nonetheless treated his portrayal of Agathon as essentially accurate. Perhaps one might think it does not make much difference one way or the other; but in fact it can lead to serious problems in the way that one approaches the fragments. If one believes that Agathon really was more or less exactly as Aristophanes describes him – that is, an outrageously camp, cross-dressing joker, spouting semi-coherent aesthetic theories – this will inevitably have an effect on one's assessment of his work. Surely enough, Agathon has generally been regarded as a trivial, pretentious dilettante, and his work has been dismissed as showy and

---

[29] Snell does not include any portions of the song in *TrGF*; but Rau (1967, 104–5) judges the song to be of high quality ('eines achtbaren Dichters nicht unwürdig') and finds it hard to judge its 'parodische Intention'; Muecke (1982, 46) says 'parody of a text of Agathon himself cannot . . . be ruled out', and adds (suggestively) that the song is not obviously funny; Austin and Olson (2005, 87) admit 'we know next to nothing about A's lyrics, including whether this song is based on a lost original.'

[30] So Austin and Olson (2005) *ad loc.*; cf. Parker (1997) 398–405.

[31] But, as Austin and Olson (2005, 96) observe, 'the instrument is confused about its gender, like Agathon and a number of other characters in the play'.

lacking in substance.[32] Unless some more of his work should come to light, of course, we have no way of giving a definitive assessment; but still it seems rather unfair to dismiss Agathon's work in this way.

So what can Aristophanes actually tell the literary historian about Agathon's lost plays? Ultimately, and perhaps depressingly, if we are looking for hard facts I believe that he can tell us nothing for certain. But elsewhere I have suggested a possible approach to comic evidence, based on Christopher Pelling's judicious discussion of Aristophanes in terms of source-material for ancient historians.[33] Pelling proposes that we ask ourselves two questions whenever faced with a difficult comic scene: first, 'what do the audience need to know if the scene is to make sense?' and second, 'what needs to be the case for the comic poet to have written the scene like this?' These questions normally turn out to have several possible answers, some of which may be mutually incompatible. But providing a range of potentially viable explanations is more realistic than attempting to identify a single definitive interpretation, and in fact the exercise may allow us to squeeze more value out of the material than we thought possible.

Aristophanes' portrait of Agathon might, I suggest, be read in several different ways, some of which are supported by independent evidence:

(*i*)   Agathon really was a transvestite or transsexual, and Aristophanes' character-portrayal, for all its exaggerations and distortions, essentially captures the real Agathon.

(*ii*)   Agathon, who is elsewhere described as a very good-looking man, was not a transvestite or transsexual; he was also 'famous', and so this fact was probably known to the audience. Therefore Aristophanes' portrayal of Agathon in this guise must be deliberately inaccurate, and so, presumably, is intended to be funny (for some reason).

(*iii*)   Agathon was a critically self-aware poet, with an interest in abstract literary theories which are represented here in some form (either faithfully or in the form of a lampoon or caricature).

(*iv*)   Agathon may have invented (or espoused) the theory that Art and Life are inherently linked; perhaps he genuinely believed that in his daily life

---

[32]   E.g. Lesky (1983) 395: 'We can form some idea, albeit a predominantly negative one, of the artistic personality of Agathon'; Knox (1985, 89): 'the surviving fragments of his works ... are, for the most part, rhetorical *jeux d'esprit* or cleverly turned moral clichés'; Muecke (1982, 49): 'Does Aristophanes want to show Agathon as a pretentious poet whose aspirations are misunderstood by the common man, or as an effeminate poet exposed by the common man, who can see what is before his eyes?'; Duncan (2006, 28): 'Agathon represents tragedy taken to what Plato sees as its extreme form ... it (he) seduces its viewers and leaves them with nothing substantive. It (he) is a tease.'

[33]   Wright (2012), esp. 4–10, 17–19; cf. Pelling (2000) 130.

he was living out artistic principles, or perhaps he believed that one should try to enter into the role of one's own characters (a sort of 'method writing', analogous to 'method acting').

(*v*)   Alternatively, Aristophanes may have invented (or espoused) the theory that Art reflects Life, and he is (for some reason) attributing it to Agathon as well as applying it to Agathon's own life and works.

(*vi*)   In a specific extension of this general theory, Aristophanes is suggesting that Art reflects its author's *Sex*-Life. In other words, any characteristics of Agathon's tragedies, including any perceived flaws or failings, can be attributed to their author's sexuality.[34]

(*vii*)   Aristophanes, rather than inventing or adopting the theory that Art reflects Life, is actually satirizing this theory (which may have been current in popular Athenian discourse at this time, or it may have been a specialized critical theory developed by serious critical thinkers not known to us). In other words, having stated the principle that Life imitates Art (and *vice versa*), Aristophanes has portrayed Agathon as the sort of poet who would have written the sort of tragedies that Agathon writes, *if the theory were valid*. But the joke lies in the fact that the theory does not hold true, either in general terms or (at least) in Agathon's case.

(*viii*) It is not Agathon's character or personal habits that are being made fun of, but some aspect of his work.

(*ix*)   Aristophanes, by a process of comic logic, is assuming that a tragedian whose work could be described as 'feminine' (in some way or another) *must* be either female or effeminate.

(*x*)   Perhaps Agathon's literary style, which was extremely unusual (see the following section), could be described as 'feminine'. In fact, the metaphor of gender to describe an author's use of language is quite widely seen in classical rhetoric, and Quintilian, Cicero and others identified distinctively 'masculine' and 'feminine' styles of diction. This theory seems to have existed in some form even as early as the fifth century, because Aristophanes elsewhere hints at a tripartite theory of 'masculine', 'feminine' and 'middle' styles.[35]

(*xi*)   Perhaps it is specifically Agathon's music and lyrics that are seen, metaphorically speaking, as 'feminine'. Certain musical styles or modes

---

[34] Cf. Aristophanes' depiction of Euripides, or (more generally) the idea that artistic creation is a gendered or sexualized activity: see (e.g.) Aristophanes, *Knights* 516–17, *Frogs* 1306–8; Pherecrates F155 K-A; Callias F117 K-A. For discussion see Wright (2012) 121–2; Baumann (2007) interprets the Agathon scene specifically in this light.

[35] Aristophanes F706 K-A; cf. Dionysius of Halicarnassus, *Demosthenes* 43, *On Verbal Composition* 17; Quintilian 5.12.17–20, 5.17.18–20. See Wright (2012) 124.

had long been associated with male or female emotions, gestures or performance styles; we know from several sources that the 'hypodorian' and 'hypophrygian' modes were thought to be inherently linked to female performance, and that Agathon made a lot of use of these modes. Note too that 'Agathonian' *aulos* music (with its sinuous sound, compared to ant-tracks) carried explicit connotations of effeminacy for more than one ancient musical writer.[36] In *Women Celebrating the Thesmophoria* (130–4) it is specifically Agathon's *song*, quoted above, that is described as feminine, as well as exercising an aphrodisiac effect on the audience.

(*xii*) It may be that Agathon was famous for (*inter alia*) writing plays containing powerful or memorable female characters. There is nothing in the fragments to support this suggestion (apart, perhaps, from F14, which might be seen as an 'enlightened' defence of women against misogynistic accusations of their stupidity). Nevertheless, the premise of the Agathon scene in Aristophanes' play is that Agathon has lots of female costumes available in his house, which must represent the costumes of characters from his tragedies (just as Euripides, who was notorious for putting beggars and cripples on stage, is depicted in *Acharnians* as having a house full of ragged costumes).

(*xiii*) It may be that Agathon acted in his own plays,[37] and was particularly good at playing female roles.

(*xiv*) Agathon is perhaps being used, more generally, as a focus for anxieties about acting and role playing – or, as one critic has put it, as 'a site for the investigation of identity'.[38] This need not imply that his work was unusual in comparison with the work of any other tragedian.

(*xv*) It is difficult to detect any qualitative or evaluative aspect to the Agathon scene. However we may choose to read it, Aristophanes' portrayal is seemingly not 'critical' in the sense of hostile or deprecatory: this is in marked contrast to many other metaliterary or parodic scenes in comedy, which often seem designed to identify and censure the work of *bad* poets.[39]

---

[36] Aristophanes, *Gerytades* F169 K-A, *Women Celebrating the Thesmophoria* 99–100 (with Σ); Hesychius A 281; Photius A 83; *Suda* A 125; [Anon.] *On Tragedy* 5.39; Diogenes, *On Music* F76 (*TrGF* 1.39 T19, T20a–c, T21).

[37] This is possibly implied by Plato, *Symposium* 194b, which describes Agathon at the *proagon* of the Lenaea, fearlessly standing before the audience on the *okribas* (a word which either refers to a theatrical stage or an actor's boot). Cf. Lévêque (1955) 63–6.

[38] Duncan (2006) 29: she sees the Agathon scene as exploring different ('essentialist' *vs* 'constructionist') notions of the self. Cf. Sommerstein (1994) 9–10.

[39] Cf. Kaimio and Nykopp (1997) on 'bad' poets in comedy; but cf. Wright (2012) 156–62 on the difficulties of judging the evaluative aspects of parody. See also the Prologue, pp. xiii–xviii.

Agathon's style

Even if Aristophanes can be treated, with caution, as providing a sort of critical reading of Agathon, his comedy tells us relatively little about the distinctive qualities of Agathon's poetry itself. Apart from the features already noted, the only specifically literary detail given by Aristophanes is that Agathon's style was unusual: the tragedian is twice described as *kalliepês* ('man of fine phrases').[40] This epithet refers to Agathon's idiosyncratic way of writing Greek – a tendency which is mentioned by several other ancient writers but is also clearly visible in the surviving fragments.[41] Elsewhere Aristophanes refers to Agathon's compositional technique using the verbs *gnômotupei* and *antonomazei*, both of which terms denote a penchant for coining new phrases or formulating quotable aphorisms; and more generally these metaphors, taken from the realm of woodworking and mould-casting, imply a high degree of verbal craftsmanship and attention to detail.[42]

Agathon's Greek is extraordinarily elegant and mannered. In particular, it makes much use of rhetorical figures and techniques such as antithesis (a marked balance or contrast between individual words or other elements), isocolon (clauses which are equally formed or share the same number of words or syllables), paradox (where the literal meaning of words or the relationship between words is implicitly questioned through the use of apparent contradiction), assonance (the juxtaposition of similar-sounding words or letters) and other sound-effects including – most unusually in classical Greek poetry – the use of rhymes at the middle or end of verses. All in all, Agathon's language would have sounded rather bizarre, a far cry from natural or normal Greek usage. Now of course no tragedian ever wrote in 'natural' Attic Greek, and even a writer such as Euripides (whose Greek is simpler than that of Aeschylus or Sophocles, and who was said to have made his characters talk like everyday men and women) wrote in highly stylized, formal verse.[43] But we can safely assume that no normal Athenian ever spoke in the manner of Agathon's characters.

Such language is difficult or impossible to reproduce in English translation: almost inevitably one has to sacrifice the exact nuance (or the style, or the wit, or

---

[40]   *Women Celebrating the Thesmophoria* 49, 60.
[41]   See also Aristophanes F326 K-A; Plato, *Symposium* 194e–197e, 198b–c; Athenaeus 5.187c; Plutarch, *Moralia* 645e; cf. *TrGF* 39 T16.
[42]   *Women Celebrating the Thesmophoria* 53–7; see Austin and Olson (2005) 69–71.
[43]   But cf. also the plain, everyday Greek used by the tragedians Sthenelus and Cleophon: see below, pp. 180, 188–90.

the rhetorical and sound-effects) in order to render the literal meaning.[44] But perhaps Agathon did not always intend his exact meaning to be literally understood. It can often seem as if the sound of a line, or the desire to be witty or provocative, is being privileged above intelligibility – as in verses such as these[45]:

τὸ μὲν πάρεργον ἔργον ὡς ποιούμεθα,
τὸ δ' ἔργον ὡς πάρεργον ἐκπονούμεθα.

We are treating what is secondary (*parergon*) as our main task (*ergon*),
and working at our main task (*ergon*) as if it were secondary (*parergon*).

τὰς συμφορὰς γὰρ οὐχὶ τοῖς τεχνάσμασιν
φέρειν δίκαιον, ἀλλὰ τοῖς παθήμασιν.

It is right to endure what befalls us not with *technasmata* (artifice, tricks,
    devices, skill, etc.)
but with *pathêmata* (emotions, feelings, sufferings, calamities, misfortunes, etc.).

In English these lines seem somewhat flat or banal, but in the original Greek they have a dazzling and decidedly odd effect because of the precise choice and arrangement of words combined with a certain level of inbuilt ambiguity or obscurity. It is impossible to know, for example, just what Agathon intended to convey here by the distinction between *technasmata* and *pathêmata*, and the problem would not be easily soluble even if we still had access to the entire scene from which the lines come. In other words, the ambiguity is not contextual or accidental; it is inherent in the way that the whole utterance is formulated. Agathon is deliberately playing around with language and its potentially misleading properties of sound and signification.

In the verses quoted above, and also several other fragments, Agathon creates a rhetorical effect by establishing or exploiting a relationship between two abstract nouns. Often the two terms in question are treated antithetically, as if they represented logical opposites – as in the case of *gnômê* (intelligence) and *rhômê* (physical strength), or *phronêsis* (intellect) and *tychê* (chance or randomness):

γνώμη δὲ κρεῖσσόν ἐστιν ἢ ῥώμη χερῶν.

Intelligence is superior to the strength of one's hands [F27].

οὐ τῆι φρονήσει, τῆι τύχηι δ' ἐσφάλμεθα.

We are tripped up not by our deliberate intention but by fortune [F20].

This latter antithesis might imply that Agathon views *phronêsis* and *tychê* as polar opposites; but in fact in a couple of other fragments *tychê* is contrasted with *technê* (art or skill), a more conventional antithesis which is widely found in the work of other contemporary writers with an interest in causation.[46] In all these examples the similarity of sound between the contrasted pairs of nouns is exploited as part of the overall effect, as if it were something more than a mere coincidence. But what does it all *mean*?

It is easy to be baffled by Agathon, even if one admires his style; but it is clear that some readers in antiquity found him just too affected for their taste. Aelian records that certain critics were displeased by his excessive reliance on antitheses[47]:

> When someone, wishing to correct this habit, tried to remove them from his plays, Agathon said: 'But, my dear chap, you have failed to see that you are taking the Agathon out of Agathon' – for he set a lot of store by these devices and felt that they made his tragedy what it was.

Even if this is another of those apocryphal quasi-biographical anecdotes, it shows that Aelian and his readers definitively associated Agathon with the antithetical style; it is less clear whether or not Aelian himself approves of this style. Athenaeus, on the other hand, also mentions the fact that Agathon has been criticized for his isocola and antitheses, but he goes out of his way to censure the practice of sneering, and implies that Agathon has not received his due measure of admiration.[48]

From the time when it was first unleashed on the Athenian public, Agathon's style was recognized as being utterly distinctive. Even now his few surviving verses are likely to strike anyone who has ever encountered them as unmistakably Agathonian: there are not many ancient writers of whom this can be said. And yet Agathon did not invent this style out of thin air. We are informed that he inherited and adapted it from Gorgias of Leontini, the sophist whose radical views of language and virtuoso rhetorical displays wowed and infuriated Athenians from the 420s onwards.

It was from Gorgias that Agathon took the use of antithesis and various other rhetorical devices, but it may be that Gorgias' influence can be detected in a

---

[46]   *TrGF* 1.39 F6, F8 (both quoted below). On *tychê* vs *technê* in various late-fifth-century writers see (e.g.) Euripides, *Alcestis* 785–6 with Parker (2007) *ad loc.*, Rood (1998) 27, Edmunds (1975), Reinhardt (2010) 365–7, etc.

[47]   Aelian, *Historical Miscellany* 14.13 (*TrGF* 1.39 T24).

[48]   Athenaeus 5.187b–d.

wider intellectual or conceptual sense as well. In his *Encomium of Helen*, Gorgias argued that the effect of language on the listener may be more important than its literal meaning, and that language, when used in the right way, can exert a powerful and mysterious force analogous to drugs or magic; and he showed how an audience may be persuaded or carried along by the power of words without necessarily understanding them. Elsewhere, in his philosophical work *On Nature* (or *On What is Not*), Gorgias seemingly argued that language is an autonomous entity completely independent of truth or reality.[49] When Plato and others refer to Agathon as a 'Gorgiastic' writer,[50] it is likely that they perceive him as sharing some of Gorgias' linguistic or philosophical outlook as well as his stylistic techniques. It is worth noting too that Gorgias, like Agathon, also seems to divide critics as to whether or not he is a writer to be taken seriously.

Gorgias is not the only significant influence on Agathon; there are signs that the sophistic movement in general may provide an intellectual framework in which to place the tragedian's output. Other 'sophistic' touches in Agathon's fragments include a preoccupation with etymology (F3, F17), which seems to connect Agathon with Protagoras, Prodicus, Antiphon and others who were concerned with the 'correctness of words' (*orthotês onomatôn*).[51] One of Agathon's characters even criticizes his interlocutor for his 'newfangled habit of using words in an inappropriate manner' (F13).[52] In a similar vein, we see signs of an interest in the alphabet and literacy (F4: see below); a sprinkling of modish concepts or intellectual buzzwords such as *tychê* (F6, F8, F20), *gnômê* (F27) and *sophia* (F19, F25); and a reworking of the 'argument from probability' (F9), which was said to have been invented by Corax but became a characteristic trope of sophistic rhetoric.[53]

Aphorisms and quotation culture

Many of the surviving lines from Agathon's plays constitute *gnômai* – that is, short, epigrammatic aphorisms which purport to embody general truths about

---

[49] Gorgias' works and fragments can now most conveniently be accessed in Graham (2010) 725–88. On all these matters (which are too complex to discuss at length here), see Wardy (1996) 6–50.

[50] Plato, *Symposium* 198c (note that Agathon's speech there is written in a pastiche of Gorgias' style); Athenaeus 5.187c; cf. *TrGF* 39 T11, T16.

[51] See (e.g.) Antiphon DK87 B14–15; Democritus DK68 B20a, B26; Plato, *Cratylus* 384b, 391b–c; *Euthydemus* 277e; cf. Guthrie (1971) 204–6. This area of interest is also reflected in Euripidean tragedy: see Wright (2005) 268–78.

[52] ἀπολεῖς μ' ἐρωτῶν καὶ σὺ χὠ νέος τρόπος
ἐν οὐ πρέποντι τοῖς λόγοισι χρώμενος.

[53] Aristotle, *Rhetoric* 2.24, 1402a10–12; cf. Wardy (1996) 32–5.

the world or about human nature. In this respect Agathon is directly comparable to many other tragedians, since (as we have already noted) a very large number of our so-called 'fragments' are *gnômai*, preserved by later writers precisely on account of their perceived quotability and wide applicability. Tragic aphorisms seem to have been designed by their authors with a dual function in mind, since they naturally lend themselves to being read either in context, as part of a particular scene within a play, or independently, as decontextualized gobbets of wisdom or advice for life; and indeed they have always been treated in both ways by readers (within antiquity and much later).[54] Nevertheless, Agathon's aphorisms have been seen as somewhat unusual. In particular, they have been thought to lack seriousness or moral profundity. Modern critical discussions of Agathon's work have tended to characterize it as teasingly insubstantial, or to dismiss his gnomic fragments as 'rhetorical *jeux d'esprit* or cleverly turned moral clichés'.[55]

Such assessments can perhaps be attributed to the influence of Aristophanes, or to the effect of Agathon's weird style. To be sure, Agathon can come across as annoyingly paradoxical and flashily self-conscious in his mode of expression, but it is too easy to dismiss him for that reason alone. At least, it is worth looking at the fragments more closely and making the effort to treat him not as a glib, superficial poseur but as a poet who genuinely had something to say. Four separate points could be made in support of this view. In the first place, rhetorical dazzle and moral seriousness are not mutually incompatible; or, at any rate, we need to be clear about whether we are talking about form or content when we criticize this material. Secondly, Agathon's aculeated style seems to be designed expressly for maximum quotability – that is to say, he especially *wanted* these lines to be quoted. Thirdly, it seems significant that respectable writers, including Plato and Aristotle, quote Agathon's aphorisms, and that they treat them as worthy of serious attention. Fourthly, the really striking fact about many Agathonian aphorisms is that, unlike the majority of tragic *gnômai*, they are *not* clichés but original formulations. Some of them, of course, do seem unremarkable in terms of their sentiments – for instance, the reflections on envy (F23, F24), wealth (F25) or parents and children (F28) – but in general Agathon relies far less than his rivals upon conventional subject-matter or hackneyed themes. He is good at coining new expressions and formulating new thoughts, and he sometimes causes the reader to look at conventional ideas in startling ways. Indeed, one explanation why Agathon's work features comparatively seldom in

---

[54] See Wright (forthcoming b).
[55] Duncan (2006) 28; Knox (1985) 89.

the ancient gnomic anthologies, despite its high level of 'quotability', may well lie
in its non-traditional, non-clichéd nature. Fragment-collectors such as Stobaeus
actually seem to *prefer* clichés and unexceptional truisms.[56]

Let us examine, for instance, the following aphorism (F9):

τάχ' ἄν τις εἰκὸς αὐτὸ τοῦτ' εἶναι λέγοι,
βροτοῖσι πολλὰ τυγχάνειν οὐκ εἰκότα.

Perhaps one might say that this very thing is probable:
that many improbable things happen to mortals.

One could read this, perhaps, as a witty but vacuous paradox with no real
significance. But in fact Aristotle, who quotes it, takes it seriously as a challenge
to received wisdom, as if Agathon was trying to make his readers think more
carefully about different *degrees* of possibility, the role of probability (*eikos*) in
rhetorical or philosophical argumentation, and the variable or contingent
meaning of what may seem to be absolute concepts.[57] It is quite true, as Aristotle
points out, that since some events happen contrary to probability, what is 'contrary
to probability' may also simultaneously be probable, however unlikely this may
sound. Thus what appear to be diametrically opposite terms ('probable' and
'improbable') may sometimes be synonymous: a fact which may have profoundly
unsettling consequences for our views about language and the nature of reality.

Several other aphorisms are concerned with the role of *tychê* in human affairs,
such as the following pithy one-liner (F6):

τέχνη τύχην ἔστερξε καὶ τύχη τέχνην.

Art likes Fortune, and Fortune Art.

This highly quotable line, with its marked antithesis, chiasmus and alliteration,
is obviously designed to look and sound unusual: but what, if anything, lies
behind the veneer of style? It is difficult to decide whether it is banal, meaningless,
or profound. As with all free-floating quotations of this sort, its effect will depend
partly on the use that a reader is inclined to make of it; and of course we have to
bear in mind that the line may have come across very differently in its original
dramatic context. But, as before, a case could be made for reading this *bon mot*
(and its implications) seriously. Perhaps Agathon is trying to make us contemplate
the relationship between two similar-sounding terms, which ostensibly signify

---

[56] On gnomic anthologies in antiquity see Wachsmuth (1881); Reydams-Schils (2011).
[57] Aristotle, *Rhetoric* 2.24.1402a10–14.

completely different entities. *Technê* (art, skill, craft, deliberate effort) ought to be diametrically opposite to *tychê* (fortune, chance, randomness), and many other authors treated them as such; but Agathon here treats them as if they are either interchangeable or inherently connected in some sort of reciprocal relationship. He seems to be suggesting, essentially, that there is always an unpredictable element in any deliberate endeavour, and always some element of contrivance in outcomes that may seem purely accidental. In another aphorism Agathon complicates the matter yet further by adding a third causative factor, *anankê* (necessity or compulsion), thus transforming the neat dichotomy between *technê* and *tychê* into a more complicated triangular relationship:

καὶ μὴν τὰ μέν γε χρὴ τέχνηι πράσσειν, τὰ δέ
ἡμῖν ἀνάγκηι καὶ τύχηι προσγίγνεται.

And indeed one must do some things by art, while certain other things
happen to us through necessity and fortune [F8].

This sort of playing-around with language could be seen as something more than a mere game. Perhaps Agathon is trying to shake up the way we think on a more fundamental level, by (in effect) rearranging the categories that we use to structure our thoughts.[58]

But there are bigger moral and metaphysical issues at stake here. Why do things turn out in the way that they do? How much of what happens is due to deliberate, conscious design on the part of human agents, how much is due to divine intervention, and how much is due to chaotic, random forces outside our control? How much meaning, or moral significance, can be attributed to our actions? These are all difficult questions which cluster around the nebulous concept of *tychê*. Agathon could be seen as one among several late fifth-century writers (including Euripides and Thucydides) who tried to grapple seriously with *tychê* and its problems.[59] Aristotle quotes Agathon's aphorism in his *Nicomachean Ethics* at just the point when he himself is discussing questions of this sort[60]: he reads it as an illustration of the fact that fortune and human agency sometimes appear to be working towards the same ends, and he adds that both *technê* and *tychê* deal with what admits of being other than it is, thus linking the fragment to broader concepts of causality.

---

[58] Cf. Adair (1997) 45 on Oscar Wilde's epigrams and the difficulty of differentiating between his best paradoxes (which 'rearrange our consciousness') and his weakest ones (which are 'platitudes performing handstands').

[59] See n. 46 above.

[60] Aristotle, *Nicomachean Ethics* 6.4.1140a19.

The paradoxical and elusive quality of Agathon's aphorisms need not be regarded as revealing a lack of seriousness. It could be seen as a deliberately aporetic strategy, a way of acknowledging the difficulty of the concepts under discussion. In other words, Agathon is trying to relate linguistic form to intellectual content, using provocative or ambiguous words as a way of representing irresolubly complex subject-matter. Or perhaps these odd verses could even be seen as an ironic response to the bland, straightforward aphorisms so often seen in the work of other tragedians. Perhaps Agathon is implying that the real answers to these enormous moral and metaphysical questions are too difficult to be summed up in dinky soundbites, and that what we need is not a collection of definitive statements which present us with the truth on a plate (as it were), but challengingly obscure pronouncements which unsettle our views and stimulate us to further thought. (A similar technique of gnomic ambiguity or paradox is also observable in the philosophical tradition – for instance, in the highly quotable, highly obscure fragments of Heraclitus, Gorgias and others.)

Many of Agathon's aphorisms might also cause us to reflect on the nature and status of tragic *gnômai* more generally. How do they function within a play? What sort of wisdom do they embody? Whose voice is imagined as uttering the sentiments that they express – is it the author, or the character, or a disembodied 'voice of wisdom'? These questions are never easy to answer (no matter which tragedian we are discussing), and there is often a significant degree of ambiguity inherent in the text. Take, for instance, F26: A young man's intellect is very prone to change its course' (νέων γὰρ ἀνδρῶν πολλὰ κάμπτονται φρένες) – a general truism, perhaps, but one which depends on speaker and context, and which takes on a completely different colour if it is specifically viewed as the work of an extremely young playwright. However, Agathon seems to make such questions even more difficult to answer than normal, not only because his aphorisms often depart from traditional wisdom or conventional popular morality, but (more significantly) because the voice which articulates the sentiments, as expressed in the distinctively Agathonian style, is so unmistakably the author's own. Whether or not these aphorisms were meant to be taken as representing Agathon's own opinions remains a moot point, but at any rate they certainly reflect an odd and oblique view of the world.

Agathon's originality

It will be clear by now that Agathon was an idiosyncratic and highly original writer of tragedy. His work seems to have been a mixture of traditional elements and bold innovations, including formal experimentation with generic conventions.

In the first place, it is clear that Agathon's plays *sounded* unmistakably modern, in terms of their music, lyrics and instrumentation. Agathon belonged to a late fifth-century movement sometimes loosely referred to as 'the New Music', the practitioners of which included Phrynis, Timotheus, Cinesias and Philoxenus: it was particularly associated with the dithyrambic genre, though tragic composers in this style also included Euripides.[61] The New Music was characterized by an innovative approach to harmony, an increased freedom in word-setting and the use of melody and metre, a marked chromaticism, a more prominent role for solo singers, a penchant for the *aulos* (a reed instrument resembling the oboe), and an increasing self-consciousness. This style of performance presented itself as radically different from anything that had gone before. Predictably, it was highly controversial: several writers, including Plato, criticize the New Music for its perceived aesthetic, social and moral defects.

None of Agathon's songs or choral odes survives, even in fragmentary form: our main evidence for the effect of Agathonian music in performance is the Aristophanic parody already mentioned (as well as certain other discussions or parodies, mostly conservative or critical in tone, which compare the sound of New Music to ant-tracks, caterpillars, birdsong or stomach-churning bends).[62] Nevertheless, it is clear that Agathon had a characteristic musical language of his own. There was even a style of *aulos*-playing sufficiently distinctive for it to be named 'Agathonian'.[63]

It was not simply their musical score that marked out Agathon's choral odes as *outré*. The poet is also associated with a major change in the content and subject-matter of choral odes, and, more specifically, with the relationship between the stasima and the plot as it unfolded in the episodes of the play. Aristotle credits Agathon with the invention of *embolima* (i.e. irrelevant 'insertions'):

> One should treat the chorus as one of the actors and a portion of the whole, as taking part in the action – that is, one should follow Sophocles' practice rather than that of Euripides. In the other plays the sung portions have nothing more

---

[61] See (most recently) D'Angour (2011) 198–206; LeVen (2014).

[62] See (e.g.) Pherecrates F155; Aristophanes, *Birds* 1372–1409, *Clouds* 829–31, 969–72, *Frogs* 1438; [Plutarch] *On Music* 1141d–f.

[63] *Suda* A 125; Photius A 83 (= *TrGF* 1.39 T20a–b): Aristophanes (*Gerytades* F178 K-A) may be the original source.

to do with the plot than with some other tragedy altogether. This explains why these days they sing interpolated songs. Agathon was the first to bring in such a practice. But what is the difference between singing *embolima* and moving a speech or an entire episode from one play to another?[64]

Thus Aristotle definitively associates Agathon with a major structural change in the composition of tragedy, which had a significant influence on later writers in terms of the way that plays were conceived of and staged. Aristotle's negative assessment of *embolima* is the consequence of his view that the most important criterion for assessing a dramatic work is *unity* (understood in a very specific sense, referring to the probable and necessary connection between every single element in a production).[65] It is because fourth-century productions seemed to lack this sort of unity that Aristotle implies that tragedy 'these days' is worse than before – a view that continues to colour modern treatments of the genre.[66] However, this is only one way of looking at dramatic structure.

Rather than seeing Agathon and his followers as simply flawed or misguided, it is worth trying to imagine what he was trying to achieve by adapting the role of the chorus. Did Agathon's choral songs have no connection at all to the other portions of his plays? Were they purely what we would call incidental music or interludes? Even if they had no *narrative* connection to the events on stage, they might have been very carefully designed to fit their dramatic setting in other ways – for example, to create a certain mood, to manipulate the emotions of the audience, to make certain thematic connections between different sections, or to punctuate the action in a carefully calculated manner. Aristotle's fixation on narrative and plot would naturally lead him to ignore or devalue such considerations. But at any rate it seems that (either deliberately or accidentally) he confuses two separate issues here, by treating Agathon's structural innovations as equivalent to the activities of interpolators. It is one thing for a single writer to structure his own plays so that the linear connection between its parts is not obvious; but it is quite another thing for someone else – as it might be a later writer, producer or actor – to mix and match material from different plays by other people. What Aristotle leaves unclear is whether Agathon himself transferred his own songs from play to play. One also wonders whether or not the *identity* of the chorus members remained important in Agathon's plays: surely it would have made a big difference whether they represented (for

---

[64] *Poetics* 18.1456a25-9.
[65] See Heath (1989) 38–55.
[66] But see Chapter 5 for a reassessment.

instance) Trojan women, Greek sailors or Furies, or whether they were just seen as an anonymous and unidentified group of musicians. Were they seen as part of the world of the play or not? At least one Agathonian tragedy, *Mysians*, was named after its chorus rather than a main character, but this does not allow us to conclude very much.

We do not know how often Agathon or others wrote *embolima* – perhaps only occasionally? – which means that they cannot be said to represent a permanent change in the way that the chorus was employed. Nor are we obliged to see the history of tragedy in the late fifth century and later as a progressive or linear process of evolution. It seems better to view Agathon's *embolima* in the context of his other formal experiments with dramatic structure. We know that from time to time Agathon tried out new types of plot. For example, Aristotle seems to imply that he once attempted to fit the material of an entire epic poem into a single tragedy.

> In epic, because of its length, the poets can have a size that suits them, but in plays things turn out quite contrary to what one expected. We can find a proof of this in the poets who have dealt with the whole of the sack of Troy and not just a part of it, as Euripides did, or with the whole story of Niobe and not just in the way that Aeschylus did. Such poets are either driven off the stage or do badly in the contest – even Agathon failed in this respect.[67]

'*Even* Agathon' seems to imply that Aristotle normally approves of Agathon's work (or that the theatre audience did); but obviously an entire epic squashed into one play would be a very strange sort of entertainment, and one can only imagine how this was practically achieved on stage. How did the timescale work? Was the resulting tragedy unusually long – a precursor, perhaps, of those gargantuan cinematic 'epics' such as *Lawrence of Arabia, Gone With The Wind* or *Ben-Hur*? Our longest surviving tragedy is Sophocles' *Oedipus at Colonus* (at 1779 lines), but it is notable that the average length of tragedies seems to have increased steadily over time (to judge by our surviving sample of thirty-two complete plays). Was Agathon deliberately setting out to break a record by writing the longest tragedy to date? This is an intriguing idea, but it is easy to see how such an experiment might have tested the limits of his audience's endurance or disrupted the organization of the festival.[68] Alternatively, it may be that this

---

[67]   *Poetics* 18.1456a18-20 (*TrGF* 1.39 T17).
[68]   The longest cinema film ever made is currently *Modern Times Forever* (2011), directed by a Finnish group headed by Bjornstjerne Reuter Christiansen: it is over 240 hours long. The International Movie Database (http://www.imdb.com) describes its subject-matter as 'the ever-slow decay of Helsinki's Stora Enso headquarters building'.

play was a radically truncated and condensed work (along the lines, perhaps, of the bizarre entertainments concocted by the Reduced Shakespeare Company).[69] However that might be, Aristotle makes it clear that Agathon's 'epic tragedy' was both a popular and an artistic failure.

Nevertheless, Agathon's boldest experiment of all is mentioned with approval by Aristotle. This was the tragedy *Anth*[ ]*s*. Owing to an ambiguity in the text of the *Poetics* at just the point at which this play is being discussed, its very title is fragmentary – a fact which may strike us as unbearably poignant (or, at any rate, ironically appropriate).[70] Was the full title *Anthos* or *Antheus*? Perhaps we shall never know, unless this lost play should miraculously come to light. Now that would be a matter for celebration, more than almost any other classical rediscovery that can be imagined, because it is clear that *Anth*[ ]*s* was an extraordinary or even unique work. Unlike any other tragedy known to us, its plot was not taken from the Greek myths but completely invented by Agathon: thus it was perhaps the earliest conscious attempt at writing fiction in antiquity.

> In Agathon's *Anth*[ ]*s* both the events and the characters' names are made up, but it gives no less pleasure. So one need not try at all costs to keep to the traditional stories which are the subject-matter of tragedy . . .[71]

Given that no trace of the play remains, it is impossible to know what its plot or characters may have been. One recent discussion states that 'presumably the characters at least existed in a world still presided over by the traditional gods and a setting somewhere in mythical time',[72] but even this is far from certain.

Scholars have sometimes suggested that the outline of *Anth*[ ]*s* may be preserved, in some form, in later works of literature.[73] Antonius Liberalis recounts the story of a youth called Anthos, son of Autonous and Hippodamia, who was killed by his father's horses. Parthenius tells of Antheus, a young man from Halicarnassus, whose story involved erotic love and calamity: the king's wife Cleobee fell in love with him and tried to seduce him, but when he rejected her advances she killed Antheus (by pushing him down a well) and then committed suicide. Of course, there is no way of knowing for sure that these writers were *not*

---

[69] This theatre troupe describes itself in its website (http://www.reducedshakespeare.com) as 'the bad boys of abridgement'.

[70] Aristotle uses only the dative form, *Anthei*, which makes it impossible to say what the nominative spelling of the word was.

[71] Aristotle, *Poetics* 9.1451b21–3.

[72] Rutherford (2012) 364.

[73] Antonius Liberalis, *Metamorphoses* 7; Parthenius, *Erotica Pathemata* 14. See Corbato (1948), Pitcher (1939) and Lévêque (1955) 105–12.

influenced by Agathon, but it does seem somewhat unlikely. Would Aristotle really have said that either of these storylines was a complete invention on the part of Agathon, given that they both bear very strong similarities to other well-known tragic myths (e.g. Phaethon, Hippolytus, Bellerophon)? Other attempts to explain the title or plot of Anth[ ]s have been even less convincing.[74] So we remain in the dark; but it is clear that this tragedy was a strikingly bold and original experiment. Indeed, it seems to have proved an unrepeatable experiment – at any rate, Aristotle mentions no other comparable attempts at fictional tragedy, and to judge by the surviving titles very few other tragedians ever seem to have strayed from the traditional myths as a source of subject-matter.[75]

How far from generic norms can a tragedy go while remaining a tragedy? After all, invented plots and characters are normally seen as characteristic of other genres such as comedy, not tragedy. It is worth recalling that strange scene at the end of Plato's *Symposium* where Socrates, in the small hours, endeavours to persuade a tired and inebriated Aristophanes and Agathon that it would be possible for the same poet to write both tragedies and comedies.[76] It is surely no accident that these two poets in particular are chosen to be Socrates' interlocutors at that point in the dialogue. Aristophanes is well known for his sustained engagement with tragedy (especially Euripidean tragedy), and his plays could be said to be more 'tragic' than any other comedians' work.[77] It may be thought that Agathon represents the converse – a tragedian who in certain respects had made his work resemble comedy.[78]

The plays

Apart from Anth[ ]s only five titles survive, all of which (on the face of it) indicate that Agathon normally treated much the same sort of mythical subject-matter as

---

[74] Crescini's (1904, 29) suggestion that the title was *Anthos*, 'au sens de "florilège": plusieurs morceaux lyriques . . . réunis par les embolima' is rejected by Lévêque (1955) 111, who doubts whether *anthos* was used in this sense in fifth-century Greek; but Lévêque's own alternative suggestion (that the title, *Anthos*, 'The Flower', is deliberately designed to be enigmatic) seems frustratingly evasive.

[75] Notable exceptions include Phrynichus, Aeschylus, Dionysius and Theodectes (see pp. 23–7, 139–43, 165–6).

[76] Plato, *Symposium* 223c–d. See Clay (1975), who thinks that the 'tragic and comic poet' of the *Symposium* is Plato or Socrates himself.

[77] See Silk (2000).

[78] Euripides is the writer normally thought of as having made tragedy more like comedy – see esp. Knox (1979) – but actually Agathon's formal experiments bring him much closer to comedy than Euripides ever ventured.

the other tragedians. The fragments can tell us nothing for certain about the way in which Agathon handled these particular stories or adapted the traditional myths. As usual we have to consult some other literary source (such as Apollodorus' *Library*) if we want to find out the basic outlines of the myth as known to writers in antiquity, though we cannot know exactly which versions or variants were current in the fifth century. It may be that Agathon's plots closely resembled the narratives in Apollodorus and elsewhere. However, there are several signs that Agathon's treatment of myth may have been eccentric. In the light of the testimonia discussed above, which tell us that Agathon sometimes broke the rules, we can cautiously speculate on ways in which this may have been so. Even from what may appear to be extremely scrappy fragments we can sometimes get a strong hint of a sophisticated and self-aware poet at work.

Two of Agathon's tragedies, *Aerope* and *Thyestes*, dramatized portions of the grotesque story of the House of Atreus.[79] Aerope, daughter of the Cretan Catreus, married Atreus but subsequently fell in love with his brother Thyestes. The two brothers were rivals for the throne of Mycenae, which Thyestes eventually won by trickery and with the aid of Aerope, who had become his lover. Subsequently Atreus re-established himself as rightful ruler, with the assistance of Zeus, and Thyestes went into exile. But when Atreus discovered that Aerope and Thyestes were lovers, he decided to punish his brother. He called Thyestes back, as if to bring about a reconciliation, and invited him to dinner – a meal which, when finished, was revealed to have consisted of Thyestes' own sons, whom Atreus had dismembered and boiled. Thyestes went off again into exile, this time vowing to have his revenge over Atreus by any means. When he consulted the oracle, he was told that he would have his revenge if he fathered a son by sleeping with (or raping) his own daughter, Pelopia. This he duly did, and the child of this union, Aegisthus, eventually killed Atreus and restored Thyestes to the throne. Later still Atreus' son Agamemnon deposed Thyestes and became king of Mycenae, until in turn he was killed by Aegisthus, who had become the lover of Agamemnon's wife Clytemnestra . . . and so on.

The story, which is impressively awful and also rather deadening when summarized in its bare bones, embodies a horrible sense of circularity and inevitability. With its powerful currents of incest, adultery, revenge, murder and cannibalism, it was among the most recurrently popular myths for tragedians of all periods. In the surviving works of Aeschylus, Euripides and Sophocles the focus is on the doings of the younger generation of descendants of Atreus and

---

[79] See (e.g.) Apollodorus, *Epitome* 2.10–16.

Thyestes. Parts of the story were dramatized by Ion (in his *Agamemnon*), Apollodorus (in *Thyestes*), Carcinus the Younger (in *Aerope* and *Orestes*), Chaeremon (in *Thyestes*), Theodectes (in *Orestes*), and many others; and the theme was still popular many years later among Roman tragedians such as Accius, Varius, Maternus and Seneca. It is easy to see why the myth exercised such an appeal, since (quite apart from its enormous narrative potential) it exemplifies some of the most characteristic tragic themes, including inherited guilt and ancestral fault, reciprocal violence, perverted kin relationships, generational conflict, and power struggles among traditional aristocratic families. But it is less easy to imagine precisely what Agathon did with the myth. Did he exploit its erotic potential by dwelling on the illicit love-affair between Aerope and Thyestes? Did he contrive to put the grotesque dinner-party on stage? Were the two plays *Aerope* and *Thyestes* somehow connected, or did they even form part of the same trilogy? It is impossible to know.

The only fragment that survives of *Aerope* consists of a single word, preserved by an etymologist on account of its grammatical form (εἰσῇισαν, F1), while the sole fragment of *Thyestes* (F3) seems to have no obvious relevance to the House of Atreus at all. It is concerned with a completely different myth, that of the suitors of Amphithea (who eventually married Adrastus, one of the Seven against Thebes).[80] Athenaeus, who preserves the fragment, quotes it apropos of his discussion of luxury[81]:

> Agathon in his *Thyestes* says that the suitors of Pronax's daughter came decked out in every way, including their hairstyle, worn long; but, when they didn't succeed in marrying her, they said:

> κόμας ἐκειράμεσθα μάρτυρας τρυφῆς,
> ἦ που ποθεινὸν χρῆμα παιζούσηι φρενί.
> ἐπώνυμον γοῦν εὐθὺς ἔσχομεν κλέος,
> Κουρῆτες εἶναι, κουρίμου χάριν τριχός.

> We sheared our hair, witness to our love of luxury,
> a thing, I suppose, that is desirable to a playful mind.
> Immediately, then, we gained a reputation in accordance with the name –
> that is to say, we are *Kouretes*, named after our shorn (*kourimou*) hair.

What is this material doing in a play called *Thyestes*? One might suppose that Amphithea's suitors were included as an incidental detail or mythical example:

80   Cf. Apollodorus 1.9.13.
81   Athenaeus 12.528d.

perhaps Aerope was being implicitly or explicitly compared to Amphithea in some way, or perhaps someone was shown as cutting their hair. However, Athenaeus does seem to imply that the incident was actually part of the plot, and the suitors' words are given in direct speech as if they were characters in the play. Would it be going too far to suggest that Agathon was experimenting by bringing together characters and events from different mythical traditions? This would have been an extraordinary thing to do, since, as Aristotle tells us in the *Poetics*, tragedians did not normally depart from the traditional myths.[82] But in the same passage Aristotle reminds us that Agathon *did* sometimes make extraordinary experiments of this kind (as discussed in the section above, with reference to *Anth*[ ]s).[83] Was Agathon having fun with his audience by putting the Kouretes in the 'wrong' play and seeing what resulted? We cannot know for sure, but it remains an intriguing possibility: one might also compare the incongruous reference to Theseus in Agathon's *Telephus* (F4, quoted later in this section).[84] Furthermore, Agathon's reference to the 'playful mind' (παιζούσηι φρενί) might also be thought to signal a certain ironical or ludic attitude to his material.

The Theban myth cycle provided the basis for Agathon's *Alcmeon*, another tragedy based on apparently unremarkable subject-matter (plays with the same title were written by Achaeus, Sophocles, Euripides, Timotheus, Astydamas, Theodectes and others). The title character was one of the Epigoni, the sons of the Seven against Thebes who mounted an expedition against Thebes to avenge their fathers' death. Alcmeon,[85] the leader of this expedition, was the son of Amphiaraus and Eriphyle, but after Thebes had been captured he discovered that Eriphyle had taken bribes to persuade her husband and her son to go to war. Following the advice of an oracle, Alcmeon killed his mother and was subsequently driven insane and pursued by the Furies, eventually reaching Psophis, where he was purified. Thus the story has obvious structural similarities with the Orestes myth (which is nowadays more familiar because of surviving tragedies by Aeschylus, Sophocles and Euripides). As before, we cannot be sure which version or aspects of the myth Agathon used in his tragedy, and slightly different accounts are given by our main literary sources.[86] Not a single trace of Agathon's plot remains, but it may be worth remembering that Aristotle, when

---

[82]   Aristotle, *Poetics* 1453b22–26.
[83]   Aristotle, *Poetics* 1451b19–22.
[84]   Lévêque (1955, 97–8) finds this detail inexplicable, and tentatively suggests that Theseus may be on the scene (which would, he says, constitute an 'insouciance' or 'flottement' with regard to chronology on Agathon's part).
[85]   Note that alternative spellings (Alcmeon/Alcmaeon/Alcmaion) exist.
[86]   E.g. Apollodorus 3.7.2–5, Pindar, *Pythian* 8.40–8, Pausanias 8.24.8 and others.

he is talking about the conventions governing the use of myth, says that 'one cannot undo the traditional stories – for example, one cannot have a tragedy in which Clytemnestra is not killed by Orestes or Eriphyle by Alcmeon'.[87] Might this imply that he has actually seen a tragedy in which Eriphyle was not killed by Alcmeon? And if so, might that tragedy have been Agathon's *Alcmeon*? (After all, as I have already pointed out, a few lines later Aristotle shows that he is thinking about Agathon's plot experiments.)

However that might be, it is certainly tempting to read the tantalizing reference to the 'lawless Muses' in *Alcmeon* (ἀθέμιστοι μοῦσαι, F2) as a metapoetic gesture. Might it be that Agathon is self-consciously drawing the audience's attention to his unorthodox handling of music and the chorus, or to some other aspect of his own extraordinary approach to the tragic art? Such a gesture would be unusual but not unparalleled in tragedy. Euripides too, on occasion, includes comparable moments of self-conscious reflection on the art of poetry, including acknowledgement of his own originality in terms of plot, poetic technique, or handling of mythical material.[88] For a similar effect one could also compare Timotheus (composer of dithyrambic nomes and exact contemporary of Agathon, to whom he has often been compared), who wrote such verses as 'Begone, ancient Muse!' and 'With my young songs I dishonour the Muse of old!' in a spirit of defiant self-promotion.[89] Of course it would not be in keeping with tragic decorum to press one's authorial claims so emphatically as Timotheus did. But it is quite plausible that Agathon (implicitly or explicitly) presented his own Muses as 'lawless' – that is, as breaking the rules or defying the normal tragic conventions. That would be a rather apt description of his work. Indeed, it is hard to think what else this phrase could signify.

At least two of Agathon's tragedies were concerned with the Trojan War, which was one of the most frequent sources of inspiration for tragedians of all periods, reflecting the ongoing appeal and cultural prestige of Homer and the poems of the Epic Cycle. The myth of Telephus, the king of Mysia and son of Heracles and Auge, was most famously dramatized by Euripides (whose *Telephus* was repeatedly quoted and parodied for decades after its first production in 438 BCE),[90] but Agathon also wrote a *Telephus* and a *Mysians*, both of which probably treated parts of the same legend. When Agamemnon and the Greeks attacked

---

[87] Aristotle, *Poetics* 1453b22–5.
[88] Cf. Euripides, *Helen* 1056, *Heracles* 38, *Orestes* 1503, *Trojan Women* 512; see Torrance (2013) for discussion.
[89] Timotheus F796, F798 *PMG*; on Timotheus and the 'New Music' generally cf. Barker (1984) 93–5, West (1992) 356–72; and on innovation in late-fifth-century lyric more generally see LeVen (2014).
[90] Tragedies called *Telephus* were also composed by Aeschylus, Sophocles, Iophon and Cleophon.

Mysia during their initial expedition to Troy, Telephus was wounded in the leg by Achilles. Since the wound would not heal, Telephus consulted the Delphic oracle and learned that he could be healed only by the man who had injured him; and so he went to the Greeks, as they assembled at Argos, and managed to persuade Achilles to heal him in return for guiding the Greeks safely to Troy.[91] As before, there is no indication of just how Agathon dealt with this story. It may be that *Mysians* dealt with the circumstances leading up to Telephus' birth, or with the Greeks' attack on Mysia, or with some other event in the Mysians' past. It may be that *Mysians* and *Telephus* were connected in some way, or even members of the same connected trilogy, but there is no way of knowing.[92] Of *Mysians* nothing survives except a comment from Plutarch to the effect that its music was highly unusual and florid, and the surviving fragment of *Telephus* gives us no help at all in reconstructing the plot.[93]

It would be surprising, given the notoriety of Euripides' *Telephus* within the fifth century, if Agathon's tragedy was not written with Euripides in mind. Indeed, the surviving fragment of Agathon's *Telephus* does seem to be quoting or adapting Euripides – but the source text, unexpectedly, is not Euripides' *Telephus* but his *Theseus*. We know this because of Athenaeus, who quotes verses from both authors in the course of his discussion of poets who showed a special interest in the alphabet and literacy.[94] Athenaeus cites various such writers – including Lasus (who wrote lipogrammatic poems), Castorion (who wrote poems in which the word-order could be rearranged without affecting the metre), and Callias (author of a late-fifth-century comedy entitled *The Alphabetic Tragedy*, which featured a chorus of letters of the alphabet) – before quoting a thirteen-line passage of Euripides (*Theseus* F382) in which an illiterate shepherd describes his first sight of the name Theseus written or inscribed in Greek letters (ΘΗΣΕΥΣ).

> I haven't got any knowledge of writing, but I shall tell you the shapes of the letters and give a clear description. There is a circle, measured out as if with compasses, and this has a firm mark in the middle. The second letter has, first of all, two lines, and then another one holding these two apart at the centre. The third letter looks like some sort of curly lock of hair; and then the fourth consists of one part standing upright and three other parts which are attached to it at all

---

[91] See e.g. Hesiod F165; Pindar, *Olympian* 9, *Isthmians* 5, 8.
[92] The relationship between plays in a trilogy is a matter of some controversy: see e.g. Wright (2006). It is not known whether Agathon wrote connected trilogies. Note that Euripides' *Telephus* was part of a 'Trojan trilogy' in 415 BCE: see Scodel (1980).
[93] Plutarch, *Table-Talk* 3.1.1 (*Moralia* 645e) = *TrGF* 1.39 F3a.
[94] Athenaeus 10.454a–f.

angle. The fifth is not easy to describe: there are two lines which stand apart from one another but then converge into a single point at the base. And the final letter is the same as the third.

Athenaeus adds that Agathon has imitated this passage in his *Telephus* (F4). This play was mentioned above apropos of the incongruity of mixing together different myths (why should there have been a description of Theseus' shield at all in a play about Telephus?). In Agathon's play another illiterate man (*agrammatos*) was made to describe an identical inscription:

> The first letter in the word was a circle with a dot in the centre;
> there were also two upright bars joined together,
> and there was a third letter also, which was similar to a Scythian bow;
> then there was a letter resembling a trident sideways-on;
> and then there were two <short bars converging together> on top of a single bar;
> and then the letter that was third appeared again at the end.

Athenaeus goes on to quote more dramatic passages which employ the same sort of idea: from the tragedian Theodectes, who recalls and reworks the lines of the Euripidean shepherd in a manner very similar to that of Agathon, and from Sophocles, whose satyr-play *Amphiaraus* featured a man who actually danced out the shape of the letters on stage.[95] In all of these dramatic works special emphasis is being placed, not just on the theme of alphabetic experimentation, but specifically on the moment at which illiterate characters come face to face with the new cultural technology of writing, and on the social and dramatic consequences of this sort of encounter.[96]

Athenaeus is a valuable source because he helps us to fill in a little more detail of Agathon's literary and intellectual context. Agathon emerges as not just an allusive and self-aware writer, but also as part of a group of poets who were active at a particularly important moment in classical civilization – the transition from performance culture to reading culture, or (as it has been called) the 'literate revolution'.[97] Furthermore, it is obvious from these quotations that Agathon is playing some sort of intertextual game with the work of Euripides. It is not clear

---

[95] Theodectes (*TrGF* 1.72 F6: see Chapter 5, pp. 172–3); Sophocles *TrGF* 4 F121. Note also Achaeus' satyric *Omphale* (*TrGF* 1.20 F33) for a similar preoccupation with letters of the alphabet.

[96] Cf. Pappas (2011) 47–9, who discusses 'visual literacy' (in these fragments and elsewhere) in terms of sophistic concerns about language and meaning.

[97] See e.g. Havelock (1982), Yunis (2003), Wright (2012), etc. Cf. also Torrance (2013) on the marked insistence upon *writing* in Euripidean tragedy in particular; Easterling (1985) interpreted this as an example of tragic 'anachronism' but Torrance goes further and views it as a metapoetical strategy aimed at drawing attention to the act of writing and the poet's own activity.

exactly what sort of relationship was being established between these two texts, or what sort of attitude Agathon was adopting towards Euripides, but this remains an important and comparatively rare example of a fifth-century tragic poet explicitly and openly responding to the work of another dramatist. Thus Agathon can be seen in this brief fragment as making his audience think about the act of writing, the question of literacy, and his own activity as an original poet who is acutely aware of his poetic predecessors.

It is not recorded how many tragedies Agathon wrote, but presumably the six known titles represent only a fraction of his total output. Most of the fragments that survive are not connected to any particular named play, and none of them gives much hint of a possible dramatic context. One fragment deals with the ethics and psychology of suicide (F7). Several fragments reveal some sort of interest in temporality and causation (F8, F9, F19, F20). Another particularly intriguing fragment (F5) even evokes the counterfactual possibility that the gods might, as it were, turn back the clock so as to undo events that had already happened. Aristotle has been taken as supplying a clue that Agathon was capable of complex character-portrayal – if it was indeed Agathon that he was talking about when he mentioned an Achilles who combined good and bad moral qualities and was compared to the Achilles of Homer.[98] Perhaps one day further literary finds will allow us to say more about how (or if?) these themes were developed, but in the meantime all we have is tantalizing glimpses of what might have been.

But it would be a shame to end this chapter on a melancholy note; and so, in lieu of a conclusion, I shall make one further (personal and highly suggestive) observation about the much lamented Agathon. Every time I contemplate Agathon, especially in his Aristophanic incarnation, I am irresistibly struck by his uncanny similarity to Oscar Wilde – his insistence on the close connection between Art and Life, his concern with beauty, his flamboyant behaviour and sexuality, and his epigrammatic and witty mode of discourse. Indeed, the sort of thing that Agathon says in Aristophanes ('I change my opinions along with my clothes'[99]) sounds exactly like the sort of thing that Oscar himself habitually said; the same is true of the aphorisms and paradoxes of Agathon's fragments.

As a recent critical study of Wilde's classical education has shown, Wilde was certainly familiar with Agathon and his reputation, primarily through his

---

[98] Aristotle, *Poetics* 15.1454b13–14 (printed by Snell as *TrGF* 1.39 F10). However, the text is corrupt, and Agathon's name cannot be confidently restored: see Lucas (1968) *ad loc.*

[99] Aristophanes, *Women Celebrating the Thesmophoria* 148.

reading of Aristophanes, though he would also have been familiar with the standard editions of dramatic fragments by Nauck, Meineke and others. What is more, he even explicitly encouraged his readers to draw a comparison between Agathon and himself, by describing Agathon, 'this brilliant man of letters and of fashion in the wittiest period of Attic social life', as 'the Aesthetic poet of the Periclean age'.[100] Of course this sort of comparison, however tempting or suggestive, is potentially dangerous and anachronistic. Nevertheless, I cannot help wondering how far Agathon – as mediated through Aristophanic comedy and the fragments – may have influenced Wilde's own work and his mannerisms. Is this a unique example of the modern reception of a lost tragedian?

---

[100] Wilde (1880) 301–2; cf. Ross (2013) on Wilde's classical education and influences, esp. p. 60 on Agathon.

4

Tragic Family Trees

Producing tragedies in classical Athens often seems to have been a family business, passed down from generation to generation. Younger members of a family, trained up from an early age in the art of tragedy, might write their own plays, or they might stage productions of their better-known relatives' work. As Dana Sutton points out, in a useful survey of the evidence, an extraordinarily large proportion of tragedians belonged to a notable theatrical family – a phenomenon that is unparalleled in any other literary genre (or indeed any other context at all, ancient or modern).[1] But it is difficult to explain this situation or to understand its precise significance in terms of theatre history. Did the younger playwrights exploit their family connections in order to get a better reception for their work? Was nepotism involved in the selection process at the festivals? Were there rivalries between different families? Did the families preserve archives or collections of scripts to draw upon as resources? Did the poets deliberately allude to the plays of other members of their own family? Were they influenced by the way in which myths and stories were told to them as children? Did they take part in their relatives' productions, as performers or assistants? These are tantalizing questions, but our scanty evidence gives few clues as to the answers. Often it is not possible to do much more than point out the familial relationships between writers, but sometimes one can say something of value about these poets' careers, their attitude to the literary and dramatic tradition, or the character of their plays.

One particular reason why these poets are worth studying together as a separate category is that they provide an unusual angle on the topic of intertextuality in tragedy. A tension between tradition and innovation can be detected in many tragedies, and can often prove to be a fruitful way of approaching the texts. But a striking feature of modern classical scholarship is that intertextual

---

[1] Sutton (1987) is an excellent discussion of the phenomenon, including a wealth of prosopographical data.

relations between authors (not just tragedians) are almost always regarded as inherently agonistic in nature, with the younger or epigonal writers attempting to outdo their earlier counterparts in some way. In part this is due to the fact that the whole enterprise of Greek literature and literary criticism can seem to be based on contests and competitions, in either a literal or a metaphorical sense. But in part it is also due to writers such as Harold Bloom, whose much-quoted book *The Anxiety of Influence* presents literary activity in starkly Freudian terms. The act of authorship is seen by Bloom as a psychological struggle to assert one's own selfhood and identity, and the relationship between younger writers and their literary predecessors is seen as an Oedipal conflict between children and parents. 'Poetry is the enchantment of incest, disciplined by resistance to that enchantment', and each new work is 'a rival poem, son or grandson of the same precursor'.[2] Bloom does not discuss any examples of writers who were literally descended from other writers, and perhaps he would say that in such a context it makes little difference whether one is talking about actual or metaphorical incest. But the apparently unique phenomenon of tragic family trees constitutes a fascinating sub-category within the 'anatomy of influence' (as Bloom calls it in a later book).

In this respect, it is intriguing to note that several younger tragedians chose to write plays on subjects and titles that had already been used by their fathers or other ancestors.[3] For instance, Sophocles and his son Iophon both wrote a *Telephus*; Philocles wrote a *Penelope* and a *Philoctetes,* as had his uncle Aeschylus before him; both Philocles and his great-grandson Astydamas the Younger wrote a *Nauplius* and an *Oedipus*; and Astydamas shared a couple of titles in common with his great-great-great-uncle Aeschylus (*Athamas, Epigoni*). It is especially wonderful to discover that Xenocles and his son Carcinus the Younger both wrote an *Oedipus*: Harold Bloom – and Sigmund Freud too, no doubt – would have rejoiced to learn of this particular literary double-act. Frustratingly, we are not in a position to compare any of these versions, so as to judge the ways in which the anxiety of influence manifested itself. But it is inconceivable that *none* of these younger poets ever alluded to (or quoted, or reflected, or plundered, or reworked, or implicitly criticized) their forebears' work.

The examples of several tragedians who actively championed their famous fathers' work, including Aristias and Euphorion, suggest that not all of these

---

[2]   Bloom (1973) 95–6.
[3]   Cf. my Epilogue (pp. 203–5) for a complete catalogue of titles and subjects that were treated by more than one tragedian.

belated writers were in need of a session on the psychoanalyst's couch. However, Sophocles' son **Iophon** represents a more problematic case. Iophon enjoyed a certain amount of success as a tragedian in his own right, during a career spanning more than thirty years. The *Suda* names him as the author of fifty plays (including *Achilles, Telephus, Actaeon, The Sack of Troy, Dexamenos, Bacchants* and *Pentheus*), and he won first prize at the City Dionysia in 435 BCE, followed by second prize at the same festival in 428.[4] It is impossible to say what his tragedies were like, because only a single three-line fragment survives.[5] However, several sources indicate that he failed to emerge completely from Sophocles' shadow.

The following extract from Aristophanes' *Frogs* (first produced in 405, just after Sophocles' death) may hint at the way in which Iophon was perceived by many Athenian theatregoers[6]:

> Dionysus: What I need is an accomplished (*dexios*) poet, but there aren't any of those left – the poets that are still writing are all bad (*kakoi*).
>
> Heracles: What do you mean? Isn't Iophon still alive?
>
> Dionysus: Yes, I suppose so. This is the only remaining good thing – if it actually *is* a good thing. I don't really know whether it is or not.
>
> Heracles: At any rate, if you must bring someone back from the underworld, why not choose Sophocles? He's preferable to Euripides.
>
> Dionysus: No – at least, not until I take Iophon by himself and see what his poetry is like without Sophocles.

The joke depends on the assumption that Iophon's success was due in large part to his father, and that Sophocles' demise will have fatal consequences for Iophon's future career. It is implied that Sophocles actually helped Iophon to write his plays, or even wrote them all himself. This is the view of the malicious ancient commentator on the passage, who explains that 'Iophon was mocked for claiming his father's works as his own; he was mocked not only for adding his own name to his father's tragedies but also for being a frigid and long-winded poet'.

As usual, it is difficult to know how seriously to take Aristophanes, or to decide just how critical or disparaging is his attitude towards Iophon. Can it really be true that this joke 'proves that father and son were working happily together till the end', as one scholar puts it?[7] Or was the relationship between Sophocles and

---

4   *Suda* I 451 (*TrGF* 1.22 T1a); cf. T2a–b (DID A1. 84; DID C13). See Millis and Olson (2012) 25.
5   From *Bacchants* (*TrGF* 1.22 F2): 'I too understand these things, even though I am a woman – that the more a person seeks to know about the gods, the less he will end up knowing'.
6   Aristophanes, *Frogs* 71–9 with scholia *ad loc.* (*TrGF* 1.22 T5).
7   Webster (1936) 15.

Iophon an uneasy one? The latter interpretation is suggested by another strand in the biographical tradition, in which Iophon is said to have taken his father to court and accused him of senile dementia in an attempt to get control of the family estate. The case allegedly collapsed when Sophocles read out extracts from *Oedipus at Colonus* (a work of his advanced old age) to great acclaim. The elderly poet is reported to have said: 'If I am Sophocles, I am not senile; and if I am senile, I am not Sophocles'. This story was obviously well known throughout antiquity, and a number of writers recount the same anecdote, with minor variations.[8] Iophon does not emerge very well from all this. He is characterized as an envious, hostile and unscrupulous nonentity. But caution is needed: as with all biographical anecdotes relating to the poets, the historical accuracy of this material is open to doubt. It has been suggested that the source of the tradition was actually 'a comedy (now lost) about Sophocles' family'.[9] This may well be true;[10] but in that case, why was such a comedy written, and why was such a scenario thought to be funny? If it did not reflect a real-life incident, it must mean that Iophon was widely *perceived* to be afflicted by the anxiety of influence. Even if his relationship with Sophocles was perfectly amiable, it must have been galling for Iophon to be in this position: whatever he did, he was doomed always to come second to his father in popular opinion. Did Iophon really quarrel with Sophocles? We cannot hope to get to the truth of the matter, but it may be relevant to note that when Sophocles' *Oedipus at Colonus* received its posthumous première in 401 BCE, it was not produced by Iophon, as one might have expected. Instead, the job went to his grandson, the younger Sophocles.[11]

This later **Sophocles** was also a relatively prolific and successful tragedian, who is said to have produced forty plays and won seven victories.[12] Epigraphic evidence confirms that two of these victories were at the City Dionysia, in 387 and 375 BCE respectively,[13] but nothing more can be said about his career.

---

8   *Life of Sophocles* §13 (incorporating Satyrus, *FGrHist* 3.162 F6); Plutarch, *Moralia* 785a; Cicero, *On Old Age* 22; Apuleius, *Apology* 37; Lucian, *Long-Livers* 24 (*TrGF* 1.22 T1c, T8a–b): sometimes Sophocles' sons (plural) are mentioned, sometimes Iophon alone is named as the accuser.

9   Lefkowitz (1981) 84–5.

10 Note that Aristophanes F591 (part of a papyrus commentary on an unknown Aristophanic comedy) includes a reference to Iophon, along with some sort of comment about dramatic prizes, but the fragment is too lacunose to interpret with any confidence.

11 *TrGF* 1.62 T3 = DID C23. But it is not known when Iophon died.

12 *Suda* Σ 816 (*TrGF* 1.62 T1): the total number of plays is also given as eleven.

13 DID A 1. 199, 244 (from the Athenian *Fasti, IG* ii² 2318. 1007, 1153): see Millis and Olson (2012) 5–58.

Aristias was the son of Pratinas, one of the earliest known tragic poets (see Chapter 1). Little is known about him or his work, though it was said that both father and son shared a particular interest in satyr-drama.[14] Aristias' first victory was won some time in the late 460s BCE,[15] but at the Dionysia in 467 he had already been awarded second prize with a trilogy consisting of *Perseus, Tantalus,* and the satyr-play *Wrestlers,* some or all of which plays were the work of his father.[16] This is an important piece of evidence in terms of the organization of the festival and the relationship between individual elements of a production, for this suite of plays evidently did not follow what we tend to think of as the normal arrangement of three tragedies plus one satyr-drama. If the 'normal' arrangement was abandoned on this occasion, perhaps it was also ignored on other occasions as well; or maybe there was always a greater degree of flexibility in the rules than is generally thought.

Aristias went on to compete against Sophocles on at least one occasion,[17] and his own plays included *Antaeus, Atalante, Fates, Cyclops* and *Orpheus.* Only a single small fragment from each of these works survives, not enough to reveal very much about the plays' content, but it has been thought that some or all of these works were satyric rather than tragic.[18] *Cyclops* was definitely a satyr-play, and it may have been similar to Euripides' later play of the same name; its sole fragment is a line spoken by Polyphemus to Odysseus, complaining that he has ruined the wine by pouring water into it.[19] The other plays show signs of an interest in various types of combat or sporting contest as well as eating and drinking, themes which may well suggest satyr-play rather than tragedy.[20] The title character of *Antaeus* was one of Poseidon's sons, a giant who wrestled all his visitors to death and was in turn defeated and killed by Heracles.[21] Wrestling-contests may also have featured in *Atalante,* since Atalante in myth was a notable huntress and a formidable sportswoman, who defeated Peleus at wrestling and challenged her would-be suitors to a foot-race (which Hippomenes eventually won only by cheating); the plot may also have featured the Calydonian boar-hunt, in which Atalante took part.[22] Some sort of Underworld scenario is

---

[14] *TrGF* 1.9 T4.

[15] *TrGF* 1.9 T2 (*IG* ii² 2325.17 = DID A3, 17). See Millis and Olson (2012) 144–8: 'the victory referred to here can date no earlier than 467/6, and most likely belongs several years after that'.

[16] *TrGF* 1.9 T1 (DID C4). See Chapter 1, p. 15 and n. 45 on the authorship of these plays.

[17] *TrGF* 1.9 T 3 (DID C5).

[18] See Snell, *TrGF* 1.9 *ad loc.,* with reference to Nauck's earlier edition of the fragments.

[19] *TrGF* 1.9 F4 (quoted by Chamaeleon in his work *On Satyr-Drama*).

[20] See Seaford (1984) 33–44 on the typical themes and subject-matter of satyr-drama.

[21] Cf. Pindar, *Isthmian* 4.56; Σ Plato, *Theaetetus* 169b; Apollodorus 2.115.

[22] Cf. Apollodorus 3.9.2.

suggested for *Fates* (*Kêres*), from which we have a two-line quotation concerning 'a fellow-diner or a reveller or a guest at Hades' dinner-table, having an immoderate appetite' (perhaps a reference to Heracles?).[23] The title *Orpheus* also suggests an interest in the Underworld or mystery religion, but its surviving fragment is concerned (once again) with wrestling and athletics: 'I had a wrestling-school and a covered running-track nearby . . .'.[24] Can one read any special significance in the number of allusions to *wrestling* (including the title of Pratinas' play of 467)? Almost certainly not – but it remains a curious coincidence.

Another odd coincidence is that there were three tragedians called **Euripides**. Apart from the famous one whose works are still well known, there were two other earlier Euripideses, an uncle and nephew. The elder of the two is listed in the *Suda* as having written twelve plays and won two victories, which counts as an extremely respectable record of prize-winning (that is, if the figures imply that he entered three tetralogies and won with two of them).[25] Less is known about the nephew, but his titles apparently included an *Orestes,* a *Medea,* and a *Polyxena.*[26] He is also alleged to have produced an 'edition' of Homer (*Homerikê ekdosis*), though this is open to doubt (it seems probable that the edition was the work of a later Euripides in the Hellenistic period).

Polyphrasmon was the son of Phrynichus, the very early fifth-century poet whose plays included the disastrous *Sack of Miletus* (see Chapter 1). Polyphrasmon himself seems to have enjoyed a certain amount of success in the dramatic competitions from the late 480s onwards: his first victory was won *c.* 482–471 BCE, he took first prize at the Dionysia in 471, and he came in third place with his *Lycourgeia* tetralogy in 467.[27] The title of this tetralogy indicates an interest in Dionysiac myth and ritual. The story of Lycurgus, as reflected in other Greek texts,[28] exemplifies a familiar pattern of resistance to the power of Dionysus followed by fatal consequences: Lycurgus, king of the Edonians, attacked Dionysus and his nurses and drove them into the sea, but he was driven insane by the god and ended up killing his own family. Aeschylus wrote

---

23   *TrGF* 1.9 F3.
24   *TrGF* 1.9 F5.
25   *TrGF* 1.16 T1 (*Suda* E 3693).
26   *TrGF* 1.17 T1 (*Suda* E 3694).
27   *TrGF* 1.7 T1–3; cf. Millis and Olson (2012) 5–58 (on *IG* ii² 2318), 141–9 (on *IG* ii² 2325.1–20).
28   Apollodorus 1.35; Hyginus, *Fabula* 132.

another *Lycourgeia* tetralogy (consisting of *Edonians, Bassarids, Young Men* and the satyric *Lycurgus*) dramatizing the same myth.[29]

Aeschylus' family included several generations of tragedians extending throughout the fifth and fourth centuries. Two of his sons, **Euphorion** and **Euaeon**, had careers as tragic poets. Nothing is known about Euaeon or his work, but Euphorion had a certain amount of success. He entered the dramatic competitions on four separate occasions with his father's plays, but also wrote his own tragedies, some of which earned him first prize at the Dionysia in 431 BCE (when his competitors were Sophocles and Euripides).[30] It has been suggested by modern scholars that Euphorion sometimes produced his own plays under Aeschylus' name, and that several 'Aeschylean' tragedies, including the surviving play *Prometheus Bound*, are actually the work of Euphorion.[31]

Euphorion's cousin **Philocles**, the father of Morsimus (see p. 100), was Aeschylus' nephew and a contemporary of Euripides. The *Suda* records that Philocles wrote one hundred plays during the course of his career, making him one of the most prolific known dramatists. Philocles is notorious for winning the first prize at the contest in which Sophocles competed with *Oedipus the King* – a verdict which many ancient and modern scholars have regarded as a prime example of the fallibility of the festival judges or the unpredictability of the voting procedure.[32] However, one can imagine several perfectly good reasons why Philocles may have won; and if Philocles was able to defeat such a masterpiece as *Oedipus the King* he cannot have been an entirely negligible poet.

Nevertheless, many of the references to Philocles in comedy are disparaging, drawing attention to his supposedly defective plots or his 'bitter' or 'wretched' style; it is even said that Philocles was nicknamed 'Bile' (*Cholê*) on account of his unpalatable use of language.[33] It is interesting to observe the comedians' use of food imagery and the metaphor of taste to describe literary aesthetics (a trait

[29]   Aeschylus *TrGF* 3 F23–4, 57–62, 124, 146–146b.
[70]   *TrGF* 1.11 T1–2.
[31]   See West (2000) for a speculative account of the relationship between Aeschylus' and Euphorion's work; cf. Müller (2002) for the suggestion that the 'surprising' result of the 431 Dionysia may have been the result of the judges' giving priority to a candidate who wanted to put on Aeschylus' plays.
[32]   *TrGF* 1.24 T3a–b (Hypothesis II to Sophocles, *Oedipus Tyrannus*; Aristides, *Oration* 46); cf. Wright (2009) 169–72 on the tendency of critics to identify 'wrong' decisions by festival judges.
[33]   Cratinus F323 K-A says that Philocles 'has ruined the plot'; cf. Aristophanes, *Birds* 281 ('bitter' or 'briny' style); *Wasps* 461–2 (bad taste of Philocles' poetry); *Women Celebrating the Thesmophoria* 167–8 (P. writes 'wretchedly'); F591 K-A ('bitter' taste); cf. also *Suda* Φ 378 (for the nickname *Cholê*): these references are found at *TrGF* 1.24 T1–2, T4, T5a, T8a, T9.

which is also seen in relation to several other tragedians' work). However, this figurative language is hard to pin down to actual details, and it is impossible to know what *specific* features of Philoclean style were thought to be bitter-tasting, or what (if any) literal meaning should be attached to this description. Aristophanes on one occasion contrasts Philocles' 'bitterness' with the 'sweet' lyrics of the older tragedian Phrynichus,[34] but we are not now in a position to make a detailed stylistic comparison between these two writers. It may be that the contrast is essentially a variation on the Aristophanic 'generation gap' theme rather than a specifically stylistic distinction – in other words, Philocles represents a modern type of tragedy which is being rejected by Aristophanes' conservative, elderly characters.[35]

Little remains of Philocles' one hundred plays, but we possess several titles, including *Erigone, Nauplius, Oedipus* and *Oeneus*. The first of these is interesting in terms of what it implies about Philocles' approach to the mythical tradition. Erigone was the daughter of Aegisthus: she does not appear in most literary versions of the myth, but according to Apollodorus she indicted Orestes for Aegisthus' murder and went on to marry him after his trial and acquittal.[36] We cannot know exactly what Philocles did with this tragedy, but the title alone seems to indicate that he took on a very well-known mythical cycle, the story of the house of Atreus, and treated it in an innovative and unexpected way. Rather like Euripides' *Orestes,* Philocles' *Erigone* seems to have provided a 'sequel' to the conventional myth, either inventing a plot completely or making use of a little-known variant.

It is particularly interesting to see that Philocles wrote an *Oedipus,* given that Philocles is most famous for the competition in which he defeated Sophocles. It is unlikely that *Oedipus* was one of the plays with which Philocles competed on that occasion (for surely our sources would have mentioned such an extraordinary coincidence), but one cannot help wondering which *Oedipus* came first. Was Sophocles' play written in the light of Philocles' version, or did Philocles write his *Oedipus* as a response to Sophocles? In the light of Philocles' *Pandionis* (see later), it is tempting to see Philocles in an ongoing dialogue or competition with the older and more successful playwright.

---

[34] Aristophanes, *Wasps* 461–2; cf. 268–9 (= *TrGF* 1.24 T5a).

[35] Note that – apart from Aristophanes' parabases, in which the poet seems to trumpet his own novelty and youth – comedians usually express a preference for older poets and disparage young or fashionable writers. Of course, this sort of stance may be ironical: see Wright (2012) 70–102. Cf. Handley (1993) on Aristophanes and the 'generation gap' theme, and Wright (2013a) on the contest of young *versus* old (and other contests) in *Wasps.*

[36] Apollodorus, *Epitome* 6.23–8; cf. Gantz (1993) 685–6.

A couple of other pieces of evidence also suggest a context of intertextual and intergenerational rivalry in which to place Philocles and his work. First of all, there is a fragment of Teleclieds' comedy *Hesiod and Friends* in which Philocles is described as 'having the mind of Aeschylus'.[37] This refers to the familial relationship that existed between the two writers, but it also hints at a connection between the intellectual content of Philocles' poetry and that of his uncle (and we have already noted the fact that both poets wrote tragedies called *Penelope* and *Philoctetes*). Secondly, there is the only other one of Philocles' productions known to us: his *Pandionis* tetralogy.[38] This group of plays dramatized the grotesque myth of Tereus, husband of Pandion's daughter Procne. Tereus raped Procne's sister Philomela and cut out her tongue to prevent her telling anybody; however, she wove a tapestry depicting what had happened to her, and Procne took revenge on Tereus by killing their son Itys and serving him up to her husband for dinner. Tereus attempted to kill both the sisters, but the gods turned them all into birds: Philomela became a swallow, Procne a nightingale, and Tereus a hoopoe. Philocles' version of this story is remarkable partly because it shows that connected tetralogies with a single consecutive storyline were still being produced in the late fifth century, but also, and more importantly, because Sophocles too produced a well-known tragedy, *Tereus*, on the same subject.

Aristophanes parodied the Sophoclean *Tereus* in his *Birds* (414 BCE), but in the same play he also alludes to Philocles' treatment. The Aristophanic Tereus, who is based directly on the Sophoclean version, makes fun of one of the other birds for the shape of his head (that is, his costume) and declares that '*he* is the son of Philocles' hoopoe, but *I* am his grandfather'. As one recent commentator observes, following the suggestion of an ancient scholar, Aristophanes' point is presumably that 'the Tereus-hoopoe created by Philocles was the offspring of (i.e. derivative from) the far more convincing character created by Sophocles'.[39] In other words, Philocles' *Pandionis* was written in the light of Sophocles' *Tereus*, and Aristophanes is drawing our attention to an intertextual relationship between the two works, which he expresses in the specific form of an intergenerational conflict. It is impossible to say more about the exact nature of this relationship, or whether Philocles' attitude to Sophocles was straightforwardly imitative, as has been supposed. Perhaps Philocles' *Pandionis* was a form of

---

[37] *TrGF* 1.24 T8b.
[38] Attested in one of the scholia to Aristophanes' *Birds* 281 (= *TrGF* 1.24 T6c), which quotes Aristotle as a source (= *Didaskaliai* F619 Rose).
[39] Aristophanes, *Birds* 279–83 (with Σ *ad loc.*) = *TrGF* 1.24 T6; cf. Sommerstein (1987) 215. This 'multilevel' joke is also discussed by Dobrov (2002) 108–9.

hommage, or (in the light of the other evidence) it might well have been an implicitly critical reworking, updating, or 'improvement' of the older poet's work. We may well be inclined to read the relationship in a different light if we are familiar with Bloom's concept of the anxiety of influence (see earlier p. 92) – and indeed Bloom's description of the 'belated' work of literature as 'a rival poem, son or grandson of the same precursor' might almost be a quotation from Aristophanes on Philocles.

Nothing else is known about Philocles' version of the Tereus story, though it is obvious from Aristophanes that his bird costumes and masks were outlandish enough to stick in the minds of theatre audiences. The only attested quotation is the opening line of the first play in the tetralogy, which was addressed to the god Helios: 'Master of all, I address you ...'.[40] A further fragment – 'he would not desist from eating brains' – might conceivably belong to a grisly banquet-scene in which Tereus dined on his own son.[41]

Morsimus is described in the *Suda* as 'the son of Philocles, a frigid (*psychros*) tragedian, and also a doctor; his plays were wretched'.[42] Another ancient dictionary entry adds the intriguing information that Morsimus specialized in ophthalmic medicine, before adding, witheringly, that he was equally talentless as a doctor and as a playwright.[43] As in other cases, these verdicts probably owe a good deal to Aristophanes, whose treatment of Morsimus was particularly scornful. One of Aristophanes' characters claims that 'being trained to sing in one of Morsimus' tragedies' is an ordeal comparable to being drenched with urine, while another discusses posthumous punishments in Hades for exceedingly wicked criminals, including 'anyone who has made somebody copy out one of Morsimus' monologues'.[44] These jokes tell us little except that the tragedian's choral and spoken sections were both equally scorned. However, Platon's metatheatrical comedy *Stage-Properties* seems to have offered more constructive criticism. One of its fragments apparently features a conversation between two literary critics – or perhaps rival producers – discussing the relative

---

40   *TrGF* 1.24 F1.
41   F5, printed among fragments of 'unknown plays' by Snell. The other fragments (also from unknown plays) are unrevealing: F2 is a paraphrase of Philocles' version of the marital history of Hermione (which differs from the plot of Euripides' *Andromache*); F3 simply gives the name of Talaos (or Kalaos), father of Parthenopaeus; F4 is a single-word epithet, *doruphonos* ('killing with the spear').
42   *Suda* M 1261 (*TrGF* 1.29 T1). Cf. Sutton (1987) 13–14, who identifies Morsimus and Melanthius (*TrGF* 1.23) as brothers. On Melanthius see Chapter 6 (pp. 184–6).
43   Hesychius K 3050 (*TrGF* 1.29 T5).
44   Aristophanes, *Knights* 400–1; *Frogs* 151–3.

merits of their favourite poets: 'Just lay a finger on my Morsimus, and I will go right ahead and smash your Sthenelus to smithereens'.[45] It may be that Platon's play involved some form of parody or extended close reading of these poets' work, but at any rate it suggests that some people, at least, took Morsimus seriously. Furthermore, the fact that jokes about Morsimus appear in comedies across the space of some twenty years hints at a certain staying power: whether or not he continued producing new tragedies for all that time, his name was not instantly forgotten.

Morsimus' son **Astydamas the Elder** and grandson **Philocles the Younger** also produced tragedies, apparently without any great success,[46] but his other grandson **Astydamas the Younger** was one of the most acclaimed tragedians in the history of Athens. In this case, apparently uniquely, the latest member of the dynasty completely outshone all the other members, which must have alleviated the anxiety of influence to a great extent.[47]

I have already discussed the significance of the fact that Astydamas was the first tragic playwright ever to be honoured with a commemorative statue in the Theatre of Dionysus at Athens: this event directly followed the success of his tragedy *Parthenopaeus*, which won first prize in 340 BCE.[48] The *Suda* records that Astydamas wrote 240 tragedies and won first prize on fifteen separate occasions – figures which, if correct, make him by some way the most prolific tragedian of all time, as well as one of the most successful (if success is judged by the number of prizes).[49] A few of these victories can be dated with the help of epigraphic evidence: he first won the City Dionysia in 372 BCE, and subsequent victories occurred at the Lenaea of 370 and the Dionysia of 347, 341 (with the plays *Achilles, Athamas* and *Antigone*) and 340.[50] The titles of some of his other plays – *Mad Ajax, Alcmeon, Alcmene, Bellerophon, Epigoni, Hector, Nauplius, Palamedes, Parthenopaeus, Tyro, Phoenix* and the satyr-plays *Hermes* and *Heracles* – are preserved in the *Suda* or

---

45 Platon, *Skeuai* F136 K-A (= *TrGF* 1.29 T6); cf. Pirrotta (2009) *ad loc.* For more discussion of Sthenelus and this comedy, see Chapter 6 (pp. 178–81).

46 Astydamas I is *TrGF* 1.59; the only fact known about his career is that his first production was in 398 BCE (Diodorus Siculus 14.43.5 = T2). Philocles II (*TrGF* 1.61) is an even more obscure figure: there is no secure evidence for his career, since T2 may refer either to *Philo*cles or *Timo*cles (*TrGF* 1.86).

47 See, however, the epigram attributed (probably falsely) to Astydamas, complaining about the burden of posterity (*TrGF* 1.60 T2a, quoted in Chapter 5, p. 120).

48 See the Prologue, pp. xv–xvi.

49 This record was apparently surpassed only by Sophocles, whose victories are variously numbered at twenty (*Life of Sophocles* §8 = Carystius, *FGrHist* 4.359) or eighteen (*IG* ii² 2325 col. i; Diodorus Siculus 13.103).

50 *TrGF* 1.60 T3–7 (*IG* ii² 2318. 1478, 1562; *IG* ii² 2325. 1, 44): see Millis and Olson (2012) 6, 141–9.

other literary sources. But in spite of the extraordinary prestige in which he was held, nothing else is known about Astydamas' life or career, and only a tiny number of fragments survive. This unusually bad fortune can be attributed to the fact that, only very shortly after his period of success, Lycurgus and the Athenians unaccountably decided that there were three 'classic' writers of tragedy and that Astydamas was not among them.[51]

Most of the fragments are disappointingly thin, consisting of nothing more than a few quotable maxims[52] and stray descriptive phrases.[53] The longest fragment from a named tragedy consists of a three-line quotation from Astydamas' *Nauplius*:

> I wish you happiness – if happiness is possible in a place below the earth.
> Yes, I think it is; for where there can be none of life's misery,
> one can rejoice, being oblivious to ills.[54]

This play's title character was the father of Palamedes, who fought in the Trojan War and was killed by his fellow Greeks as a result of the intrigues of Odysseus; Nauplius took his revenge on the Greeks by lighting false beacons along the dangerous coast of Euboea, thus wrecking many ships as they sailed home from Troy.[55] The myth had already been dramatized by Aeschylus, Sophocles and Euripides,[56] and Astydamas' tragedy may have engaged with any or all of these earlier versions. But the lines above, presumably addressed by Nauplius to the spirit of his dead son, tell us very little.

Astydamas, along with several other tragedians, dramatized the myth of Alcmeon, who killed his mother Eriphyle and was driven insane by the Furies. All that survives from his *Alcmeon* is a single line, based on the conventional contrast between reality and appearance: 'It's the truth I care about; appearances don't mean anything to me'.[57] Aristotle in the *Poetics* also mentions this as an example of a tragedy in which the murder takes place during the play itself (rather than prior to the dramatic action, as in Sophocles' *Oedipus Tyrannus*); he also implies that Astydamas' *Alcmeon* was unaware of Eriphyle's identity when

---

[51]   See the Prologue, pp. xvii–xix.
[52]   *TrGF* 1.60 F7–8: see Xanthakis-Karamanos (1980) 140–1.
[53]   *TrGF* 1.60 F6, F9; F3 and F4 are satyric.
[54]   *TrGF* 1.60 F5, playing on the dual meaning of *chairein*: (1) to rejoice or be happy; (2) to give a greeting.
[55]   See Apollodorus, *Epitome* 6.7-11.
[56]   Aeschylus, *Palamedes* (*TrGF* 3 F180a–182); Sophocles, *Nauplius* (*TrGF* 4 F425–34); Euripides, *Palamedes* (*TrGF* 5 F578–89).
[57]   *TrGF* 1.60 F1c.

he killed her.[58] This evidence is rather paltry, but it has been thought to point towards a significant plot innovation. If Alcmeon was portrayed here as acting out of ignorance, or even suffering an insane delusion (like Ajax, for instance), the moral and psychological aspects of the play would have been very different from previous well-known versions of the story in which Alcmeon killed his mother deliberately as an act of revenge.[59]

The only other one of Astydamas' tragedies about which something definite can be said is his *Hector*. A single book fragment from this play survives, but this gives us the valuable information that the play dramatized a specific episode from Homeric epic:

> Hector: Servant! Take my helmet, please,
> so that the boy is not frightened.[60]

This obviously relates to a famous scene in the sixth book of the *Iliad,* in which 'Hector of the flashing helmet' visits his wife Andromache and infant son Astyanax and reflects sombrely on his forthcoming death. Astydamas must surely have had the following lines in mind:

> Glorious Hector stretched out his arms to his son, but the child let out a shriek and shrank back into the bosom of his fair-girdled nurse, distressed at the sight of his own father and terrified by the bronze and the horse-hair crest as he saw it nodding terribly from the top of the helmet. And his dear father laughed aloud, and his royal mother too, and straightaway glorious Hector took the helmet from his head and laid it, bright-shining, upon the ground. And he kissed his dear son, and held him in his arms.[61]

Even on the basis of one small fragment, it is possible to imagine something of the plot, and the emotional potential, of Astydamas' tragedy. However, scholars have identified several other pieces of evidence that may tell us a little more. First of all, there is an Apulian red-figure vase-painting that depicts Hector's departure for battle. This picture shows Hector reaching out his arms to the infant Astyanax while an attendant holds his helmet, and thus it may have been inspired (in some sense) by Astydamas' play.[62] Secondly, there are several papyrus fragments, from

---

[58] Aristotle, *Poetics* 14. 1453b29–32 (*TrGF* 1.60 F1b) – though it seems to me that Aristotle's phrasing is ambiguous (it may be that only Oedipus is named as one who killed in ignorance).

[59] See Webster (1954) 305 and Xanthakis-Karamanos (1980) 38–41.

[60] *TrGF* 1.60 F2: the text is slightly corrupt, but the meaning is clear.

[61] Homer, *Iliad* 6.466–74. Cf. Carrara (1997) for discussion of Astydamas' play in relation to the fourth-century reception of Homer.

[62] Berlin, Staatliche Museen, Antikensammlung inv. 1984.45 = Taplin (2007) no. 101, pp. 252–55. For discussion linking the painting to the play see also Taplin (2009) and (2014) 148–9.

separate sources, which appear to come from tragedies about the confrontation in battle between Hector and Achilles. Since no other tragedian is known to have written a *Hector*, it has been suggested that all these fragments belong to Astydamas' play.[63] (Note, however, that both Sophocles and Antiphon wrote plays entitled *Andromache*, and Aeschylus and Dionysius wrote plays entitled *The Ransoming of Hector*: it could plausibly be claimed that the papyrus relates to one of these lost tragedies, or to another unknown to us.)

These lacunose fragments are not easy to interpret, and contain almost no consecutive meaning, but they include several significant features. F1h includes part of a speech by a character who admits to feeling fear at the sight of something; it contains an appeal to Apollo and references to the seer Helenus and the god Hephaestus; and it mentions a spear and someone 'bereft of armour'. The speaker of F1i, identified as Hector by Snell and others, seems to be calling on someone to bring his weapons and the shield of Achilles, and telling someone not to impede his progress. F2a is part of a report of the battle between Hector and Achilles: Hector attacks first but misses Achilles with his spear, which sticks in the ground, and then Achilles hits Hector's shield. A further papyrus fragment has more recently been connected to this group by Oliver Taplin[64]: this very badly preserved text contains part of a dialogue between Cassandra, Priam and Deiphobus, and makes reference to some sort of confrontation beneath the walls of Troy, including the phrase 'Hector(?) has perished'; it appears that Cassandra is describing events on the battlefield as seen in some sort of vision or hallucination.[65] If these fragments really do belong together, they can help us to fill in a few more gaps in our knowledge, and it is clear from F2, at least, that Astydamas' tragedy culminated in the death of Hector.

Another interesting feature of these papyrus fragments is that they contain indications of the way in which the scenes were performed. F1h begins with the performance direction 'choral ode' (*chorou melos*), followed by spoken or chanted lines in an unusual rhythm;[66] and the Cassandra fragment contains not only spoken contributions from the Chorus but also the repeated stage direction 'song' (*ôidê*) in between Cassandra's lines. Taplin argues that what we are seeing here is an innovative approach to word-setting and performance, and he

---

[63] *P.Hib.* 2.174; *P.Amh.* 2.10; *P.Strasb. WG* 304.2 (printed by Snell as *TrGF* 1.60 F1h–i and F2a). For detailed discussion see Snell (1971) 138–53; Xanthakis-Karamanos (1980) 161–9; Taplin (2009).

[64] *P.Oxy.* 2746 (= *TrGF* 2 adesp. F649); see Taplin (2009) 259–63.

[65] Line 25: Ἕκτωρ ἐξόλωλ[(the reading is not certain).

[66] Taplin (2009) 258 diagnoses the metre as a mixture of ionics and stichic galliambics, though the lacunose and incomplete lines make it impossible to be certain.

specifically suggests that *ôidê* signifies that 'the actor of Cassandra should improvise some suitably mantic singing whenever the signal appears.'[67] Whether or not he is right, it remains a possibility that the chorus played an important function in Astydamas' work, and that the poet continued to make innovations in music and staging at a period in which these elements of drama are usually thought to have diminished in importance.

The tragedian **Carcinus the Elder** had at least three sons who were tragic poets or actors. Carcinus himself was a prominent Athenian politician as well as a poet – he served as *stratêgos* in 431 BCE – a fact which may account, at least in part, for his largely hostile treatment in contemporary comedy.[68] The entire family was ridiculed by Aristophanes on two separate occasions, and these passages have normally been taken as evidence that the sons (Xenocles, Xenotimus and Xenarchus) performed in their father's plays. In *Peace* Carcinus is described as dancing with his sons, and they are all compared to quails or hunchbacked dwarves – which is simultaneously a comment on their physical appearance and their style of dancing.[69] In the final scene of *Wasps* Carcinus and his sons – or rather comic actors impersonating them in cruelly caricatured form – actually appear on stage, dressed up as crabs, and perform a ludicrous dance which seems to incorporate detailed parody of specific dance moves by Carcinus.[70] This is significant because it shows that Carcinus had a distinctive and instantly recognizable choreographic style, though it was obviously not universally admired. It is hard to imagine just what this type of dance looked like on stage, but some sort of scuttling or sideways movement seems to be implied by the comparison to crabs: a further comic description of Carcinus' sons as 'twisty' (*stroboloi*) was interpreted in precisely this way by one of the ancient commentators.[71]

Apart from this, not much can be said about Carcinus' tragedies. It is said by one source that one of them was called *Mice*, which looks more like a comic than

[67] Taplin (2014) 149.
[68] *TrGF* 1.21 T6 (Thucydides 2.23.2). Cf. my remarks on Dionysius of Syracuse (*TrGF* 1.76) in Chapter 5 below, pp. 130–138. Millis and Olson (2012) 5–58 restore Carcinus' name as victor at the Dionysia in 446 BCE (*IG* ii² 2318.297).
[69] Aristophanes, *Peace* 781–95 with Σ *ad loc.* (*TrGF* T3a–b).
[70] Aristophanes, *Wasps* 1498–1532 with scholia *ad loc.* (*TrGF* 1.21 T2a–f). Note that the Greek *karkinos* means 'crab'. See Borthwick (1968) 47–51 and Roos (1951) 76–88 for tentative attempts to reconstruct the specific details of the dancing; cf. Sommerstein (1983) and MacDowell (1971) *ad loc.* Several scholars have assumed that the *real* Carcinus and his family actually appeared in *Wasps*, but this seems highly unlikely to me, given the hostile and derisory attitude to them adopted here and elsewhere: see MacDowell (1971) 327; Henderson (1998) 410–11.
[71] Aristophanes, *Peace* 863 with Σ *ad loc.* (*TrGF* 1.21 T4).

a tragic title – a fact which has led some scholars to suggest that Carcinus was actually a comedian.[72] But the ending of *Wasps* shows that this cannot be correct; and in any case the title *Mice* seems to be merely a scholiast's unreliable inference from an obscure Aristophanic joke (which says that an unsuccessful play by Carcinus was 'throttled by a weasel').[73] There are a couple of other, more secure pointers to features of Carcinus' work. A passing reference in Aristophanes' *Clouds* implies that the gods in Carcinus' tragedies made strange noises, or that they were depicted as uttering laments.[74] Another ancient commentator draws attention to the fact that both Carcinus and his son Xenocles were celebrated, or reviled, for their use of special effects such as theatrical machinery (*mêchanai*) and astonishing spectacles (*terateiai*). This fact is illustrated by a fragment of Platon's comedy *Sophists* in which Xenocles is given the epithet *dôdekamêchanos* ('the poet of the twelve devices'), a description implying that he repeatedly drew upon a distinctive – but finite – repertoire of theatrical tricks.[75]

Xenocles himself is listed among the supposedly inferior generation of modern-day tragedians at the start of Aristophanes' *Frogs* (405 BCE), where Dionysus complains that all the decent writers are now dead. 'What about Xenocles?' asks Heracles, to which Dionysus replies scornfully: 'To hell with him, by Zeus!'[76] Other references to him are similarly disparaging: in *Women Celebrating the Thesmophoria* he is simply 'a bad man, who writes bad poetry'.[77] In fact Xenocles was judged worthy of first prize at the Dionysia of 415 BCE, where he triumphed – against no less a writer than Euripides – with a tetralogy of plays consisting of *Oedipus*, *Lycaon*, *Bacchae*, and the satyr-play *Athamas*. (Euripides' entry on this occasion consisted of the 'Trojan tragedies' *Alexandros*, *Palamedes* and *Trojan Women*, and the satyric *Sisyphus*).[78] Nevertheless, even this victory is devalued by Aelian, who reports the result of the competition and expresses incredulity that Euripides should have been defeated by Xenocles, 'whoever he is'.[79]

Aristophanes mentions Xenoclean tragedy again in his *Women at the Thesmophoria*, where the subject under discussion is the clever female character

---

See Rothwell (1994), referring to Nicole (1884); but Olson (1997) provides an effective rebuttal, which I summarize here.

[73]   Aristophanes, *Peace* 794–6 with Σ *ad loc.* (*TrGF* 1.21 T3d–e). Admittedly, the joke still eludes explanation.

[74]   Aristophanes, *Clouds* 1259a–1261; cf. Dover (1968) 242–3.

[75]   Σ Aristophanes, *Peace* 791, quoting Platon, *Sophists* F143 K-A (*TrGF* 1.21 T3c).

[76]   Aristophanes, *Frogs* 86 (*TrGF* 1.33 T5).

[77]   Aristophanes, *Women at the Thesmophoria* 169 (*TrGF* 1.33 T4).

[78]   See Scodel (1980).

[79]   Aelian, *Historical Miscellany* 2.8 (*TrGF* 1.33 T3).

called Mica and her impressive and persuasive command of rhetoric – 'so that if
Xenocles, son of Carcinus, should speak in opposition to her, I think that all of
you would find that he was talking absolute nonsense'.[80] This oblique reference is
hard to interpret: an ancient commentator on this passage speculates that
Xenocles was famous for writing about feminine wiles, but it seems more likely
that the point relates to Xenocles' command of rhetoric. Another Aristophanic
character actually quotes a couple of lines which are obviously taken (with
alterations) from Xenocles' tragedy *Licymnius*:

> Oh, cruel deity! Oh, misfortune that shattered my chariot-rail and put my horses
> to flight! Oh, Pallas, how you have ruined me!

In Aristophanes the speaker is a creditor who is being cheated out of his money,
but in the Xenoclean original the lines appeared in a speech by Alcmena, whose
half-brother Licymnius had been killed by Tlempolemus.[81] It is not quite clear how
much of this quotation is Xenocles and how much is Aristophanes, but it seems
that the tragic lines are meant to seem ridiculous because of their new context
rather than because of any inherently wretched quality of their own. Note too that
Aristophanes does not identify the tragic source or its author, but both must have
been sufficiently well known for the audience to get the joke in the next line – 'and
what harm has Tlempolemus ever done to you?' – without any further clue.

Xenocles' son, **Carcinus the Younger**, was apparently one of the most prolific
tragedians ever, with a total of 160 plays to his name. This fact comes from the
Suda, which is not altogether trustworthy (and it mixes up Carcinus with the
much later poet Carcinus of Acragas).[82] However, epigraphic evidence also
seems to indicate that Carcinus was a frequent competitor in the dramatic
festivals, since he won eleven first prizes at the Dionysia, the first of which was *c.*
372–365 BCE.[83] Other biographical testimonia are thin on the ground, but a
couple of sources tell us that Carcinus was active not just in Athens but also in
Syracuse: he was one of the illustrious poets whom Dionysius, tyrant and
tragedian, attracted to his court in an effort to boost his own cultural prestige.[84]

---

[80]   *Women Celebrating the Thesmophoria* 440–3 with Σ *ad loc.* (*TrGF* 1.33 T4b); the scholiast adds that
Xenocles was a talentless (*aphuês*) poet.

[81]   Aristophanes, *Clouds* 1264–5 with Σ *ad loc.* (= *TrGF* 1.33 T1; cf. F2). Snell prints only part of the
couplet as it appears in Aristophanes.

[82]   *Suda* K 394 (*TrGF* 1.70 T1).

[83]   *IG* ii[2] 2325. 43 (*TrGF* 1.70 T2 = DID A3a 43): see Millis and Olson (2012) 141–9 (the name is
restored but accepted by all editors). Carcinus may also have competed at the Lenaea *c.* 376, but the
evidence is unclear (DID A2 b86; *IG* ii[2] 2319–2323).

[84]   *TrGF* 1.70 T3–4; on Dionysius (*TrGF* 1.76) see Ch. 5, pp. 133–6.

In particular, we are told that Carcinus took a special interest in the religious and ritual customs of Syracuse, and became a devotee of the mystery-cult of Demeter and Persephone there. This experience seems to have inspired one of his tragedies. The historian Diodorus of Sicily quotes a revealing passage which narrates the myth of Persephone's abduction by the god of the Underworld and links it to current-day religious practices[85]:

> Concerning the rape of Kore (Persephone) many ancient historians and poets bear witness to the fact that it happened in the way that we have described. The tragic poet Carcinus – who was often a visitor to Syracuse and saw the enthusiasm which those who lived there showed in their sacrifices and festivals of both Demeter and Kore – includes the following verses in his works:
>
> λέγουσι Δήμητρός ποτ' ἄρρητον κόρην
> Πλούτωνα κρυφίοις ἁρπάσαι βουλεύμασιν
> δῦναί τε γαίας εἰς μελαμφαεῖς μυχούς·
> πόθωι δὲ μητέρ' ἠφανισμένης κόρης
> μαστῆρ' ἐπελθεῖν πᾶσαν ἐν κύκλωι χθόνα·
> καὶ γῆν μὲν Αἰτναίοισι Σικελίας πάγοις
> πυρὸς γέμουσαν ῥεύμασιν δυσεμβόλοις
> πᾶσαν στενάξαι, πένθεσιν δὲ παρθένου
> σίτων ἄμοιρον Διοτρεφὲς φθίνειν γένος,
> ὅθεν θεὰς τιμῶσιν ἐς τὰ νῦν ἔτι.
>
> Once upon a time, they say, Pluto secretly snatched away Demeter's daughter, whom none may name; and then he went down into the depths of earth, where light is darkness. Meanwhile her mother, in her longing for the vanished girl, went round to every region of the earth in search of her. And the whole land of Sicily by Aetna's crags was filled with unapproachable streams of fire, and let out a groan; and in their grief for the maiden the people of Sicily, beloved by Zeus, were perishing through shortage of grain. Henceforth people still honour the goddesses even right up to the present day.

This unknown play by Carcinus, whatever else it may have contained, obviously provided an aetiological account of mystery-cult with a specific local significance for the inhabitants of Syracuse. This is a vivid description, full of geographical detail and colour, and it also contains a couple of specific echoes of the language of mystic initiation. The description ἄρρητον ('whom none may name') is an apotropaic formula to avoid ill omen, and the oxymoron μελαμφαεῖς ('where light is darkness') not only recalls other antithetical formulas from mystic contexts

---

[85]　Diodorus Siculus 5.51 (*TrGF* 1.70 F5).

but more generally evokes the concept of light from darkness which was central to the Orphic and Eleusinian mysteries.[86] All of these motifs had been seen before, especially in the tragedies of Aeschylus,[87] but this fragment from Carcinus constitutes valuable evidence for the continuation of ritual motifs in the tragedy of the fourth century – a period which has been linked to the gradual disappearance of religious drama in favour of secular themes.[88] In this respect it is relevant to note that Carcinus also wrote a tragedy called *Semele*. Nothing remains of this play apart from its opening words ('O nights . . .') and a two-line quip from some weary misogynist ('O Zeus, why is it necessary to say out loud that women are an evil thing? It would be enough if one were just to say the word *woman*').[89] Nevertheless, a play with Dionysus' mother as its central character would be likely to centre on the god's birth and the emergence of Dionysiac cult.

Unusually, we happen to possess information about two particular performances of Carcinus' plays: in both cases something happened which the author could not or did not predict. A production of *Ajax* is mentioned by Zenobius, the second-century CE collector of proverbs, apropos of the proverb 'the laughter of Ajax'. When the actor playing Odysseus said 'One ought to do the right thing', it is said that the actor Pleisthenes, who was in the starring role, burst out with ironical laughter that was not in the script.[90] Elsewhere Aristotle mentions the première of Carcinus' *Amphiaraus*: this was spoiled by a staging problem that ought to have been spotted and ironed out during the rehearsal process.

> When putting together plots and working them out in terms of verbal expression, it is very important that the poet should (as it were) put it all before his eyes, because by doing this he will be able to see the events being acted out most clearly, just as if he were actually present; and conversely, if there is anything out of place, it will not escape his attention. A good example of this is the criticism suffered by Carcinus when his Amphiaraus came out of the temple: no one would have noticed this unless they were watching the play, but in performance it fell flat because the theatre audience kicked up a fuss about it. Thus, as far as possible, the poet should work it all out with the appropriate gestures and movements.[91]

---

[86] Oxymorons: cf. (e.g.) the Ostian bone tablets from Orphic cult, containing antitheses such as 'life death life', 'peace war', 'body soul': see Graf and Iles Johnston (2013), Appendix 4. Mystic light from darkness: cf. (e.g.) Aristophanes, *Frogs* 343–4, 446–7, 454–7; Plutarch F178; Apuleius, *Metamorphoses* 11.23, Diodorus Siculus 1.11.3. See Burkert (1987) 89–115 on all such matters.

[87] See Seaford (2003) and (2005).

[88] Xanthakis-Karamanos (1980) 3–4.

[89] *TrGF* 1.70 F2, F3.

[90] *TrGF* 1.70 F1a (Zenobius 1.61).

[91] Aristotle, *Poetics* 17.1455a26-30 (*TrGF* 1.70 F1c).

It is interesting to note that Aristotle explicitly distinguishes between two types of audience for Carcinus' work – spectators in the theatre and readers of books – and he implies that Carcinus himself was more interested in the script than in the technicalities of production and staging. In some ways this is comparable with Aristotle's discussion of another fourth-century tragedian, Chaeremon, whom he describes as *anagnôstikos* (that is, an author who is especially suitable for reading),[92] and more generally it chimes in with Aristotle's own opinion that the visual element is the least fundamental part of tragedy.

Nevertheless, the main point here is that some specific aspect of the plot of *Amphiaraus* was disastrously misjudged. It is obvious that some sort of continuity error was involved, and it is easy to see why this only made itself apparent in performance – for a reader would not naturally tend to visualize the exact details of entrances and exits in each scene, or to pay attention to the number of characters or actors who were required to be in a certain place at a certain time. Thus Amphiaraus 'came out of the temple' (or perhaps 'came up from the temple'[93]) when he ought to have been elsewhere. Scholars have argued inconclusively about what Amphiaraus was doing or where he ought to have been, but until such time as the play should miraculously reappear we cannot know enough about its plot to solve the problem definitively.[94] However, if we ask ourselves why no one noticed the mistake in advance, the obvious answer is that the rehearsal process was inadequate. Even if Carcinus himself was not a very meticulous director, the actors themselves would surely have noticed if the entrances and exits at any point did not work. The obvious conclusion is that there was no opportunity to carry out a full dress rehearsal in the Theatre of Dionysus before the start of the festival.

Nevertheless, there is no sign that *Amphiaraus* was thought to be a bad play in other respects, and in general when Carcinus' plays are mentioned by other writers it is in a tone of apparent approbation.[95] Aristotle quite often cites Carcinus to illustrate a point (see later), and authors as diverse as Lysias, Menander and John of Stobi seem to treat selected verses from his tragedies as the embodiment of gnomic wisdom and authority.[96] Plutarch regarded Carcinus'

---

[92]   Aristotle, *Rhetoric* 3.12, 1413b8–13 (*TrGF* 1.71 T3): see Chapter 5, pp. 126–30.

[93]   The verb ἀνῄει can bear either meaning: see Davidson (2003) 117–18.

[94]   See Green (1990) and Davidson (2003), with reference to earlier discussions.

[95]   One exception is Philodemus (*On Poems* 2, *P.Herc.* 994, col. 25, 6–15: Janko (2011) 88–9 = *TrGF* 1.70 T7), who contrasts 'bad' writers Carcinus and Cleaenetus with the 'best' writers such as Euripides and Homer: this represents a predictable Hellenistic ranking of 'canonical' authors *versus* all the rest.

[96]   F4 (Stobaeus 4.39.3); F5a (Menander, *Shield* 415–18: see Chapter 5, pp. 124–5 for discussion); F6 (Lysias, *Against Mnesimachus* F68); F7 (Stobaeus 3.33.1); F8 (Stobaeus 3.38.18); F9 (Stobaeus 4.31.60); F10 (Stobaeus 4.31.63).

Aerope (along with Astydamas the Younger's *Hector*) as one of the crowning glories of classical theatre, and thought that a day of celebration ought to have been established to mark the anniversary of its first production, while Aelian reports that *Aerope* could even move tyrants to tears with its emotional power.[97]

Carcinus' *Alope* seems to have been noted for its pathos and psychological subtlety, not to mention a surprising central plot twist. Not a single word of this play survives. However, our main piece of evidence is Aristotle's *Nicomachean Ethics*, in which *Alope* is cited during a discussion about endurance *versus* surrender[98]:

> There is nothing to cause amazement if a person is overcome by violent and excessive pleasures or pains: such a person should be forgiven if he has tried to resist, as in the case of Cercyon in Carcinus' *Alope*. But it is amazing if a person is not able to resist, and is overcome by, the sort of pleasures and pains which most people are able to resist.

Some further contextualization and a partial plot summary is provided by an anonymous commentator on the passage:

> Cercyon had a daughter, Alope. When he found out that Alope had been raped, he asked her who it was who had violated her, saying that if she were to tell him the identity of her rapist he would not feel so entirely undone by grief. But when Alope told him the name of the rapist – Poseidon – Cercyon's own grief was such that he could not bear to live on, and he chose to commit suicide.

In other words, the plot of this tragedy contained a major departure from the more usual version of the myth, as previously dramatized by Choerilus and Euripides, in which Cercyon killed Alope and was himself killed by Theseus.[99] A scenario in which the great wrestler Cercyon committed suicide because of unbearable grief and shame would have marked an extraordinary reversal of expectation. Far from being a harsh parent, a brutal tyrant or a paradigm of physical strength, Cercyon was apparently transformed into a figure of sympathy and compassion, a loving father driven beyond the limits of endurance.[100]

---

[97] Plutarch, *On the Glory of the Athenians* 7.349f (*TrGF* 1.70 T5). Cf. Aelian, *Historical Miscellany* 14.40, though this may possibly refer to the *Aerope* of some other poet: see Snell, *TrGF* 1 pp. 221, 330.

[98] *Nicomachean Ethics* 7.7.1150b10 (*TrGF* 1.70 F1b).

[99] Choerilus, *Alope* (*TrGF* 1.2 F1); Euripides, *Alope* (*TrGF* 5 F105–111); cf. Hyginus, *Fabula* 187 (= *TrGF* 5 test. *iib). See Collard and Cropp (2008) I.115-23.

[100] This is made clear by Karamanou (2003) 37–9; see also Xanthakis-Karamanos (1980) 36–8, who explains Carcinus' changes as resulting from a wish to avoid repulsive subject matter.

Alope is not the only play in which we can detect an impulse towards mythical innovation. Another unexpected variation on a well-known myth is seen in Carcinus' *Medea*, in which Medea did not murder her children. This alternative to the more familiar version of the story is mentioned by Aristotle in his *Rhetoric* (during a discussion of the use by prosecutors or defendants of arguments based on mistakes committed):

> In Carcinus' *Medea,* some characters accuse Medea of having killed her children – or, at any rate, they had disappeared – for Medea made the mistake of sending them out of the way. And Medea herself says in her defence that she would not have killed her children but would have killed Jason instead; for indeed it would have been a mistake not to have done this, if she had actually done the other killings of which she was accused.[101]

On the basis of this evidence, we may surmise that Medea sent her children away from Corinth for their own protection, fearing, perhaps, that Jason's new wife Glauce would do them harm. When the children could not be found, the characters in the play made the assumption that Medea had killed them: this is precisely the same assumption that the audience members would be bound to make, on the basis of their prior knowledge of the mythical and dramatic tradition. It also seems likely that the tragedy contained an *agon* or trial scene in which Medea was seen confronting her accusers and offering a forensic-style self-defence.[102]

Very recently another piece of evidence for this play has come to light: this is a second-century CE papyrus fragment first published in 2004,[103] containing a number of lines of tragic dialogue between Jason, Medea and a third character (probably Creon). This has plausibly been attributed to Carcinus' play, since the scenario fits more or less exactly with Aristotle's description. The text is full of gaps and is difficult to interpret with complete confidence, but Martin West's recent edition (with supplements) allows us to understand a fair amount of the meaning.[104] Jason begins by saying to Medea: 'If, [. . .] as you say, you did not kill the children, save yourself: produce these ones you have not killed, let us see them'. Medea replies: 'I swear to you that [. . .] I have not destroyed the boys that I myself bore, but sent them away to safety in the care of an aged(?) nurse'. Creon (or some other hostile character) repeats the accusation against Medea, saying that she is clearly guilty: 'the Colchian woman has killed Glauce with fire – she

---

[101] *Rhetoric* 2.28. 400b9–12 (*TrGF* 1.70 F1e).
[102] Duchemin (1968) 105–8, followed by Xanthakis-Karamanos (1980) 66–70.
[103] P. Louvre (Antiquités égyptiennes inv. E 10534): see Bélis (2004).
[104] See West (2007) for full details: I quote West's reconstructed text and translations here.

admits as much – so there is no doubt that she has done this too, killed the children. So what are you waiting for, Jason? You are free to take this barbarian woman to be executed'.

It is not clear how the plot developed after this, or what actually happened to the children: did they live or die? West suggests that they were taken for protection to the shrine of Hera Akraia but slaughtered there by the Corinthians, a version of the myth attested in later sources.[105] Oliver Taplin suggests that they were taken by Medea to the sanctuary at Eleusis, on the basis that there is a late fourth-century vase-painting depicting such a scene, which may have been influenced by tragedy.[106] There is no way of knowing which (if either) suggestion is right, but Taplin's version makes Carcinus' play come to seem even more extraordinary, since no other Medea play is known to have taken place at Eleusis, and very few of any other tragedies involve a change of scene part-way through. Another odd feature of the papyrus is that it contains notation for musical accompaniment, even though the lines are part of an iambic dialogue (which would normally be assumed to be spoken, not sung). It has been suggested that Carcinus himself wrote this music, which would imply that the performance style of this *Medea* was as innovative as its content.[107] However, it would be more natural to suppose that the musical notation was added much later in antiquity.[108]

Perhaps unsurprisingly, Euripides' *Medea* is normally assumed to be the main source or model for Carcinus. Indeed, Taplin argues that 'there could hardly be a bolder departure from the authority of the Euripidean version', and he goes as far as to call Carcinus' tragedy 'anti-canonical' on this account.[109] But there is no reason to assume that Euripides' play was *already* canonical, or that it already represented the 'authorized version' of the myth, in Carcinus' time. We have to remember that rather a lot of other playwrights also treated this well-known story – including Dicaeogenes, Diogenes, Neophron and Melanthius.

Indeed, it could be thought more generally that modern discussions of intertextuality or epigonality in fourth-century drama have exaggerated the importance of Euripides.[110] It is easy to think, on the basis of his quasi-canonization in the Lycurgan period and his later reception history, that

---

[105] West (2007) 5, citing the historian Creophylus of Ephesus (*FGrHist* 417 F3); cf. Σ Euripides, *Medea* 9.
[106] Taplin (2014) 150–3, citing an Apulian red-figure volute-krater (Princeton inv. 1983.13 = Taplin (2007) no. 94, pp. 238–40).
[107] Bélis (2004) 1328, Taplin (2014) 152–3.
[108] West (2007) 8.
[109] Taplin (2014) 151.
[110] See also Chapter 5 (pp. 121–2).

Euripides represented the 'classic' tragedian *par excellence* for Carcinus and his contemporaries. But (as I have been at pains to emphasize throughout this book) Euripides was only one among many tragedians. Even if it could be demonstrated that in the mid-fourth century he was already the best-known author of tragedy, it is not plausible that all these belated writers would invariably choose the best-known plays for intertextual reworking. Surely one would expect at least some of the more bookish poets to have made use of relatively obscure or little-known works, in order to show off their knowledge and appeal to a similarly learned or bookish contingent within their audience.

All of this is highly speculative, of course. But it is worth making the effort to search for other likely models or points of departure that the later tragedians might have chosen; and it is often possible to identify some plausible candidates. For instance, Euripides' *Orestes* is normally assumed to have been the main inspiration for Carcinus' play of the same name. But the one piece of evidence we possess for Carcinus' version – the fact that when Orestes was accused of matricide, he defended himself in *riddles* – suggests very strongly that Theodectes' *Orestes* may have been an even more significant intertext, since Theodectes was obsessed by riddles and included them in several of his plays.[111] Similarly, it might be assumed that either Euripides' *Oedipus* or Sophocles' *Oedipus Tyrannus* was the main model for Carcinus' *Oedipus*. Perhaps in this case Sophocles rather than Euripides may seem to be the more obvious candidate, given that nowadays his play is so very famous, and that even as early as the fourth century it was regarded by Aristotle as a model tragedy. Nevertheless, Aristotle's view cannot be treated as identical with that of Carcinus' audience, and it is easy to forget that Sophocles' was far from the only tragedy on the subject. There were *Oedipus*es by Achaeus, Philocles, Meletus, Theodectes, Timocles and no doubt others during the fifth and fourth centuries. But in this particular case an even more obvious precursor presents itself: the *Oedipus* of Carcinus' own father, Xenocles.

There is little material for further speculation, since Xenocles' *Oedipus* is completely lost and Carcinus' *Oedipus* is known only from a brief reference in Aristotle's *Rhetoric*:

> If there is anything incredible, one should immediately undertake to give an explanation for it at once, and also to arrange the argument in a way that is acceptable to the audience – such as, for example, Jocasta in Carcinus' *Oedipus*,

---

[111] *TrGF* 1.72 F5. See Chapter 5 for discussion of Theodectes and his penchant for riddles (pp. 172–3).

who is always promising to do this when the man who is looking for her son makes inquiries of her.[112]

This is one of our most tantalizing testimonia, because it hints at a treatment of the myth that is quite different from Sophocles' play and the other versions that are known to us. What portion of the myth was included in Carcinus' play, and what was the timeframe covered by the plot? Who was the mysterious man in search of Oedipus? One possibility is that this tragedy covered the early part of the myth shortly after Oedipus' birth, and that the scenario above involved Jocasta's concealment of the baby Oedipus to prevent his exposure.[113] But this is not the only possible explanation: it may be that the play adopted a whodunit-style plot, rather along the lines of Sophocles' version, with the crucial difference that this time the 'detective' was someone other than Oedipus himself.

Alas, there is no way of answering these questions, and there is no way of proving whether Carcinus consciously – or subconsciously – made use of his father's work. But it is inevitable that he would have known Xenocles' *Oedipus*, or (at least) known of its existence. Even if Carcinus had completely *ignored* his father's play, this in itself would have constituted a significant gesture of self-assertion and defiance on the part of the younger poet. And there would certainly have been some among the audience who would have noted the gesture. Could one imagine a more aptly Oedipal example of the anxiety of influence?

---

[112] Aristotle, *Rhetoric* 3.16.1417b18–21 (*TrGF* 1.70 F1f).
[113] Webster (1954) 301; Xanthakis-Karamanos (1980) 45–6.

5

Some Fourth-Century Tragedians

If one's impression of the tragic genre is formed exclusively on the basis of the few plays that survive, or the accounts that are offered in the standard handbooks or surveys of Greek literature, it is easy to imagine that tragedy was essentially a fifth-century phenomenon, and that it more or less died out at the end of the fifth century.[1] But this would be a serious mistake.

There are several obvious reasons why this point in time can *seem* to represent the end of an era, not just in literary history but in other respects too. Sophocles and Euripides both died in 406–405 BCE, which means that none of the writers that we have come to see as canonical were producing plays any more. In 405 Aristophanes produced his *Frogs*, a comedy that has exerted a disproportionately large influence on the later reception history of drama: in this play a character claims that all the good tragedians are dead, leaving behind only awful amateurs who have brought the tragic art into disrepute. In 404 the Athenians were finally defeated after the long and exhausting Peloponnesian War. At around the same time their democratic system of government was seriously destabilized by a series of oligarchic revolutions. And thus the fifth century came to a close.

This last fact, at least, is irrelevant, since the classical Greeks did not count in years BCE, but it is difficult to resist the problematic periodization that is so conveniently implied by the labels 'fifth-century' and 'fourth-century'. Indeed, it is hard to think of an alternative way of referring to the authors discussed in this chapter without automatically marking them with the taint of posteriority. 'Later writers', 'tragedy after the Peloponnesian War', 'post-Euripidean tragedy' or similar titles would all carry the same undesirable implications – of a crucial cut-off point somewhere around the year 405, of 'before' and 'after'. Nomenclature remains a problem, then, but tragedy certainly did not come to an

---

[1] Note that most Handbooks or Companions to Greek tragedy omit fourth-century material or relegate it to footnotes or parentheses: Easterling (1997) is an exception. For the current purposes I assume that all the surviving tragedies belong to the fifth century, though there is some doubt about the date and authorship of Aeschylus' *Prometheus Bound* and Euripides' *Rhesus*: see e.g. Griffith (1977); Fries (2014) 22–8.

end after the fifth century. We must take Aristophanes' humorous assessment of the situation with a large pinch of salt.

Athens may have been undergoing a political crisis, but the theatre continued to flourish and expand throughout the fourth century and beyond. Many successful, prolific and talented new playwrights emerged during this period, and a quick glance at the contents page of *TrGF* shows there are almost as many tragedians attested for the fourth century as for the fifth.[2] It is true that from 386 BCE the archon in charge of the City Dionysia introduced 'old tragedy' alongside the other categories of performance – a change that has sometimes been seen as implying a lack of confidence in new writing.[3] But new tragedies continued to be produced for several more centuries yet,[4] and it is hard to see why this revival of interest in earlier poets and their work should have affected the way in which contemporary playwrights were perceived. All that it proves is that the Athenians were developing a keener sense of the theatre as an institution with its own history and traditions. The really important fact is that there were now more plays being performed than ever before.

For many years the conventional scholarly view (as expressed, for example, by T.B.L. Webster in his book *Art and Literature in Fourth-Century Athens*) was that after the fifth century 'tragedy had practically ceased to be a live art'.[5] The label 'fourth-century' came to seem synonymous with decline, creative stagnation, a tendency towards imitative or derivative writing, and a general falling-off in standards of literary taste. The most detailed and comprehensive treatment of the subject remains Georgia Xanthakis-Karamanos's *Studies in Fourth-Century Tragedy*.[6] This is a major scholarly achievement, and it is still indispensable in many ways, but it is also seriously misleading, in that it presents fourth-century tragedy as essentially a decadent art form. According to Xanthakis-Karamanos,

> tragedy began to take a new direction which might be called 'anti-tragic'. It started to reject the seriousness of classical drama and paid attention to dramatic technique and elegance of style . . . The tragic element was replaced by a complex, carefully designed plot and spectacular effects . . . Classical tragedies with highly

---

[2]   *TrGF* 1 p. xi lists forty-eight poets in the fifth century, forty-five in the fourth: this list presumably represents only a fraction of the total.

[3]   *IG* ii² 2318.1009–11; see Pickard-Cambridge (1988) 72, 99–100.

[4]   See now Kotlińska-Toma (2014) on the riches of Hellenistic tragedy; cf. *TrGF* DID I (pp. 3–16) and Pickard-Cambridge (1988) 82 for evidence of new tragedies in competition up to the first century BCE; cf. *TrGF* 1.95-200 for evidence of tragedians active all the way down to the fifth century CE.

[5]   Webster (1956) 135–6. No doubt Nietzsche's *Die Geburt der Tragödie* is partly responsible, with its influential but idiosyncratic portrait of tragedy's *Todeskampf* ('death-struggle') at Euripides' hands: see Nietzsche (1872), esp. §12. This is seen by Csapo et al. (2014) 1–3; cf. Michelini (1987) 3–51 on Nietzsche's influence on modern tragic scholarship.

[6]   Xanthakis-Karamanos (1980).

tragic issues, appreciated for their merits, but not really understood, were replaced by rhetorical tragedies with intensely pathetic overtones or romantic dramas with intrigue and coups de théâtre ... Serious tragedy was gradually replaced by melodramatic intrigue plays in response to people's wish to relax and enjoy light entertainment.[7]

Leaving aside the question of what is meant by such ambiguous and suggestive terms as 'serious' drama, 'the tragic element' or 'highly tragic issues', the main problem is that there is no real evidence for this supposed change of direction. As Xanthakis-Karamanos demonstrates, the remains of fourth-century tragedy do contain elements and motifs which might broadly be called 'emotional', 'pathetic' or 'rhetorical', and they do sometimes allow us to say a certain amount about the authors' handling of their plots. But the fragments are not substantial enough to allow us to make the bigger claim that these elements came to predominate, let alone the more radical assertion that the entire character of tragedy was altered or overturned. Furthermore, in any case, we could point to similar elements in tragedy of *any* period: that is, we can hardly deny the importance of emotion, or the influence of rhetoric, or the presence of intrigue or exciting plot twists, in the works of earlier tragedians from the fifth century. Nor is there enough evidence to allow us to say that these later plays were not 'serious', or that they privileged style or plot-construction above meaning. It is hard to avoid the conclusion that this 'new direction' is the creation of scholars who have approached the material with certain inherited preconceptions about the inferiority of fourth-century culture.

It is only comparatively recently that classical scholarship has started to reassess the evidence and react against earlier views. This welcome trend seems to have begun in 1993, with an influential article by P.E. Easterling, and more recently a series of important studies by Eric Csapo, H.R. Goette, J.R. Green, Peter Wilson, Oliver Taplin, Johanna Hanink and others has shown beyond doubt that the fourth century, far from being a period of decline, was a boom period for tragedy.[8] Nevertheless, it is fair to say that all of these discussions have been primarily historical and social rather than literary in focus: they have tended to concentrate on the organisation of the festivals, the institution of the *chorêgia*, the rise of the acting profession, the spread of theatre beyond Athens,

---

[7] Xanthakis-Karamanos (1980) 3–4, 58; cf. Webster (1954) 297 for a similar assessment.
[8] See Easterling (1993) and (1997); Taplin (1993); Le Guen (1995); Deardon (1999); Hall (2007); Csapo (2010); Hanink (2014a) and (2014b). Csapo, Goette, Green and Wilson (2014) is a major new collection of essays which completely reassesses fourth-century theatre and its social context: see especially the editors' Introduction (pp. 1–12).

the archaeological and artistic evidence for tragic performance, and other material aspects of theatre history and reception. Here we are mainly concerned with what can be said about the plays themselves.

My aim, in this chapter and elsewhere, has been to present the fourth-century material in a clear and unbiased way. I have tried to avoid preconceptions about the nature or character of these plays, instead letting the evidence speak for itself as far as possible. What seems to emerge very clearly, and rather surprisingly, is that there is no sign of any general trends or patterns at all. Here and there we can make out remarkable features or signs of individuality in the work of specific poets, but it is not possible to detect any significant changes or developments in the character of the tragic genre *as a whole* during the years up to *c.* 322 BCE. Every key feature of the later material finds a parallel in earlier tragedy. Of course, we have to keep reminding ourselves of the inadequate nature of the evidence and the limitations of the argument from silence. It remains perfectly possible that the traditional scholarly accounts were right all along, and that fourth-century tragedy really was derivative, turgid stuff, but it must be very clearly emphasized that there is no evidence to support such a view. I tentatively conclude that the overall character of fourth-century tragedy – if we can even talk in such broad terms – was not significantly different from that of fifth-century tragedy. The type of literary history that we can construct from this evidence is above all a narrative of continuity and stability across the decades.

It might reasonably be thought that one way in which the fourth-century writers differed from their earlier counterparts was in a heightened sense of their own epigonal status and the 'anxiety of influence'.[9] Did the weight of the literary tradition press down upon them more heavily than upon the fifth-century poets? This is certainly suggested by the epigram attributed to the fourth-century tragedian Astydamas the Younger:

> If only I had been born among them, or they had lived in our time,
>> those poets who are thought to bear the first prize with their speech,
> then I could have been judged on a true basis, starting level with my competitors;
>> but as it is they run ahead, taking the lead given by time, and no envy attaches
>> to them.[10]

---

[9]   This aspect of fourth-century tragedy in general, or of specific authors' work, is stressed by (e.g.) Del Grande (1934); Webster (1954) 303–5; Xanthakis-Karamanos (1979); Grossardt (2005) 227–8; Hall (2007) 280.

[10] *TrGF* 1.59 T2a; see Hanink (2014a) 183–8 on the rhetorical contrast of 'classic' *versus* 'epigonal' poetry. Page (1981) 33–4 doubts the poem's authenticity. On Astydamas cf. the Prologue and Chapter 4: pp. xv–xvi, 101–5.

Whether these lines are genuinely the words of Astydamas or a later invention, they have often been quoted as a typical illustration of the difficulties faced by later classical poets, who found themselves having to strive ever harder to be seen as original or worthwhile because so many fine and celebrated works had already been written.

Nevertheless, this aspect of their poetry has probably been overstated. In the first place, the anxiety of influence is not a characteristically 'fourth-century' phenomenon: it is present throughout the whole of Greek poetry. About a century before Astydamas, Bacchylides had already expressed similar sentiments: 'One poet is heir to another, now as in days of old; for it is no easy matter to find gates of verse that have never been uttered before'.[11] Every tragedian who ever produced a play, from Thespis onwards, would naturally have been conscious of the need for innovation. Because every playwright drew on the same repertoire of mythical material, if they chose a subject that had been dramatized before, they would invariably handle it in a way that was different (in large or small ways) from earlier treatments. This is an inherent feature of the art of tragedy at all periods, and it has even been regarded as tantamount to a universal rule of the genre.[12] Perhaps we might expect to find signs that the fourth-century tragedians were signalling their own originality in a markedly self-conscious or metapoetic way, drawing special attention to their own literary knowledge or their departure from specific models. But there are surprisingly few examples of this sort of self-conscious literariness among the fragments. In this respect, the later writers actually seem to provide a contrast with the practice of fifth-century poets such as Euripides.[13]

It has also been suggested that Euripides became an especially important model for fourth-century writers, reflecting this poet's increasing popularity in the years following his death.[14] This is perfectly plausible, and the evidence from

---

[11] Bacchylides, *Paeans* F5 Maehler; cf. Wright (2012) 77–8 on the tension between tradition and originality in early Greek poetics.

[12] Sommerstein (2010) 65: 'Every lost tragedy told a story that differed to a greater or lesser degree from that of every other tragedy based on the same slice of myth' (this observation is actually used as a general principle for reconstructing lost plays); cf. Burian (1997) and see the Epilogue below (pp. 203–5).

[13] See Torrance (2013) on Euripidean metapoetics and originality. Cf. my own earlier attempts to detect self-conscious literary innovation in other fifth-century tragedians: see pp. 42–5, 98–100.

[14] E.g. Del Grande (1934), Webster (1954) 305, Xanthakis-Karamanos (1980) 29–34, Hall (2013) 76, Hanink (2014a) 159–78. The (limited) evidence for fourth-century revivals of Euripides' plays includes Demosthenes 18. 180, 267; 19. 246, 337; Plutarch, *On the Fortune of Alexander* 328d; Lucian, *On the Writing of History* 1; cf. *TrGF* 1 DID A1, 292; A2a, 1; see also Pickard-Cambridge (1988) 100.

fourth-century comedy certainly points to a strong preoccupation, even an obsession, with Euripides and his work;[15] but again it has to be said that there is no evidence that Euripides *in particular* was the main model or source for later writers, except in the case of Polyidus and Theodectes (see related sections below). It is true that many fourth-century poets wrote plays on subjects that Euripides had treated – including Medea, Orestes, Helen, Iphigenia and others – but Euripides was far from being the only fifth-century writer to dramatize these myths. It is important to bear in mind that it was only rather later, towards the end of the fourth century, that Euripides officially achieved classic status, and in fact these later tragedians had a much bigger range of tragic and poetic material available to draw upon.

In the pages below I explore the work of most of the fourth-century tragedians whose work can be described with a reasonable amount of confidence. A couple of others, Carcinus and Astydamas the Younger, have already featured in the previous chapter, and several more are included in the following chapter on 'the very lost'. As before, I have adopted a poet-by-poet structure, but lack of evidence, combined with the fact that most of these authors seem to cluster together during the first few decades of the century, makes it impossible to arrange the authors in order of chronology. What follows, then, is in a more or less random order, beginning with the playwright who is best preserved.

Chaeremon

When discussing Ion and Achaeus in an earlier chapter,[16] I made the observation that our knowledge of lost tragedies is often out of proportion with the amount of evidence that survives. Paradoxically, the poets who are represented by the greatest number of fragments are among the most obscure. Chaeremon, with forty-three fragments to his name, is the best-preserved fourth-century tragedian, but comparatively little can be said about his drama or how it compared with that of his contemporaries. It is also striking that (as in the case of Ion and Achaeus also) there are hardly any biographical or critical testimonia. Chaeremon's entry in the *Suda* lists him, incorrectly, as a comic poet, and includes an incomplete list of his works: *Oeneus, Alphesiboea, Centaur, Dionysus, Odysseus,*

---

[15]   See Wright (2013b) 620–2; Hanink (2014a) 159–78.
[16]   Chapter 2, pp. 29–36.

Thyestes and *Minyans* (it omits *Achilles the Killer of Thersites* and *Io,* titles which are known from other sources).[17] There are a couple of brief references to Chaeremon in the comedies of Ephippus and Eubulus, apparently making fun of his literary style and his drinking habits: these jokes tell us that he was reasonably well known (at least), and the two comedians are known to have won their first victories in 368 and 370 BCE respectively, which gives us a very loose basis on which to date the tragedian.[18] Otherwise almost nothing else is known about Chaeremon's life or career, and the fragments themselves tell us nothing whatsoever about the plays' plots or his treatment of the myths.[19] Christopher Collard, whose discussion of the evidence is the most detailed and comprehensive treatment available, is right to describe him as 'a shadowy figure'.[20]

Shadowy he may be, but Chaeremon can be seen as a particularly interesting figure in relation to ancient reading habits and quotation culture. The majority of our fragments are one- or two-line gnomic maxims, on familiar topics such as anger, wisdom, time, fortune and the relationship between parents and children. For example:[21]

> Chance, not judgement, governs the affairs of men. [F2]

> Need has made her home not far from Necessity. [F18]

> Time, proceeding at a leisurely pace, always gets there in the end. [F20]

> It is the mark of wise men to exercise fair judgement upon sins,
> but to judge rashly and impetuously is a bad thing. [F31]

The frequency with which Chaeremon's *gnômai* were quoted by John of Stobi and other anthologists demonstrates that, along with other tragedians (including, notably, Agathon and Euripides), he was thought to be unusually skilled at packaging well-worn sentiments in a neatly quotable and memorable form. It also suggests that Chaeremon's tragedies were perceived by later readers as a particularly authoritative source of moral wisdom or inspiration for life. Indeed, it may well be that Chaeremon and these other tragedians deliberately designed

---

[17] *Suda* X 170 (*TrGF* 1.71 T1). The list also incorrectly includes *The Wounded Man* (*Traumatias*), which is the title of comedies by Alexis and Antiphanes.

[18] Ephippus F9 K-A, Eubulus F17 K-A (*TrGF* 1.71 T2).

[19] Apart from the fragments, an Apulian red-figure vase (Boston 03.804) has been thought to constitute evidence for Chaeremon's *Achilles the Killer of Thersites*: see Morelli (2001) for a very speculative discussion.

[20] Collard (2007b) 31.

[21] See Appendix 1 for a complete translation of Chaeremon's fragments.

their work in such a way that it lent itself to selective quotation and excerption, in the knowledge that many readers would tend to treat their plays in precisely this manner.[22]

The popularity of excerption as a reading habit in the fourth century, as well as the status of Chaeremon as quotable/quoted author *par excellence,* can be observed in the following extract from a scene in Menander's comedy *The Shield.* Here the slave Daos – who is attempting to bamboozle another character, Smikrines, into thinking that a 'tragic' event has taken place – quotes a large number of verses excerpted from several different tragedies by Chaeremon and others.[23]

> *Daos:* And then there's this one: '**Chance, not judgement, governs the affairs of men**'.[24] Oh yes, that's jolly good! '**The god sows guilt among men, whenever he wishes to destroy a household utterly**'[25]: that one's from Aeschylus, the one who solemnly –
>
> *Smikrines:* You thrice-wretched creature! Spout maxims, will you (*gnômologeis*)?
>
> *Daos:* '**Incredible! Senseless! Terrible!**'[26]
>
> *Smikrines:* Won't he ever stop?
>
> *Daos:* '**Among the evils of human life, is there anything that is beyond belief?**' – that's what Carcinus says – '**for in a single day the god brings the fortunate to misfortune**'.[27] All this is well said, Smikrines.
>
> *Smikrines:* What do you mean?
>
> *Daos:* Your brother – o Zeus! How am I going to tell you? – is on the verge of death.
>
> *Smikrines:* What? My brother, who was just here now, talking to me? What happened to him?
>
> *Daos:* Bile, grief, a nervous breakdown, choking . . .
>
> *Smikrines:* Poseidon and the gods! What a terrible affliction!
>
> *Daos:* '**There is nothing that is so dreadful, to tell the truth or to suffer** . . .'[28]
>
> *Smikrines:* You're getting on my nerves now.
>
> *Daos:* '. . . **for the divine powers have determined unexpected outcomes**'.[29] These aren't from just any old poets (*tôn tuchontôn*). One is from Euripides, and the other from Chaeremon.

---

[22] See Chapter 3 on Agathon and quotation culture (pp. 73–7), and cf. Wright (forthcoming b) on 'excerptability' as a seemingly deliberate characteristic of Euripidean tragedy.
[23] Menander, *Aspis* 399–436: see Cusset (2003) 144–58, Ireland (2010) 100–102.
[24] Chaeremon, *Achilles, Killer of Thersites TrGF* 1.71 F2.
[25] Aeschylus, *Niobe TrGF* 3 F154.15–16.
[26] Carcinus *TrGF* 1.70 F5b.
[27] Carcinus *TrGF* 1.70 F5b.
[28] Euripides, *Orestes* 1–2.
[29] Chaeremon *TrGF* 1.71 F42.

These verses are non-consecutive, irrelevant to the comic context, and completely unrelated to one another, but the point is that they already resemble extracts from a gnomic anthology. People in Menander's time were well accustomed to making use of tragedy in this way, the verb *gnômologein* ('to collect maxims') was obviously in common usage, and the excerpts in question had already become 'popular tags' (in the words of one commentator). In this respect, it is worth reflecting that our own present-day encounters with Chaeremon's maxims as '*fragments*' are not necessarily very different from the reading experiences of many ancient Greeks, who often encountered these same maxims as '*excerpts*'. This would remain true even if we rediscovered the full texts of Chaeremon's plays, and thus were able to judge the effect of all these excerptable quotations within their original context. The point is that a distinction can be made between two modes of reading, which are not mutually exclusive – the 'linear' (complete, consecutive, unitary) and the 'non-linear' (disconnected, fragmentary, selective).[30] An aphoristic author such as Chaeremon especially lends himself to this second mode.

Note also that all four poets here, Euripides, Aeschylus, Carcinus and Chaeremon, are being quoted side-by-side. Perhaps we might have expected to see some sort of contrast between the 'classic' fifth-century authors and their 'minor' fourth-century counterparts, but there appears to be no sense in which these authors are being differentiated in terms of status or function. In fact, Menander goes out of his way to stress that Euripides and Chaeremon are *not* 'just any old poets', implying that both tragedians are seen as comparable in terms of status and authority. All these playwrights are apparently being treated equally, as typical representatives of the tragic genre, and their plays are all seen as texts to be dipped into at random as a source of moral wisdom, truth or guidance.

One of the most curious fragments is F14b, a lacunose and incomplete scrap of papyrus dating from the mid-third century BCE and first published in 1955.[31] The passage consists entirely of hexameter maxims, and – uniquely among tragic fragments – it also contains an acrostic spelling out the name of the author.

Χρὴ τιμᾶν θ[
Ἀρχὴ γὰρ θνητ[οῖς
Ἱμείρου πάση[ς

---

[30] See Wright (forthcoming b), drawing on Hunter (2014) and Konstan (2011).
[31] *TrGF* 1.71 F14b = *P.Hib.* 2.224 = Pack (1965) 1613.

Ῥώμην τιμῶμεν μ[
Ἦθος ἔχειν ὅσιον ζῃ [
Μὴ πᾶν κέρδος ὅρα [
. [. .]γ [.]. κιαν σαυτ [

One must honour . . .
For humans the beginning . . .
Of a desire for every . . .
We honour strength . . .
To possess a pious character . . .
Do not fix your eye on every sort of gain . . .
. . . (?) . . . yourself . . .

This odd-looking text has been discussed by several modern scholars, some of whom argue that it does not represent a continuous passage written in just this way by Chaeremon himself: it is suggested instead that we are dealing with a mélange of one-line maxims, excerpted from different places within Chaeremon's work and stuck together by the later editor of a gnomic anthology.[32] If this is true, the fragment is still valuable in that it provides further confirmation of the importance of quotation culture for understanding Chaeremon's work and its ancient reception; it also shows that collections of decontextualized maxims were circulating in Egypt, in the form of papyrus books, a century or so after Chaeremon's death.

　　Nevertheless, it remains probable that Chaeremon himself did assemble the lines in this way.[33] Indeed, the fact that these acrostic verses are preceded in the papyrus by the phrase Χαιρήμων ἐν [('[as] Chaeremon writes in [ ] . . .') suggests to me that they almost certainly do belong to a single work. (The *Centaur*, mentioned below, has been cited as a possible source, but this is far from certain.[34]) If we are prepared to entertain such a suggestion, the fragment becomes even more interesting.[35] Not only can it be seen as the earliest attested acrostic in Greek literature, but it also seems to provide a rare example of a tragic author explicitly signalling his authorial presence within the text, in the form of a signature or seal (*sphragis*).[36] Even more significantly, the fragment suggests

---

[32]　See most recently Schubert (2013); cf. Collard (2007b) 32–3. See also West (1977) 37–8, who fills in the missing words with speculative conjectures (cf. Snell *TrGF* 1 p. 222).

[33]　Euripides' *Phoenician Women* provides a partial parallel for the use of consecutive *gnômai* in tragic dialogue, either in stichomythia (390–407) or continuous dialogue (529–58).

[34]　See Snell *ad loc.* (*TrGF* 1, p. 222); cf. *P.Hib* (ed. Turner) 2.224; Snell (1971) 166.

[35]　See Luz (2010) 7–15, whose main points I summarize here.

[36]　Rare but perhaps not unique: compare, in slightly different ways, Diogenes and Dionysius (pp. 140,

that Chaeremon was envisaging an audience consisting, at least in part, of book-readers, since the effect of the acrostic is purely visual: it would have been imperceptible in live theatre performance or oral recitation. Despite the fact that many scholars prefer to treat the classical Greek theatre exclusively in terms of performance culture, it seems perfectly possible that Chaeremon wrote his plays in such a way that they could be enjoyed either as written texts for private reading or as scripts for performance, with slightly different effects available to each type of consumer.

The idea of a reading public for poetry and drama during the classical period is nothing new. Even as early as the fifth century there is evidence of a small but significant sub-category of readers within Athenian literary culture, and it is generally accepted that literacy and book-ownership will have increased considerably by the mid-fourth century when Chaeremon was writing, even if the majority of the citizens were still unable to read or afford books.[37] At this period it would still, I think, be somewhat anachronistic to regard Chaeremon as writing *exclusively* for book-readers. But there are two additional pieces of evidence which may point towards Chaeremon as the original author of the acrostic. The first is a passage of Aristotle's *Rhetoric* which discusses the 'written style' in drama and also identifies a special category of poets – including Chaeremon – who are especially suitable for reading[38]:

> The written style (*lexis graphikê*) is the most precise, and the debating style is the most suitable for spoken delivery. For this reason actors look for plays written in this latter style, and poets look for such actors. But the poets who are especially suitable for reading (*hoi anagnôstikoi*) are constantly in our hands – for example, Chaeremon, for he is as precise in his writing as a speechwriter, and also the dithyrambic poet Licymnius. If we compare the two types of writing side-by-side, the speeches of the 'written' sort of author appear constrained in debates, whereas those of the 'rhetorical' sort seem eccentric when they are read in the pages of a book.

Of course (as critics have been quick to point out) the term *anagnôstikos* does

---

163); and note the presence of passages in Euripides which have sometimes been read as authorial gestures, e.g. *Heracles* 673–96, *Andromache* 476–7, *Helen* 1056, *Erechtheus* F369: see Torrance (2013).

[37] These matters are too big to explore in depth here; but for sources and extensive discussion see Harris (1989) 43–146, Thomas (1992), and (with specific reference to drama) Wright (2010) 178–9, (2012) and (2013b) 608–12.

[38] Aristotle, *Rhetoric* 3.12, 1413b8–13 (*TrGF* 1.71 T3).

[39] See Collard (2007b) 35, citing earlier scholars.

not mean that Chaeremon wrote his plays exclusively for reading,[39] but Aristotle's contrast between two distinct sorts of tragic writing is certainly suggestive. The second piece of evidence is the fact that Chaeremon, like Theodectes (see section below), was interested in riddles, which fall into the same category as acrostics and other sorts of wordplay.[40] One of his fragments is a riddle on the subject of the vine: '†In summer the daughter of springtime gives birth to a child for the future†, but in winter she is gone, cut off along with the wind'.[41] Several other fragments contain rather strained circumlocutions (or 'kennings') which seem designed to tease or intrigue: ivy is 'the lover of choruses', garlands are described as 'the messengers of good news'; water is 'the body of a river'; flowers are 'children of the florid spring', or 'children of the meadows', or 'offspring of the seasons', and so on.[42] It is also significant to note that Chaeremon's vocabulary is inventive and often odd, including as many as nine unique words (*hapax legomena*) in the seventy-five lines that survive.[43] Furthermore, he is said to have had a penchant for metrical experimentation, as in his *Centaur* (described by Athenaeus as a 'polymetric drama' and Aristotle as a 'mixed rhapsody').[44] It would hardly be surprising if a poet of this sort made use of acrostics or other verbal games as well.

Aristotle's description of Chaeremon as an especially 'readable' poet encourages us to search for other reader-friendly qualities in his work. As already noted, the remains are frustratingly unrevealing, but it is striking that a couple of longer fragments contain extended visual descriptions. Perhaps these scenes might be regarded as more akin to narrative than dramatic poetry. The first of these is from *Alphesiboea*, a tragedy which evidently dealt with the relationship between Alcmeon and his first wife (as in Theodectes' tragedy *Alcmeon* – see p. 169–70). All that can be said about the context of this fragment is that a beautiful young woman is being described: it has been suggested that this is

---

[40]   On all aspects of *technopaignia* (wordplay, puns, acrostics, pattern poems, riddles, etc.) see the excellent study of Luz (2010).

[41]   *TrGF* 1.71 F41 (quoted as an example of an *ainigma* by Cocondrius, *On Tropes* 11): the fragment is highly corrupt, and the translation offered here is only a rough approximation.

[42]   *TrGF* 1.71 F5, F6, F17, F9, F10, F13. Eubulus F128 K-A quotes Chaeremon F17, perhaps in order to mock this tendency?

[43]   See Collard (2007b) 38–40 on these *hapax legomena* and Chaeremon's style more generally.

[44]   *TrGF* 1.72 F9a; cf. F43, where the 'Chaeremonian metre' (hypercatalectic iambic pentameter) is cited. Athenaeus 13.608e calls *Centaur* a *drama polumetron*. Aristotle, *Poetics* 1.1447b21 calls it a *miktê rhapsôidia* and says it combines several metres; cf. 24.1460a2. No clear conclusion has emerged about the genre and character of this work, though several scholars treat it as satyric: see Snell (1971) 167–9, Collard (2007b) 36.

Alphesiboea herself, or Alcmeon's second wife Callirhoe, but it might just as well be anyone at all.[45]

> †She put a lot of effort into her appearance, making her body gleam with its white complexion.† Modesty added a sense of proportion, bringing a very gentle blush to her bright complexion. Just like an image sculpted in wax, hair and all, her tresses waved in the breeze and glowed luxuriantly.

A similar effect is created in a longer fragment (also without any indication of dramatic context or the identity of the characters described) from Chaeremon's *Oeneus*[46]:

> One girl, her shoulder-piece loosened, revealed a white breast to the moonlight as she lay. Meanwhile another girl danced and laid bare her left flank. Naked, she appeared in full view in the open air, and she resembled a living picture; her white complexion met the eye with an answering gleam, the work of dark shadow. Another girl exposed her lovely arms, throwing her hands around another's feminine neck, and this one showed a glimpse of thigh beneath the folds of a torn cloak; and hopeless love set its seal upon her smiling bloom. Drowsily they sank down upon calamint, crushing the dark-petalled violets and the crocus which smeared the shadowy trace of its sunny image on their woven garments, and the sturdy marjoram, nurtured by the dew; and they lay there, stretching out their necks in the soft meadows.

Both of these passages show the powerful influence of visual art. The young women are being described as if they were sculptures or figures in a painting. Much emphasis is placed upon colours and textures, contrasting shades, and the effects of light and shadow. It has been thought that these extraordinarily vivid images reflect contemporary developments in the world of painting, and that they are specifically meant to evoke the techniques of *skiagraphia* or *chiaroscuro*.[47] Note the recurrence, in both passages, of the language of appearance, showing, revealing and exposing, while in the second fragment the viewer is explicitly mentioned ('her white complexion . . . *met the eye*'). Note also that it is impossible to tell whether the narrator in either case is describing an actual event that he has seen or a physical artwork.

---

[45] *TrGF* 1.71 F1. The first two lines of text are corrupt and not entirely intelligible; I have been guided by Collard (2007b) 42. The ungainly repetition of 'complexion' (*chrôma*) in the space of two lines is surely wrong.

[46] *TrGF* 1.71 F14. Athenaeus (13.608b) names the speaker as Oeneus. There is no particular reason to think that the girls depicted are bacchants (Snell *TrGF* p. 221; Collard (2007b) 44–5) or girls dancing in honour of Aphrodite (Dolfi (2006) 48–54).

[47] Collard (2007b) 46–7, Piatowski (1981) 207–8, Snell (1971) 159–62.

It cannot be claimed that these passages are unique. In fact several tragedies by Euripides, including *Ion* and *Iphigenia at Aulis,* feature similar visual descriptions of art: such scenes have been interpreted as a means of focusing attention on the activity of spectatorship and the nature of illusion, underlining the analogy between the act of viewing artworks and the act of watching plays in the theatre (both of which acts require us to interpret stylized symbols and codes).[48] No doubt Chaeremon's work adopted a similar sort of strategy. Nevertheless, the level of detail in the passages above goes beyond anything that we find in Euripides. Indeed, Chaeremon can even be seen as foreshadowing the later Greek novels, not just in his narrative technique but also in the markedly sensual and erotic tone of these descriptions.[49] But at any rate it seems obvious that Chaeremon's use of *ekphrasis* and narrative description (as opposed to mimetic enactment) is precisely the sort of technique that would work particularly well in a written text for private reading. It does not require performance but imagination to make the scene come alive.

Dionysius

A well-known article by Alan Sommerstein has posed the question of 'how to avoid being a *komoidoumenos*' (that is, the object of mockery or personal abuse by comedians) in classical Athens.[50] There seem to have been few completely reliable ways of avoiding this fate – not being famous for anything at all was probably the safest option – but by far the most common butts of comic ridicule were politicians and poets. Anyone who was both a politician *and* a poet was simply asking for it. Of course, many poets may have performed some sort of official function in public life from time to time: Sophocles, who served a term as *stratêgos* of Athens, is a prominent example. Nevertheless, Dionysius must be seen as an unusual or even unique case, since he was not only a tragic playwright but also Dionysius I, tyrant of Syracuse from 406 to 367 BCE.[51]

---

[48] E.g. Euripides, *Ion* 184–236, 1129–66, *Iphigenia at Aulis* 164–302; cf. *Andromeda* F125 (which is similar to Chaeremon F1 in its comparison of the real-life Andromeda to a statue). For rich discussion see Zeitlin (1994) and Stieber (2011).

[49] E.g. Longus, *Daphnis and Chloe* pr. 1–4; Achilles Tatius, *Leucippe and Clitophon* 1.1.2–13, 3.7.1–9. The connection between Chaeremon and the Greek novels is seen by Xanthakis-Karamanos (1980) 78 and Dolfi (2006). Piatowski (1981) 208–9 also sees Chaeremon as a precursor of Roman erotic elegy (e.g. Ovid, *Amores* 14.21-3).

[50] Sommerstein (1996). Specialized studies or catalogues of *komoidoumenoi* were undertaken by scholars from the Hellenistic period onwards, including Ammonius, Herodicus et al.

[51] On the historical and political aspects of Dionysius' career see Stroheker (1958), Sanders (1987), Caven (1990).

This (as it were) dual identity made Dionysius an easy target for contemporary comedians, who mercilessly mocked the tyrant and his poetry. Eubulus' *Dionysius* evidently featured a caricature of the tyrant as its main character, and this comedy seems to have quoted or parodied Aeschylus and Euripides as well as Dionysius' own tragedies.[52] A lost comedy by Polyzelus made fun of Dionysius' penchant for fine costumes and luxurious fabrics.[53] An obscure joke about facial hair in Strattis' comedy *The Burning of Zopyrus* has been seen as an irreverent allusion to the tyrant's fear of barbers.[54] One of the characters in Ephippus' *Lookalikes* begins what looks like a list of exaggeratedly terrible scenarios or punishments by saying 'May I be compelled to learn the plays of Dionysius by heart …' (the same list also includes having Euripides as a dinner-guest, and being forced to listen to speeches from the tragedies of Theodorus, another of Dionysius' contemporaries and rivals).[55] The dithyrambic poet Philoxenus of Cythera (see below, pp. 133–7) also wrote a work called *Cyclops*: this seems to have been some sort of humorous allegorical fantasy, in which Dionysius appeared in the guise of Polyphemus, serenading his sweetheart Galateia, while Philoxenus himself was Odysseus. If so, it may well be that the several fourth-century comedies with related titles – including Nicochares' *Galateia,* Antiphanes' *Cyclops* and Alexis' *Galateia* – also incorporated an element of political satire or literary parody (of the works of either poet).[56] But it is clear, at any rate, that the comedians had a field day with Dionysius.

Why begin a general discussion of Dionysius' work by emphasizing his role as a *komoidoumenos?* Because it is important to acknowledge the enormous influence that these comedies had upon the biographical and critical tradition. Dionysius has emerged from the historical record as the tyrant *par excellence* – cruel, unjust, capricious, selfish, paranoid and (if all that were not bad enough) wretchedly lacking in poetic talent. But this image is predominantly the product of hostile and derisive source-material, including, above all, comedy – a fact that

---

52 Eubulus F25a–29 K-A; see Hunter (1983) 116–22 for discussion. F25a alludes to Aeschylus and/or Aristophanes; F25 concerns flatterers; F26–7 parody the excessive use of the letter sigma by Euripides (and perhaps also Dionysius). Cf. Suess (1966) 306–10.
53 Polyzelus F12 K-A; cf. Timaeus (*FGrHist* 562 F1 *apud* Polybius 12.24.1 = *TrGF* 1.76 F13), where Dionysius' love of expensive fabrics is reported as historical fact.
54 Strattis, *Zopyrus Perikaiomenos* F9 K-A; cf. Cicero, *Tusculan Disputations* 5.58 for Dionysius' fear of barbers. Both Webster (1970) 29 and Duncan (2012) 140 state, incorrectly, that a similar joke ('Dionysio-beard-conflagration') is found in a fragment of Strattis' *Atlanta*, but this is a mistake based on misattribution of the fragment in older editions (Strattis F6 Kock = Cratinus F223 K-A), combined with a doubtful emendation. See K-A *ad loc.* and Orth (2009) 77–8 for further discussion.
55 Ephippus, *Homoioi* F16 K-A (*TrGF* 1.76 T5).
56 See Webster (1970) 21; cf. Arnott (1996) 139–49, who concludes that Alexis' play (at least) was probably 'a non-political myth travesty'; LeVen (2014) 233–4 believes that Philoxenus is a more likely source for these comedians than Dionysius.

has been widely acknowledged in recent scholarship.[57] Leaving aside Dionysus'
life and political career, it is particularly noticeable that almost every one of the
sources that relate specifically to his poetry has a decidedly comical or anecdotal
flavour.

The most extended discussions of Dionysius' literary career are found in the
work of Diodorus, the Sicilian historian of the first century BCE. Diodorus'
Historical Library contains a vivid account of how the tyrant unexpectedly met
his end: he supposedly drank himself to death during the party that he held to
celebrate his victory at the Athenian Lenaea of 367.[58] Thus Dionysius comes
across as, in the first place, an example of dangerous excess and a warning against
overindulgence; but Diodorus also takes the opportunity to disparage the tyrant
and his work yet further, showing that he was the victim of a grave delusion:

> Dionysius was in possession of an oracle from the gods to the effect that he
> would meet his end 'when he had conquered his superiors', but he interpreted the
> oracle as referring to the Carthaginians, assuming that they were his 'superiors'.
> For this reason, in the wars that he had waged against them on many occasions,
> it had been his habit to retire just as he was on the point of winning, and to
> accept defeat willingly, so that he would not seem to have conquered his
> 'superiors' who were stronger. And yet, for all his trickery, he was unable to
> outwit necessity, imposed on him by Fate. As it turned out, even though he was
> a bad (*kakos*) poet, and even though this competition was adjudicated at Athens,
> he managed to defeat poets who were better than himself. And so, in accordance
> with the oracle, Dionysius met his death as a direct result of 'conquering his
> superiors'.

It is not enough that Dionysius should have died in an embarrassing manner; it
is crucial that his dramatic victory should also be devalued. Diodorus explicitly
states, as if we needed to be reminded of the fact, that Dionysius was a bad poet,
but he also notes that this first prize was won at Athens, where critical standards
are assumed to be higher than elsewhere. According to this reasoning, the success
of Dionysius' tragedy (*The Ransoming of Hector*) must be presented as a freakish
anomaly; or maybe it is an illustration of the inexplicable randomness of the
adjudication process (a feature of dramatic festivals which is remarked upon by

---

[57]   See (e.g.) Stroheker (1958) 11–31; Suess (1966) 305–7; Sanders (1987) 2–3, 21 (though he also
       stresses other hostile sources, such as Timaeus of Tauromenium); Caven (1990) 222; Arnott (1996)
       139–41; Duncan (2012) 137–43, etc. Cf. also Lefkowitz (1984) for comedy's disproportionate and
       distorting influence on literary history more generally.
[58]   Diodorus Siculus 15.73–4 (*TrGF* 1.76 T1); cf. Pliny, *Natural History* 7.180 (*TrGF* 1.76 T9), who
       reminds us that the story is suspiciously similar to the traditional account of Sophocles' death.

many indignant critics throughout antiquity).[59] Typically, we are not told who Dionysius' rivals or 'superiors' were, or what was so good about their work in comparison with *The Ransoming of Hector*. Probably Diodorus does not know or care. The point of the anecdote is that Dionysius was a 'bad' poet who got his comeuppance in the end. Indeed, the judgement of literary critics on earth is seen here as being endorsed on a cosmic level. The detail of the misunderstood oracle underlines the fact that Dionysius' fate embodies divine justice, since his undeserved victory was ultimately the cause of his death: it is just as if the gods themselves were drawing attention to Dionysius' lack of talent or even punishing him for it.

Elsewhere Diodorus makes a point of emphasizing Dionysius' insecurity and need for approval, as in his account (15.7.3) of how the tyrant fell into a severe depression after hearing some adverse criticism of his poetry. This account ties in with another strand in the biographical tradition, attested by Aristotle, Plutarch and others, in which Dionysius was accused of murdering a rival tragedian, Antiphon (sources differ as to whether Antiphon had plotted against the tyrant or merely presumed to criticize his plays).[60] These same traits of jealousy and insecurity are also highlighted in Diodorus' account of Dionysius' encounter with Philoxenus – a well-known and funny anecdote which is worth quoting at length.[61] Diodorus begins by explaining how the tyrant came to take up literary pursuits at a time when Syracuse was enjoying peace and leisure:

> He began composing poetry with great enthusiasm, and he sent for other poets, the ones who enjoyed a good reputation, spending time with them, giving them honours, and using them as literary advisors and critics of his poetry (*tôn poiêmatôn epistatas kai diorthôtas*).

By filling his court with talented and prestigious people, and generally giving support to cultural and artistic activities, Dionysius was only doing what many other Greek tyrants had done before him. But in this account the tyrant is said to have his own unusual motives for surrounding himself with such people. He does not simply want to make Sicily a haven of elite culture, but he wants to improve the quality of his own writing – as if by placing himself in close proximity to the best poets he could somehow absorb some of their talent.

We are told that Dionysius' generosity led to a great deal of praise and flattery (which, naturally, is said to be misguided) on the part of these other writers. One

---

[59] See Wright (2009) on the 'anti-prize mentality' in ancient literary criticism.
[60] *TrGF* 1.76 T4; *TrGF* 1.55 (Antiphon) T1–6. On Antiphon himself see section pp. 143–5.
[61] Diodorus Siculus 15.6 (*TrGF* 1.76 T1).

poet, however, stands out from the crowd. This is Philoxenus, the dithyrambist from Cythera, who is said to have a very great reputation on account of the refinement of his own poetry, in contrast with the tyrant's 'wretched' (*mochthêra*) poems.

> Philoxenus refused to indulge the tyrant, but gave a rather frank reply when asked for his opinion. The tyrant took offence, accused him of slandering him from motives of envy, and ordered him to be taken off to the stone-quarries.
>
> On the next day his friends prevailed on him to pardon Philoxenus, so he relented and had him brought back to the table. As the drinking progressed, Dionysius once again began to boast about his poetry, and he quoted some verses which, in his own view, were particularly successful. However, when he asked Philoxenus: 'What is your opinion of the quality of these verses?', Philoxenus said nothing. He just summoned the attendants and asked them to take him back to the stone-quarries.
>
> At the time Dionysius tolerated the poet's freedom of speech, for the joke took the edge off the criticism. But afterwards, when his friends and Dionysius too tried to make him take back his inappropriate frankness, Philoxenus made a paradoxical offer: he said that he would give a response that would simultaneously observe both the truth and Dionysus' reputation. And he was not lying; for when the tyrant quoted a few verses describing pitiable occurrences, Philoxenus replied: 'They are pathetic (*oiktra*)' – thus maintaining both the truth and Dionysius' reputation through the use of ambiguity. Dionysius took 'pathetic' to mean 'full of pathos and pity', and he interpreted Philoxenus' verdict as an accolade, since such qualities are the characteristics of good poets. Everybody else, however, picked up the true meaning and understood that the word 'pathetic' was used by Philoxenus to denote a failure.

This anecdote has most recently been interpreted, by Pauline LeVen, as a commentary on the politics of literary criticism and a meditation on the value, and the danger, of free speech (*parrhêsia*). Dionysius' poetry is seen as 'a synecdoche for his power', while Philoxenus emerges as 'a master of discourse, who can act successively as critic, wise man and court poet, and is unwilling to compromise on any position'.[62] This reading is a compelling one, but, along with other interpretations, it privileges Philoxenus over Dionysius and accepts Diodorus' own rhetoric and presentation of the situation (no doubt partly because LeVen is predominantly interested in Philoxenus). However, this is not the only way of reading the anecdote, and we are not obliged to accept Diodorus' assessment at face value.

---

[62]   LeVen (2014) 113–49 (quotations from 148).

Politics aside, the story embodies a profoundly competitive and hierarchical model of literary criticism. Along with all the other testimonia, it is based on a contrast between two figures who supposedly represent polar opposites, a technique which is fairly common in ancient literary criticism (a particularly good example from drama is the contest of Aeschylus *versus* Euripides in Aristophanes' *Frogs*). Here a first-rate, professional, clever, avant-garde poet is seen as competing against a 'wretched' amateur who is supposed to represent all the opposite values. Unsurprisingly, Philoxenus emerges as the 'winner'. But why should this be a foregone conclusion? As elsewhere, we are not told anything at all about the content, style or character of either poet's work, which makes it impossible to engage in a true comparison or critique. What we really need to know is which specific features of Dionysius' poetry were judged to be 'wretched' or 'pathetic'. But at any rate we do not need to accept Diodorus' heavily stylized, cartoon-like account on its own terms.

One notes that Diodorus' anecdote finds a close parallel in a scenario from Eubulus' comedy *Dionysius*. This is shown by a fragment from that play quoted by Athenaeus apropos of people who try to ingratiate themselves with others by showering them with hospitality and being amusing.[63] Dionysius is cited as an example of this sort of person:

> Dionysius behaved in a similar fashion, as the comic poet Eubulus makes clear in his play named after the tyrant:
>
>> With solemn people and all flatterers he is rather difficult to deal with,
>> but to anyone who makes fun of him he is perfectly pleasant;
>> indeed, in his opinion, these are the only people who are free,
>> even if they are slaves.

It is not clear exactly how this fragment fitted into the plot, but it seems that the whole situation and setting – including the underlying assumptions about mockery, free speech, the uneasy relationship between tyrants and flatterers, and the image of Dionysius as a figure of fun – is very closely comparable to Diodorus' narrative. It may even be that the whole Philoxenus story ultimately derives from Eubulus' comedy.

The story obviously became very well known throughout antiquity, and it is recounted or alluded to by other writers, often with variants which seem designed to add humour by further emphasizing the wretchedness of Dionysius' poetry.

---

[63] Eubulus F25 K-A (Athenaeus 6.260c) = *TrGF* 1.76 T12. See Hunter (1983) 118–19, who suggests that the fragment comes from the play's prologue.

Plutarch, for instance, repeats the anecdote about the stone-quarries, but adds a different punchline: 'when Dionysius ordered the poet to go through one of his tragedies and make improvements, Philoxenus crossed out the whole play from the first word to the final full stop'.[64] The 'letter of Philoxenus' (*Philoxenou grammateion*) became a proverbial expression, denoting those who refuse to accept an invitation on the terms offered. The *Suda* illustrates the expression by explaining that when Dionysius invited Philoxenus to make a return visit to Syracuse, the poet replied by sending a papyrus scroll containing nothing but the letter omicron (i.e. *No!*).[65]

Lucian's variation on the theme, in *The Ignorant Book-Collector*, repeats the same motifs but adds the curious detail that Dionysius attempted to improve his poetry by obtaining writing-tablets once owned by Aeschylus[66]:

> It is said that Dionysius wrote tragedy in a very feeble and risible style (*phaulôs panu kai geloiôs*), with the result that Philoxenus was thrown into the stone-quarries because of it on many occasions, as he was unable to control his laughter. And so Dionysius, when he realized that he was being laughed at, went to great lengths to get hold of the wax tablets on which Aeschylus used to write: he believed that he too would be inspired and possessed with divine madness if he owned these tablets. However, the verses that he wrote on the tablets were much more risible than before.

The phrasing here ('on many occasions') suggests that by this time the Philoxenus narrative had assumed paradigmatic status, but Lucian is more interested in its sequel. The most interesting thing about his own anecdote is that it assumes a world in which Aeschylus had already attained high cultural status as a 'classic' and in which there was already a fascination with collecting the memorabilia of famous authors.[67] It is hard to decide whether this is an accurate description of the first few decades of the fourth century, or whether Lucian is reflecting the cultural currents of his own time.[68] Nevertheless, a very similar detail is preserved in the anonymous ancient *Life of Euripides*, attributed to the third-century BCE scholar Hermippus[69]:

---

[64] Plutarch, *On the Fortune of Alexander* 2.1, 334c (*TrGF* 1.76 T13).
[65] *Suda* Φ 397 (*TrGF* 1.76 T14).
[66] *TrGF* 1.76 T11.
[67] See Gekoski (2004) for critical discussion of the mania for collecting writers' memorabilia in more recent times.
[68] Hanink's (2010) view is that these classicizing narratives 'do seem to have begun to coalesce relatively early on in the history of drama's reception' (41; cf. 46–8 on Dionysius).
[69] *Life of Euripides* 5 (*TrGF* 1.76 T10 = Hermippus F84 Bollansée).

Dionysius, after the death of Euripides, purchased from his heirs, for the sum of one talent, Euripides' writing-tablet, pen and lyre. He instructed those who had procured these items for him to place them in the Muses' temple and to label them with Euripides' name and his own.

In Lucian's account in particular, Dionysius is portrayed as an ignoramus, who believes that poetic talent can be acquired for money, or that inspiration can somehow be transferred to him via special objects. These items of memorabilia are thought to possess a magical or talismanic property because of their association with Aeschylus and Euripides; but whether or not this is actually true, it is made plain, either implicitly or explicitly, that Dionysius did not derive the expected benefit from his acquisitions. As in the case of the Philoxenus anecdote, the motif of competition underpins these accounts, along with a hierarchical distinction between the two earlier dramatists (good, inspired, venerated, classic) and Dionysius himself (bad, uninspired, deluded, epigonal). In other words, it is set up in advance as a 'generation gap' contest which the younger poet is bound to lose. But we are not bound to accept the evidence at face value. It is important to bear in mind that the writers who recount these anecdotes were predisposed to accept the notion of the 'classic' fifth-century triad and the inevitable inferiority of fourth-century tragedians.

It will be obvious by now that the task of writing a balanced general introduction to Dionysius' work presents serious problems. It is unusually hard to find a critical perspective on the source-material, practically all of which is comical, fictional, exaggerated, anachronistic, or downright hostile in its nature. In general, the factual content of this material is probably minimal. As we have seen, most of the testimonia are based on certain questionable preconceptions – not just the usual banal distinctions between 'good' and 'bad' poetry, or 'major' and 'minor' status, that have dogged the posthumous reputation of almost all our tragedians, but also certain underlying assumptions about the interface between politics and poetics. The challenge facing the literary historian is to try to read beyond all these jokes and simplistic put-downs, and to ask whether our sources can tell us anything at all about Dionysius' work.

As we have seen, many of the testimonia explicitly label Dionysius as a *bad* poet.[70] In general this sort of value-judgement is extremely problematic, as I have already observed in an earlier chapter. But in this particular case, at least, we

---

[70] *TrGF* 1.76 T1, 4, 5, 11, 13, 14, 15; only Cicero seems ambivalent (or ironical), saying that 'it scarcely matters how good a poet he was' (*Tusculan Disputations* 5.22 = T7). Cf. Webster (1954) 298 on Dionysius ('an exceedingly bad dramatist').

should try to avoid falling into the trap of assuming that an unpopular leader, being generally open to criticism in other ways, will inevitably produce inferior art. This is not only a lazy and prejudicial assumption; it is also precisely the assumption that a comedian such as Eubulus would make. No doubt we could list examples that seem to prove the point: such a list might include Nero's ludicrous acting, Hitler's watercolours, Mussolini's embarrassing foray into romantic fiction (*L'Amante del Cardinale*), and so on. But it can hardly be that all politicians and rulers are by nature untalented artists, or that it is impossible for a person to be successful in more than one field. It is hard to resist the conclusion that, essentially, criticism of a politician's artistic activities is equivalent to criticism of his politics: it tells us comparatively little about the art itself, and it tends to have a powerfully distorting effect.

We may prefer to make the more inconvenient assumption that Dionysius' tragedies were perfectly respectable or even better. After all, despite what these uncharitable anecdotists would have us believe, Dionysius did not merely inflict his poetry upon a small group of timorous yes-men or sycophantic dinner-guests in Syracuse. He competed much further afield, in front of audiences who were not obliged to admire him, and he won prizes at major festivals, including at least one first prize at the Athenian Lenaea of 367 and second or third prize in many other competitions.[71] Dionysius remained well known as a writer throughout posterity, and his works were quoted and anthologized more frequently than those of many other tragedians, which suggests that his plays remained in circulation for a long period.[72] We also happen to know that his literary activities were not confined to drama: he wrote in other genres including paeans, lyric poetry and history.[73] In other words, then, it is possible to see Dionysius as a versatile and successful writer, not a trivial dilettante or an embarrassing failure.

The question of how 'good' or 'bad' his plays really were would be impossible to answer definitively, even if all his plays survived complete, but the fragmentary remains do not suggest that Dionysius' poetry was egregiously bad. A number of lexical fragments reveal a fascination with etymological wordplay and unusual

---

[71]   Tzetzes, *Chiliades* 5.178 (*TrGF* 1.76 T3). It has been suggested that political motives lay behind these awards – see Suess (1966) 317–18; Sanders (1987) 16; Caven (1990) 209 – but there is no evidence for such a view, nor any reason to make this uncharitable assumption.

[72]   Stobaeus includes seven gnomic fragments by Dionysius (F2, 3, 4, 5, 6, 7, 8); F4 was also quoted as a maxim or proverb by Plutarch, Zenobius and others; F11 was quoted by both Lucian and Tzetzes; F1 is quoted by Athenaeus; various grammarians and etymologists cite one-word lexical fragments (F12a–l).

[73]   *TrGF* 1.76 T2, 8, 6, 15.

vocabulary,[74] which might lead us to expect that his style was difficult or odd, but all the other surviving fragments are written in clear and elegant Greek without any obvious tics or mannerisms.

More generally, the evidence seems to point to a poet of considerable originality.[75] Take, for example, the three verses which Lucian tells us were composed on Aeschylus' writing-tablets:

Doris, the wife of Dionysius, is dead.[76] [F9]

Alas! I have lost a useful wife. [F10]

Foolish people make sport of themselves. [F11]

The third of these fragments may seem to be a fairly conventional maxim, of a type widely found throughout tragedy. However, it becomes considerably more interesting when we learn (from the Byzantine scholar and poet Ioannes Tzetzes, who also quotes the verse) that it came from a play in which Dionysius criticized the philosopher Plato.[77] Tzetzes comments that this play was 'more comic than a proper tragedy'. Perhaps he is making some sort of comparison between Dionysius' play and Aristophanes' *Clouds*, which famously attacked Socrates, though it is not certain that he would have had access to the complete text of this tragedy: he is more probably repeating an anecdotal 'fact' handed down in the biographical tradition. Nonetheless, following Tzetzes' lead, Dionysius' play has been seen as a strange generic experiment, blurring the boundary between tragedy and comedy.[78] Unless this play should miraculously resurface, it is impossible to know whether or not this was the case. However, it is also possible that Dionysius' surprising choice of subject-matter is not a bold, genre-bending innovation but actually a deliberate return to an earlier type of tragedy, which is not attested since the time of Phrynichus and Aeschylus: that is, the real-life, contemporary historical drama previously exemplified by *Phoenician Women*, *The Sack of Miletus* and *Persians*. Either way, it is apparent that Dionysius was attempting something out of the ordinary – which suggests another explanation

---

[74] *TrGF* 1.76 F12a-l; cf. Suess (1966) 310–11, who finds parallels in Aristophanic wordplay and the nonsense verse of Christian Morgenstern.

[75] This is made clear by Suess (1966), though the word that Suess repeatedly uses to describe Dionysius and his work is 'weird' (*seltsam*). Cf. Duncan (2012) for an excellent recent attempt to rehabilitate the tyrant and his plays.

[76] Translating Hermann's conjecture Δωρὶς τέθνηκεν (the transmitted text, †Δωρικὸν ἦκεν, is corrupt): see Suess (1966) 302. Cf. Kannicht in *TrGF* 5, p. 1113.

[77] Tzetzes *Epistle* 1.4.5; cf. *Chiliades* 5.185 (see *TrGF* 1.76 F11 *ad loc.*).

[78] Both Suess (1966) 300 and Duncan (2012) 147 refer to this play as a 'tragicomedy'. Note also a certain amount of confusion in the ancient sources as to whether or not Dionysus wrote comedies: T2, T6.

why his work (regardless of its perceived quality) might have prompted strong reactions from critics or the general public.

The other two fragments quoted by Lucian (if they are indeed genuine) also relate to real-life subject-matter, but in an even more extraordinary manner. This is apparently not just contemporary tragedy but *autobiographical* tragedy, with Dionysius himself and his wife Doris appearing among the characters. If one can tentatively reconstruct something of the plot from these two lines, it seems that Dionysius composed the play about his wife's death and his subsequent lamentation.[79] Such a public display of grief, and the elevation of Dionysius' life and emotions to tragic or quasi-mythological status, must have made a big impact on the play's original audience (perhaps at Syracuse rather than Athens). This lost play also hints at the different uses to which tragedy could be put. Discussions of Athenian tragedy often centre around the political aspects of drama in relation to the state, but it seems that Dionysius' tragedy, at least on occasion, might have a very specific sort of political function in terms of the image of the tyrant that it projected to the public.

Was this the only tragedy in which Dionysius presented his audience with a portrayal of himself and his own thoughts? It has been thought that drama in Dionysius' Sicily functioned more generally as a vehicle for 'propaganda', and that in fact the tyrant routinely used tragedy in order to project a rose-tinted image of his own regime as one of justice and morality.[80] There is no way of knowing whether or not this was so, but it may be relevant that the fragments contain gnomic pronouncements such as the following:

> The eye of Justice, looking out from a quiet face, as it were,
> always sees all things equally. [F5]

> Tyranny is the mother of injustice. [F4]

Plutarch quoted the second of these fragments as an example of hypocrisy, or supreme irony, on the part of a tyrant who had killed tens of thousands of people,[81] and it may well be that some of Dionysius' original audience members shared Plutarch's opinion; but this does not preclude the possibility that these sentiments were specifically intended to show Dionysius and his rule in a positive light. Nonetheless, it is equally possible that these verses are no more than conventional restatements of moral truisms found elsewhere in tragedy and

---

[79] So Suess (1966) 302–3.
[80] Sanders (1987) 2–3; cf. Monoson (2012), Duncan (2012) 148.
[81] Plutarch, *On the Fortune of Alexander* 5. 338b.

Greek literature.[82] To treat these decontextualized quotations as if they had a privileged status – as the play's message or the author's personal opinions – is a somewhat simplistic way of reading dramatic texts, which are usually a good deal more subtle in the way they articulate their meaning. There is really no reason to assume that the lines just quoted reflect Dionysius' message to his subjects any more than do the other maxims in his plays, concerning the contrast between divine and human existence (F2), the old cliché that one cannot judge a man's fortune aright until he is dead (F3), the reflections on the value of silence (F6) and on envy (F7), or the contrast between rich and poor (F8).

Dionysius' attested play titles are *Adonis, Alcmene, The Ransoming of Hector, Leda,* and the satyr-play *Limos* ('Hunger').[83] All of these denote mythological subject-matter, which shows that not all of his plays were of the contemporary or autobiographical type – unless we are to suppose that he introduced real-life characters into mythical scenarios, a possibility which seems outré but not completely out of the question. The fragments are too meagre to allow us to say anything substantial about Dionysius' treatment of the myths. *Alcmene* presumably dealt with some aspect of the birth of Heracles, and *Leda* with the birth of Helen, but it is impossible to do more than guess at their plots. *Adonis* obviously dramatized the story of the archetypally beautiful youth Adonis, whose prowess as a hunter led to his downfall when he was killed by a wild boar sent by the jealous Artemis. Its single fragment is as follows:

> As I bring the newly-born wild boar
> beneath the covered cavern of the nymphs,
> I am spoken of as a lucky hunter,
> and I bring the boar's hooves to offer as first-fruits.

These lines were apparently spoken by Adonis himself early on in the play, and they refer to the custom whereby hunters would offer up the head and feet of their captured prey as gifts to Artemis or Pan.[84] No doubt the play exploited the

---

[82] E.g. Sophocles, *Oedipus Tyrannus* 873, F11; Euripides *TrGF* 5 F486; *TrGF* 2 *adesp.* F421; Philemon F246 K–A; see Olivieri (1950) 99–100 and Duncan (2012) 148, Xanthakis-Karamanos (1980) 123–6 compares other tragic texts concerned with retribution, e.g. Theodectes *TrGF* 1.72 F8, Aeschylus, *Eumenides* 538–44, Euripides, *Ion* 1619–22, etc.

[83] The title *Limos* presumably relates to the proverbially hungry Heracles, a character commonly featured in satyr-drama: see Suess (1966) 301–2; cf. Snell *TrGF* 1.76 *ad loc.* (p. 243).

[84] *TrGF* 1.76 F1. See Suess (1966) 313–16. I translate Suess' conjecturally reconstituted text (rather than the corrupt text transmitted by Athenaeus 9.401f and printed by Snell):

> νυμφῶν ὑπὸ σπήλυγγ' ἄγων αὐτόστεγον
> σύαγρον τὸν ἐκβόλειον, εὔθηρος κλύω
> ὁπλάς τ' ἀπαρχὰς ἀκροθινιάζομαι

poignant and ironical contrast between Adonis' prowess as a hunter and his later transformation into the prey. It is equally quite probable that it also contained an aetiological element, showing how Adonis came to be worshipped in religious cult,[85] but that is about as far as one can go.

Dionysius' most successful tragedy, *The Ransoming of Hector,* shared its title and some of its subject-matter with an earlier play by Aeschylus.[86] This fact is particularly suggestive in the light of Lucian's anecdote about the lengths to which Dionysius went to obtain Aeschylus' writing-tablets (discussed earlier). Even if the exact details of Lucian's story cannot be trusted, its main significance is that it presents Aeschylus as an established author with whom Dionysius wants to align himself in a special relationship. It may well be that in this play (and perhaps elsewhere) Dionysius deliberately set out to produce some sort of creative response, or *hommage,* to the older tragedian.[87] *The Ransoming of Hector* was a tragedy about Priam's visit to Achilles in order to recover the body of his son Hector. Something of its plot can be inferred from Ioannes Tzetzes' commentary to his own poem *Homerica,* which obviously treated this Iliadic story in a manner similar to Dionysius.[88] Tzetzes records that in Dionysius' play Priam came to Achilles on foot and alone, in contrast to Homer's version, in which Priam arrived on a chariot and with an entourage. He also says that Polyxena guided Priam and that Hector's wife Andromache and their two sons (Astyanax and Laodamas) accompanied them. All these characters were thus (somehow) involved in the plot, perhaps in central roles, though no precise details are supplied, and the text is corrupt and partly unintelligible. This is all that can be said for certain, despite speculative attempts that have been made to reconstruct the play's contents.[89]

In conclusion, it is hard to rescue Dionysius' poetic reputation from the very thorough demolition-job that was carried out by the comedians and other writers throughout antiquity. Perhaps he really was a rotten poet, and perhaps

---

[85] For the myth see Apollodorus 3.14.4; cf. Ovid, *Metamorphoses* 10. 519–741. On the cult of Adonis see Burkert (1985) 176–7.

[86] Aeschylus *TrGF* 3 F263–72. The play had an alternative title (*Phrygians*).

[87] This is the view of Grossardt (2005), esp. 228: 'eine solche kreative Bezugnahme auf Aischylos ist nicht verwunderlich bei einem spätklassischen Dichter, der bekannt war für seine Bewunderung für den einstigen Dichterfürsten'.

[88] Tzetzes, *Homerica* 311–19 with Σ *ad loc.* (Leone (1995) 200–201) = *TrGF* 1.76 (Addenda) pp. 354–5; Dictys of Crete (3.20–27) and Ptolemy Chennus (39.9) offer similar accounts. For exhaustive discussion of this evidence, including various different attempts to solve the textual problems, see Bühler (1973) and Papathomopoulos (1981).

[89] Most recently, Grossardt (2005) speculates that Philostratus (*Heroicus* 51) and Dictys of Crete (3.20–22) took the main elements of their account of the love affair of Achilles and Polyxena, and Achilles' subsequent death, from Dionysius' play.

his creative experiments did, on the whole, fail to please the public. There is not quite enough evidence to allow us to rebut these accusations. Nevertheless, careful and unbiased study of the remains, such as they are, can reveal tantalizing glimpses of a fascinating and in some ways unique tragedian.

Antiphon

Apart from the tradition, mentioned above, that Antiphon was murdered by Dionysius from motives of jealousy or self-preservation, biographical information about this tragedian is entirely lacking.[90] Presumably he is not the same person as the sophist and/or speechwriter of the same name, though these various Antiphons are often confused with one another.[91] Nevertheless, the tragedies of Antiphon are quite frequently discussed and quoted by Aristotle, who is the source of most of our fragments.

In his *Eudemian Ethics* Aristotle discusses the question of reciprocity in relation to love and friendship. His argument is too complex to summarize adequately here, but in essence he is talking about the sort of feeling described by Auden in his poem 'The More Loving One' ('If equal affection cannot be, Let the more loving one be me'). Aristotle maintains that 'a *philos* [i.e. friend, lover or relative] would choose to know a loved one rather than to be known, if it were not possible to do both – just as, say, women do in situations where they have given away their babies, as in the case of Antiphon's *Andromache*, for instance'.[92] It is clear that Antiphon's heroine was seen as a paradigm of motherly love, and that during the course of this tragedy she gave away one or other of her children (Molossus or Astyanax) to someone else – either by her own decision, in order to keep them out of the way and safe from harm, or because they were forcibly taken away from her after the capture of Troy.[93]

It may be that another Aristotelian passage (from the *Nicomachean Ethics*) is also connected to Antiphon's *Andromache*.

> The essence of friendship (*philia*) seems to consist more in loving than being loved. This is indicated by the joy that mothers experience in loving their

---

[90]   *TrGF* 1.55 T1–7.
[91]   How many Antiphons were there (one, two or three)? See Pendrick (2002) 1–25.
[92]   Aristotle, *Eudemian Ethics* 7.4, 1239a35–7 (*TrGF* 1.55 F1).
[93]   Xanthakis-Karamanos (1980) 45 compares Euripides, *Andromache* 47–8, 68–70, 309–10, which mentions Andromache's attempt to hide Molossus and so save him.

children; for some mothers hand over their own children to be brought up by other people, and they keep an eye on their progress and keep on loving them, not seeking to be loved in return (if they cannot have both), but it seems to be sufficient for them to see their children prospering. Such women love their children even if these children, on account of ignorance, give them nothing of the affection that is due to a mother.

This time there is no explicit mention of Antiphon or Andromache, but this discussion is very similar to the other passage, and most critics have accepted it, with caution, as evidence for the plot of the lost play.[94] A further, more doubtful piece of evidence is provided by a papyrus fragment first published in 1936.[95] This very badly preserved text represents part of an anapaestic lament sung by a woman who is mourning the death of Hector. As far as one can reconstruct the meaning, it seems that the singer is bewailing her own misery and the destruction of Troy, blaming Helen for everyone's current sufferings, and presenting herself as a mother addressing her son. This scenario corresponds (in a very broad sense) to what we know of Antiphon's play, but there is no real basis on which to make an identification, and the singer is not necessarily Andromache: it might just as well be Hecuba, apostrophizing her dead son at the side of his tomb.[96] In sum, then, our evidence for *Andromache* is far from secure, but there is just enough to allow us to say that it featured a striking, or even definitive, portrayal of motherly love and loss.

Antiphon's other tragedies included *Jason* – a title which could hint at another painful portrayal of the parent–child relationship, if its plot was anything like that of the numerous tragic *Medea*s by Euripides and others – but this play may have dealt with a quite different portion of the myth of Jason and the Argonauts, and the one-word lexicographic fragment that survives can tell us nothing.[97] Apart from a rather uninteresting gnomic fragment,[98] all that remains of Antiphon's other work is a two-line quotation from his *Meleager*, one of a number of tragedies which dramatized the myth of the Calydonian boar-hunt

---

[94] Aristotle, *Nicomachean Ethics* 8.9.1159a27–34: see e.g. Snell, *TrGF* 1 *ad loc.*, pp. 194–5; Webster (1954) 299; Xanthakis-Karamanos (1980) 41–6.

[95] Rejected by Snell but included as *TrGF* 2 *adesp.* F644; see Lobel (1936); Webster (1954) 299–300; Pack (1965) 1710; Xanthakis-Karamanos (1980) 42–5.

[96] See Kannicht *ad loc.* (*TrGF* 2, pp. 211–12) for discussion of various possibilities (though Kannicht thinks Hecuba an unlikely candidate).

[97] *TrGF* 1.55 T1a: 'they disposed' (*dietithoun*, an alternative form of *dietithêsan*).

[98] *TrGF* 1.55 F4: 'By skill (*technê*) we overcome those who would defeat us by nature (*phusis*)'. A further title (*Philoctetes*) and a couple of other lexicographic fragments (F5–6) are misattributed to Antiphon.

and Meleager's death at the hands of his mother Althaea.[99] These verses are quoted by Aristotle, who records that

> men picked out from the Aetolians came to Oeneus, Meleager's father,
>> not in order to kill the wild beast, but
>> to bear witness to Greece of the virtue of Meleager.[100]

Elsewhere Aristotle helps us to fill in a little more detail of *Meleager*'s plot[101]:

> Inferiors ought not to speak slightingly of their superiors; and they are angry with their friends, if they do not speak kindly or treat them kindly; and they are even angrier if they are actually unkind, or if they fail to perceive that they want something from them, just as Plexippus in Antiphon's tragedy was angry with Meleager. For failure to see this is a sign of contempt: when we have a proper regard for people, such things do not escape our notice.

This discussion is somewhat dense, but it shows that Antiphon's Meleager had failed to realize that Plexippus, his maternal uncle, wanted the Calydonian boar's hide for himself. In other accounts it is said that Meleager gave the hide to Atalanta, the virgin huntress who joined the expedition and with whom Meleager fell in love: it was this impulsive action that angered Meleager's relatives and fellow-huntsmen and set in motion the events that led to his death.[102] The clash of wills between Meleager and his uncle seems to have been at the centre of Antiphon's tragedy. Athenaeus also suggests this when he makes a passing reference to a book by Adrastus of Aphrodisias, a Peripatetic scholar of the second century CE. This work is *On Questions in Aristotle's Nicomachean Ethics*,

> in which Adrastus sets out a number of ideas about the Plexippus who appears in the work of the tragedian Antiphon, and also says a good deal about Antiphon himself.[103]

In other words, the character of Plexippus was considered interesting enough, and Antiphon himself was considered an important enough author, to be the subject of scholarly discussion five centuries after the original production of *Meleager*.

---

[99] As treated also by Phrynichus (*TrGF* 1.3 F5–6: see pp. 20–21 above), Aeschylus (*TrGF* 3 F241–4), Sophocles (*TrGF* 4 F401–2) and Euripides (*TrGF* 5 F515–37).

[100] *TrGF* 1.55 F2.

[101] *Rhetoric* 2.2. 1379b13–15 (*TrGF* 1.55 F1b).

[102] See Apollodorus 1.8.2–3.

[103] Athenaeus 14.673f (*TrGF* 1.55 F1b).

Dicaeogenes

Relatively little is known about Dicaeogenes. He is named in the *Suda* as a writer of tragedies and dithyrambs, though no more information is supplied; and a fourth-century inscription of uncertain date commemorates his victory at a rural Dionysia in the deme of Acharnae.[104] Nevertheless, his work was known and apparently admired by Aristotle, who discussed it on a couple of occasions, and selected excerpts were still being anthologized many centuries later.

In the *Poetics* Dicaeogenes' *Cyprians* is mentioned during the discussion of different types of recognition-scene in tragedy. The play is cited as an example of Aristotle's third type of recognition, in which some sort of visual stimulus jogs a character's memory – 'just as in Dicaeogenes' *Cyprians*, where he wept at the sight of the picture'.[105] This tantalizingly brief description tells us almost nothing about the play, not even the name of the man who experienced the recognition and wept. The play's title is unrevealing, and no other tragedy of that name is known to us, which means that we can only guess at its characters and plot. Teucer, who founded the city of Salamis on Cyprus, has been suggested as a possible candidate, as have Demophon and Acamas, who were also named as legendary settlers of the island, but nothing in their mythical traditions (as narrated in other sources) seems to suggest that recognitions or pictures were involved in their stories.[106] It is just possible that the word translated as 'picture' (*graphê*) refers to some form of written text, such as a letter, but this uncertainty seems to make matters more, rather than less, obscure.

But this evidence is not completely frustrating. In fact, it reveals three very significant facts about *Cyprians*. First of all, the play's plural title shows that it was named after its chorus, and thus demonstrates that (despite what is sometimes thought) the chorus had not altogether declined in importance within fourth-century tragedy. Secondly, if *graphê* really does mean 'painting' (the most natural reading), it shows that Dicaeogenes was capable of using props and visual aids in a striking way. A number of later classical tragedies show a preoccupation with visual art and the detailed description (*ekphrasis*) of artefacts,[107] but it is hard to think of another tragic example of a painting being

---

[104] *TrGF* 1.52 T1, T2; cf. Pickard-Cambridge (1988) 49–50 (who inclines toward the view that this inscription commemorates a dithyrambic victory, but this is far from clear).

[105] Aristotle, *Poetics* 16.1454b37–8 (*TrGF* 1.52 F1).

[106] See Lucas (1968) 170, Karamanou (2010) 392; cf. Sophocles' *Teucer* (*TrGF* 4 F576–8).

[107] See Zeitlin (1994), Stieber (2011), with particular reference to Euripides' *Phoenician Women* and *Ion.*; cf. Chaeremon (pp. 128–30 above).

used in quite this manner, in order to influence a major plot development. It also suggests that Dicaeogenes may have been interested in exploring the complex cognitive and emotional effects that an aesthetic object may have on the beholder.[108] Thirdly, the very brevity of Aristotle's reference to *Cyprians* suggests that this play – and the recognition-scene in particular – made an impact on its audience. The fact that Aristotle only needed to use this form of shorthand reference shows that his own audience or readers would immediately know what he meant without being reminded.

Aristotle also discussed Dicaeogenes in his lost work *On Poets*, and his discussion was in turn criticized by the Hellenistic writer Philodemus, as follows[109]:

> When Aristotle claims that 'tragedy contains several elements', that 'elements that are shared belong to the same art', and that 'Dicaeogenes used to compose lyrics that are not inferior to anybody's', let it be granted that 'tragedy includes several elements'. But no one will agree that 'elements that are shared belong to the same art', and everyone will burst out laughing upon hearing that Dicaeogenes used to compose lyrics not inferior to – let alone superior to – those of Simonides and Pindar, although he was so unsuccessful in his tragedies.

Richard Janko, Philodemus' most recent editor, remarks on the polemical or sarcastic-sounding tone employed here: 'Philodemus uses *praeteritio* to lambast Aristotle for comparing this mediocre tragedian with great lyric poets like Simonides and Pindar'.[110] Quite so; but it is important to remember that this is a first-century BCE writer, who saw literature as divided neatly into classic *versus* non-classic authors, and whose opinions (or prejudices) about what counted as good or bad tragedy had been formed in the post-Lycurgan tradition. Aristotle, writing three centuries earlier, had different priorities, and he at least seems to have viewed Dicaeogenes as an important and talented writer.

Perhaps Dicaeogenes really was a mediocrity, judged by some criterion or other. One notes that, as usual, no explanation or illustration is offered by Philodemus for his withering negative evaluation. But even if Aristotle's admiration for Dicaeogenes was misplaced, this extra piece of evidence shows us that Dicaeogenes' plays were still known in some sense, and their merits were still being debated, several centuries after his death. Even more importantly, it

---

[108] Cf. O'Sullivan (2008) on the way in which artistic imagery is used as a way of arousing emotions elsewhere in tragedy (Aeschylus, *Agamemnon* 239–42 and Euripides, *Hecuba* 807–8).

[109] Philodemus, *On Poems* 4 §119 Janko (= Aristotle, *On Poets* F27–30 Janko, pp. 422–3); cf. Dicaeogenes *TrGF* 1.52 T3: see Janko (2011) 220–1, 306–9, 422–3. I quote Janko's translation here.

[110] Janko (2011) 309.

confirms that Dicaeogenes' plays included lyrics and maintained a significant role for the chorus.

Apart from *Cyprians*, the only play that Dicaeogenes is known to have written is *Medea*. This powerful myth was obviously a popular subject for tragedians: apart from Euripides' famous version, we know of *Medea*s by Neophron, Carcinus, Melanthius, Diogenes and Theodorides. No doubt each subsequent treatment in turn reacted to the others, introducing new twists on the well-known material. Only the tiniest fragment of Dicaeogenes' version is preserved, in an ancient commentary on Euripides' *Medea*, but this source tells us that Dicaeogenes did indeed alter at least one detail of the myth, calling Medea's brother Metapontios (whereas other writers name him Apsyrtus).[111]

There are also four short gnomic fragments from unnamed plays, all of them preserved in John of Stobi's anthology.[112] These mostly embody conventional popular wisdom about parents and children. The first of them, though hopelessly corrupt, is a little more interesting, since it represents a rare tragic appearance of an erotic metaphor from archaic lyric poetry.[113]

> Whenever we are caught fast in love's hunting-nets
> †we are quicker to show gratitude to strangers
> than to those to whom gratitude is necessary, being members of the family†
>   (F1b).[114]

Patrocles

The few sources that mention Patrocles describe him either as a Thurian or as an Athenian, an inconsistency which may suggest that there were actually two tragedians of that name. The Athenian Patrocles was subjected to mockery in two Aristophanic comedies. In *Storks* (normally dated to about 390 BCE) Patrocles was described as a wealthy man but also tight-fisted, miserly, base-living and money-loving. In *Wealth* (produced in 388) the god Wealth is asked why he smells so bad, and he answers: 'Because I've just come from the house of Patrocles, who hasn't had a bath since the day he was born'. The ancient

---

[111] Σ Euripides, *Medea* 167 (*TrGF* 1.52 F1a).
[112] *TrGF* 1.52 F1b, F2, F4, F5. F3 consists of a heading only: Stobaeus was obviously intending to include verses from Dicaeogenes in his section entitled 'That it is a fine thing to have children' (4.24), but the quotation is missing.
[113] See Wright (forthcoming a).
[114] The text is corrupt, and this translation cannot be regarded as definitive.

commentator on this passage elucidates the joke by explaining that Patrocles was rich but too stingy to waste money on new clothes or laundry; and he adds that the expression 'from the house of Patrocles' had become a proverbial way of referring to dirty or smelly people.[115] As ever, it is hard to know exactly what to make of the comedian's jokes. Perhaps they simply denote the fact that Patrocles was a well-known poet and an easy target for ridicule (hostile or good-natured as it might be); or perhaps they are to be read literally, as evidence that the real-life Patrocles was indeed miserly and indifferent to personal hygiene; or perhaps they are equivalent to a form of critical comment on some aspect of his tragedies. Even if the last explanation is true, it remains difficult to see what sort of critical judgement is being expressed.

The other evidence is too meagre to tell us what Patrocles' tragedies were like. One source records that Patrocles ('the Thurian') wrote a play that featured the Dioscuri,[116] while another source cites a poignant seven-line fragment on the subject of frustrated hopes and the vanity of human endeavour[117]:

> But now all these extraordinary deeds and all these words
> have ended up gathered by fortune into this container so very small.
> Why, then, do we mortals utter many vain threats,
> letting fly terrible speeches at one another,
> and why do we think we can accomplish anything by our efforts,
> looking forward into the future? We do not perceive fortune standing by,
> under our very noses, nor do we see the approach of our wretched fate.

Here, as so often elsewhere in later classical drama, particular emphasis is placed on the unpredictable but inescapable power of Fortune (*tychê*). Perhaps this may seem to be a somewhat hackneyed theme, but the way in which the sentiments are framed here gives them an extra level of interest. It appears that the speaker is addressing these words to an urn full of ashes, using this small object as a physical focus for large reflections on mortality and as a simple but powerful way of evoking pathos. Perhaps Patrocles was influenced by a famous scene in Sophocles' *Electra* in which a funerary urn is used in a similar manner (Electra is seen holding and talking to what she imagines to be the remains of her brother); but the scenario also irresistibly calls to mind Hamlet addressing the skull of Yorick.[118]

---

[115] Aristophanes, *Storks* F455 K-A, *Wealth* 83–5 (with Σ) = *TrGF* 1.57-8 T1a–b.

[116] *TrGF* 1.57-8 F2 (Clement of Alexandria, *Protrepticus* 2.30.4).

[117] *TrGF* 1.57-8 F1 (Stobaeus 4.47.3).

[118] Sophocles, *Electra* 1126–59; cf. Shakespeare, *Hamlet* V.1. On the Sophoclean scene see Ringer (1998) 185–99, esp. 187: 'The urn compacts the fictitious corpse into a little room, much as the art of tragedy compacts into a small performable space the crises of existence'.

Cleaenetus

Like Patrocles, Cleaenetus is known to us partly because he was the subject of an obscure joke in a contemporary comedy. The following odd little exchange comes from a lost play by Alexis[119]:

> (*A*.) Bah to the man who ate the lupins! May he come to an untimely end! He's left the pods right by our front door, but did he choke when he was scoffing them? No – but in particular <. . .>

> (*B*.) I know that the tragic poet Cleaenetus hasn't eaten them, because he never threw away even a single seed pod – he's just such an omnivorous fellow!

Why was this supposed to be funny? Arnott, in his commentary on the fragment, says: 'we may safely guess that the tragic Cleaenetus had such a reputation for gourmandizing on every dish put before him that he would even consume lupin seeds, pods and all (and so never drop the pods as litter)'. This is the most literal interpretation of the joke, but there may be a less literal explanation. As I have pointed out in other chapters, there are in fact several other tragedians who were mocked by comedians on account of their supposed gluttony, including Melanthius, Morychus and Nothippus.[120] This further occurrence of the same joke makes it seem ever more likely that this is a stock theme or 'running joke' rather than a literal description of these poets' personal habits. In the other cases it was suggested that 'gluttony' may function as a metaphor for literary style, indicating prolix, bombastic or 'overweight' language. So it may be that Alexis is indirectly criticizing Cleaenetus' style, or that he is making some sort of connection between Cleaenetus and these earlier tragedians.

Sadly, the two surviving fragments of Cleaenetus' work tell us nothing about his style or any other aspect of his work. They are brief, quotable, utterly conventional maxims that might have been written by any tragedian[121]:

> It is a fine thing to die for the sake of one's parents.

> Anger and grief, when they come together in a single place within the soul,
> turn into madness for those who experience them.

Otherwise very little is known about this poet. The Hellenistic critic Philodemus dismissed him, along with his fellow-tragedian Carcinus, as 'good-for-nothing'

---

[119] Alexis F268 K-A (*TrGF* 1.84 T1): see Arnott (1996) 750–4.
[120] *TrGF* 1.23, 1.30, 1.26: see pp. 184–6, 193 below.
[121] *TrGF* 1.84 F1–2 (Stobaeus 4.25.5, 4.35.2).

(*ponêros*),[122] but as usual it is impossible to see just why these writers deserve such scorn: perhaps it is just that they have the bad luck not to be Aeschylus, Sophocles or Euripides. A speech by Aeschines makes reference to a 'chorus-trainer' (*chorodidaskalos*) called Cleaenetus who bought a house from the comedian Nausicrates: this may or may not be the same person as the tragedian. Finally, an inscription commemorates the fact that Cleaenetus won third prize at the Lenaea in 363 BCE with *Hypsipyle* and another play whose title – *Ph*[ ] – is only partially preserved. (*Phoenician Women? Phoenix? Phineus? Phrixus? Philoctetes?* Who can say?) Snell believes that this production was a 'dilogy', reflecting changes in the organization of the festival in the mid-fourth century,[123] but it may be that the didascalic record is incomplete, and in any case no one really knows what the normal programme of the Lenaea was, at this or any other period.[124]

Polyidus

Doubt has been expressed whether Polyidus wrote tragedies or not. He is mentioned in a few literary sources as the writer of dithyrambs and musically inventive lyric poetry, and he is commemorated in the Parian Marble as the winner of the dithyrambic competition at the City Dionysia *c.* 398-380 BCE.[125] None of these testimonia actually says that Polyidus was a tragedian, and the only surviving tragic fragment attributed to him is probably from Euripides' tragedy about Polyidus the Corinthian seer.[126]

The most significant piece of evidence comes from Aristotle's *Poetics*, where Polyidus is cited in connection with the fourth category of recognition-scene, i.e. the sort that involves reasoning alone. ('He said that it was probable for Orestes

---

[122] Philodemus, *On Poems* 2, col. 25.10 (*P. Herc.* 994) = *TrGF* 1.84 T3, 1.70 T7.

[123] *SEG* xxvi 203 col. ii.13 (=*TrGF* 1.84 T4; DID A2b 97): see Millis and Olson (2012) 118–21. Theodorides, commemorated in the same inscription, also seems to have entered two tragedies in 363: cf. apparent 'dilogies' by Timocles and Euaretus later in the 300s (*TrGF* 1.78a; 1.86 T3; 1.85 T2: see p. 192 below).

[124] Pickard-Cambridge (1988, 41) stated that even in the fifth century the Lenaea normally featured two tragedians competing with two plays each (and no satyr-play), but this is now disputed: see Luppe (2009), who suggests that the norm was three tragedies plus satyr-play, just as at the City Dionysia.

[125] See *TrGF* 1.78 T1–6. On the type of lyrics and music practised by Polyidus (including what ancient writers call his 'patchwork' style), see West (1992) 372; cf. Borthwick (1968) 61–2.

[126] *TrGF* 1.78 F2 *dubium* = Euripides, *Polyidus*, *TrGF* 5 F642, quoted with ambiguous attribution by Stobaeus 4.31.12 ('Money gives pleasure to people, and not just at a symposium or a banquet: it brings no little strength amid troubles').

to infer that his sister had been sacrificed and that he himself would be sacrificed'.)
The problem is that Aristotle's mode of citation here is ambiguous: he writes of
'the sophist Polyidus' work about Iphigenia', which some have taken as a reference
to a commentary on Euripides' *Iphigenia among the Taurians*, though it could
also be taken as some other sort of sophistic composition (along the lines of the
mythical speeches of Gorgias and Alcidamas, perhaps).[127] Nevertheless, it seems
much more likely that Aristotle is describing a tragedy. This is shown by another,
more extended discussion of Polyidus' work a little later on in the *Poetics*. Here
Aristotle is discussing the tragedians' use of myths: he advises that 'even myths
that have been the subject of previous tragedies would be set out in general
terms and then turned into episodes and elaborated'.[128] As an example of what he
means, Aristotle describes the plot of Euripides' *Iphigenia*, but he also mentions
Polyidus by way of comparison:

> A young woman has been sacrificed and disappeared, but those who sacrificed
> her do not realize this; she is removed and placed in another country, in which it
> is the custom to sacrifice foreigners to the deity; she becomes a priestess, and it
> later comes about that her brother arrives – the fact that the god made him go
> there and the purpose for which he went is external to the myth – and her
> brother arrives there and is captured; but when he is just about to be sacrificed,
> he brings about the recognition, either as Euripides or as Polyidus composed it;
> and Orestes says, in accordance with probability, that he (and also his sister too)
> had to be sacrificed; and this is how he escapes.

It is hard to see what this could mean except that Polyidus wrote a tragedy,
Iphigenia, which followed Euripides' play very closely in the outline of its plot.

It appears that Polyidus' version not only recalled Euripides' tragedy but also
made a significant modification to its most famous scene. The recognition-scene
in *Iphigenia among the Taurians* evidently became very well known in the fourth
century: not only was it discussed by Aristotle, but it was also the inspiration for
several vase-paintings depicting the very moment at which Orestes hands over
the letter to Iphigenia.[129] The point of Aristotle's discussion seems to be that in
Polyidus' play the recognition was brought about *solely* by means of inference,
and that the letter device was not used. This version chimes in with Aristotle's

---

[127] Aristotle, *Poetics* 16. 1455a6 (*TrGF* 1.78 F1): ἡ Πολυΐδου τοῦ σοφιστοῦ περὶ τῆς Ἰφιγενείας. See
       Lucas (1968) 170–1 and Karamanou (2010) 392–3 for a sceptical approach: Polyidus is seen as a
       commentator suggesting ways in which Euripides' version might have been improved.
[128] *Poetics* 17.1455b1–11.
[129] Trendall and Webster (1971) 3.27, 3.30(a), 3.30(b) (Ferrara Spina T1145, Moscow 504, Sydney
       51.17); cf. *LIMC* (s.v. 'Iphigenia' 19–26, 56–7) and Taplin (2007) no. 48, pp. 152–3.

view that the best recognition-scenes do not involve tokens or other such 'contrivances', though in that case it seems a little odd or inconsistent that he still admires Euripides' version the more. However that may be, Polyidus comes across as an interesting and original poet: he was responding to the well-known earlier play and perhaps also drawing attention to his own novelty, in much the same way as Euripides himself had done before. As we have already seen, this sort of intertextual activity is well attested throughout classical tragedy, and we can only guess at Polyidus' exact aims, but it has been suggested that his main innovation was to introduce an increased level of verisimilitude or psychological plausibility.[130]

Diogenes of Sinope

Diogenes of Sinope is another example of a tragedian who is famous chiefly for his non-dramatic activities. He was one of the founders of the philosophical movement known as Cynicism, which was concerned with practical ethics and, in particular, with the benefits of a simple life lived in accordance with nature. Diogenes and other Cynics advocated such ideas as the rejection of custom and the conventions of civilized society, the criticism of existing political structures, the importance of free speech, and the virtues of self-sufficiency, poverty and asceticism. Because of their antinomian views, the Cynics often came across as shocking or outrageous in their attitudes and behaviour.[131] Diogenes in particular seems to have deliberately set out to cause maximum provocation or offence. Much of our evidence for Diogenes' life and philosophical ideas is found in the sixth book of Diogenes Laertius' *Lives of Eminent Philosophers*. In this extraordinary account he is portrayed as a highly eccentric and independent-minded person, who habitually uses obscene language or bad behaviour in order to make a point. He gratuitously insults Plato and interrupts his lectures; he defecates in the theatre; he openly masturbates in public; he urinates on his fellow guests at a dinner-party; he encourages people to rob temples.[132]

Diogenes is said to have been the author of many literary works, including *The Republic* and *The Art of Ethics,* several philosophical dialogues, a number of letters, treatises on subjects such as wealth, love and death, and seven tragedies,

---

[130] Hall (2013) 71–4.

[131] See Desmond (2008) for an excellent recent survey of the Cynics and their beliefs; cf. Dudley (1937) on Diogenes' place within the movement.

[132] See esp. Diogenes Laertius 6.24–6, 46, 73; cf. Dio Chrysostom 8.36, Epictetus, *Discourses* 3.2.11.

which Diogenes Laertius lists as *Helen, Thyestes, Heracles, Achilles, Medea, Chrysippus* and *Oedipus*.[133] However, it is also stated that the authorship of some or all of these works was doubted in antiquity: the tragedies, in particular, were sometimes said to be the work of Diogenes' pupil Crates, his friend Philiscus of Aegina, or the later writer Pasiphon.[134] Indeed, it has been thought odd that Diogenes, who famously eschewed possessions and scorned all forms of conventional activity, should have left behind any written works at all.[135] Nevertheless, a substantial number of testimonia and fragments shows that Diogenes was widely regarded as a tragedian and that his plays were well known – or even notorious.

Furthermore, the evidence suggests that these plays (whoever really wrote them) were closely connected to Diogenes' life and activities as a philosopher, and that they were actually used as vehicles for propounding the precepts of Cynicism.[136] Of course many Greek tragedies have been seen as 'philosophical' in a general sense, but this description does not normally imply that they provide fully worked-out treatments of philosophical precepts, or that their aim is primarily didactic. In this respect Diogenes can be seen as considerably more philosophical than any other classical Greek tragedian known to us, and he also emerges as an important precursor to the Stoic tragedies of Seneca, several hundred years later.[137]

The remains of Diogenes' tragedies show that these plays were designed to be profoundly provocative and shocking. For instance, his *Thyestes* defended or even recommended the act of cannibalism, while his *Oedipus* lauded incest and parricide, and another of his plays was criticized for its obscene language.[138] According to Philodemus, in these plays 'Diogenes outlines most of the shameful and unholy deeds that are actually recommended as doctrines in his *Republic*'.[139] Another ancient critic, the emperor Julian, was appalled by these tragedies: 'what reader, coming to these works, would not abhor them, and judge them to contain an excess of unspeakable behaviour even worse than that of prostitutes?'[140] One

---

[133] Diogenes Laertius 6.80 (*TrGF* 1.88 T1).

[134] Diogenes Laertius 6.73; cf. *TrGF* 1.88 T3 (Julian, *Against the Cynics* 6.210c, 7.186c). Crates is listed separately as a tragedian in his own right by Snell (*TrGF* 1.90); cf. Diog. Laert. 6.98, who says that Crates 'wrote tragedies with a very lofty philosophical character'. Philiscus (*TrGF* 1.89) is discussed in Chapter 6: p. 198.

[135] Desmond (2008) 22; cf. Diogenes Laertius 6.80.

[136] Cf. Diogenes Laertius 6.87, where Crates is said to have turned to philosophy after watching a tragedy (*Telephus*).

[137] See Marti (1947).

[138] *TrGF* 1.88 T2–3, F1d, 1h.

[139] Philodemus, *On the Stoics* 16.29–17.4 (*TrGF* 1.88 T2): my translation is based on Hook (2005) 30–1 n. 59.

[140] Julian, *To the Cynic Heracleius* 6.210 (*TrGF* 1.88 T3).

could say, perhaps, that Diogenes' tragedies represented the literary equivalent of masturbating in public. Indeed, they have been called anti-tragic, parodic or comic in their outlook, or compared to the transgressive genres of satire and gangsta rap.[141] But this is not to say that they were not also serious in their outlook and purpose. They can be seen as making a profound philosophical point about the artificiality or arbitrariness of conventional morality, or the need for reasoned discussion (rather than socially conditioned prejudice) when forming ethical judgements. It seems likely that Diogenes employed shock tactics in order to make this point with the greatest possible impact. As one recent scholar points out, tragedy would have been a particularly good medium to adopt if one had such a strategy in mind, because 'for the Greek world of the fifth and fourth centuries BCE, it is the principal public articulation of the social and religious conventions that Diogenes attempted to undermine'.[142] Diogenes can be seen as appropriating an established and authoritative art form to reach a wider audience and to give rise to a greater amount of controversy or debate.

Nevertheless, there is no record of Diogenes' ever having produced any of his plays at a festival, and one cannot help wondering whether he would ever have won a prize, or made it onto a competition shortlist, with plays of this sort. It has been suggested that the plays were written for non-competitive performance or recitation: a possibility that cannot be proved or disproved, though there is no positive evidence in its support.[143]

Although several fragments survive (some of which are of doubtful provenance), not a single line is definitely preserved from any of the tragedies named by Diogenes Laertius. Nevertheless, we can assemble a rough idea of the plays' character and content from a miscellaneous collection of ancient summaries and critical discussions. For instance, Diogenes' *Thyestes* is (apparently) mentioned by Theophilus, Bishop of Antioch during the second century CE, in his *Apology to Autolycus*[144]:

> Since you have read much, what is your opinion of the teachings of Zeno, Diogenes and Cleanthes, which their books contain, inculcating the practice of eating human flesh? – that fathers be cooked and eaten by their own children, and that if anyone should refuse or reject a part of this abominable food, he

---

[141] Noussia (2006) 234–6; López Cruces (2003); Sluiter (2005).

[142] Hook (2005) 30.

[143] Bartalucci (1970–1) 133–4, followed by Noussia (2006) 230–2. Both scholars base this suggestion on Diogenes Laertius' description of Diogenes' tragedies as *tragôidaria* (6.80, apparently quoting Satyrus). But this diminutive form is more obviously interpreted as a sign of condescension or scorn; it does not (*pace* Bartalucci and Noussia) signify 'short dialogue-text dramas in iambic trimeters without choral parts' or 'brief self-contained dramas'.

[144] *Apology to Autolycus* 3.5 (*TrGF* F1d).

himself will be eaten? An utterance even more ungodly is found in the works of Diogenes, who teaches children to lead their own parents to sacrifice and then eat them.

Theophilus – if he has actually read the play rather than someone else's account of it – has evidently not been won over by its arguments.[145] It is significant that he regards the play as didactic in its intentions; but what *was* the lesson? Did Diogenes really aim to influence his more impressionable audience members into personally committing what most people would regard as atrocious acts? Or was he trying to encourage them towards a more complex or nuanced assessment of Atreus' and Thyestes' behaviour?

Diogenes Laertius' biography fills in a little more of the context, and gives us a better sense of the way in which the play represented the subject of cannibalism[146]:

> Diogenes argued that there was nothing irregular about stealing from a temple, or tasting the flesh of any animal. He even argued that there was nothing impious about eating human flesh, since (he said) this is a conspicuous habit among certain foreign races. Furthermore, he argued that, according to correct reasoning, all elements are contained in all other things and pervade everything: the constituents of meat are contained in bread; and the constituents of bread are contained in vegetables; and the constituents of all things are contained in other bodies, and by means of invisible particles and passages they make their way in and unite with all substances in the form of vapour. He makes this plain in the *Thyestes* – if the tragedies are really his work.

In other words, Diogenes (or his characters) attempted to explain and justify cannibalism by means of rational arguments. These arguments are not in themselves particularly novel: the blurring of the conventional distinction between Greeks and foreigners is quite common in Euripidean tragedy as well as the writings of sophists such as Protagoras and Antiphon, while the quasi-scientific content finds parallels in the cosmological theories of Anaxagoras.[147] But the application of such arguments to the myth of Atreus and Thyestes is apparently new. This subject had been dramatized by many earlier tragedians, but this was almost certainly the first time that anyone had attempted to show

---

[145] It remains possible that Theophilus is referring not to the play *Thyestes* but to a philosophical discussion: note that in 3.2 he refers to the 'philosophy' of Diogenes but the 'tragedies' of Sophocles and Euripides.

[146] Diogenes Laertius 6.73.

[147] See Dudley (1937) 30–1, who says that 'this is clearly a bit of popularized Anaxagorean physics, and it is strange to find it in Diogenes, who was so opposed to the natural sciences.'

Atreus in a favourable light, rather than taking the obvious and conventional course of presenting his butchery of Thyestes' children as a horrific crime.[148]

In a sense, of course, Diogenes was doing what all tragedians had always done: that is, finding new angles on old and well-worn material. His plays were undoubtedly brash, tasteless and idiosyncratic, but they were also ingeniously original reworkings of myths that had been presented in tragedy many times before – and in this respect they obviously achieved a certain *succès de scandale*. If we look at the evidence for the other plays, a similar picture emerges. In several places Diogenes' work reveals an unexpected attitude to famous myths. His own new versions might be described as counterfactual (in that they question or overturn facts that were normally accepted as the truth) or rationalizing (in that they question the specific details of myths and suggest alternative, down-to-earth explanations for unusual phenomena).

Diogenes' *Heracles*, for example, appears to have poked fun at traditional accounts of Heracles, especially his birth and apotheosis.[149] The play was almost certainly a source for Lucian's *Dialogues of the Dead*, in which Diogenes appears as a character in conversation with Heracles and asks some awkward questions. How is it possible for anyone to be half god and half dead? How is it that Heracles can live on, in a sense, after his death? How did Alcmene come to bear two Heracleses at the same time? Lucian's work concludes by showing Diogenes 'making fun of Homer and nonsensical stories (*psychrologia*) of this sort', a description which no doubt reflects his assessment of the character and tone of the playwright's work.

If F3 comes from Diogenes' play (rather than some other tragedy or author), this may help us to fill in some more detail about his treatment of Heracles. These verses are cited by Plutarch, in a mixture of quotation and paraphrase, in the course of a discussion about whether virtue (*aretê*) and vice (*kakia*) are substantial entities[150]:

ὦ τλῆμον ἀρετή· λόγος ἄρ' ἦσθ', ἐγὼ δέ σε
ὡς ἔργον ἤσκουν, σὺ δ' ἄρ' ἐδούλευες τύχηι,
ἀφεὶς τὴν πλουτοποιὸν ἀδικίαν καὶ τὴν γόνιμον ἁπάσης ἡδονῆς ἀκολασίαν.

Heracles: O wretched virtue! So you were a mere word, though I practised you as a reality – and yet all the time you were a slave to fortune . . . and so I gave

---

[148]　Cf. Hook (2005) 28: 'Diogenes evoked the horror to contradict it'.

[149]　Tertullian, *Apology* 14.9 (*TrGF* 1.88 F1c); cf. Lucian, *Dialogues of the Dead* 11.

[150]　Plutarch, *On Superstition* 1.165a (*TrGF* 1.88 F3 *dubium*). The same fragment is also quoted by Dio Cassius (47.49.2), who names Heracles as the speaker.

up wealth-producing injustice and also licentiousness that gives birth to every sort of pleasure.

It is hard to judge how much of this is quotation from Heracles' speech and how much is Plutarch's own description or interpretation. It is also difficult to see exactly how the figure of Heracles was depicted in this work. It may be that these lines are calling into question Heracles' traditional status as a paradigmatic embodiment of virtue.[151] Perhaps the play presented Heracles' fabled physical strength as an inadequate means of coping with life's challenges, or perhaps it showed Heracles' realization that his dedication to virtue could not save him from the superior power of fortune (*tychê*). Note that the second line of the fragment contains an intertextual echo of Euripides' *Heracles*[152]: this suggests that the play was not just a revisionist response to the mythical tradition in general, but it was also a sophisticated and self-aware piece of literature, designed to make its readers recall and re-evaluate Euripides' portrayal of the great hero.

No fragments of Diogenes' *Oedipus* survive, but part of its outline is suggested by Dio Chrysostom, the first-century CE orator who was heavily influenced by Cynic philosophy. Diogenes appears as a character in Dio's tenth oration (*On Household Servants*), in which it is argued that it is harmful and unnecessary to consult the gods. As an example of the dangers involved in the interpretation of oracles, Dio cites the myth of Laïus and Oedipus. It has plausibly been suggested that this narrative reflects the plot of Diogenes' *Oedipus*, since Diogenes is the speaker at this point in the dialogue.[153]

> [Diogenes said:] 'Oedipus did not go to Delphi to consult the oracle, but encountered Teiresias and suffered great misfortune through prophecy because of his own ignorance. For he realized that he had slept with his own mother and had had children by her; and later, when perhaps he ought to have concealed this fact or to have made it legal in Thebes, first of all he let everyone know what he had done, and then he became agitated and said, in a loud voice, that he was father and brother of the same children and husband and son of the same woman. And yet cockerels do not object to such relationships, nor do dogs, nor any donkey; nor do the Persians, even though they are held to be the finest race in Asia. And furthermore Oedipus blinded himself and then wandered around blind – as if he could not go wandering while he still had his eyesight.'

---

[151] See the illuminating discussions of Bartalucci (1970–1) and Noussia (2006) 237–40.
[152] Euripides, *Heracles* 1357: 'Now, so it seems, we must be slaves to fortune'.
[153] Dio Chrysostom 10.29–32. Snell does not include this text in *TrGF*, but Dudley (1937), Marti (1947), Hook (2005) and Noussia (2006) treat it as a significant piece of evidence.

On hearing all this, Diogenes' interlocutor replied: 'You, Diogenes, make Oedipus seem to be the stupidest person in the world! But the Greeks believe that, while he may not have been a fortunate person, he was the most intelligent of all men. At any rate, they say that he alone solved the riddle of the Sphinx.'

Diogenes let out a laugh and said: 'You're telling me that he solved the riddle? Haven't you heard that it was the Sphinx who told him to give the answer "man"? He didn't say or realize what he meant by saying "man", but when he said it he thought he was answering the question. It was just the same as if someone were to ask you "What is Socrates?" and you were to give no reply except the name "Socrates". I have heard someone saying that the Sphinx is synonymous with stupidity (*amathia*), and that this was what led to the downfall of the Boeotians in the past, just as it does now: their stupidity prevents them acquiring any knowledge, since they are the most stupid of all people. But anyway – while these others had some realization of how ignorant they were, Oedipus, believing that he was very clever, and that he had eluded the Sphinx, and had made all the rest of the Thebans believe him, perished in the most wretched way. For any who, despite their ignorance, believe that they are wise are much worse off than everyone else.'

We must treat this evidence with caution, but if it really is based on Diogenes' tragedy, it suggests that this play handled its myth in an original and surprising way. In the first place, it seems to have offered a justification of mother-son incest by reference to nature, through parallels from the animal world and from non-Greek civilizations; it even seems to have advocated the legalization of incest. In that case, its presentation of the issues will have been strikingly similar to the cannibalism debate in Diogenes' *Thyestes*. More strikingly still, the play apparently changed certain key aspects of the myth: Oedipus, who is elsewhere famed for his cleverness, is said by Diogenes to have been unusually stupid, and it is also implied that he had full knowledge of his own guilt from the start. The outline of the story remains more or less the same, but some details are undermined or treated with scepticism, even derision: Oedipus' self-blinding is seen as unnecessary ostentation, while the riddle of the Sphinx is exposed as a banal and childish misunderstanding. That the Oedipus myth in particular should be questioned or altered in this way is a further sign of Diogenes' status as a *provocateur*, since Oedipus is repeatedly cited throughout antiquity as the quintessential example of a myth that was universally well known and seemingly incontrovertible.[154]

As in the case of Heracles' lines quoted above (if genuine), it may well be that Diogenes was engaging with, or reacting against, specific earlier tragedies on the

---

[154] E.g. Aristotle, *Poetics* 13.1453b3–7; Antiphanes, *Poetry* F189 K-A.

same theme. Sophocles' *Oedipus Tyrannus* is the best known example in modern times, and perhaps also in Diogenes' own time (if Aristotle's *Poetics* is a reliable guide to fourth-century tastes), but several other tragedians wrote plays about Oedipus that might have served as sources, including Meletus, Nicomachus, Euripides, Aeschylus and Timocles. If, as seems likely, the riddle of the Sphinx played a prominent part in Diogenes' play, perhaps a special connection can be detected between Diogenes and his contemporary Theodectes. We happen to know that Theodectes' tragedies were famous for containing many riddles, and we also know that he too wrote an *Oedipus,* the only surviving fragment of which is a riddle.[155] It is tempting to suppose that Diogenes' scornful debunking of the Sphinx's riddle and its solution was not just a rationalizing account of the myth but also a polemical dig at Theodectes' version.

A further parallel for Diogenes' attitude to myth can be found in a rather different sort of writer. This is Palaephatus, whose work *On The Incredible* is conventionally dated to the mid- to late fourth century BCE.[156] Palaephatus is not thought to be a Cynic, but in his rationalizing approach to mythology and his contemptuous attitude towards credulous people he is closely comparable to what we know of Diogenes. In his book Palaephatus discusses several dozen well-known myths, first describing the normally accepted version before going on to offer an alternative, 'commonsensical' explanation of any abnormal or seemingly miraculous details. One of the mythical characters that comes under Palaephatus' microscope is the Sphinx, and, as in Diogenes' version, the riddle is seen as an implausible feature of the story.[157] Furthermore, writes Palaephatus, it is childish to imagine that those who cannot solve riddles would be devoured; and why did the Thebans not just shoot the Sphinx anyway?

It is not really necessary to claim that Palaephatus and Diogenes knew or influenced each other's work, any more than it is necessary to prove that Diogenes was consciously responding to Theodectes or any other tragedian. The value of these parallels is that they help us to place Diogenes' writing more securely within a fourth-century intellectual and literary context. He is not just to be seen as a freakish one-off, in other words, but he shares certain traits and preoccupations with other contemporary writers. Nevertheless, a further parallel between Palaephatus and Diogenes does seem to hint at a closer connection between the two.

---

[155] *TrGF* 1.72 T10, F4. See pp. 172–3 below.
[156] See now Hawes (2014) 37–92.
[157] Palaephatus, *Peri Apistôn* §4. Cf. Apollodorus 3.5–8 for what may be regarded as the standard version.

A later section of *On The Incredible* is devoted to the myth of Medea, and, in particular, the legend that Medea was a sorceress.[158] 'They say that Medea made old men young again by boiling them', Palaephatus reports. 'However, there is no proof that she ever rejuvenated anybody, and if she actually boiled anyone, surely this would have killed them'. His own more down-to-earth explanation is that Medea was the first inventor of hair dye and therapeutic steam baths. But in this case Palaephatus' rationalizing version of the myth is actually identical to that which was offered in Diogenes' *Medea*. According to John of Stobi's summary,[159]

> Diogenes said that while Medea may have been clever (*sophê*), she was not a sorceress. That is, she took on weak and feeble people, whose bodies had been ruined through overindulgence, and she made them strong and vigorous again by means of gymnastic exercises and steam baths. It is for this reason that the story arose that she boiled people's flesh and rejuvenated them.

A broadly similar explanation of Medea's actions is also given by Dio Chrysostom, whose work (as we have seen) shows affinities with Diogenes in other respects[160]:

> It is said that Jason anointed himself with a certain potent substance that he obtained from Medea, and afterwards, I believe, no harm came to him, either from the dragon or from the fire-breathing bulls. And so this is the potent substance that we ought to get from Medea – that is to say, from intelligence (*phronêsis*) – and from then on we ought to treat all such things with scorn. If we don't do this, absolutely everything will be for us as fire and unsleeping dragons.

This explanation, like that of Diogenes, removes the magical or supernatural element from the myth and replaces it with a more straightforward or realistic explanation, this time of an allegorical nature. It has been suggested that Diogenes allegorized the myth in order to exemplify the benefits of hard work (a Cynic virtue),[161] or that he portrayed Medea and Jason in the guise of ideal Cynics.[162] Until some more evidence should come to light, it is impossible to confirm these suggestions, but what is clear is that Diogenes' *Medea* rejected certain key aspects of the traditional myth. He seems to have removed the magical and supernatural element entirely and replaced it with an emphasis on rational intelligence and practical knowledge. No doubt he was aiming to surprise his audience, here as elsewhere, but it is interesting to note that he was not the only fourth-century

---

[158] *Peri Apistôn* §43.
[159] Stobaeus 3.29.92 (*TrGF* 1.88 F1e).
[160] Dio Chrysostom 16.10 (*On Pain*).
[161] Dudley (1937) 33.
[162] Noussia (2006) 234.

writer to offer a radically alternative account of Medea. Carcinus the Younger seems to have portrayed her, perhaps even more surprisingly, as innocent of the murder of her children.[163]

There remains very little more that can be said. Plutarch quotes a *bon mot* about a certain Melanthius, who, when he was asked to give an account of Diogenes' tragedy, replied that he couldn't see it clearly because there were so many words in the way.[164] This suggests that the plays contained a lot of rhetorical and argumentative content – a suggestion which would fit in well with their philosophical purpose and controversial themes. But (alas) hardly any of these words survive.

Only two fragments are definitely attributable to Diogenes' plays. The first, quoted by the early Christian writer Clement of Alexandria,[165] is an attack on luxury and self-indulgence from a typically Cynical perspective:

> What is luxury, other than voluptuous gluttony and the excessive abundance of people who have abandoned themselves to self-indulgence? Diogenes makes the following trenchant remark in one of his tragedies:
>
> > Those whose hearts have been stuffed full
> > of the pleasures of effeminate and filthy luxury
> > do not want to exert themselves even in the smallest way.

The second is a quotable gnomic two-liner about the power of fortune (*tychê*).[166]

> I wish for a drop of fortune rather than a whole jar of intellect;
> if fortune is absent, intellect fares badly.

To what extent does human experience depend on luck or on other factors? This theme may have featured in Diogenes' *Heracles* (F3: see above), but it was important to the Cynics and other fourth-century thinkers more generally.[167] It is recorded that Diogenes himself, when asked what he had learned from philosophy, answered: 'If nothing else, it has taught me to prepare for every change of fortune'.[168]

---

[163] *TrGF* 1.70 F1e; see pp. 112–14 above.
[164] Plutarch, *On Listening to Lectures* 41c–d (*TrGF* 1.88 T4). Is this Melanthius one of the tragic poets of that name (*TrGF* 1.23, 1.131)? See Hunter and Russell (2011) 114–15 on the problems of identification.
[165] *TrGF* 1.88 F1h (Clement, *Stromata* 2.20).
[166] *TrGF* 1.88 F2 (Theodore Hyrtakenos, *Epistle* 17).
[167] See Desmond (2008) 162–83 on the Cynics' interest in *tychê*; cf. Demetrius of Phaleron's treatise *On Tychê* (fr. 81 Wehrli = Diodorus Siculus 31.10, Polybius 29.21). See also Xanthakis-Karamanos (1980) 132–5 on *tychê* in other fourth-century tragedies. However, it was already a theme of tragedy in the fifth century: see the discussion of Agathon above (pp. 75–7).
[168] Diogenes Laertius 6.63.

A couple of further fragments are more difficult to place. They are definitely attributed to Diogenes by the writers who quote them, but it is not certain whether they are lines from his tragedies. These quotations certainly look like tragic verses, but in each of them Diogenes is apparently describing himself. The first one comes from Diogenes Laertius' biography[169]:

> He used to say that he was assailed by tragic curses, or, at any rate, that he was
> > Cityless, homeless, deprived of his fatherland,
> > a beggar, a wanderer, living from day to day.

The second comes from Plutarch, who says that it was a description by Diogenes of the philosopher Antisthenes[170]:

> He who clothed me in rags and forced me
> to become a beggar and an outcast from my home ...

It may be that the author was simply comparing himself to tragic characters, for the sake of wit, irony or genuine pathos. But if these really are quotations from a play, it seems that Diogenes may have been experimenting with the 'autobiographical' type of tragedy otherwise exemplified only by Dionysius of Syracuse.

The remaining two less securely attested fragments (F6 and F7, both from John of Stobi) are tentatively assigned to Diogenes because of their preoccupation with the Cynic virtues of hard work and a simple lifestyle in accordance with nature,[171] but they might be the work of anyone at all.

Theodectes

The interface between drama and oratory has long been recognized as an important aspect of Greek culture.[172] From the fifth century onward a number of tragic and comic dramas reveal the influence of the law courts, forensic oratory or the rhetorical theories of the sophists (one thinks particularly of Aeschylus' *Eumenides,* Euripides' *Orestes,* and Aristophanes' *Wasps* and *Clouds*). Several

---

[169] Diogenes Laertius 6.38 (= *TrGF* 1.88 F4); cf. Aelian, *Historical Miscellany* 3.29 for the same story and quotation.

[170] Plutarch, *Quaest. Conv.* 2.1.7. 632e (*TrGF* 1.88 F5).

[171] See Desmond (2008) 150–9 on various Cynical ideas associated with these fragments, e.g. self-sufficiency (*autarkeia*), natural toughness, adaptation to the environment, the ability of nature to supply all bodily needs, etc.

[172] See esp. Hall (1995) and the contributors to Harris, Leão and Rhodes (2010).

tragedies, especially those by Euripides, involve their central characters in set-piece debates (*agônes*), making prominent use of the latest modes of forensic argumentation to set out or defend a position.[173] Conversely, many real-life law court speeches also made use of quotations or tropes from tragedy as a way of making their case more persuasive or adding colour to their arguments.[174] Nevertheless, hardly any tragedians ever seem to have practised as professional orators themselves: Theodectes is one of only two known examples.[175]

The *Suda* and several other sources tell us that Theodectes was a native of Phaselis in Lycia who moved to Athens to study rhetoric under Isocrates (and perhaps also Aristotle, though this fact has been doubted since Aristotle was younger than Theodectes). He was a famously beautiful young man (compared to Alcibiades in this respect), who achieved success in his own right as an orator before turning to tragedy relatively late in his career and making an even bigger success as a dramatist.[176] He is said to have written numerous speeches, treatises on the art of rhetoric (*rhêtorikai technai*), and fifty plays. After his death his achievements were lavishly commemorated. A statue of Theodectes stood in the market-place at Phaselis, where Alexander the Great came to pay homage to it.[177] At Athens a monument to Theodectes was erected by the side of the sacred road to Eleusis, adjacent to the statues of Homer and other famous poets.[178] And when he died, the following funerary epigram was composed in his honour[179]:

> This patch of earth hides in its bosom Theodectes of Phaselis,
>> he whom the Olympian Muses made to flourish.
> In thirteen sacred contests of tragic choruses
>> I put on eight immortal crowns of victory.

Eight first prizes in thirteen competitions certainly constitutes an unusually high success rate. The information in this epigram is supplemented by independent epigraphic evidence from the Athenian Dionysia victors' list.[180] In this inscription it is said that 'Theodectas' (apparently the Doric spelling of his name, which is adopted by Snell in his edition) won *seven* Dionysia victories, the first of which

---

[173] E.g. Sophocles, *Ajax, Antigone, Electra*; Euripides, *Alcestis, Medea, Electra, Hippolytus, Hecuba, Orestes, Cretan Women*, etc. See Duchemin (1968); Conacher (1981); Lloyd (1992) for detailed analysis.

[174] See Perlman (1964) and Wilson (1996) for references and discussion.

[175] The other is Aphareus (*TrGF* 1.73 T1–2; see Chapter 6, p. 188); Astydamas (*TrGF* 1.60 T1) is said, more vaguely, to have been influenced by Isocrates.

[176] *Suda* Θ 138 (*TrGF* 1.72 T1); cf. T2, T5–13.

[177] Plutarch, *Alexander* 17. 674a (*TrGF* 1.72 T4).

[178] [Plutarch] *Lives of the Ten Orators* 837c; Pausanias 1.37.4 (*TrGF* 1.72 T7).

[179] Eustathius, *On Dionysius Periegetes* 855 (*TrGF* 1.72 T2).

[180] *IG* ii² 2325. 45 (*TrGF* 1.72 T3 = DID A3a. 45).

was shortly after 372 BCE. This figure does not contradict the epigram; it simply means that one of Theodectes' victories was won at another festival.[181]

Theodectes' fame as an orator spread beyond Athens, and there is a tradition that in 353 he was invited to enter a competition to compose a funeral oration for Mausolus, the ruler of Caria. This competition is mentioned by Aulus Gellius when he is discussing the Mausoleum at Halicarnassus[182]:

> When Artemisia dedicated this monument, which was sacred to the deified spirit of her husband Mausolus, she established a competition to sing his praises, and offered very substantial prizes of money and other valuable goods to the winner. It is reported that three men, distinguished for their outstanding talent and eloquence, came forward to compete with eulogies to Mausolus: these were Theopompus, Theodectes and Naucrates. There are even some who say that Isocrates himself entered the competition alongside these men. However, Theopompus was judged the winner in this contest: he was Isocrates' pupil. Theodectes' tragedy *Mausolus* is still extant today; and Hyginus in his *Exempla* writes that in this play Theodectes was more pleasing than in his prose works.

It is interesting to see that Theodectes wrote both a eulogy and a tragedy on the same theme, though the relationship between the two works, and the circumstances in which the tragedy *Mausolus* was performed, are not quite clear. Was there a separate tragic competition alongside the rhetorical contest? There is no parallel for such a scenario, in which several different tragedians would have to be imagined as competing with plays on exactly the same topic, but the possibility is an intriguing one. Whatever its exact circumstances of production, it seems certain that *Mausolus* was an unusual tragedy in several respects: it was performed in Halicarnassus, and has been seen as part of a wider cultural programme of Hellenization there;[183] it was a comparatively rare example of a tragedy based on historical or real-life themes rather than myth;[184] it was written by appointment to the ruling family; and it had a straightforwardly commemorative or eulogistic function. Furthermore, it was still being admired a couple of centuries later by Hyginus, a Roman historian and literary scholar of

---

[181] Cf. Pickard-Cambridge (1988) 41; but there is no way of knowing what the other festival was. See Snell (*TrGF* 1 pp. 227–8) for various inconclusive attempts to divide the attested total of fifty plays into tetralogies/trilogies/dilogies.

[182] Aulus Gellius, *Attic Nights* 10.18.5–7 (*TrGF* 1.72 T6); cf. T1, 5.

[183] See Hornblower (1982) 333–6, who also makes the intriguing (but unprovable) suggestion that this tragedy linked Mausolus with an eponymous local hero and river-god as a way of legitimizing his rule (cf. Euripides' *Archelaus* for a similar strategy).

[184] Cf. Phrynichus (*Phoenician Women* and *Sack of Miletus*), Aeschylus (*Persians*), Dionysius of Syracuse and (perhaps) Diogenes of Sinope (see pp. 23–7, 139–41, 163 above); the Hellenistic tragedian Moschion later wrote a *Themistocles* (*TrGF* 1.97 F1; cf. Kotlińska-Toma (2014) 128–30).

the first century BCE: this implies that *Mausolus* was deemed to be more of an artistic success than other contemporary-themed tragedies (which might be dismissed as propaganda, as in the case of Dionysius' plays, or banned, as in the case of Phrynichus' tragedy about the Milesians). Sadly, nothing of it survives except its title.

The fact that Theodectes was an orator might lead us to assume that his tragedies had a notably 'rhetorical' character, and that they were enlivened (or deadened as it might be) by a preponderance of *agôn*-scenes and polished argumentation,[185] but this is not conclusively demonstrated by the fragments. It is true that they are cited several times by Aristotle as providing examples of specific rhetorical devices or types of argument, but this does not prove that Theodectes' plays were *pervasively* rhetorical in their style, and after all Aristotle cites many other tragedians to illustrate individual points here and there. It is also true that many of Theodectes' fragments take the form of quotable maxims, which are viewed by Aristotle as especially effective rhetorical devices to win over an audience,[186] but (as we have seen many times before) tragedy is full of maxims. The most rhetorical fragment is F10, which explicitly mentions an *agôn* ('contest', 'debate' or 'trial'), 'words', 'accusation' and 'judging', but this quotation, a mere seven lines in length, comes down to us without any sort of context.[187] We would need to have a complete play in front of us, or at least a whole scene, in order to make a proper assessment of the function of rhetoric or its prevalence within Theodectes' work.

Theodectes' *Ajax* is mentioned on three occasions in Aristotle's *Rhetoric* with regard to some of the arguments used by its characters. Aristotle does not quote directly from the play, but his summaries and descriptions tell us a small amount about its contents. The three relevant passages are as follows[188]:

> Another topic consists in treating one possible cause of something as if it were the actual cause – such as might be the case if one were to give a present to somebody in order to cause him distress by depriving him of it [...] for example, as in the situation that we find in Theodectes' *Ajax*: that Diomedes chose Odysseus in preference to anyone else, not in order to honour him, but in order that his companion might be someone inferior, for it is conceivable that this was his reason.

---

[185] Cf. Xanthakis-Karamanos (1980) 59–69.
[186] Aristotle, *Rhetoric* 2.21, 1394a–95b; 3.17, 1418a.
[187] There is no reason to think, as Xanthakis-Karamanos (1980) 67–8 seems to do, that the fragment comes from Theodectes' *Helen*.
[188] Aristotle, *Rhetoric* 2.23, 1399b28, 1400a27–8; 3.1416b12–17 (*TrGF* 1.72 F1).

Another topic consists in explaining the reason for the misapprehension, whenever people or things have been (or seem to have been) slandered; for there is always some reason why things appear as they do. [...] For example, in Theodectes' *Ajax*, Odysseus speaks to Ajax, explaining why, even though he is braver than Ajax, he is not considered to be braver.

Another method of argumentation is shared by prosecutor and defendant alike. Because the same act might have been committed for several different reasons, the accuser must criticize it by attaching the worst possible interpretation to it, whereas the defendant must show it in a better light. For example, when Diomedes chose Odysseus as his companion, on the one hand it may have been because he considered him the best of men, but on the other hand it may have been only because Odysseus was no rival for him, since he was a mean sort of fellow.

The most familiar tragic version of Ajax's story is Sophocles' *Ajax,* which centres on the unbearable humiliation suffered by Ajax on account of the Greeks' decision to award the arms of Achilles to Odysseus, whom he considers his inferior. Towards the end of Sophocles' play, after Ajax's suicide, Odysseus comes on stage to talk about the long-standing hostility that existed between Ajax and himself, and he concedes that Ajax was the best and bravest of all the men who fought at Troy.[189] This speech has some features in common with the content of Theodectes' play, as described by Aristotle. However, in Sophocles' version the award of the arms has already taken place before the plot begins, and the action concentrates on the aftermath of this decision. It is possible that Theodectes' play dramatized an earlier stage in the story. The arguments reported above could be seen as corresponding to an episode in the tenth book of the *Iliad* (also known as the 'Doloneia'), in which Diomedes goes in search of a companion to accompany him on a dangerous night mission behind Trojan lines. A number of leading Greek heroes volunteer their services, including Ajax and Menelaus as well as Odysseus, but Odysseus, fearing that someone else will be chosen instead of him, wins Diomedes over with the following speech[190]:

Diomedes, son of Tydeus, dear to my heart, it is up to you to make a free choice of your companion, and you must choose whoever seems the best of those that offer themselves: there are many eager volunteers, at any rate. But in your reverent heart do not leave the better man behind and take as your companion one who is worse, yielding to reverence and looking only to birth, not even if someone here is more kingly.

189 Sophocles, *Ajax* 1334–45.
190 Homer, *Iliad* 10. 218–53 (esp. 234–40).

Diomedes consequently chooses Odysseus to go by his side, a decision that marks another stage in the developing enmity between Odysseus and Ajax. It may be that Theodectes' play was based on the Doloneia or other material from the epic tradition, avoiding Ajax's later madness and suicide as dramatized by Sophocles. However, Ajax is not a major character in the Doloneia, which makes it hard to imagine how Theodectes would have constructed his plot on such a basis.

Another (I think more likely) possibility is that Diomedes' choice of Odysseus as his comrade was referred to by Theodectes in some sort of flashback scene or narrative of past events. Aristotle leaves it unclear whether or not Diomedes was among the characters, but he does explicitly say that the play included a scene in which Odysseus speaks to Ajax. It is clear that they argued about how Diomedes could have come to choose Odysseus over Ajax, but it may be that this was part of a dispute about which of the two heroes should win the arms of Achilles, or even a formal *agôn* on this topic between the two characters.[191] This is suggested by the fact that precisely such a scene is found in other literary texts. In Ovid's *Metamorphoses*, for instance, the two heroes confront one another in a balanced pair of long speeches, each arguing that they themselves deserve the prize.[192] Ovid's Odysseus (Ulixes) says to Ajax:

> Who among the Greeks praises you or seeks you out? But the son of Tydeus shares his exploits with me, gives me his approval, and always chooses Ulixes as his special companion. That is something – to be singled out by Diomedes from so many thousand Greeks!

Could it be that Ovid used Theodectes' tragedy as his inspiration when writing this scene? As usual, there is no way of proving such a suggestion, but a formal debate over the award of Achilles' arms seems to provide a plausible context into which the arguments mentioned by Aristotle would fit. In that case, it is also possible to identify a couple of other possible sources or parallels for Theodectes' play: Aeschylus wrote a tragedy called *The Award of the Arms* in which Ajax and Odysseus were seen as in dispute, and we know that the lost epic known as the *Little Iliad* dealt with the same incident.[193]

---

[191] This is suggested by Xanthakis-Karamanos (1980) 65–6.

[192] Ovid, *Metamorphoses* 13. 1–122 (Ajax) and 123–381 (Ulixes); lines 238–42 are quoted here. Quintus of Smyrna, *Posthomerica* 5.1–332 also includes a similar debate between the two heroes. But the motif of the clash over the arms goes back at least as early as the fifth century BCE, as in (e.g.) Antisthenes' *Ajax* and *Odysseus*: see Caizzi (1966) F14–15.

[193] Aeschylus, *Hoplôn Krisis* (TrGF 3 F174–8); cf. *Little Iliad* F2 Davies (in which Greeks below the Trojan walls 'eavesdrop on conversation concerning the respective bravery of Ajax and Odysseus'): see Davies (1989b) 61–3.

Theodectes' *Alcmeon* was based on the well-known myth of Alcmeon, the leader of the Epigoni (sons of the Seven against Thebes), who killed his mother Eriphyle after discovering that she had accepted bribes to persuade her husband and son to go to war, and was subsequently hounded by the Furies. This myth was a popular subject for tragedians throughout the classical period – including Achaeus, Agathon, Sophocles, Astydamas and others – and it was cited by Aristotle in the *Poetics* as an example of a story that was universally familiar (and thus impossible to change or modify).[194] It is hard to imagine what new perspective Theodectes managed to bring to the myth, but it seems that his version involved some sort of attempt by Alcmeon to justify his behaviour. Aristotle's *Rhetoric* once again supplies the vital evidence[195]:

> One must consider separately whether the sufferer deserved to suffer, and whether the one who acted was right in acting as he did, and then one must make use of the argument as it fits best in either case. This is because there is occasionally a difference in cases of this sort, and there is nothing to prevent such an argument – just as in Theodectes' *Alcmeon*:
>
> Was there no one among the human race who hated your mother?
>
> Alcmeon said in reply:
>
> Yes, of course there was, but first we must make a distinction and look.
>
> And when Alphesiboea asked 'How?', Alcmeon responded:
>
> They judged that she should die, but that it was not for me to kill her.

The presence of Alphesiboea as a character shows that the action of the play took place long after the matricide. Alcmeon, having been driven from Argos and having travelled far and wide across the Greek world in search of purification, arrived at the home of king Phegeus in Psophis and married Phegeus' daughter Alphesiboea. But that was not the end of his story: various accounts of the myth detail Alcmeon's subsequent wanderings and adventures, as well as a further marriage (to Achelous' daughter Callirhoe).[196] So it is not quite clear what portion of the story was dramatized by Theodectes, but perhaps the fragment above belongs to a point soon after Alcmeon's arrival in Psophis, when he is still a relative stranger to Alphesiboea

---

[194] Aristotle, *Poetics* 1453b22–5. Cf. my discussion of Agathon's *Alcmeon* in Chapter 3 (pp. 85–6).
[195] Aristotle, *Rhetoric* 2.23, 1397b3–7 (*TrGF* 1.72 F2).
[196] The myth is narrated by Pausanias, *Description of Greece* 8.24.7–10; cf. the longer account in Apollodorus 3.6–7 (where Phegeus' daughter is called Arsinoe), Thucydides 2.102, Ephorus *FGrHist* 70 F123, etc. Cf. also Euripides' *Alcmeon in Psophis* (*TrGF* 5 F65–72).

and giving her an account of his past life and misdeeds. The only other surviving lines from the play (F1a) take the form of a gnomic reflection:

> It is true, the saying that is recounted far and wide among mortals,
> that there is no creature more wretched than womankind.

Obviously the myth involves its fair share of female characters who might be called unfortunate, but it is impossible to connect this utterly conventional sentiment with any particular character or situation.

The myth of Alcmeon obviously shares many of its central elements – revenge, matricide, madness, exile and purification – with the better attested myth of Orestes.[197] Thus Theodectes' *Orestes* must have had certain similarities with his *Alcmeon*, and though even less is known about this other tragedy, it is clear that his Orestes also attempted to explain or justify his crimes. Aristotle quotes part of Orestes' self-defence apropos of what he calls the fallacy of combination or division (i.e. treating several separate points as one, or dividing a single point up and treating it as several separate points)[198]:

> For example, the fallacy of division is seen in Theodectes' *Orestes:*
>
> 'When a woman has killed her husband, it is right'
>
> that she should be put to death, and that the son should avenge his father –
> and accordingly these deeds that have been done are also just. But perhaps it is
> *not* right if the two acts are combined. It may be that this is also an example of
> the fallacy of omission, since it is not stated by whom the woman should be put
> to death.

But it is impossible to tell from this brief account whether Theodectes' Orestes came up with any original arguments that had not already been made in Aeschylus' *Eumenides*, Euripides' *Orestes* or elsewhere; nor is there any evidence for the suggestion that this play contained a courtroom trial scene.[199]

Theodectes' other plays included a *Tydeus*, known only through Aristotle's brief mention of it in the *Poetics* as an example of his fourth type of recognition-scene (the type that arises from reasoning or inference alone, as in Polyidus' *Iphigenia*). We are told that one of the characters inferred that 'having come in search of his son, he himself was going to die', but nothing more is said. It is not

---

[197] See Delcourt (1959) for a comparative study.
[198] Aristotle, *Rhetoric* 2.24, 1401a35–b3 (*TrGF* 1.72 F5). The second line of the quotation is reconstructed by Snell from Aristotle's prose paraphrase.
[199] Xanthakis-Karamanos (1980) 66–7.

even clear whether Aristotle is talking about Tydeus himself (going in search of Diomedes) or Tydeus' father Oeneus (going in search of Tydeus following the latter's banishment from the kingdom of Calydon),[200] and nothing resembling the situation so cryptically described here seems to be attested elsewhere in the literary tradition.

Theodectes also wrote a *Helen*, in which the central character apparently appeared in the guise of a slave. This suggests a scenario similar to that of Euripides' *Women of Troy*, where Helen is rounded up along with all the other captured women from the sacked city, to be assigned as slaves or concubines to the conquering Greeks.[201] Yet again Aristotle is our only source for this tragedy: he quotes a couple of lines from it in his *Politics*, when he is discussing the question of whether people can be slaves by nature[202]:

> It is just the same when one considers nobility (*eugeneia*): our aristocrats consider themselves noble not only among their own people but wherever they happen to be; but they think that barbarian noblemen are noble only in their own country – making the assumption that there are two separate types of nobility and freedom, one absolute and the other relative, as for instance Theodectes' Helen says:
>
> > Who would think it right to address me as a servant, when I am
> > the descendant of divine ancestors on both sides?
>
> But whenever people talk in this way, what they bring about is precisely a distinction between servile and free, and between noble and ignoble, for they believe it right that, just as from a person comes another person and from an animal another animal, so also from noble parents comes a noble child. Nature may wish to do this, but often it cannot.

In other words, this may well represent a variation on themes familiar from Euripidean tragedy – not just in terms of the general situation depicted in *Women of Troy*, but also the paradox of the 'noble slave', and (more generally) the sophistic contrast between nature (*physis*) and convention (*nomos*), which is exploited or questioned in several of Euripides' other plays.[203] It seems likely that

---

[200]   Aristotle, *Poetics* 16. 1455a4–11 (*TrGF* 1.72 F5a). See Karamanou (2010) 393–4 for possible literary sources and parallels. Cf. Polyidus (pp. 151–3 above).

[201]   See esp. *Women of Troy* 34–6, 870–3; cf. Gregory (1991) 155–79.

[202]   Aristotle, *Politics* 1.6. 1255a37–b4 (*TrGF* 1.72 F3).

[203]   On the *nomos/physis* contrast (especially in relation to slavery *versus* freedom), cf. Euripides, *Women of Troy* 614–15, 1021–7; *Helen* 729–30, 1627–41; *Ion* 854–6; *Hecuba* 592–9, 864–9; *Antiope* F185, 206, 217–8, *Auge* F265a; cf. also Sophocles *TrGF* 4 F940. On the *nomos–physis* dichotomy in fifth-century discourse more generally see Ostwald (1986) 260–6. Cf. Lee (1975) 9–10 on the motif in *Women of Troy*.

Theodectes' Helen, by insisting on her own superior status despite her reduced circumstances, was reaffirming the importance of *physis*.

Was Theodectes' *Helen* conceived of specifically as a reworking of Euripidean material? It may well have been so, but, as in most other cases, it is impossible to say for certain. The only instance in which an intertextual relationship between the two tragedians can definitely be detected is a fragment from an unknown play, quoted by Athenaeus in his discussion of dramas which make use of wordplay based on letters of the alphabet. It is said that in one of his tragedies Theodectes brought on stage an illiterate peasant, who was nonetheless able to describe the shape of the letters that spell out the name Theseus (ΘΗΣΕΥΣ):

> The first letter in the inscription was a †soft-eyed circle†, then there were two upright lines, exactly equal in length, and a horizontal bar in between joined them together; the third letter was similar to a curling lock of hair. Then the next letter appeared to be a trident on its side, and fifth came two wands of equal length up above, and these converged into a single base. Sixth came the letter which I mentioned before, the lock of hair. [F6]

This peculiar fragment is virtually identical with a passage in Euripides' *Theseus*[204]:

> I haven't got any knowledge of writing, but I shall tell you the shapes of the letters and give a clear description. There is a circle, measured out as if with compasses, and this has a firm mark in the middle. The second letter has, first of all, two lines, and then another one holding these two apart at the centre. The third letter looks like some sort of curly lock of hair; and then the fourth consists of one part standing upright and three other parts which are attached to it at an angle. The fifth is not easy to describe: there are two lines which stand apart from one another but then converge into a single point at the base. And the final letter is the same as the third.

In fact, these Euripidean lines had already been quoted, with slight alterations, by Agathon in his *Telephus*, suggesting that they had made a big impression on audiences and readers. In their original dramatic context, the lines have been interpreted as a calculated anachronism, drawing attention to the growth of literacy as a topic of particular social or intellectual interest in Euripides' own time (perhaps in the mid-420s BCE or earlier).[205] But it is not entirely clear what the point of the allusion is in either Agathon or Theodectes, apart from giving a

---

[204] Euripides *TrGF* 5 F382; cf. Agathon (*TrGF* 1.39 F4) and my discussion above: pp. 87–9.

[205] See e.g. Wright (2010) 176–9; cf. Easterling (1985) on reading and writing among other types of anachronism in tragedy. *Theseus* was produced earlier than 422 BCE, when it was parodied in Aristophanes' *Wasps* (312–14): Cropp and Fick (1985) estimate a date between 455 and 422.

very obvious signal of these authors' literary knowledge. Perhaps Theodectes was criticizing Euripides in some way (for example, by implying that this alphabetic motif was far-fetched or incongruous), or perhaps he was playing a more complex, multi-layered intertextual game (by quoting Agathon quoting Euripides), but there is not enough evidence to pursue such ideas further.

A rather simpler explanation is provided by Athenaeus, who tells us that Theodectes was generally fond of linguistic games – including riddles.[206]

> Hermippus, in his book *On the Students of Isocrates,* says that Theodectes of Phaselis was extremely adept at solving any riddle put in front of him, and also at skilfully posing riddles for other people to solve, such as the one about the shadow. He said that there was a creature that is at its biggest around the time of its birth and death, but at its smallest when at its prime. This is what he says:
>
>> What creature is it that does not fall among those that are born by the protecting earth or the sea, that doesn't have limbs that grow like those of mortals, but is biggest at the time of its first sowing and generation, small at the very mid-point of its prime, and in old age once again even larger than at all other times in shape and size? (=F18)
>
> And also in his tragedy *Oedipus* Theodectes describes the night and day in a riddling fashion:
>
>> There are twin sisters, of whom one gives birth to the other, and having given birth she herself is born from the one she bore. (=F4)

It is hard to imagine the effect of tragedies full of riddles: no doubt many people would have found them difficult or distracting.[207] There are, however, certain contexts in which riddles could be dramatically appropriate. Given the prominence of the Sphinx and her riddle in the mythical tradition, the choice of Oedipus as a subject would have given Theodectes an ideal opportunity to integrate riddles into the plot in a thematically apt way. Nothing else is known about Theodectes' *Oedipus* apart from Athenaeus' citation; but see above (p. 160) for the suggestion that Diogenes' *Oedipus*, which poked fun at the Sphinx and her riddle, may have been some sort of polemical response to Theodectes.

Apart from a number of less interesting short fragments (including a brief ethnographic description of the Ethiopians and eight gnomic maxims on

---

[206] Athenaeus 10. 451e–452a (*TrGF* 1.72 T10 = Hermippus F77 Wehrli); cf. 452e, where Theodectes is mentioned again in a long section on the use of riddles in various literary genres.

[207] It may be relevant that Antiphanes' comedy *Carians* (F111 K-A = *TrGF* 1.72 T9) made fun of someone who is 'the only person who can understand the art (*technê*) of Theodectes', though *technê* could refer to one of his rhetorical treatises (cf. T2, *rhêtorikai technai*) rather than his tragedies.

traditional subjects such as parents, children and wives, the gods' justice, the power of time, and the vicissitudes of fortune),[208] the only other known work of Theodectes is his *Philoctetes*. This play was about the Thessalian hero who was grievously wounded by a snake-bite and abandoned on the isle of Lemnos until the Greeks realized that they needed his services (or his bow and arrows) to defeat the Trojans. The subject had already appeared in Homer and the epic cycle, and tragic versions had been produced by Achaeus, Aeschylus, Sophocles and Euripides.[209] These versions differ in a number of details, but in all of them Philoctetes was wounded in the foot, whereas in Theodectes' play he was wounded in the hand. This detail is preserved by Aspasius, one of the ancient commentators on Aristotle, who writes[210]:

> In Theodectes' play Philoctetes, having been bitten by the snake, bears it up to a certain point, because he wishes to conceal it from Neoptolemus and his men, but later on he comes to suffer visibly because the magnitude of the pain becomes unbearable. Sophocles and Aeschylus also portrayed Philoctetes in the same way, and Carcinus too appears to have portrayed Cercyon as being overwhelmed by great pain. These men are not soft, but they would be judged soft if they could not endure the sort of pain that everyone can endure, but were overcome by it. [. . .] Theodectes brings on stage Philoctetes having been bitten in the hand by a snake, and though he bears up under the pain and suffering for a long time, eventually he is overcome and cries out: 'Chop off my hand!' (=F5a)

This is a small but significant difference, because without both his hands Philoctetes would have been unable to use his bow and arrows: this would have had a crucial bearing on the question of whether Philoctetes himself was needed by the Greeks (a question that is central to the surviving play by Sophocles). It has been suggested that the alteration was made in order to provide a sharp contrast with Euripides' crippled heroes, whom Aristophanes criticized for their lack of dignity.[211] As elsewhere, however, there is no reason to think that Euripides was more of an influence (or point of departure) for Theodectes than Achaeus,

---

[208] F17 (quoted and criticized for its inaccuracy by Strabo 15.1.24) attributes the Ethiopians' black skin and curly hair to the effects of the sun; F7–9 and F11–15 are *gnômai*: cf. Xanthakis-Karamanos (1980) 123–6, 130–2 on their conventional or clichéd character. Translations of all fragments are provided in Appendix 1.

[209] Homer, *Iliad* 2. 721–5; Proclus, *Cypria* arg. §9; Achaeus *TrGF* 1 F37 (see Ch. 2 above); Aeschylus *TrGF* 3 F249–57; Sophocles, *Philoctetes*; Euripides *TrGF* 5 F787–800; cf. Pausanias 8.33.4, Dio Chrysostom, *Oration* 52. On the myth in general cf. Ogden (2013) 145–6.

[210] Aspasius, *On Aristotle, Nicomachean Ethics 1–4, 7–8* XIX 1.133, XX 436.33 = Konstan (2015) §133, pp. 133–4 (I quote Konstan's translation here). The passage of Aristotle under discussion is *Nicomachean Ethics* 7.7. 1150b10–12 (*TrGF* 1.72 F5b), which conveys similar information.

[211] Xanthakis-Karamanos (1979) 100, comparing Aristophanes, *Acharnians* 411ff., *Peace* 146ff. etc.

Aeschylus or Sophocles. Otherwise it appears that Theodectes' play followed familiar lines, with a focus on the noble endurance of Philoctetes and the detailed portrayal of physical suffering.

In general, then, Theodectes emerges as a tragedian firmly in the established tradition. Like earlier dramatists, he was clearly interested in exploring myths from new angles, and in presenting his characters' backgrounds and motivations in a subtle and sensitive way. The remains include definite signs of creative vitality and risk-taking (most notably in his tragedy about Mausolus), as well as a few quirky oddities such as his penchant for wordplay and riddles. However, there is no sign of the rhetorical excesses that we might have expected from our external knowledge of Theodectes' career or from the conventional scholarly stereotype of fourth-century drama.

6

The Very Lost

Even in such a context as this it is possible to speak of *degrees* of loss. We can differentiate between tragedians whose work lives on in frustratingly tiny fragments and those whose work has completely vanished. From the playwrights whose work is discussed in this chapter *not a single word* survives. And yet – astonishingly – it is sometimes still possible to say something of value and interest about their lost plays. In the pages that follow, several important facts or suggestive pieces of evidence emerge from the ruins, throwing light upon (*inter alia*) the prize-winning records of certain authors; the continuing development or evolution of the tragic genre throughout the fifth and fourth centuries; the variable number of plays in a production; various attempts to expand the limits of dramatic realism; the range of subject-matter and themes handled by different playwrights; the characterization of major characters; the evocation of emotion; and the use of music to create different effects. All of these tiny scraps of evidence can enrich and expand our overall view of tragedy throughout the classical period, giving us small but revealing glimpses of an extraordinarily rich and varied genre of drama.

This chapter, inevitably, has rather less narrative continuity than the others. At times, it assumes the character of an annotated list or roll call. I have divided these very lost tragedians into three sections: (i) those attested in literary sources, (ii) those attested only in epigraphic sources, and (iii) those who are not attested with complete certainty. Within each section I have tried to adopt a loosely chronological arrangement, though of course this is not always possible to ascertain. Several of the tragedians are discussed at some length, while others have very brief entries indeed. But all of them in their day were important and worthwhile artists, and it is a bittersweet pleasure to be able to give them one more evanescent moment in the limelight.

Tragedians attested in literary sources

Euetes was among the earliest writers of tragedy – he was producing plays right at the beginning of the century, before the Persian Wars, and he won first prize at the Dionysia *c.* 483 BCE[1] – but this is the sum total of our knowledge about him.

Hieronymus, son of Xenophantes, is described in an ancient encyclopedia entry as an 'uneven' (*anômalos*) writer of tragedy and lyric poetry, and he is criticized for his penchant for excessively emotional plots and terrifying characters; nevertheless it is said that he won the applause of audiences.[2] It would be good to know more about the ways in which Hieronymus manipulated the spectators' emotions, but not a trace of his plays remains. Unusually, we know what he looked like, for Aristophanes mentions him twice, each time in relation to his long, shaggy hair. In *Clouds* he is ridiculed for his unkempt hairstyle and mad appearance, while a character in *Acharnians*, more puzzlingly, talks about 'the darkshaggystouthairy cap of Hades, in the style of Hieronymus'.[3] This latter joke seems to be a reference not just to Hieronymus' appearance but also to his poetry: the ludicrous compound adjective *skotodasupuknotricha* may be a parody of the tragedian's fondness for long compound words, in much the same way that Aristophanes also parodied Aeschylus' diction elsewhere,[4] and the 'cap of Hades' could be an oblique allusion to some detail in a tragedy by Hieronymus.

Sthenelus illustrates the potential value of snippets of evidence from comedy, even when such snippets appear to be unrevealing or crudely pejorative.[5] A character in Aristophanes' *Wasps,* produced in 422 BCE, makes a withering, throwaway reference to 'Sthenelus shorn of his props (*skeuaria*)', which is ostensibly a negative value-judgement implying that the tragedian ought to have paid more attention to other aspects of his plays, such as the plot or the script. The ancient commentator on the passage elaborates on the reference, explaining that the tragedian was forced by poverty to give away his collection of *skeuai*

---

[1]   *Suda* E 2766 (*TrGF* 1.6); cf. DID A3a.12 (*IG* ii² 2325.12): see Millis and Olson (2012) 141–9.
[2]   *Suda* A 676; Σ Aristophanes, *Acharnians* 388 (*TrGF* 1.31 T1).
[3]   Aristophanes *Clouds* 348, *Acharnians* 388 (*TrGF* 1.31 T1, T2).
[4]   This is how Olson (2002, 175) interprets it: he calls it 'a deliberately absurd compound in dithyrambic style', and indeed Hieronymus is said to have written dithyrambs as well as tragedies (Σ Aristophanes, *Clouds* 348). Snell (*TrGF* 1.31, p. 149) notes the dochmiac rhythm in Aristophanes and suggests that the comedian is also drawing attention to Hieronymus' use of metre. Cf. *Frogs* 923–42 for parody of Aeschylean compound words.
[5]   *TrGF* 1.32.

(props, costumes, or theatrical paraphernalia) and consequently did badly at his art.[6] There may not be much factual value to this claim, since many comic scholia seem to be fabrications or extrapolations from the text itself; or it may even represent the plot of a lost metaliterary comedy in which Sthenelus was a character.[7] However that may be, the specific value of the comic evidence is that it tells us that Sthenelus was famous for his use of props. Indeed, since a brief parenthetic reference is all that is needed to make the point, it is obvious that Aristophanes' audience in 422 already firmly associated the name of Sthenelus with theatrical props. A few years later the comedian Platon even wrote an entire play called *Skeuai*, which also featured at least one joke about Sthenelus.[8]

This evidence is more revealing than it might seem. The fifth-century stage essentially adhered to minimalist conventions, and even though props, objects and scenery did sometimes have a meaningful function in drama, they were comparatively rare.[9] Thus it is highly significant that Sthenelus used them often, for he was evidently concerned with theatricality and the *mise-en-scène* more than many other tragedians. Was Sthenelus striving towards greater realism or illusionism? Were his performances characterized by representational, visual, physical elements and special effects, in contrast to the more static or conventional focus of so much other tragedy? Did his props and theatrical objects have an interesting semiotic function within their plays? Were they unusually charged with meaning? One can only speculate, but it seems likely that the answer to all these questions is yes, and that Aristophanes is indirectly reflecting this side of Sthenelus' drama.

Perhaps Aristophanes' pejorative value-judgement is really pejorative only to someone who does not rate the visual or theatrical aspects of drama very highly. Indeed, the fact that his character sneers at Sthenelus and his props may be seen as aligning Aristophanes' outlook with that of Aristotle, who also preferred well-constructed plots to spectacle or special effects.[10] This little joke may well hint at a couple of possible explanations why Sthenelus' work did not survive for posterity: either it didn't work quite so well on the page as on the stage, and thus

---

[6]   Aristophanes, *Wasps* 1313 with Σ *ad loc.* (*TrGF* 1.32 T1).
[7]   Note that the scenario mentioned by the scholiast is uncannily reminiscent of the plot of Cratinus' *Pytine* (T ii–iii K-A), in which the author appeared as a character: see Olson (2007) 80–7, Bakola (2009) 59–63.
[8]   Platon F136 K-A – 'a play with a theatrical theme', according to its most recent editor: see Storey (2011) III.154–5. Cf. Pirrotta (2009) 272–83. This comedy also ridiculed Morsimus (F136), Melanthius (F140) and Euripides (F142).
[9]   See Noel (2012).
[10]   Aristotle, *Poetics* 7.1450b, 26.1462a; cf. Lucas (1968) *ad loc.*

failed to appeal to a reading public,[11] or it passed out of circulation owing to the dominance of Aristotelian ideas about what constituted the best type of tragedy.

It seems, alas, that Sthenelus' writing style also failed to please Aristotle. We are told in the *Poetics* that excellence in poetic diction consists in clarity: the clearest language of all is taken from ordinary, everyday speech (*kuria onomata*), but this is also said to be 'low' (*tapeinê*) and undesirable. The tragedians whom Aristotle cites as illustrations of this 'low' language are Sthenelus and Cleophon.[12] Of course, some people in the audience may have preferred to hear down-to-earth language at the theatre, and it may well be that diction was another area in which Sthenelus was deliberately aiming at a more realistic or naturalistic style of tragedy. However, there are other signs that Sthenelus' style of writing was unpopular. The following exchange occurred in another Aristophanic comedy, *Gerytades* (normally dated to 408 BCE):

A: How might I eat the words of Sthenelus?
B: You'd have to dip them in vinegar and dry salt.

This joke is based on the conceit, quite frequent in old comedy, that literature is 'food' and poets are 'chefs', and it is clearly implied that Sthenelus' overly plain writing style is completely lacking in 'flavour'.[13]

All the same, Sthenelus cannot have been such a terrible poet: he had a career which stretched across two decades, to judge by these comic references, and many more decades after his death he was still being discussed seriously by Aristotle and featuring in other didascalic works.[14] He may also have been noted for his reworking of other people's plays, given that the only other surviving reference to him is found in a fragment of Platon's comedy *Laconians* which apparently mocks Sthenelus for plagiarism. As we have already noted in an earlier chapter, comic or scholarly accusations of 'plagiarism' tend to denote overt intertextual activity rather than covert literary theft.[15]

A further tiny piece of evidence is presented by an Apulian red-figure vase dating from *c.* 380 BCE.[16] This vase depicts three figures in wrinkly costumes,

---

11   Demetrius, *On Style* 163 distinguishes between the type of drama that works well on stage and that which better suits an audience of book-readers; cf. Chapter 5 above (pp. 127–30) on Chaeremon as an especially 'readable' (*anagnôstikos*) playwright.

12   Aristotle, *Poetics* 22.1458a18–20 (*TrGF* 1.32 T3). See pp. 188–90 below for more on Cleophon (*TrGF* 1.77).

13   Aristophanes, *Gerytades* F158 K-A; for further discussion in the context of fifth-century stylistic theory see Wright (2012) 136–7.

14   Harpocration 166.3 (*s.v.* 'Sthenelus') = *TrGF* 1.32 T2; this source also contains the reference to Platon's *Laconians* (= F72 K-A) mentioned here.

15   See Chapter 2, pp. 43–5 above.

16   Richmond, Virginia Museum 78.83. See Green (2003), whose conclusions I summarize here.

padding and phalluses: this iconography clearly marks them out as comic actors, and the overall appearance of the picture suggests that it was inspired by a scene from some comedy or other. The crucial point is that one of the figures has the letters ΣΘΕ on his forehead. As J.R. Green suggests, this probably represents the common practice of tattooing runaway slaves with their owner's name; but the only attested Athenian names beginning *Sthe-* seem to be Sthennon and Sthenelus. What we have here, then, could be evidence for a comedy in which Sthenelus and his slave appeared as characters. Platon's *Skeuai* is named by Green as a likely candidate for such a comedy, though *Laconians* is another possibility. If Green is correct, this evidence is very significant, because it confirms that this supposedly 'minor' tragedian was important enough to appear prominently in comedy – and comic iconography – over a number of decades.

Little is known about **Acestor**. It seems that, like several other tragedians, he came from outside Athens. Several comedians from the 420s onwards made fun of him for his supposed foreignness, calling him a 'Mysian' or 'Scythian', depicting him as a barbarian slave, accusing him of being a non-citizen trying to force his way into the city, or giving him the oriental-sounding nickname 'Sakas'.[17] It is hard to know what (if anything) these jokes say about Acestor's plays themselves. A little more detail is supplied, or hinted at, by a couple of other comic references. In Cratinus' *Cleoboulinai* it was said that 'Acestor deserves a beating unless he gets his plots in order', implying that his storylines or plot structures had been criticized. A character in Callias' *Men in Fetters* said that 'choruses hate him', which is more difficult to interpret: perhaps he was known for writing difficult music, or for handling the choreography in an unusual way.[18]

Several centuries later Acestor appears in a literary-biographical anecdote which is specifically concerned with the survival (or non-survival) of certain tragedies. Valerius Maximus records the following conversation between Euripides and Acestor[19]:

> He grumbled to Acestor that in the past three days he had been able to compose only three verses, and those with a very great amount of effort. Acestor boasted that he had written one hundred lines with the utmost ease. 'But there is a

---

[17]　Aristophanes, *Wasps* 1219–21, *Birds* 31–5; Theopompus, *Tisamenos* F61 K-A; Metagenes, *Philothytes* F14 K-A; Eupolis, *Kolakes* F172 K-A (*TrGF* 1.25 T1–4).

[18]　Cratinus F85 K-A; Callias F13 K-A (*TrGF* 1.25 T2).

[19]　Valerius Maximus 3.7 ext. 1b (*TrGF* 1.25 T5b).

difference,' said Euripides, 'in that your verses will only last for three days, but mine will last for all time.' And indeed the works of Acestor, for all his fecundity, perished before memory's first measuring-post, whereas the works of Euripides, written late into the night with hesitant pen, will be borne with sails full of glory through the ages.

This anecdote is suggestive, but it tells us nothing about the nature or specific qualities of Acestor's plays themselves. It is implied that Acestor wrote too much, but was he prolific or merely prolix? It is impossible to say. Valerius does not tell his readers what was so good about Euripides or so bad about Acestor; perhaps he thinks it is self-evident. He is more interested in their respective posthumous status in the world of letters, and he obviously expects his readers to share his underlying assumption that authors can be divided into 'classics' (possessed of genius, lasting value, and the acclaim of posterity) *versus* 'non-classics' (regarded as ephemeral or inferior). In this respect Valerius' outlook is very similar to that of many ancient critics, especially Longinus, who in his treatise *On the Sublime* included an explicit discussion of genius *versus* mediocrity.[20] When Valerius says that the plays of the non-classic Acestor have 'perished', he may mean that no one valued them or bothered to read them any more, or that by the first century CE they were already lost works. Nevertheless, it is interesting to note that the name and reputation of Acestor were still known to first-century Romans.

Nicomachus, an Athenian poet whose tragedies included an *Oedipus*, is given short shrift in his entry in the *Suda*, which records that he 'astonishingly' (*paradoxôs*) defeated Euripides and Theognis.[21] It is not clear whether he beat them both on a single occasion, but he evidently won at least one victory and maybe more.[22] The writer of the *Suda* exhibits the same prejudice against 'non-classic' writers as Valerius Maximus (quoted above): he takes it for granted that a 'classic' writer such as Euripides automatically ought to have won on every occasion, regardless of the specific quality of the individual plays in question. But why assume that Euripides was naturally bound to win? In his own day, before his fourth-century reinvention as one of the canonical triad of great

---

[20] Longinus, *On the Sublime* 33.5: in this case the 'classic' Sophocles and the 'non-classic' Ion are the authors contrasted.

[21] *Suda* N 397 = *TrGF* 1.36 T1.

[22] *SEG* xxvi 203 col. ii. 3 (*TrGF* 1.36 T2) records that a Nicomachus also won third prize at the Lenaea of 364 BCE with a production including *Amymone*, but the late date may be suspect: Millis and Olson (2012) 120–1 suggest that perhaps another Nicomachus is denoted.

geniuses, Euripides was certainly not seen as a sure-fire winner.[23] Admittedly, the adjudication and voting procedure at the Athenian festivals was a chancy affair and not a reliable guarantee of literary merit, and it may be that the 'wrong' candidate won; but it still seems unfair to Nicomachus to rule out the possibility that he might have achieved a genuine literary success.

Spintharus, like Acestor, seems to have been mocked by Aristophanes for being a 'barbarian' or 'Phrygian'.[24] Beyond that his life and career are obscure, though we do know the titles of three of his plays. Two of them are unusually descriptive, revealing more information about their content and use of myth than most tragic titles. *Heracles on the Pyre* obviously dramatized the very end of Heracles' myth after the death of his wife Deianeira: his journey to Mount Oeta, his construction of his own funeral pyre, and his eventual apotheosis. *Semele Struck By Lightning* must have dealt with the birth of the god Dionysus: Zeus had a secret liaison with the mortal woman Semele, daughter of Cadmus, but caused her death by hurling thunder and lightning; he snatched the unborn six-month-old embryo from her body and sewed it into his own thigh, and eventually Dionysus was born. The myth is a well-known one, and it provides a comparatively rare example of a tragedy on a theogonic theme (plays about the birth of gods were apparently more characteristic of comedy).[25] The third known title, *Parthenopaeus*, was evidently another tragedy centering on the popular Theban cycle of myths: its title character was one of the Seven against Thebes.

Dorillus (or Dorilaus, or Doriallus, or Doryallus) is known only from ancient dictionary entries, which spell his name in a variety of ways, and from a vulgar joke in Aristophanes, which uses the tragedian's name as a slang term for the female genitalia.[26] We may or may not choose to treat this as a qualitative aesthetic evaluation of his work.

---

[23]   Euripides won only four first prizes in his lifetime (and another posthumously), far fewer than either Sophocles or Aeschylus: see Stevens (1956), and cf. Wright (2009) for broader discussion of fifth-century dramatic prizes in relation to literary criticism and an author's standing.

[24]   Aristophanes, *Birds* 762–3 (*TrGF* 1.40 T2a; cf. T2b). It has been suggested that the target of mockery here is not the tragedian but a different Spintharus (*PA* 12855): see Storey (1977) 246.

[25]   The *Suda* records that Philiscus wrote plays on the birth of Zeus, Pan, Hermes and Aphrodite, but these may be comedies rather than tragedies, and the evidence is disputed (*Suda* Φ 357 = *TrGF* 1.89 T5). On the 'birth of gods' theme and mythological comedy, see Nesselrath (1995). Aeschylus, Diogenes (see Chapter 5, p. 153) and the younger Carcinus (Chapter 4, p. 109) also wrote tragedies called *Semele*.

[26]   *TrGF* 1.41 T1; Aristophanes, *Lemnian Women* F382 K-A.

Hippias is mentioned by Plato as a writer of lyric poems, tragedies and dithyrambs.[27] No trace of his work survives, despite this generic versatility.

Morychus is known to us entirely through jokes in comedy, all of which make fun of his gourmandism.[28] Nothing is said by the comedians about Morychus' plays, and we know that he was a tragedian only because the ancient commentators on these comedies tell us so.[29]

Melanthius, author of tragedy and elegiac poems,[30] was another noted bon viveur, who, like Morychus, was mercilessly mocked by the comedians for his appetite.[31] In one comedy in particular, Archippus' *Fish*, Melanthius featured as a character: the plot involved his being tied up and thrown to the fish, to be eaten by them in turn, seeing that he had eaten so many of them.[32] This shows that, like Euripides, Aeschylus, and other tragedians, Melanthius was sufficiently well known for a comic plot to be based around him – and indeed it has been pointed out that he featured in *all* the comedies performed at the Dionysia in 421 BCE, which seems to indicate a certain notoriety or vogueish appeal at that time.[33]

A choral song in Aristophanes' *Peace* links together Melanthius with another tragic poet, Morsimus,[34] implying that both are terrible poets who should never have been chosen to compete in the festivals. It also implies that Melanthius sometimes co-produced plays with his brother (whose name is not known).[35]

> The skilful poet must sing this sort of public song of the lovely-haired Graces, whenever the swallow sings spring songs with her delightful voice, and whenever Morsimus doesn't get a chorus, and neither does Melanthius, whose extremely bitter voice I heard speaking when he and his brother were awarded a chorus – that pair of gluttonous Gorgons, skate-watching Harpies, disgusting shooers-away

---

[27] Plato, *Hippias Minor* 386b (*TrGF* 1.42 T1).

[28] *TrGF* 1.30 T1–5 (Aristophanes, *Acharnians* 885–7, *Wasps* 503–7, 1141, *Peace* 1008; Platon, *Perialges* F114 K-A).

[29] Olson (2002) 295 doubts whether Morychus was a tragedian at all.

[30] A couple of lines from his elegiac poem in honour of Cimon are quoted by Plutarch (*Cimon* 14, 481b = *TrGF* 1.23 T1): 'for at his own expense he decorated the gods' temples and the Cecropian agora with the valour of the demi-gods . . .'.

[31] Aristophanes, *Peace* 803–13, 1009; Leucon, *Phrateres* F3 K-A, Eupolis F178 K-A, Pherecrates, *Petale* F148 K-A. Cf. Athenaeus 1.6b, 12.549a for similar information (and the report that Melanthius' death was due to choking): see *TrGF* 1.23 T7a–b.

[32] Archippus F28 K-A: the plot is described by Athenaeus 8.343c (= *TrGF* 1.23 T2).

[33] Olson (1998) 229.

[34] *TrGF* 1.29: see Chapter 4, pp. 100–101.

[35] *Peace* 796–816 (*TrGF* 1.23 T3); cf. Olson (1998) 229. However, Sutton (1987) 13–14 identifies Melanthius' brother as Morsimus himself, which produces a slightly different reading of this passage.

of old women, fish-destroyers with armpits stinking of goat. Spit a big fat gob of phlegm on them, divine Muse! – and come and play with me in this festival.

This is an extraordinarily negative portrayal. The comedian ridicules Melanthius' voice, his appearance, his personal habits, and even his body odour. But this is not a unique passage. Elsewhere in comedy Melanthius is also mocked as a sexual pervert, a parasite, a talker of drivel, a sufferer of leprosy, and the father of sons 'with pale arses' (whatever that may signify).[36] Few other literary figures are subjected to such a level of personal abuse. But can it tell us anything about Melanthius' work?

All of these insults may be an indirect form of qualitative critical judgement. By not only showering Melanthius with all these insults but also inviting the muse of poetry to spit at him, Aristophanes may be saying that, in his view, Melanthius' work is simply beneath contempt. But what was wrong with it? It is hard to say; but perhaps we could see all these gluttony-related jokes as a metaphorical indication of some specific quality (or defect) of the poetry itself. Indeed, the fact that several different poets are called gluttons suggests that this is not literally a joke about the personal habits of individuals. As I have already noted, it is significant that in comic imagery poetry is often assimilated to food.[37] In this case, a 'gluttonous' writer might be one with a penchant for (as it were) rich, luxurious, fattening poetry, to be produced or consumed in great quantity, in contrast with the more 'frugal' sort of poet who might write more plainly or at shorter length. This is precisely the type of contrast seen elsewhere in Aristophanes, most notably in a stylistic comparison between Aeschylus' 'overweight' tragedy and Euripides' 'slimmed-down' version.[38] If this interpretation is valid, the same sort of reading could also be extended to other tragedians who are called 'gluttons', including Morychus (see above, p. 184); and it may even be that the use of the same joke is meant to hint at an essential similarity between these two poets' work. The likelihood that Aristophanes is criticizing Melanthius' verbal style in particular, rather than some other aspect of his work, is increased by his reference to the tragedian's tone of voice, since 'bitterness' (*pikrotês*) is a stylistic metaphor found elsewhere (though it remains

---

[36] Eupolis F178 K-A, Platon *Skeuai* F140 K-A, Aristophanes, *Birds* 150, Callias, *Pedetai* F14 K-A. It has been suggested, plausibly, that the adjective denotes cowardice: see O'Sullivan and Collard (2013) 479–80, 485 n. 9 (citing e.g. Alexis F322 K-A).

[37] See Wright (2012) 129–39, where the theme is linked to Callimachean literary aesthetics; and cf. above on Sthenelus' 'flavourless' poetry.

[38] *Frogs* 939–44; cf. *Knights* 537–9, F347; Metagenes F15 K-A.

unclear precisely what sort of verbal effect the label denotes).[39] But in addition there may be an oblique allusion to the *content* of some of Melanthius' tragedies in these references to Gorgons, Harpies, and old women.

Later on in *Peace* Melanthius' name pops up once again in a list of gluttons[40]:

> ... and then let Melanthius arrive late at the market and find that everything has been sold, and let him wail in his despair, and then sing a monody from his *Medea*: 'I am ruined! I am ruined and bereft of her that gave birth among the beetroots!' – and let everyone rejoice at his misfortune.

This passage is even more revealing than the previous one, since it tells us that Melanthius (like Neophron, Euripides and others) wrote a *Medea*. It seems likely that the words quoted above contain some sort of mangled version of a couple of lines from Melanthius' *Medea*.[41] In that case it has been suggested that the speaker is Jason, mourning his new wife: 'did she die in childbirth, perhaps with the aid of drugs given by Medea ostensibly meant to ease her labour?' asks Douglas Olson.[42] This is a plausible suggestion, though one notes in addition that Aristophanes is explicitly referring to a *monody*. By far the majority of solo songs in late fifth-century tragedy were performed by female or barbarian characters, which implies that Melanthius was attempting something rather striking here in his characterization of Jason. For a male character to express heightened emotion in a passionate lyric outburst, especially one with strong overtones of a ritual lament (*thrênos*), would have seemed an unusual or even feminized gesture.[43] This would surely have affected the audience's understanding of the gender relationship and power dynamic between Jason and Medea – an aspect of the myth which is also made into a particular focus of attention in other dramatic versions (not only Euripides' play but also Neophron's, which 'feminized' Jason by the manner of his suicide).[44]

Pythangelus is known from a single, disdainful reference in Aristophanes' *Frogs*, where he is mentioned as an example of the allegedly talentless generation of

---

[39] Aristophanes, *Wasps* 461–2, F591 K-A (of Philocles' style). Cf. (from later in antiquity) Quintilian 8.3.89, 10.1.117, 11.3.169; Diogenes Laertius 5.5.

[40] Aristophanes, *Peace* 1009–14 (*TrGF* 1.23 T4).

[41] Snell, inexplicably, attributes the quotation to Morsimus, and prints the lines (minus the reference to beetroots) as *TrGF* 1.29 F1.

[42] Olson (1998) 263.

[43] See Hall (1999), esp. 112–13 and 116: 'It is striking that tragedy's other "manly" female, Euripides' Medea, is ... given anapaests but never lyric song'. Hall compares tr. adesp. F6 Nauck for another monodic Jason from a lost tragedy.

[44] See Chapter 2, p. 37.

tragedians still active in 405 BCE (after the death or departure of all the good poets such as Aeschylus, Sophocles, Euripides and Agathon).[45]

The philosopher **Plato** is said to have begun his career as a poet, writing dithyrambs, lyrics and tragedies. Both Diogenes Laertius and Aelian tell a similar anecdote about the moment at which Plato abandoned tragedy for philosophy: it is said that he intended to compete at the Dionysia with a tragic tetralogy that he had composed, and that he even got as far as distributing the scripts to the actors and beginning rehearsals; but when Socrates listened to the rehearsals he dissuaded him from going ahead, saying that these plays were fit only to be burned.[46] It is impossible to guess what Plato's plays were actually like – assuming that we give any credence to this story in the first place. It may well be that Plato never wrote tragedies at all, and that the anecdote is a subsequent invention designed to explain his idiosyncratic treatment of tragedy in his philosophical writings (such as the *Republic*, where poetry and drama are, notoriously, banished from the ideal state).

The *Suda,* that compendious but not always accurate source of obscure knowledge, contains an entry on **Apollodorus**, described as a tragic poet from Tarsus. Several of Apollodorus' titles are listed, including *The Greeks, Thyestes, Suppliant Women* and *Odysseus,* as well as two others which are obviously incomplete.[47] The full title of *Akanthoplex* was probably *Odysseus Akanthoplex* ('Odysseus Wounded by the Spine'), which is also the title of a tragedy by Sophocles: this play dramatized Odysseus' death at the hands of his son Telegonus, who struck Odysseus with a spear tipped with a poisonous stingray spine.[48] *Teknoktonos* ('The Child-Killer') is more difficult to pin down, but it may have featured (for example) Heracles, Medea or Atreus. Snell identifies Apollodorus with the playwright who is commemorated in a couple of didascalic inscriptions as having won five victories at the Lenaea (the first in *c.* 380 BCE) and perhaps six at the Dionysia: this would represent a highly successful competitive career.[49] However, the name in the inscriptions is almost illegible, and the identification is very doubtful.

---

45 *Frogs* 87 (*TrGF* 1.44 T1).
46 Diogenes Laertius 3.5; Aelian, *Historical Miscellany* 2.30 (*TrGF* 1.46 T1). Aristotle (*Topics* 6.2.140a3) quotes three single-word fragments supposedly taken from Plato's tragedies, but they are thought to be spurious.
47 *Suda* A 3406 (*TrGF* 1.64 T1).
48 *TrGF* 4 F453–461a.
49 *IG* ii². 2325.21 (*TrGF* 1.64 T2 = DID A3b, 38; cf. DID A3a, 41): see Millis and Olson (2012) 204–7.

Isocrates' adopted son **Aphareus** was both a rhetor and a tragedian. Apart from the *Suda*, our main evidence for his career comes from incidental references in the pseudo-Plutarchian *Life of Isocrates*.[50] According to Plutarch,

> Aphareus wrote a few speeches, both forensic and deliberative, and he also wrote about thirty-seven tragedies, of which the authorship of two is doubted. Beginning in the archonship of Lysistratus [363 BCE] and going up to the time of the archonship of Sosigenes [341 BCE], a period of twenty-eight years, he put on six productions and won the first prize twice, with Dionysius as his producer; and he put on two other productions at the Lenaea with other people as his producers.

This respectable prize-winning record is confirmed by epigraphic evidence, which also suggests the further detail that Aphareus took third prize at the Dionysia of 341 – perhaps his last ever production? – with a trilogy comprising *Daughters of Pelias, Orestes* and *Auge*.[51] It seems that Aphareus, no doubt overshadowed by his famous father, achieved greater success as a dramatist than as a speechmaker, but it may be that, in common with certain other playwrights (including Aristophanes), he preferred to write the script and leave others to act as *didaskalos* and direct the performance (unless Dionysius et al. are seen as *chorêgoi*).

Cleophon is listed in the *Suda* as an Athenian tragic poet and the author of *Actaeon, Amphiaraus, Achilles, Bacchantes, Dexamenos, Erigone, Thyestes, Leucippus, Persis* and *Telephus*.[52] Not a word of these plays survives, but Cleophon's work was obviously well known to Aristotle, who discusses it in a number of places. Aristotle's testimony is extremely revealing, because it tells us that Cleophon's plays were seen as unusually naturalistic or realistic in comparison with other tragedies. This increased naturalism was achieved both through diction (as in the case of Sthenelus, to whom Cleophon is compared[53]) and through character portrayal.

---

[50] *TrGF* 1.73 T1 (*Suda* A 4556), T2 (Plutarch, *Lives of the Ten Orators* 4.16, 838a–b, 839b–c; the quotation here is from 839c).

[51] *IG* ii². 2325 col. i.46; *IG* ii². 2320. 13–16 (DID A 3a, 46; 3b, 43; A2, 11): see Millis and Olson (2012) 64–7 (the name is plausibly restored).

[52] *Suda* K 1730 = *TrGF* 1.77 T1. Snell (p. 246) points out that this information may be defective, since it overlaps with what is known about Iophon's plays (*TrGF* 1.22). It has been thought that Cleophon was an orator rather than a tragedian, but the testimonia seem to make better sense if they are describing a tragedian.

[53] *TrGF* 1.32 T3; see pp. 178–81 above.

In his discussion of *mimesis* in the *Poetics,* Aristotle mentions Cleophon's characters as furnishing a typical example of 'ordinary' people:[54]

> Those who imitate produce imitations of people doing things; and these people must be either admirable or inferior ... Homer imitates people better than us, Cleophon imitates people just like us, and Hegemon of Thasos (the inventor of parody) or Nicochares (the author of the *Deiliad*) imitate people worse than us. In just the same way tragedy and comedy are distinguished from one another: tragedy's aim is to show better people, comedy's aim is to show worse people.

This is a somewhat ambiguous description. Does Aristotle mean to imply that Cleophon is failing to achieve the proper aim of tragedy, or that he occupies an intermediate position in between tragedy (or epic) and comedy? Perhaps so, but it is clear, at least, that to Aristotle's readers Cleophon's plays were sufficiently familiar to serve as representative examples of a recognizable character type.

I have already quoted Aristotle's comparison of Sthenelus and Cleophon in terms of their tendency to use 'ordinary' language (*kuria onomata*) – a tendency which Aristotle does not admire, judging this sort of language to be lacking in dignity. In his *Rhetoric* Aristotle recommends a style of diction which has clarity but is neither excessively low nor excessively grand, and here again he cites Cleophon as an example of the sort of style which seems inappropriate[55]:

> Style will possess appropriateness (*to prepon*) if it is expressive of emotion and character, and if it is in proportion to the subject-matter. By 'in proportion' I mean that it should not be casual when serious matters are under discussion, nor should it be solemn when dealing with trivialities, and no embellishment should be added to an ordinary word. If this rule is not observed, the effect comes across as if it were comedy – as, for example, in the poetry of Cleophon. He used a number of expressions that were just as if someone were to address a fig as 'Your Royal Highness'.[56]

Presumably none of Cleophon's characters really did address a fig in this manner: Aristotle is making a rare joke, in order to underline the point that Cleophon's tragedies (in his opinion) used inappropriate language. It seems clear that Cleophon favoured 'low' or 'ordinary' speech in situations where more elevated diction would normally have been expected. Aristotle implies that this tendency

---

[54] Aristotle, *Poetics* 2.1448a1–13 (*TrGF* 1.77 T2); cf. Lucas (1968) 65.
[55] Aristotle, *Rhetoric* 3.7.1408a10–16; cf. 3.2.1404b.
[56] (Lit.) 'as if someone were to say *potnia sukē*': i.e. the joke seems to lie in the application of a formal term of address to a piece of fruit. See Freese (1926) 378.

is to be seen as an artistic failure or lapse of taste, but it may well have been a deliberate literary strategy – unless one assumes that Cleophon simply had a tin ear for dialogue.

Aristotle (apparently) mentions Cleophon once more, in his work *On Sophistical Refutations*, in a passage where he is discussing a particular method of rhetorical argumentation:

> Just as people responding to their opponents often make fine distinctions, if they are just on the point of being refuted, so people asking questions should do the same thing from time to time, when dealing with objections: if the objection is valid against one meaning of the word but not the other, they should pretend to assume that their opponent meant it in precisely the other sense. For example, Cleophon does this in the *Mandroboulos*.

If this source actually relates to the tragedian, it seems that Aristotle did not always disapprove of his deployment of language. Perhaps this could be taken as a sign that Cleophon's tragedies were noted for their rhetorical character or content.[57] However, the myth of Mandroboulos does not seem like an obvious subject for a tragedy,[58] and it has been thought that Aristotle is referring not to the tragedian but to a philosophical dialogue by Plato's nephew Speusippus, in which there was a character named Cleophon.[59]

Mamercus was tyrant of Catane during the 340s BCE, at the time when Timoleon invaded Sicily. Plutarch, in his *Life of Timoleon*, provides the sole surviving reference to his literary activities[60]:

> Mamercus, who thought a great deal of himself as a writer of poems and tragedies, boasted of his victory over the mercenaries, and when he dedicated their shields to the gods he composed an insulting elegiac couplet for the occasion:
>
>> These shields, painted purple and decorated with gold, ivory and amber,
>>   we captured with our simple shieldlets.

Plutarch clearly does not share Mamercus' own opinion of the merits of his poetry; but perhaps the couplet quoted above does not represent the pinnacle of

---

[57] See Xanthakis-Karamanos (1980) 59–69 for the view that there was an increased emphasis on rhetoric (at the expense of character) in fourth-century tragedy.

[58] See Aelian, *On Animals* 12.40: Mandroboulos found some treasure on Samos, and dedicated to Hera a golden sheep one year, a silver one the next year, and a bronze one the year after that.

[59] See Diogenes Laertius 4.5; cf. Taràn (1981) 242–4.

[60] Plutarch, *Timoleon* 31.1 (*TrGF* 1.87).

his achievement, and it seems likely that Mamercus' work and reputation will have suffered in much the same way as the reputation of that other tyrant-tragedian, Dionysius I of Syracuse (see Chapter 5).

Tragedians in epigraphic sources

A tragedian called **Callistratus**, who shares his name with the man who co-produced some of Aristophanes' earliest plays,[61] won second prize at the Lenaea in 418 BCE with a set of plays including *Amphilochus* and *Ixion*.[62] This fact is known from epigraphic evidence only, and no trace of Callistratus or his work appears in any literary text. There are several other names which are seen only in inscriptions. From the fifth century these include **Mesatus**, who won at least two victories at the Dionysia, the first soon after 468, and also took third prize at the same festival (behind Aeschylus and the 'Danaid trilogy' of Sophocles) at some date between the mid-460s and mid-450s;[63] there is also **Menecrates**, who won the Dionysia in 422 and may have been a successful tragic actor as well as a poet.[64]

After the fifth century the number of tragedians known chiefly from epigraphic evidence increases. A certain **Ariphron** and **Polychares** are commemorated as victors at the rural Dionysia in Acharnae at an unknown date near the beginning of the fourth century (though it is not quite certain that they were tragedians).[65] **Megaclides** took first prize at the Lenaea at around the same period.[66] Other Lenaea victories were won, during the 350s, by the otherwise obscure **Philinus**, **Asclepiades**, **Caerius** and **[Tim]ostratus**,[67] as well as the younger **Achaeus** (the Syracusan poet who is mentioned by the *Suda* as the author of ten tragedies and distinguished from his older namesake).[68]

---

[61] See Kassel-Austin (*PCG* IV, p. 56). It would be odd if this Callistratus were the same person, given the fact that the two genres normally kept themselves so very separate: e.g. no playwright wrote both comedies and tragedies (*pace* Socrates in Plato, *Symposium* 223c–d), and no actor performed in plays of both genres (Plato, *Republic* 396a).

[62] *TrGF* 1.38 (DID A 2b, 80: *IG* ii² 2319 col. ii.80-1): see Millis and Olson (2012) 116–17.

[63] *TrGF* 1.11 T1–2, DID A 3a, 16 (*IG* ii² 2325.16); C6 (*P.Oxy.* 2256 fr. 3): see Millis and Olson (2012) 147–8.

[64] *TrGF* 1.35 (DID A1, 118; T1–3: *IG* ii² 2318.585): see Millis and Olson (2012) 54.

[65] *TrGF* 1.53-4; cf. 1.52 (Dicaeogenes) T2 (DID B6 = *IG* ii². 3092). Snell suggests that the record may refer to the dithyrambic competition.

[66] *TrGF* 1.56a (DID B 5a: *IG* ii² 3091).

[67] *TrGF* 1.80-83 (DID A3b: *IG* ii² 2325 col. iii.35–9): see Millis and Olson (2012) 204–7, who suggest Demostratus as a more likely name.

[68] *TrGF* 1.79 T1, T2 (DID A3b).

Theodorides won second prize at the same festival in 363 BCE with the plays *Medea* and *Phaethon* – a production which Snell and others treat as a 'dilogy'.[69] If this is true, it may be that the competition rules at the Lenaea had altered by this date, to allow entrants to exhibit fewer plays than before.[70] Other didascalic inscriptions, relating to the City Dionysia, also appear to credit certain competitors with just two plays. **Timocles**, for example, apparently took second prize at the Dionysia in the mid-330s with *Phrixus* and *Oedipus* (the inscription also records the names of the two star actors, Thessalus and Neoptolemus).[71] **Euaretus** also took third prize at the 340 Dionysia with two plays whose titles are illegible (also starring Thessalus and Neoptolemus);[72] but at the same festival in the previous year he won second prize with *Teucer, Achilles* and a third play. Either the rules for entry must have been fairly flexible (though it is worth noting that all three competitors in 340 produced two plays apiece), or some of these records are incomplete.

Perhaps the most lost and lamentable of all are a number of tragedians whose names appear only incompletely in inscriptions that are mutilated and lacunose. [ ]**ippus** was the victor at the 470 Dionysia.[73] **Hera**[ ] won second prize at the 419 Lenaea, with plays including a *These*[*us?*].[74] [ ]**es** won first prize at the Lenaea on two occasions, the first of which was *c.* 382. This is commemorated on the same inscription as the victories of several other poets, whose names are also partly illegible, between the years *c.* 377–360: [ ]**as**, [ ]**as**[, [ ]**des**, [ ]**crates**, [ ]**des**, and [ ]**on**.[75]

Less securely attested tragedians

This final section deals with a number of individuals who are included in *Tragicorum Graecorum Fragmenta* but cannot be identified with absolute certainty.

---

[69]   *TrGF* 1.78a (DID A2b, 94: SEG xxvi 203): see Millis and Olson (2012) 118–21.
[70]   See, however, p. 151 with n. 124 above; cf. Luppe (2009).
[71]   *TrGF* 1.86 T3 (*IG* ii² 2320.19). However, the name is incomplete: Snell suggests that this victory may be attributable to Philocles (*TrGF* 1.61). Millis and Olson (2012) 68 are similarly undecided. Timocles won first prize at the 340 Dionysia with his satyr-play *Lycurgus*.
[72]   *TrGF* 1.85 T2 (DID A2a: *IG* ii² 2320. 9, 28): see Millis and Olson (2012) 67.
[73]   *TrGF* 1.8 (DID A 3a, 14: *IG* ii² 2325.14). Snell tentatively suggests that this may be the same person as Nothippus (*TrGF* 1.26), despite the early date; he is followed by Millis and Olson (2012) 144–7.
[74]   *TrGF* 1.37 (DID A 2b, 73: *IG* ii² 2319 col. iii.7). Millis and Olson (2012) 115–17 suggest Hera[cleides] for the poet's name. *Children of Theseus* would be another possibility for the play's title.
[75]   *TrGF* 1.63, 65–9, 74 (*IG* ii². 2325. 235–46): see Millis and Olson (2012) 204–7. All attempts to restore these names are doubtful.

The available evidence is ambiguous or muddled, and in some cases there is some confusion over the identity of the writer(s) in question. But even this material, for all its problems, can fill in a number of small and large gaps in our knowledge of the tragic genre.

Snell's edition of the remains lists **Datis** among the fifth-century tragedians, but it is unlikely that a person of this name ever wrote tragedies. Trygaeus, one of the characters in Aristophanes' *Peace* of 421 BCE, says that he once sang what he calls 'a song of Datis', and he quotes one feeble line – 'How I rejoice and celebrate and make merry!' – which does not sound particularly tragic or paratragic.[76] We would not make any connection at all with the world of tragedy were it not for the fact that an ancient commentator on this passage believed that 'Datis' (actually the name of a Persian satrap or commander) was a nickname for one of the sons of Carcinus. As Douglas Olson has pointed out, 'if Xenocles or one of his brothers came to be called Datis as the result of a series of ill-received linguistic innovations, this could only have happened if the name already meant "one who speaks Greek like a barbarian".'[77]

Nothippus is another name featured in comedy but suspected of being some sort of joke rather than the genuine name of a tragedian. The character Nothippus features as a gluttonous tragic poet in two comic fragments,[78] but nothing else is known about him; and it was pointed out by Wilamowitz that his name is oddly reminiscent of another tragic poet, Gnesippus.[79] Indeed, it seems possible that the name Nothippus is a play on words, since *nothos* in Greek ('bastard') is the opposite of *gnêsios* ('legitimate'). Is 'Nothippus' an insulting inversion of Gnesippus' name? Perhaps so; but, as Snell points out, Athenaeus, who quotes these two comic references, apparently treats Nothippus as a genuine person.

Gnesippus himself has caused problems of identification, largely because Athenaeus, our main source of information about his career, calls him a witty writer of *jeux d'esprit* (*paigniagraphos*).[80] This ambiguous description is hard to

---

[76] Aristophanes, *Peace* 289–91 with Σ *ad loc.* (= *TrGF* 1.34 T1).
[77] Olson (1998) 128. However, Sutton (1987) 18 takes Datis to be the genuine name of one of Carcinus' sons.
[78] Hermippus, *Moirai* F46 K-A; Telecleides, *Hesiodoi* F17 K-A, both quoted by Athenaeus 8.344c (= *TrGF* 1.26 T1).
[79] Wilamowitz (1870) 27–8.
[80] Athenaeus 14.638d–f (*TrGF* 1.27 T1).

interpret, but it has been taken as indicating that Gnesippus was actually a comedian or writer of mimes.[81] However, the evidence of comedians, also quoted by Athenaeus, points to his having been a tragic poet. This seems clear from a direct comparison between Gnesippus and Sophocles in Cratinus' *Cowherds*, where a character makes fun of an archon '... who didn't award Sophocles a chorus when he applied for one, but did award a chorus to Cleomachus' son [i.e. Gnesippus], whom *I* wouldn't have judged worthy of training a chorus – even at the Adonia'.[82] This is scarcely flattering to Gnesippus – and it suggests that even in his own lifetime he was seen by some people as naturally occupying an inferior position in the tragic hierarchy – but the point is that the joke does not work unless Gnesippus is a tragedian who can be imagined as directly competing with Sophocles. Note also that this joke is our sole piece of evidence suggesting that tragedies may have been performed at the Adonia in the late fifth century.

Other comic references to Gnesippus are (on the face of it) similarly unflattering, but they reveal two significant facts about his works. The first is that they were remarkable for including erotic subject-matter. Telecleides in his comedy *Hard Men* joked that Gnesippus spent all his time seducing women (a comment which probably reflects the content of his plays), while a character in Eupolis' *Helots* said[83]:

> It's old-fashioned to sing the poetry of Stesichorus, and Alcman, and Simonides; but it is possible to listen to Gnesippus – he came up with nocturnal songs for adulterers to serenade women with, holding an *iambykê* and a *trigônos*.

Here Gnesippus is treated as representative of a new, fashionable type of poetry, in contrast with the outdated older lyric poetry of Stesichorus et al., and his poetry is characterized by its erotic themes and sexy music. This is a particularly significant piece of evidence because the tragedian who is normally associated with this sort of subject-matter is Euripides. Ancient comedians, critics and biographers repeatedly draw attention to the erotic and romantic aspects of Euripides' drama, or the poet's own love life, while modern scholars have seen Euripides as a forerunner of New Comedy in the sense that his

---

[81] Davidson (2000); but see the response by Prauscello (2006), who reaffirms the case for seeing Gnesippus as a tragic poet.

[82] Cratinus, *Cowherds* F17 K-A (*TrGF* 1.27 T1). Cratinus, *Seasons* F276 K-A also explicitly names Gnesippus ('the son of Cleomachus') as a *tragic* poet.

[83] Telecleides, *Sterroi* F36 K-A; Eupolis, *Helots* F148 K-A. Cf. Cratinus' *Malthakoi* F104 K-A, a corrupt fragment which is (somehow) concerned with erotic love in relation to Gnesippus.

plots often involve love-affairs, rapes, seductions, supposititious children, and so on.[84] Nevertheless, the evidence of comedy suggests that Gnesippus may have been equally important in this respect; and it has even been thought that his tragedies deliberately (or incongruously) incorporated cross-generic elements from lyric or sympotic poetry.[85] Perhaps Gnesippus can be seen as a writer whose aim was to expand the emotional and thematic range of tragic plots.

The second remarkable feature of Gnesippus' work was its music. It seems that Gnesippus, along with certain other late fifth-century dramatists including Euripides and Agathon, was an exponent of the 'New Music', a controversial style of theatre music with a novel approach to instrumentation and word-setting.[86] These comic testimonia identify several specific aspects of the music and sound-world of Gnesippus' tragedies. Eupolis explicitly mentions the unusual instrumentation used for some of his erotic lyrics – the *iambykê* and *trigônos* were innovative and exotic stringed instruments – and it is implied that this music had a markedly feminine, sensual effect.[87] Cratinus also refers to Gnesippus' chorus as 'plucking their awful songs in the Lydian mode' (a tonality elsewhere associated with a 'relaxed', 'slack', or 'soft' sound),[88] while a character in Chionides' *Beggars* complains after hearing some music that 'neither Gnesippus nor Cleomenes could have made this sound sweet, not even with nine strings!' – another indication of Gnesippus' penchant for stringed instruments.[89] It is obvious that this style of music did not suit everyone's tastes, but if we discount these qualitative aesthetic judgements we are left with an important piece of factual information: Gnesippus' tragedies incorporated quirkily orchestrated and highly distinctive choral songs and monodies.

---

[84] E.g. Aristophanes, *Women at the Thesmophoria* 85, 383 (and *passim*), *Clouds* 1371–2, *Frogs* 52–5, 1042–55; Plutarch, *Moralia* 177a; Longinus, *On the Sublime* 15.3; Quintilian 10.1.68–9; Satyrus, *Life of Euripides* F39 col. vii; see Knox (1979) and Seidensticker (1982) 15–19 for Euripides' influence on the erotic plots of New Comedy. Cf. Wright (forthcoming a) for a broader discussion of erotic love in tragedy.

[85] Prauscello (2006, 62) argues that the comedians' treatment of Gnesippus stems from indignation at his 'appropriation of the civic social body represented by the chorus itself, transferring his indecent muse from the private sphere of symposia (*kitharoidia*) to the institutionalized one of public space (tragedy)'.

[86] See West (1992) 356–72; Barker (1984) 93–116 presents a useful collection of contemporary source-material relating to the fifth-century 'musical revolution'. Cf. the discussion of Diogenes above (pp. 49–50).

[87] West (1992) 75–7 describes these harp-like instruments in detail, and refers to their 'image of sensuality and low hedonism'.

[88] Cratinus, *Seasons* F276 K-A; cf. Plato, *Republic* 3.398e–399a; [Plutarch,] *On Music* 15.1136b–c.

[89] Chionides, *Beggars* F4 K-A.

A tragedian by the name of **Meletus** produced an *Oedipodeia* – i.e. a trilogy or tetralogy based on the myth of Oedipus – in the same year as Aristophanes' *Storks* (a comedy which jokingly referred to Meletus as 'the son of Laius' on account of his choice of subject-matter).[90] This fact is significant in terms of the way in which dramatists' approach to trilogies and tetralogies changed and evolved over time. It is often thought that connected trilogies or tetralogies disappeared after the time of Aeschylus, but the case of Meletus makes it clear that even at a comparatively late date, perhaps in the last decade of the fifth century,[91] some tragedians, at least, were still writing suites of plays connected by a single narrative thread.[92]

There are a number of other references to Meletus, including a few scurrilous jokes from comedy and a few descriptions of his work as 'frigid' (*psychros*) or 'slender' (*leptos*) in character. The problem is that some of these references may relate to different people of the same name. Sometimes it is obvious that a tragedian is denoted – as in the case of Aristophanes' *Gerytades*, where Meletus is treated as the representative of the tragic genre down in the Underworld (alongside the comedian Sannyrion and the dithyrambist Cinesias), or Sannyrion's comedy *Laughter*, in which Meletus is referred to as 'the corpse from the Lenaea festival'.[93] But elsewhere it appears that the Meletus in question is a writer of erotic lyric poetry after the manner of Sappho, or a composer of drinking-songs.[94] Now it may be that Meletus wrote in more than one genre, or that (like Gnesippus) he incorporated cross-generic elements into his tragedies; but it may also be that there were several poets called Meletus. The situation is confused further by the fact that Meletus was also the name of the notorious character who brought the prosecution against Socrates in 399 BCE, and a few scholars (both ancient and modern) have debated whether or not this Meletus

---

[90] *TrGF* 1.47 T1, incorporating Aristophanes, *Storks* F453 K-A; cf. *Frogs* 1302, *Farmers* F117 K-A.

[91] *Storks* and the *Oedipodeia* are conventionally dated to c. 400–399 BCE, but this is probably incorrect. The detail that *Storks* and Meletus' *Oedipodeia* appeared in the same year derives from Aristotle [*TrGF* 1.47 T1 = *Didaskaliae* F628 Rose] and so should probably be regarded as accurate. However, Meletus was clearly dead by 408 BCE, when he appeared as one of the dead poets in Aristophanes' *Gerytades* (F156 K-A). This means that the latest possible date for his tetralogy and *Storks* is 409.

[92] Note also that Sophocles the Younger wrote a *Telepheia* in the fourth century (*TrGF* DID B5, 8). See Wright (2006), esp. 27–30, for more detailed discussion about the evidence for different types of connection between plays in a production (including a table showing every complete production known to us).

[93] Aristophanes, *Gerytades* F156 K-A; Sannyrion, *Laughter* F2 K-A. See Wright (2012) 135–9 for discussion of Meletus' treatment in comedy and its possible implications for his poetic style.

[94] Epicrates, *Antilais* F4 K-A; cf. Aristophanes, *Frogs* 1301 (which Sommerstein [1994, *ad loc.*] takes as a reference to a different Meletus, not the tragic poet).

had anything to do with the tragic Meletus. Unless some more evidence should come to light, it is impossible to reach any firm conclusion about these matters.[95]

The name **Demetrius** appears on the so-called 'Pronomos Vase', a large piece of Athenian red-figure pottery from around 400 BCE which apparently commemorates a specific performance or victory at a festival. The images include chorus members, actors, and other members of the production team.[96] Most of the figures on the vase are helpfully labelled by the artist, including Demetrius, who is depicted with several papyrus rolls representing the scripts of his plays: this character is probably the playwright, though it is not impossible that he was a chorus trainer or coach.[97] Even though the performance evoked by this vase-painting is clearly a satyr-play, it is normally assumed that Demetrius wrote tragedies as well, and that the satyr-play in question would have formed part of a tragic tetralogy; but even this assumption is open to doubt.[98]

An **Empedocles**, grandson of the philosopher of the same name, is listed in the *Suda* as the author of twenty-four tragedies, though nothing at all is known about these plays or their author.[99]

A reference, in Aristophanes' *Wealth*, to **Pamphilus'** *Children of Heracles* has sometimes been taken as implying that this work was a tragedy, but it has also been thought to refer to a painting: ancient scholars clearly resorted to guesswork when explaining the reference.[100] If Pamphilus was a tragedian, he has left no other trace on the historical record.

Plutarch, in his *Life of Aristides*, says that in his own times there remained in the Athenian theatre some choregic tripods that had been left there as victory-offerings by Aristides. He even quotes the inscription, which he says was still

---

[95] Snell's edition differentiates between 'Meletus I' (1.47) and 'Meletus II' (1.48), but it is hard to be confident that he is right. For the evidence (such as it is) see *TrGF* 1.47 T1, T4 and 1.48 T1–3; for further discussion of these identification problems cf. Blumenthal (1973).

[96] Naples, Museo Archeologico Nazionale 81673 (H3240) = *TrGF* 1.49. See Taplin and Wyles (2010) for discussion of the significance of this artefact for theatre historians.

[97] As pointed out by Hall (2010), who discusses many other points of interest in these images.

[98] Satyr-plays might well have been performed separately – if not at the major festivals, then at minor festivals or other performance venues; and even the Dionysia dropped satyr-plays from the tragic part of the competition during the mid-fourth century and perhaps earlier: see *IG* ii². 2319–23; cf. Pickard-Cambridge (1988) 72–3, Hall (2010) 163. There is no direct evidence that the Lenaea ever included satyr-plays, but see Luppe (2009).

[99] *Suda* Σ 1001 = *TrGF* 1.50 T1.

[100] Aristophanes, *Wealth* 382–5 (with Σ) = *TrGF* 1.51.

legible: 'The tribe Antiochis was victorious; the *choregos* was Aristides, and the poet was **Archestratus**'.[101] However, Plutarch goes on to say that there was some uncertainty regarding the date, for Archestratus was active at the time of the Peloponnesian War rather than during the lifetime of Aristides the 'Just' (who died in 468). The only other reference to a poet of this name occurs in an inscription from the theatre at Tegea, commemorating a much later contest: an individual whose name is not recorded won the prize for Best Actor at the Delphic Soteria festival in the mid-third century BCE, performing in Euripides' *Heracles* and Archestratus' *Antaeus*.[102] If this evidence relates to the same Archestratus mentioned by Plutarch, it tells us the significant fact that his plays were still being read and reperformed a couple of centuries after their first production. Incidentally, it is also interesting to note that this Delphic production consisted of a 'thematic' pairing of two tragedies by different playwrights on the same subject (the various exploits of Heracles).

There were apparently two tragedians called **Philiscus**. The younger and more famous one, Philiscus of Corcyra, was a Hellenistic tragedian.[103] According to the *Suda*, his namesake, perhaps a generation older, was born in Aegina and moved to Athens to become a disciple of Diogenes, the Cynic philosopher and tragedian (see Chapter 5); there was even a tradition that Philiscus had written the tragedies attributed to Diogenes.[104] Unfortunately the testimonia relating to these two Philiscuses are rather confused, and it is not always clear which of the two writers is being referred to.

---

[101] Plutarch, *Aristides* 1.3. 318d (*TrGF* 1. 75).
[102] *IG* v. 2.118 (DID B11): the estimated date is *c.* 276–219 BCE. Snell *ad loc.* records other possible references to Archestratus, but these may relate to someone else of the same name.
[103] *TrGF* 1.104. See Kotlińska-Toma (2014) 66–73.
[104] *TrGF* 1.89 T1–5; cf. Snell, *TrGF* 1, p. 258 on the confusion between the two.

Epilogue

Generalizing about tragedy is a risky business, as is the attempt to come up with catch-all generic definitions of 'tragedy' or 'the tragic'. If any conclusion can be drawn from the chapters above, it is that the lost plays make it more difficult than ever to attempt such an undertaking. As I have been arguing, the study of lost tragedies and neglected playwrights only makes us more aware of the polymorphous diversity of the genre throughout the classical period. It also reminds us, if reminder were needed, of the many differences between classical Greek *tragôidia* and the later forms of literature and drama that indirectly descend from it. These later 'tragedies', though diverse in terms of origin and historical context, are considerably more restricted and more narrowly defined in terms of content, theme, treatment and tone. Throughout the classical period, from its earliest origins through to the late fourth century BCE, tragedy is characterized above all by *variety*. It does not seem to have a single pattern, form or purpose. It does not have a rigidly fixed repertoire of themes, plot-types or subject-matter. It ranges widely across the whole mythical tradition, and even (on rare occasions) incorporates contemporary events from real life. But there is no evidence of anything resembling a generic master-narrative, nor of any recurrent preoccupations of a particularly significant sort (such as, for instance, Dionysiac themes or Athenian politics), and I can find no hint that the classical Greeks ever discerned or looked for any special meaning or essence at the heart of tragedy.

Another very striking feature which seems to present itself is the continuity and stability of the genre during the whole of the classical period. Despite the fact that we are dealing with material stretching across two centuries or more, and despite what has often been thought about developments in Athenian political and artistic life after 404 BCE, it is hard to discern any major or meaningful changes in the character of tragedy throughout the period. In particular, none of the traits conventionally attributed to fourth-century drama – its rhetorical excesses, its melodramatic plots, its reliance on mawkish emotionalism, or similar – can actually be detected in the fragments or other evidence. Of course individual playwrights came along from time to time, with their own unique characteristics and original ideas, but the overall character of the genre remained more or less the same.

One potentially major development, in terms of performance conventions, relates to the function of the tragic chorus from the late fifth century onwards. It has often been thought that the chorus was used much less than before, in a way that was less integrated into the plot, and that there was a drastic reduction in the overall amount of lyrics and music in drama. But in fact there is very little definite evidence for this supposed change or decline. Against Aristotle's brief remarks about non-integrated choral odes (*embolima*) in Agathon and some later tragedians, we have to consider the evidence that the chorus persisted into the fourth century. Several plays are named after their chorus (e.g. Apollodorus' *Greeks* and *Suppliant Women,* Astydamas the Younger's *Epigoni,* Dicaeogenes' *Cyprians,* Timocles' *Phorcides,* Chaeremon's *Minyans* and so on), and some later tragedians were still particularly celebrated for composing choral songs and lyrics (e.g. Carcinus the Younger, Dicaeogenes). If there is a dearth of choral fragments from the fourth century, this could just as easily be attributed to the poor quality of the evidence (and the fact that most tragic fragments, from *all* periods, are from the dialogue portions of the text, especially *gnômai*).

Here and there one can discern hints that some of the 'facts' or generic 'norms' that have conventionally been accepted by scholars are subject to doubt. Against the supposed Athenocentrism of tragedy we have to consider the substantial and growing presence of non-Athenian tragedians throughout the classical period (e.g. Pratinas, Aristias, Aristarchus, Neophron, Achaeus, Ion, Acestor, Spintharus, Diogenes, Dionysius, Theodectes), as well as the evidence of lively theatrical traditions further afield (e.g. Macedon, Halicarnassus, Syracuse and the Greek West). Against the normal assumption that connected trilogies or tetralogies were the norm during the early fifth century but were later abandoned, we can point to certain instances where a relatively late author produced a connected tetralogy (such as Philocles' *Pandionis,* Meletus' *Oedipodeia* or the Younger Sophocles' *Telepheia*); but more generally, in fact, there seems to have been a wide variety of practice, not just in terms of the relationship between plays in a trilogy/tetralogy but also in terms of the number and arrangement of plays in a complete production. Sometimes a satyr-play might be put on as the third play in a set (as Aristias' *Wrestlers* apparently was) or a tragedy as fourth play (e.g. Euripides' *Alcestis*); even though we do not always possess complete records, it is seldom the case that a playwright's attested titles divide neatly into 75 per cent tragedies plus 25 per cent satyr-plays (as one would expect if tetralogies consisting of three tragedies-plus-satyr-play had been normative); and at certain periods both trilogies and dilogies seem to be attested (see e.g. the records for Cleaenetus, Theodorides, Timocles and Euaretus). All of this evidence may make us wonder what the 'normal' competition rules were at any particular period, or whether there was always a certain amount of flexibility.

In every chapter, despite the shortage of information, one can see tantalizing glimpses of original or curious features in the work of individual poets. For instance (to take just a few examples from many), some tragedians strove towards greater dramatic realism in terms of dialogue or stagecraft (Sthenelus, Cleophon); some introduced new perspectives on myth and religion (Critias, Diogenes, Carcinus the Younger); some indulged in verbal experimentation or stylistic oddities (Agathon, Theodectes, Diogenes, Chaeremon); some made creative use of the 'curtain' and other opening devices (Phrynichus, Aristarchus); some expanded the range of character types or the psychological range of their characters (Phrynichus, Neophron, Carcinus the Younger, Theodectes); some introduced innovations in the staging, special effects or use of props (Patrocles, Dicaeogenes, Sthenelus, Xenocles); some incorporated extraordinary mimetic choreography into their work (Carcinus the Elder); some introduced erotic themes into the world of tragedy (Gnesippus, Chaeremon); and others seem to have begun exploiting the tension between reading and performance (Carcinus the Younger, Chaeremon).

A number of our neglected tragedians were obviously fascinating maverick figures, whose work one would dearly love to be able to read in full – I am thinking particularly of Diogenes of Sinope, whose plays endeavoured to make incest and cannibalism seem appealing; or Agathon, with his bizarrely mannered Greek style and his one-off fictional experiments; or Dionysius, with his autobiographical drama and his dirge for the dear departed Doris. But as well as these literary curiosities there are many other lost tragedies which give the impression of having been works of major historical or dramatic importance. Everyone who has ever spent any time thinking about this material will have their own fantasy wish-list of plays for retrieval. If a few lost plays could be recovered tomorrow from the sands of Oxyrhynchus or the Villa of the Papyri at Herculaneum, my own list would include Phrynichus' *Sack of Miletus* (for its historical interest, and as a prime example of early-period tragedy), Aristarchus' *Asclepius* and Diogenes of Athens' tragedy about Cybele (for what they might be able to tell us about the obscure world of Greek religion), the plays with which Xenocles defeated Sophocles' *Oedipus Tyrannus* and its companion pieces (so as to try to decide whether the judges really were having an off day), Neophron's *Medea* (to compare it with Euripides' version), and Astydamas the Younger's

Parthenopaeus (in order to try to understand why it catapulted its author to super-stardom). Of course this is wishful thinking, but it is a pleasant and diverting game – and one which can also, incidentally, help one to articulate and clarify just what was so extraordinary about the lost works in question.

One feature of the genre which will have become very obvious on the basis of the discussions above is the extent to which tragic playwrights repeatedly used and reused the same material as one another. The same myths, characters and play titles are encountered over and over again. One notes especially that certain mythical figures – including, above all, Alcmeon, Telephus, Oeneus and Meleager – were extremely prominent in the genre as a whole, even though they are not represented at all by extant tragedy.

Sometimes it has been possible to detect significant variations in the treatment of this material. We have seen alternative treatments of characters and situations that are well-known from surviving plays, including a non-murderous Medea (Carcinus the Younger), an emasculated Jason (Neophron and Melanthius), a stupid Oedipus (Diogenes of Sinope), a sensitive and suicidal Cercyon (Carcinus the Younger), and an Alcmeon who did not mean to kill his mother (Astydamas the Younger). The surviving versions of these myths, in tragedy and elsewhere, can seem to represent the 'definitive' version, but it is clear that things were not so simple. There were multiple versions of these stories – not just because the mythical tradition was unusually capacious and full of contradictions and variants, but because each new literary or dramatic version presented an opportunity for the poet to re-examine the myth and bring his own perspective or new twist to it.

It comes to seem almost certain that each successive dramatization of a myth will have differed in some way from the previous ones,[1] and it may be that certain later writers deliberately and self-consciously set out to define their own originality in terms of departure from specific earlier treatments (a technique that Harold Bloom called *clinamen*). But there is no reason whatsoever to see this tendency as a special characteristic of 'epigonal' (i.e. fourth-century) authors, as is sometimes claimed, nor is there any reason to suppose that the main sources or points of departure were the so-called 'classic' versions by Euripides, Aeschylus or Sophocles. In the chapters above I have tried to avoid this sort of assumption and to suggest alternative ways of looking at intertextual relationships between playwrights. In particular, I have tried to go beyond straightforwardly agonistic models of intertextuality based on the 'anxiety of influence', and instead to ask

---

[1] See Sommerstein (2010), who assumes that this is a universal rule of the genre.

the more interesting question of what it might have *meant* to rework an earlier version or versions. Of course we are often unable to answer this question or to identify the exact relationships or sources that were most important to the poets. But the evidence seems to suggest that *some sort* of intertextual dialogue between authors may have been central to the whole genre. Indeed, even the work of the three 'classic' authors is often characterized by mythical innovation or intertextual responses to other poets' work. Much of the pleasure for the spectators or readers will have lain in noting the differences between the new version and the old (which may often have been quite subtle), detecting new depth and nuance in the treatment of characters and their situations, and looking at the myths from a new and unexpected angle each time.

With this in mind, it may be useful for readers to have a conspectus of classical (i.e. pre-Hellenistic) tragedies which share the same titles or subject-matter[2]:

Aerope: Agathon, Carcinus the Younger; cf. Euripides, *Cretan Women.*

Agamemnon: Aeschylus, Ion.

Athamas: Aeschylus, Sophocles, Xenocles (satyric), Astydamas the Younger.

Ajax: Sophocles, Carcinus, Theodectes, Astydamas the Younger; (cf. Aeschylus, *The Award of the Arms, Thracian Women*).

Actaeon: Iophon, Cleophon; cf. Aeschylus, *Female Archers.*

Alexandros: Sophocles, Euripides.

Alcestis: Phrynichus, Euripides.

Alcmeon: Achaeus (satyric), Sophocles, Euripides, Agathon, Astydamas the Younger, Theodectes, Timotheus; cf. Sophocles, *Eriphyle, Epigoni*; Aeschylus, *Epigoni*; Astydamas the Younger, *Epigoni*; Achaeus, Timotheus and Chaeremon, *Alphesiboea.*

Alcmene: Ion, Euripides, Dionysius, Astydamas the Younger; cf. Sophocles, *Amphitryon.* (Cf. *Heracles.*)

Alope: Choerilus, Euripides, Carcinus the Younger; cf. Aeschylus, *Cercyon* (satyric?).

Antaeus: Phrynichus, (Aristias,) Archestratus. (Cf. *Heracles.*)

Auge: Euripides, Aphareus.

Achilles: Aristarchus, Iophon, Astydamas the Younger, Carcinus the Younger, Chaeremon (*Achilles, Killer of Thersites*), Cleophon, Euaretus, Diogenes of Sinope; cf. Aeschylus, *Weighing of Souls.*

---

[2] This is (inevitably) an indicative rather than exhaustive list: many titles are lost, and even those titles that survive do not always give an obvious indication of the play's content. For titles of Hellenistic and later tragedies see Kotlińska-Toma (2014) and Snell's *TrGF* 1, pp. 259–334. I omit titles collected in the second volume of *TrGF* (*adespota*) because it is impossible to give an exact date for any of this material.

Bacchae: Xenocles, Cleophon, Ion, Euripides; cf. Thespis(?), Aeschylus and Iophon, *Pentheus*; Chaeremon, *Dionysus*.

Bellerophon: Euripides, Astydamas the Younger; (cf. Euripides, *Stheneboea*).

Children of Pelias: Euripides, Aphareus.

Chrysippus: Euripides, Diogenes of Sinope.

Danae: Euripides, Sophocles.

Danaids: Phrynichus, Aeschylus.

Erigone: Sophocles, Philocles, Cleophon.

Hector: Aeschylus (*Phrygians* or *Ransoming of Hector*), Dionysius (*Ransoming of Hector*), Astydamas the Younger; cf. Sophocles, *Andromache, Hermione*; Euripides, *Andromache*; Antiphon, *Andromache*. (Cf. *Achilles*).

Helen: Euripides, Theodectes, Diogenes of Sinope; cf. Dionysius, *Leda*; Sophocles, *The Demand for Helen's Return, The Rape of Helen* (?), *The Wedding of Helen* (satyric?).

Heracles: Sophocles (*Heracles, Trachiniae*), Spintharus, Euripides, Diogenes of Sinope; cf. Ion, *Omphale* (satyric), Achaeus, *Omphale* (satyric); cf. Aeschylus, Euripides and Pamphilus(?), *Children of Heracles*.

Hypsipyle: Aeschylus, Euripides, Cleaenetus.

Ixion: Aeschylus, Sophocles, Euripides.

Iphigenia: Aeschylus, Sophocles, Euripides, Polyidus(?).

Licymnius: Xenocles, Euripides.

Lycaon: Xenocles, Astydamas the Younger.

Lycurgus: Polyphrasmon (*Lycourgeia*), Aeschylus, Timocles (satyric). (Cf. *Bacchae*.)

Medea: Neophron, Euripides II, Euripides, Melanthius, Dicaeogenes, Carcinus the Younger, Diogenes of Sinope, Theodorides; cf. Antiphon, *Jason*.

Meleager: Euripides, Antiphon; cf. Phrynichus, *Pleuronian Women*; Aeschylus, *Atalanta* (cf. *Oeneus*).

Mysians: Aeschylus, Agathon, Sophocles.

Momus: Achaeus, Sophocles.

Nauplius: Sophocles, Philocles, Astydamas the Younger (cf. *Palamedes*).

Niobe: Aeschylus, Sophocles.

Odysseus: Apollodorus, Chaeremon, Sophocles; cf. Aeschylus, *Penelope, Circe* (satyric), *Bone-Gatherers, Ghost-Raisers*; Philocles, *Penelope*; Ion, *Laertes*; Sophocles, *Nausicaa* (satyric?); also cf. *Philoctetes* below.

Oedipus: Aeschylus, Sophocles, Achaeus, Xenocles, Euripides, Carcinus the Younger, Timocles, Theodectes, Diogenes of Sinope; cf. Meletus, *Oedipodeia*; Aeschylus, *Laius, Sphinx* (satyric); Sophocles, *Antigone*; Euripides, *Antigone, Phoenician Women*; Astydamas the Younger, *Antigone*.

Oeneus: Philocles, Ion(?), Euripides, Sophocles, Chaeremon; cf. Sophocles, *Hipponous*; Theodectes, *Tydeus* (cf. *Meleager*).

Oenomaus: Euripides, Sophocles.

Orestes: Euripides II, Euripides, Theodectes, Aphareus, Carcinus the Younger; cf. Aeschylus, *Oresteia*; Sophocles, *Electra*; Euripides, *Electra*.

Palamedes: Aeschylus, Sophocles, Euripides, Astydamas the Younger (cf. *Nauplius*).

Persians: Aeschylus; cf. Phrynichus, *Phoenician Women*.

Perseus: Pratinas; cf. Sophocles and Euripides, *Andromeda*.

Phaedra: Sophocles, Euripides (*Hippolytus I* and *II*). (Cf. *Theseus*.)

Phaethon: Euripides, Theodorides.

Philoctetes: Aeschylus, Achaeus, Sophocles, Philocles, Euripides, Antiphon(?), Theodectes.

Phineus: Aeschylus, Sophocles.

Phoenix: Euripides, Ion (maybe two separate plays?), Astydamas the Younger.

Phrixus: Achaeus, Sophocles, Euripides (*Phrixus I* and *II*), Timocles.

Polyxena: Euripides II, Sophocles; cf. Euripides, *Hecuba*.

Scyrians: Sophocles, Euripides.

Semele: Aeschylus, Spintharus, Diogenes of Athens, Iophon (?), Carcinus the Younger; cf. Chaeremon, *Dionysus*.

Sisyphus: Aeschylus, Critias, Euripides (satyric), Sophocles.

Tantalus: Phrynichus, Pratinas, Aristarchus, Sophocles. (Cf. *Thyestes*.)

Teucer: Sophocles, Ion, Euaretus; cf. Aeschylus, *Women of Salamis* (cf. *Ajax*).

Telephus: Aeschylus, Sophocles, Iophon, Agathon, Euripides, Cleophon.

Tereus: Sophocles; cf. Philocles, *Pandionis*.

Theseus: Achaeus, Sophocles, Euripides; cf. Critias, *Peirithous*; Sophocles, *Aegeus*.

Thyestes: Sophocles, Agathon, Euripides, Carcinus the Younger (*Thyestes* or *Aerope*), Chaeremon, Cleophon, Apollodorus; cf. Agathon, *Aerope*; Diogenes of Sinope (*Thyestes* or *Atreus*); Ion, *Agamemnon*. (Cf. *Orestes*.)

Trojan Women: Euripides; cf. Iophon, *Sack of Troy*; Sophocles, *Cassandra, Priam*; Philocles, *Priam*.

Tyro: Sophocles, Astydamas the Younger, Carcinus the Younger(?)

This list does not prove that any of these individual poets knew, or consciously responded to, the work of any of the others, but it does demonstrate that in many cases there was a fairly wide range of possibilities to choose from — and of course there will have been many other titles that are unknown to us. (Aeschylus, Sophocles and Euripides do feature more often than the other names, but this is simply because far more plays and titles survive from their output than from any of the others.)

To conclude: Volume 1 has deliberately set out to give an account of the tragic genre *without* Aeschylus, Sophocles or Euripides, and thus to redress some of the imbalances and distortions of two and a half millennia. Volume 2 will rewrite the triad back into literary history, but it will demonstrate that even the work of these 'classic' writers has been radically misrepresented by later scholarship and seriously affected by accidents of survival. In the meantime, what is absolutely clear is that we would have a very different view of Greek tragedy today if all these plays – or a different selection of them – had survived.

APPENDIX 1

Translations

For the benefit of students and other general readers, this section provides English translations of all the fragments of the neglected tragedians, since no other English version exists in print. In most cases the paucity of the material made it possible to incorporate the translations into the main text or footnotes at the relevant point in each chapter, but in the interests of convenience and completeness this Appendix contains the tragic fragments of every neglected author in their entirety. (Spurious fragments, testimonia and satyric fragments are omitted.) In order to avoid confusion or exasperation, I present the fragments in the same order as Snell's *Tragicorum Graecorum Fragmenta,* even though this is not the order in which the tragedians are discussed in this book.

I have aimed to provide a clear English version of the fragments, insofar as such a thing is possible. The nature of the material means that it would be impossible to produce a completely reliable or definitive version. In many cases the intended meaning is unclear because of the brevity or incomplete state of the fragment, or textual uncertainties, or the lack of interpretative context. Often it is impossible to reproduce the stylistic effect of the Greek in English (and in general, English must use rather more words than Greek in order to get the meaning across). Some will no doubt regret that I have not attempted to produce stylish or elegant translations; I have simply concentrated on trying to convey a reasonably accurate sense of what I think these authors meant. The reader is warned that many of these versions are fairly tentative or provisional in nature. A few specific difficulties or special features are mentioned in footnotes.

Choerilus (*TrGF* 1.2)

F1   *The Athenian Choerilus wrote a play called* Alope *in which it is said that Cercyon and Triptolemus were brothers, and that Amphictyon's daughter* *was their mother, but Rharus was Triptolemus' father, whereas Poseidon was Cercyon's father.*[1]

F2 scraping [his?] foot against the earth's bones (i.e. rocks)

F3 the veins of the earth (i.e. rivers)

Phrynichus (*TrGF* 1.3)

Note that some of the items labelled 'F' by Snell in *TrGF* are strictly testimonia rather than actual quotations from Phrynichus, so they are not included here (but they are discussed in Chapter 1). As Snell acknowledges, some of the fragments (especially F20–24) are doubtful and may be misattributed: there was also a comic playwright called Phrynichus, and perhaps some of these quotations are from his work. I think this is almost certainly true of F21a (printed with a question-mark by Snell), since it is highly unlikely that any character in a tragedy would make an explicit reference to the stage-machinery – or, at any rate, if the tragic Phrynichus' characters *were* indulging in metatheatrical games right at the start of the fifth century, this would have important consequences for our understanding of the development and changing limits of the genre.

Egyptians

F1 Aegyptus came to Argos with the Aegyptioi.

F1a . . . is provoked

Alcestis

F2 [he] exhausts his fearless body, limb-shaken . . .

F3 *Death enters with a sword, with which he cuts off a lock of Alcestis' hair.*[2]

Daughters of Danaus

F4 fruitful (?) *or* cuttings (?)

---

[1] Strictly a testimonium rather than a fragment (Pausanias 1.14.3).
[2] A description from Servius' commentary on Vergil's *Aeneid* 4.694, rather than a fragment as such.

Women of Pleuron

F5   Once upon a time a body of men made their way to this land,
an ancient people, who inhabited the land of Hyas;
and rapid fire consumed in its wild jaws
the whole of the open country and the coastal plain.

F6   [Meleager] did not escape his chill fate;
but as the wooden brand was destroyed by his terrible mother,
contriver of evil, the flame swiftly consumed him.

Tantalus

F7   sitting down (?) *or* seats (?)

Phoenician Women

F8   *Eunuch*: All this belongs to the Persians, who have long ago gone . . .[3]

F9   leaving the Sidonian city and dewy Arados

F10   abandoning the temple of Sidon

F10a . . . round about evening . . .
. . . men were killed up until evening . . .

F11   singing songs in response to the sound of the harp

F12   to pinch in tightly at the waist

From unknown plays

F13   The light of love shines brightly on his [Troilus'] crimson cheeks.

F14   The women, after giving him entertainment, as the story goes,
killing [him] and chopping off [his] head with a sharp bronze sword

F16   a quick-witted (*or* white?) bull

F16a a messenger delivering good tidings rather than ill

---

[3]   Or: 'These are the [ ] of the Persians . . .' or 'This is the [ ] of the Persians . . .'

F16b   worth seeing

F16c   misdemeanour

F17   The cock crouched, bending his wing in servile fashion.

F20   Dearest of men, do not behave disrespectfully towards me.

F21   But, since he hates me, I shall get out of his sight.

F21a   the push-out stage [*exôstra,* another name for the *ekkyklêma*]

F22   knowledgeable people

F23   Semele [a sort of table]

F24   bracelets

Pratinas (*TrGF* 1.4)

F1   the sweet-voiced [quail]

F3   What is this noise? What is all this dancing? What is this excessive behaviour that has come to the much-resounding altar of Dionysus? Bromios is mine, he is mine! It is my duty to cry out, my duty to make a loud noise as I rush about all over the mountains with the Naiads, like a swan leading the subtle, winged song. The Pierian Muse established song to rule over us, so let the *aulos* dance in second place – for it is but a servant. Would that the *aulos* might restrict its martial ambitions to the revel and the fisticuffs of young drunkards fighting at their lovers' front doors!

Strike the man who makes a breathy noise like a spotted toad! Burn the reed that squanders saliva as it chatters away with its deep voice, discordant and arhythmical, its shape fashioned by the bore!

Look here! See, I fling my right hand and foot in your honour, o thriambodithyrambic one, lord of the ivy wreath! Listen to my Dorian song and dance![4]

---

[4]   The genre of this fragment – described as a *hyporchêma* by Athenaeus, who quotes it (14.617b–c) – is disputed. See Chapter 1, pp. 15–16.

F4   the Laconian cicada, well-suited to dancing

F5   ... Not going over land that has already been ploughed,
but in search of untouched soil ...

F6   Pursue neither the tense nor the relaxed Muse,
but as you are ploughing the middle of your field,
make an Aeolian sound with your song ...
Indeed, an Aeolian harmony is fitting
for all those who are greedy for poetry.

Aristias (*TrGF* 1.9)

Antaeus

F1   son of Poseidon of the Aegean, my father ...

Atalante

F2   ... and untying the thread of the loom ...

Fates[5]

F3   a fellow-diner or a reveller or a guest at Hades' dinner-table,
having an immoderate appetite ...

Orpheus

F5   I had a wrestling-school and a covered running-track nearby ...

From unknown plays

F6   the stony ground was swelling with mushrooms

F7   is parched *or* is sought (?)[6]

---

[5]   This play is probably satyric: see O'Sullivan and Collard (2013) 504.
[6]   Meaning disputed: see Snell, *TrGF* 1 *ad loc.*, p. 87.

Aristarchus (*TrGF* 1.14)

Achilles

F1a   (*Agamemnon:*) Rise up, herald! Make sure that the people hear!
(*Herald:*) Be silent and keep quiet and pay attention![7]

Tantalus

F1b   In this matter it makes no difference whether you speak well or whether
you don't. Whether you try to find things out or fail to find out anything
at all, it's all the same. Wise men do not understand any more about these
matters than those who are not wise. If anyone claims to be better than
anyone else, he is an excellent speaker [but] . . .

From unknown plays

F2   Among human beings whoever has no experience of love is ignorant of
the law of necessity – in obedience to which I am overwhelmed to such
an extent that I make this journey here. For the god of love has the power
to make sick people healthy, and to make the helpless man find a way . . .

F3   O death, the restoration of good sense to those who lack judgement . . .

F4   [I say this to you] not as a preliminary but in return for what has gone
before.

F5   Talaos *or* Kalaos [the father of Parthenopaeus]

F6   companion *or* beloved one (?)

Neophron (*TrGF* 1.15)

Medea

F1   *Aegeus:* Indeed I came here in person to find out some solution from you,
for I have no means of interpreting the prophetic voice which Apollo's

---

[7]   Tentatively reconstructed from a Latin adaptation by Plautus (*Poenulus* 1–12): these lines cannot be
absolutely trusted. See Snell, *TrGF* 1 *ad loc.* (p. 90) and pp. 45–7 above.

priestess revealed to me. By coming to speak to you I hoped that I might learn.

F2   *Medea:* Well, then – what will you do, my heart? Think hard before you slip up and turn your dearest friends into bitterest enemies. Wretched heart, whither have you rushed forth? Restrain your impulse and your terrible strength that is hateful to the gods.

And why is it that I am crying about all this, when I can see my soul desolate and forsaken by those who least of all ought to have abandoned me? Am I, then, to become weak, indeed, as I undergo such awful sufferings? My heart! Do not betray yourself, even among such evils! [*She sighs.*] Alas! My mind is made up.

[*Speaking to her children*] Out of my sight, boys! Get away from here! For by now a murderous madness has already sunk deep within my heart.

Oh, hands! My hands! What sort of deed is this to which we are steeling ourselves! Ah! I am wretched even in my daring, I who now set out to destroy my long travail in a short moment.

F3   *Medea:* In the end you will kill yourself and meet a most shameful fate, tying a knotted noose around your neck – this is the sort of destiny that awaits you in return for your evil deeds, and acts as a lesson to others for countless days to come: that mortals should never try to raise themselves above gods.

Ion (*TrGF* 1.19)

I have included only those fragments which are, or which have a claim to be, tragic. Satyric fragments are excluded, but for these and other fragments see Leurini (2000), Krumeich et al. (1999), and O'Sullivan and Collard (2013).

Agamemnon

F1   You will carry off a gift worthy of the running:
an indented drinking-cup, undefiled by fire,
the great prize of Pelias, to commemorate the achievement of Castor's feet.

F2   Let death stand apart from other evils, so that he may see what evil is.

F3   splendour of a horseman[8]

F4   in light, gentle slumber

F5   eagle

Alcmene

F5a   And indeed all creatures are inexperienced when at first they are born, but gain in knowledge through experience.

F6   with their souls imprisoned

F7   a pack containing life's necessities

F8   (women) who admire themselves

Men of Argos

F8a   Nobody escapes accusation if he comes bearing bad news.

F9   how old †a broom …[9]

F9a   radiant

Children of Eurytus

F10   Glug out the potent wine, drawing it off
from sacred jars into flasks.

F11   untouched young girls

F12   lamentable

F13   illustrious

F13a   touch(ing) it lightly[10]

---

[8]   Hesychius (I 806), who cites the fragment, says that this phrase refers to clothing.
[9]   Referring to someone who is perceived as useless because of old age.
[10]   Probably a reference to a stringed musical instrument.

Laertes

F14   Go, slave, if you please,
        with winged swiftness, and shut up the house,
        so that no person at all may enter.

Mega Drama

F15   a brittle fennel-stalk

F16   †black-haired (?)

F17   blaming (*or* disdaining)

Teucer

F34   And we, in our ignorance, stumbled against the rocks.

F35   noised abroad

Phoenix (*or* Caineus *or* Oineus)

F38, 36 But on dry land I admire the skill of the lion
        in preference to the miserable craft of the hedgehog,
        who, whenever he apprehends an attack by any other larger animals,
        rolls his thorny body up into a ball, curled right round,
        and lies still, impossible for the attacker to bite or touch ...

*   *

        ... and I detest that creature the octopus who lives among the rocks,
        with its bloodless coils, changing its skin colour.

F37   But, o gods, you who dwell beside these doors ...!

F39   And the *aulos*, like a cockerel,
        resounds with a Lydian tune.

F40   The exudation of the oak-tree nourishes me,
        and so does the branch with its dense foliage, and also the Egyptian
        garment of spun linen that I use to catch wild beasts.[11]

---

[11]   Athenaeus (10.451d), who quotes these lines, tells us that they are a riddle: the reference is to
    mistletoe and a hunting-net.

F41   If I am right to see the life of a man, o citizens . . .

F41a from ignorant men

F41b Manifestly I have acted well in every respect.

Phoenix II (?)

F42   I made my loud, deep-voiced *aulos* resound with a running rhythm . . .

F43   incurring honour

Guards

[**F43a** *Odysseus, having disguised himself, goes to Troy on a spying mission; when he is recognized by Helen, he comes to an arrangement with her concerning the capture of the city. After killing several of the Trojans he arrives back at the ships.*[12]]

F43b And how did the stranger arrive in the bedchamber?

F43c The †luxurious things (?) caused me to retreat in fear . . .

F44   *Helen:* It's silent, but rancorous; yet, at any rate, it wants him.

F45   The cock crows like a pan-pipe from Mount Ida.

F46   snow-white Helen

F47   a watch-tower

F48   wreaths on their arms (*or* garlanded arms)

F49   summoner

F49a beneficial

From unknown plays

F50   these unexpected happenings have made your heart dance

F51   a cup full of wine

---

[12]   Not strictly a fragment but a testimonium (from Proclus' summary of the *Little Iliad*: §53 Davies).

F52   the hill of the nymphs[13]

F53   Nor, at any rate, stricken as he is in body
and in both eyes too, does he forget his courage,
but he makes a noise as his strength is waning;
he has chosen death in preference to slavery ...

F53a   bedimmed

F53b   Now at the time when I do not yet see dawn's light close by,
nor is the break of day dimly visible ...

F53c   concerning kings (?)

F53d   hostile

F53e   We are facing destruction unprepared and unarmed.

F53f   of one mind and sharing the same cup

F54   I came out here ... †and our ... † a nurse of children,
leaving behind the pits of despair.

F58, 55 The strength of a dolphin on dry land is useless.

*   *   *

That proverb, 'Know thyself', is a phrase of no great size,
but Zeus alone of the gods understands how great a thing it is in practice.

F56   Each friend that comes to visit causes vexation, but at the same time
the friend who goes away is also hard to bear.

F57   The dark cluster of grapes does not ripen [in the moon's beams].

F59   Dressed in a short linen frock which reached half-way down his (*or* her)
thigh ...

F60   When I race across the level surface of the Aegean sea ...

F61   strike your own head

[**F62**   *Ion believes that Eridanus is in Achaea.*[14]]

---

13   A mountain in Arcadia (according to Hesychius, who cites the fragment).
14   Not technically a fragment but a testimonium (Σ Vergil, *Georgics* 1.482).

F63 For the city of Sparta is not built with words;
  but on each occasion when Ares descends anew upon the people,
  it is good counsel that reigns,
  while physical might adds extra assistance to the action.

F64 bumblebee[15]

F65 the Pnyx (*or* dense)

F66 easy

F67 rough

F68 purple-edged[16]

Achaeus (*TrGF* 1.20)

As above, only fragments which are, or have a claim to be, tragic are included: cf. Krumeich et al. (1999). Plays or fragments that are *probably* satyric are marked with an asterisk (*).

Adrastus

F1 a serpent

Azanians

F2 [*Chorus:*]
  And so we suppliants place the branches of our garlands
  before your feet and reverence you, begging you
  to put a stop to the sacrifice demanded by unfeeling Zeus.

*Contests

*F3** [A.] Are you talking to the religious ambassadors or to the contestants?
  [B.] They are eating a lot, as men in training are wont to do.

---

15 According to Pollux (6.98), the name of a small drinking vessel that makes a buzzing noise when poured.
16 An epithet used of the *pênelops*, a kind of duck with a purple neck and throat.

[A.] Where do these visitors hail from?
[B.] Boeotia.

*F4   For they †go about naked, their splendid arms bursting with the prime of
        life,
        their powerful shoulders gleaming, their youth in full flower;
        they anoint their chests and† feet with oil in abundance,
        as if they were used to luxury at home.

*F5   They will place into your hand an ornament of emerald
        worth its weight in silver, and Egyptian unguents . . .

Alphesiboea

F16   Like a maenad, among the stars . . .

Theseus

F18   Saronian [Artemis][17]

F18a   with a sharp prow[18]

The Attack (Katapeira)

F23a   opinions of divergent humour

Cycnus

F24, 43 In the first place we have come to the house of Cycnus . . .

*   *

You have come to the house of such a man . . .

F25   To a hungry man a barley cake is more valuable than either gold or ivory.

*Fates

*F27   . . . a great crowd of sea-creatures whirling around,
        a marine embassy, churning up the calm of the sea with their tails.

[17] So named after the Saronic Bay at Troezen.
[18] Of the bull which gored Hippolytus (i.e. sharp-horned).

*F28 *Babai babai!* I shall go in pursuit of women.

Blame (Mômos)

F29 the thief Ares, with spear and with shield . . .

Oedipus

F30 unclean (*or* insane)

F31 (s)he is decked out with lotus flowers

Peirithous

F36 a jar fenced around on all sides[19]

Philoctetes

F37 [*Agamemnon:*]
The hour has come to offer help.
I shall take charge. Let someone take up the sword by its handle!
Someone else, make a signal with the trumpet as quickly as possible!
It is time to make haste! *Eleleleu!*

Phrixus

F38 Peleos

From unknown plays

F40 Tarantine dyes

F41 He made a toast with a drinking-vessel full of unmixed Bibline wine.

F42 Does Aetna nourish horned snails of such a size?

F44 I came here having perpetrated terrible crimes; but now – farewell!

F45 people who force the unafflicted to join them in their own grief

---

[19] I.e. worked into a circular shape (according to Hesychius, who cites the fragment).

F46   [*Achaeus numbers the Hyades as four; Euripides as three.*[20]]

F47   a calf with its mouth wide open in hunger, like a swallow[21]

F48   glittering

F49   more timely

F50   cells of a honeycomb

F51   barley-meal

***F52**   [Silenus] in pursuit of women

F53   the all-seeing one [Zeus]

F54   *aliapous* (a sea-bird, probably the stormy petrel)

F55   diadrachm (?)

F56   vine

Iophon (*TrGF* 1.22)

Bacchae (*or* Pentheus?)

F2   (*Agave?*) I too understand these things, even though I am a woman –
         that the more a person seeks to know about the gods,
         the less he will end up knowing.

Philocles (*TrGF* 1.24)

Pandionis (*tetralogy*)

F1   Master of all, I address you . . .

From unknown plays

F2   [*Philocles relates that Hermione was given in marriage by Tyndareus to
         Orestes, and that she was already pregnant when Menelaus gave her in*

---

[20]   Technically a testimonium (quoted apropos of Euripides' *Phaethon*).
[21]   Or perhaps the young of a swallow is called a 'calf': Aelian, *History of Animals* 7.47.

marriage to Neoptolemus, and gave birth to Amphictyon; later she dwelt with Diomedes . . .[22]]

F3 Talaos *or* Kalaos [the father of Parthenopaeus]

F4 killing with the spear

F5 he would not desist from eating brains

Theognis (*TrGF* 1.28)

F1 a lyre that plays no tune [i.e. a bow]

Xenocles (*TrGF* 1.33)

Licymnius

F1 *Alcmene:* Oh, cruel deity! Oh, misfortune that shattered my chariot-rail and put my horses to flight! Oh, Pallas, how you have ruined me![23]

Agathon (*TrGF* 1.39)

One can only appreciate the extraordinary subtlety and elegance of Agathon's style by reading the fragments in the original language. What follows is merely a provisional attempt at an English translation, which tries to convey the literal meaning of what Agathon wrote. (Sometimes this is difficult or impossible: see Chapter 3, pp. 70–77, for further discussion.)

Aerope

F1 They were making their entrance . . .

Alcmeon

F2 lawless Muses

---

[22] A plot-summary (rather than a fragment as such) quoted by Σ Euripides *Andromache* 32.
[23] Reconstructed from an Aristophanic parody (*Clouds* 1264–5): it may be that these verses are not exactly what Xenocles originally wrote.

Thyestes

F3   We sheared our hair, witness to our love of luxury,
a thing, I suppose, that is desirable to a playful mind.
Immediately, then, we gained a reputation in accordance with the
name –
that is to say, we are *Kouretes*, named after our shorn (*kourimou*) hair.

Telephus

F4   The first letter in the word was a circle with a dot in the centre;
there were also two upright bars joined together,
and there was a third letter also, which was similar to a Scythian bow;
then there was a letter resembling a trident sideways-on;
and then there were two <short bars converging together> on top of a
single bar;
and then the letter that was third appeared again at the end.

From unidentified plays

F5   . . . for the god is prevented from doing just this one thing –
from undoing any deeds that have already been done.

F6   Art likes Fortune, and Fortune Art.[24]

F7   The base among mankind, overcome by toil,
are in love with death.

F8   And indeed one must do some things by art, while certain other things
happen to us through necessity and fortune.

F9   Perhaps one might say that this very thing is probable:
that many improbable things happen to human beings.

F11   We are treating what is secondary as our main task,
and working at our main task as if it were secondary.[25]

---

[24] The words *technê* (art, skill, etc.) and *tychê* (fortune, chance, randomness, etc.) are hard to render into English, as is the similarity of sound between the two words, which creates such a neat balance in the original Greek: cf. F8, F20, F34 below (where *tychê*/*technê* or cognate words are found).

[25] This couplet contains a number of rhymes in the middle and at the end of its lines (involving the nouns *ergon* and *parergon* and the verbs *poioumetha* and *ekponoumetha*) which cannot be reproduced in English.

F12 If I speak the truth, I shan't make you glad;
but if I make you glad at all, I shan't be speaking the truth.

F13 You'll be the death of me, asking all these questions, you and your newfangled habit
of using words in an inappropriate manner.

F14 ... but a woman, just because her body is lazy,
doesn't carry about a lazy intellect within her soul.

F15 Bring forth light-bearing pinewood torches ...

F16a ... but the gratitude that will be given will not go unwitnessed ...

F17 *The Amphictyones gather at the place called* Pylaia, *concerning which Agathon says that Pylades, son of Strophios, was the first to establish it when he was in Phocis, purifying himself of the pollution resulting from Clytemnestra's murder; and it is from him that Agathon says that this meeting-place was called* Pylaia.

F18 I never thought it right to †adopt such habits†[26]

F19 They say that time is by nature a clever thing.[27]

F20 We are tripped up not by our deliberate intention but by fortune.

F21 Those who are by nature industrious seek out their own individual ways.

F22 Being accustomed to sin I am ashamed of being seen by my friends.

F23 May he perish, whoever envies those who possess good things.

F24 Envy would never have existed in human life,
if all of us had been born equal.

F25 It is a fine thing to be grudging of cleverness rather than wealth.[28]

F26 A young man's intellect is very prone to change its course.

F27 Intelligence is a greater thing than the strength of one's hands.

F28 How pleasant it is when children are obedient to the one who bore them!

---

[26] The translation is extremely conjectural, and the text uncertain (see *TrGF ad loc.*).
[27] The word *sophon*, which can mean either 'wise' or 'clever' (in various senses), is hard to translate or evaluate: see discussion above, and cf. Gladigow (1964), Origa (2007).
[28] Cf. on F19 above.

F29   ...for among mortals love comes into being from a glimpse [at the beloved].[29]

F30   unjollity

F31   Hybris or Cypris
†... in payment, whence comes either toil for our native land [or] ...†[30]

F32   O bright eye of the charioteer ...

F34   It is right to endure what befalls us not by artifice
but by our emotions.[31]

Critias (*TrGF* 1.43)

The authorship and genre of some of these fragments has been questioned: see my discussion in Chapter 2, pp. 50–58.

Peirithous

F1

Aeacus: Hey! What is happening here? I spy someone making his way here in haste and with an exceedingly bold demeanour. Stranger, you who approach this region, it is right that you should tell me who you are and what is the purpose of your journey.

Heracles: I shall reveal the whole story to you without any hesitation: my native land is Argos, my name is Heracles, and I am sprung from Zeus, father of all the gods – for Zeus came to my mother's noble bed, as it is

---

[29]   The Greek verse uses the similarity of the words *esorân* (glimpse) and *erân* (love) to create an internal rhyme (or pun) which cannot be reproduced in English.

[30]   The force of this verse seems to come from the equivalence in both sound and (so it is implied) meaning between *Hybris* (arrogance, sin, etc.) and *Cypris* (another name for Aphrodite, the goddess of love), but English possesses no such equivalent terms ('amours' and 'misdemeanours' does not quite achieve the desired effect). Also the text is problematic; our source (Dionysius of Halicarnassus, *Demosthenes* 26) quotes what may be two separate fragments (perhaps by Licymnius and/or Agathon): see *TrGF ad loc.*

[31]   The distinction between *technasmasin* (artifice, tricks, devices, etc.) and *pathêmasin* (emotions, feelings, sufferings, calamities, misfortunes, etc.) in the original is hard to understand; it is also impossible to reproduce the rhyme in English.

told to us by a true account. I have come here under compulsion, obedient to the command of Eurystheus, who sent me with instructions to bring back alive the hound of Hades to the gates of Mycenae. Eurystheus did not actually wish to see Cerberus, but he imagined that he had come up with this task as an impossible challenge for me. In pursuit of such a task I have travelled all around Europe and into the secret places of the whole of Asia.

F2   . . . so that in silence we may pour these water vessels into the chasm in the earth.

F3   [*Chorus:*] And unwearying time moves on its course
in an everlasting stream, in all its fullness, regenerating itself,
and the twin Bears, with quick wandering movements of their wings,
keep watch over Atlas' celestial pole.

F4   [*Chorus:*] You, the self-begotten, who in the whirling of ether
have woven together all natural things, and around whom daylight,
and dark-spangled night, and the innumerable host of stars
perpetually do dance . . .[32]

F5   . . . tripped up . . . coming . . . Greek . . . altars . . . the god . . . madness . . . sent ruin . . . a cloud as a wife . . . sowed among the . . . had sexual intercourse with a daughter . . . of such boasts . . . he paid the gods penalty . . . for madness on a wheel . . . in frenzy [gone?] . . . unnoticed by people . . . hid, but Boreas . . . his body was torn to pieces . . . father offending against the gods . . . and I . . . his sufferings . . .

F6   He is bound fast in honour's fetters, forged not of bronze . . .

F7   . . . labour . . . now seems pleasant to you . . .
[*Theseus:*] I shall (not) blame you, Heracles, for to betray a dear and faithful friend when he has been evilly captured is. . . .
[*Heracles:*] You have spoken, Theseus, in a manner which befits both yourself and the city of the Athenians – for you have always been an ally to those suffering misfortune. But it is a disgrace for me to return to my home country and to have to make excuses. If Eurystheus discovered that you had shared in this toil with me, just imagine what pleasure he

---

[32] Addressed to Mind (*Nous*) as creator of the universe, according to Clement of Alexandria (5.115), who cites the fragment: see *TrGF* 1.43 *ad loc.*

would take in saying that I had failed to complete this labour, for all my struggles!

[*Theseus:*] But that which you desire ... you have my good will; it is not unstable but freely given, in enmity to my enemies and favour towards friends. It is said that formerly ... to me ... and you would say ... the words ...[33]

F10　He had a finely-trained mind, that man who first tossed off the saying, coining a new phrase – that fortune is an ally to sensible people.

F11　An honest character is more steadfast than a law:
no public speaker could ever manage to twist its meaning,
whereas a speaker might often corrupt the law,
distorting it this way and that with his arguments.

F12　Is it not better, then, not to live at all, rather than to live badly?

F13　a pretext

F14　to vex

Rhadamanthys

[**F15**　*After Polydeuces' death, Castor was killed when fighting alone. While Rhadamanthys was rejoicing at the victory but also grieving for his daughters, Artemis appeared and commanded Helen to establish rituals honouring her two dead brothers; and she announced that his daughters would become goddesses.*[34]]

F16　those who possess the land of Euboea, the neighbouring state.

F17　In life all sorts of desires come upon us: one man yearns to gain nobility, while another cares nothing for rank but longs to be called the father of many possessions in his house; it pleases another to persuade those around him to embark on daring crimes, but his words contain no decent sentiment, meanwhile others among mortals seek shameful gain rather than good. Such are the ways in which human life is fallible. But for

---

[33]　The fragment tails off with a few unintelligible words. F8 and F9 are unintelligible papyrus fragments.

[34]　Not a fragment but a portion of an ancient plot-summary (*hypothesis*): see *TrGF* 1.43 *ad loc.*

myself I desire none of these things; rather, I should wish to have the renown of a good reputation.

F18   ... for there is no one who shall remove them from us.

Sisyphus

F19   *Sisyphus:* Once upon a time human life lacked order: it was bestial and subservient to physical force, and there was no reward at that time for good behaviour, neither was there any punishment for the wicked. But then, so it seems to me, humans established laws for punishment, so that justice might be their ruler <...> and reduce wilful aggression to servitude. If anyone still did wrong, he was punished. Then, when laws prevented them from committing violent crimes out in the open, they began to commit them in secret; then at last (so it seems to me) some ingenious and clever man invented the fear of the gods for the benefit of mortals, so that terror might be implanted in the hearts of the wicked, even if they were doing or saying or thinking anything in secret. And thus it came about that he introduced religion – the belief that there exists a deity, flourishing in eternal life, who hears and sees in his mind, who considers and pays attention to these things, who has a divine nature, who will listen to everything that is said among humans and will be able to see everything that is being done; and that if you silently concoct some wicked plan, it will not go unnoticed by the gods, for they have the power of thought. By telling such tales as these, he introduced the pleasantest of teachings, concealing the truth with his lying speech. And he said that gods dwell in such a place as would be most likely to inspire terror in people, a place that he knew to be the source of mortals' fears and the source of benefits for their miserable existence: he said that they proceed from the encircling vault above, where they saw that there were lightning-flashes, and dreadful thunderclaps, and the starry countenance of heaven, the fine, intricate ornament of the clever craftsman Time. This is the region, he said, whence come stars in their gleaming mass, and whence the moist rain travels down to earth. Such were the fears with which he encircled humans; and by these fears, and with his words, he located the deity in an appropriate place and also put out the fire of lawlessness with his laws. <...> And so it was, I believe, that someone first persuaded mortals to believe in a race of deities.

Tennes

[**F20** . . . *shutting . . . witness of . . . repented . . . when he heard that Tennes had safely reached the island opposite. At Apollo's instruction he named the island Tenedos and killed the woman who had deceived him.*[35]]

F21 Ah! There is no justice at all in the present race of men.

From unknown plays

F22 Time is a drug that cures all anger.

F23 The man who in his dealings with his friends does everything to please them might be giving immediate pleasure, but he is laying up enmity for a later date.

F24 It is a terrible thing for an unintelligent person to think that he is intelligent.

F25 It is better to share one's home with stupidity, if it is accompanied by wealth, rather than with poverty, even if it is clever.

Diogenes of Athens (*TrGF* 1.45)

Semele

F1 And indeed I hear the female followers of Asian Cybele, wearing their headbands, the children of wealthy Phrygians, making a loud noise with their drums and rattles and the clashing of bronze cymbals that they hold in both hands <. . .> the gods' wise songstress and healer. And I hear the Lydian and Bactrian maidens who dwell beside the River Halys worship the Tmolian goddess Artemis in her sacred grove in the shadow of laurel trees, entertaining her with notes played in counterpoint[36] on the triangular *pêktides*, plucking the strings of the *magadis*, where the *aulos*, entertained as a guest, joins in with the choruses in a Persian tune.

---

[35] Another plot-summary (imperfectly preserved in papyrus form) rather than a fragment as such.
[36] The word which I tentatively translate here as 'in counterpoint' is ἀντιζύγοις, which might alternatively refer to harmony, balance, contrast (or perhaps even 'unison'): without hearing the music it is impossible to say precisely what effect is denoted.

Dicaeogenes (*TrGF* 1.52)

Cyprians

F1   [*Then there is recognition by means of memory, in which a visual stimulus
         makes someone realize something, just as in Dicaeogenes'* Cyprians, *where
         he wept at the sight of the picture.*[37]]

Medea

F1a   Metapontios [said to be the name of Medea's brother]

From unknown plays

F1b   Whenever we are caught fast in love's hunting-nets
         †we are quicker to show gratitude to strangers
         than to those to whom gratitude is necessary, being members of the
           family†.[38]

F2   Blessed is the man who remains powerful in his own right
         but also has mighty children to fight beside him.

F4   . . . but you, having been brought up well by your parents,
         give them the same fine treatment in return.

F5   To those with good sense, 'the greatest god' is one's parents.

Antiphon (*TrGF* 1.55)

Andromache

F1   [Aristotle, *Eudemian Ethics* 7.4, 1239a37; *Nicomachean Ethics* 8.9,
         1159a27: see Chapter 5, pp. 143–5]

---

[37]   Aristotle's (*Poetics* 16.1454b37–8) brief allusion to the plot of Dicaeogenes' play, not a fragment as
       such.
[38]   The text is corrupt, and this translation cannot be regarded as definitive.

Jason

F1a they disposed

Meleager

F1b [Aristotle, *Rhetoric* 2.2, 1379b13–15: see Chapter 5, pp. 143–5]

F2 ... <They came> not in order to kill the wild beast, but
to bear witness to Greece of the virtue of Meleager.

From an unknown play

F4 By skill we overcome those who would defeat us by nature.

Patrocles (*TrGF* 1.57–8)

F1 But now all these extraordinary deeds and all these words
have ended up gathered by fortune into this container so very small.
Why, then, do we mortals utter many vain threats,
letting fly terrible speeches at one another,
and why do we think we can accomplish anything by our efforts,
looking forward into the future? We do not perceive fortune standing by,
under our very noses, nor do we see the approach of our wretched fate.

Astydamas the Younger (*TrGF* 1.60)

Alcmeon

F1c It's the truth I care about; appearances don't mean anything to me.

Hector

F2 *Hector:* Servant! Take my helmet, please,
so that the boy is not frightened.[39]

---

[39] See Chapter 4, pp. 103–5, for discussion and interpretation of **F1h-1i** and **F2a** (attribution uncertain).

Nauplius

F5   I wish you happiness – if happiness is possible in a place below the
          earth.[40]
          Yes, I think it is; for where there can be none of life's misery,
          one can rejoice, being oblivious to ills.

From unknown plays

F6   He revealed to humans the grapevine,
          mother of wine and taker-away of sorrow.[41]

F7   Gossip is when a tongue goes a-wandering.

F8   Praise of a family is safest when one praises each person individually;
          whoever is just and of excellent character,
          this person should be called well-born.
          It would scarcely be possible to find one such man in a hundred,
          even if countless people are searching for him.

F9   the brazen way[42]

Carcinus the Younger (*TrGF* 1.70)

Semele

F2   O nights . . .

F3   O Zeus, why is it necessary to say out loud that women are an evil
          thing?
          It would be enough if one were just to say the word *woman*.

Tyro(?)

F4   Practise excellence and ask the gods for good fortune:
          the person who has both these things at the same time
          will be able to live and will be called blessed and good.

---

[40]   There is a play on the dual meaning of *chairein:* (1) to rejoice or be happy; (2) to give a greeting.
[41]   A description of Dionysus.
[42]   A reference to the boundary of Colonus.

From unknown plays

F5   Once upon a time, they say, Pluto secretly snatched away Demeter's daughter, whom none may name; and then he went down into the depths of earth, where light is darkness. Meanwhile her mother, in her longing for the vanished girl, went round to every region of the earth in search of her. And the whole land of Sicily by Aetna's crags was filled with unapproachable streams of fire, and let out a groan; and in their grief for the maiden the people of Sicily, beloved by Zeus, were perishing through shortage of grain. Henceforth people still honour the goddesses even right up to the present day.

F5a   Incredible! Senseless! Terrible! <...>
Among the evils of human life, is there anything that is beyond belief?
... for in a single day the god brings the fortunate to misfortune.

F6   †It was not that man who drove him out of his senses;
for no opportune situation could induce those of fixed mind to go
   astray.[43]

F7   For many people silence is a drug to cure ills,
and in particular it is the mark of a sensible disposition.

F8   I rejoice to see that you are envious, because I am aware that
among all the things that envy causes there is only one that is just:
it is †a possession that brings suffering to those who possess it.

F9   Wealth is an evil thing: it makes men cowardly and craven.

F10   †Oh! Wealth is a most unfortunate thing in every respect,
and yet it is pursued very enthusiastically by mortals.

Chaeremon (*TrGF* 1.71)

Alphesiboea

F1   †She put a lot of effort into her appearance, making her body gleam with
its white complexion.† Modesty added a sense of proportion, bringing a

---

[43]   Seriously corrupt/incomplete; F8 and F10 are also corrupt and hard to translate definitively.

very gentle blush to her bright complexion. Just like an image sculpted in wax, hair and all, her tresses waved in the rustling breeze and glowed luxuriantly.

Achilles the Killer of Thersites

F2   Chance, not judgement, governs the affairs of men.

F3   As one not throwing the first punch, but taking revenge.

Dionysus

F4   Pentheus, named for the fate that would befall him.[44]

F5   Ivy, lover of choruses and child of the year

F6   Culling garlands, messengers of good news

F7   Twisted wreaths, thrice-coiled in a circle with ivy and narcissus

Thyestes

F8   A bright-shining rose together with while lilies

Io

F9   Scattering the children of the florid spring all around.

Centaur

F10   Some of the women made war on the boundless, unarmed army of
           flowers,
           hunting the <?> children of the meadow in their delight.

F11   The children prepare wreaths, heralds of holy silence, which they cast
           forth
           along with their prayers to the gods.

---

[44] Alluding to the supposed etymological connection between Pentheus and *penthos* (misery).

Minyans

F12   It was possible to see much of Cypris' harvest,
        turning dark at the topmost parts of time's vines.

Odysseus

F13   In their hair they wore roses, the season's fair-flowering bodies,
        most pre-eminent nurselings of spring.

Oeneus

F14   One girl, her shoulder-piece loosened, revealed a white breast to the
        moonlight as she lay. Meanwhile another girl danced and laid bare her
        left flank. Naked, she appeared in full view in the open air, and she
        resembled a living picture; her white complexion met the eye with an
        answering gleam, the work of dark shadow. Another girl exposed her
        lovely arms and hands, embracing another's feminine neck, and this one
        showed a glimpse of thigh beneath the folds of a torn cloak; and hopeless
        love set its seal upon her smiling bloom. Drowsily they sank down upon
        calamint, crushing the dark-petalled violets and the crocus which
        smeared the shadowy trace of its sunny image on their woven garments,
        and the sturdy marjoram, nurtured by the dew; and they lay there,[45]
        stretching out their necks in the soft meadows.

From unknown plays

F14b   One must honour . . .
        For humans the beginning . . .
        Of a desire for every . . .
        We honour strength . . .
        To possess a pious character . . .
        Do not fix your eye on every sort of gain . . .
        . . . (?) . . . yourself.

---

[45]   I have adopted Scaliger's *exeteinon* (rather than Athenaeus' *exeteinen,* accepted by Snell).

F15   (Athenaeus 2.35e) *The tragic poet Chaeremon says that wine provides those who consume it with* 'laughter, wisdom, wit, judgement'.[46]

F16   Wine is mixed with the characters of those who drink it.

F17   When we had passed the boundaries of the sacred enclosure (*or* sheepfold)
and crossed over the water, body of the river . . .

F18   Need has made her home not far from Necessity.

F19   Fortune overcomes and reverses everything.

F20   Time, proceeding at a leisurely pace, always gets there in the end.

F21   There is nothing in human life that cannot be discovered
in the course of time by those who seek after it.

F22   Time softens up everything and fashions it to its own end.

F23   I say that the most powerful man should be honoured in all circumstances,
for the prudent man has everything in his possession.

F24   People who understand nothing of wisdom are not truly alive.

F25   You have not yet acquired good sense,
but you know how to look down on other people.

F26   No one who has failed is held to have planned ahead well.

F27   It ill beseems noble men to tell lies.

F28   Consider this, that all evil acts are committed in anger.

F29   Anger compels a man to do many evil deeds.

F30   In general a superior power does not allow arrogance.

F31   It is the mark of wise men to exercise fair judgement upon sins,
but to judge rashly and impetuously is a bad thing.

---

[46]   Snell combines F16 and F15 (in that order) into a single fragment, and also cites Athenaeus 13. 562e: 'Theophrastus, in his *Erotica*, says that the tragedian Chaeremon describes Love (*Erôs*) as like the mixing of wine: when he is mixed moderately, he is charming, but when he is intense and disturbing, he is very intractable'.

F32   Better to bury your wife than to marry her.

F33   May it fall to me to pay back my father for his kindness.

F35   A good father does not show anger towards his son.[47]

F36   Wealth, when it †meets with every sort of honour,
           has no dignity, such as would lead to good repute,
           but is lacking in gravity; but in the homes of men†
           it is pleasant to dwell, and having obtained gratitude . . .[48]

F37   A wise man does not grieve over trifles.

F38   Every old man is bad at being a slave to anger.

F39   Veins issuing underground from roots of the palm tree with its unpleasant
           smoke . . .

F41   †In summer the daughter of springtime gives birth to a child for the
               future†,
           but in winter she is gone, cut off along with the wind.[49]

F42   For the divine powers have determined unexpected outcomes . . .

Theodectes (*TrGF* 1.72)

Ajax

F1   (Aristotle, *Rhetoric* 2.23, 1399b28, 1400a27–8; 3.1416b12–17: see
           pp. 166–7 above.)

Alcmeon

F1a   It is true, the saying that is recounted far and wide among mortals,
           that there is no creature more wretched than womankind.

---

[47]   There is no F34. Stobaeus cites Chaeremon's name in a section of his anthology entitled 'That one must hold one's parents in high esteem' (4.25), but the quotation is missing.

[48]   The fragment is corrupt and not entirely intelligible: this is an approximate translation which tries to convey the general sense (adopting Hense's δώμασιν for the manuscript reading δόσει as in *TrGF*). Cf. Xanthakis-Karamanos (1980) 154–5.

[49]   Another highly corrupt fragment: this translation aims only at an approximate sense of the meaning. (Note that there is no F40.)

F2   *Alphesiboea:* Was there no one among the human race who hated your
          mother?

          Alcmeon: [Yes, of course there was,> but first we must make a distinction
          and look.

          [*Alphesiboea:* How?>

          Alcmeon: They judged that she should die, but that it was not for me to
          kill her.

Helen

F3   *Helen:* Who would think it right to address me as a servant, when I am
          the descendant of divine ancestors on both sides?

Oedipus

F4   There are twin sisters, of whom one gives birth to the other,
          and having given birth she herself is born from the one she bore.

Orestes

F5   When a woman has killed her husband, it is right . . .

Tydeus

F5a   (Aristotle, *Poetics* 16. 1455a4–11: see p. 170–1 above.)

Philoctetes

F5b   *Philoctetes:* Chop off my hand!

From unknown plays

F6   *Peasant:* The first letter in the inscription was a †soft-eyed circle†, then
          there were two upright lines, exactly equal in length, and a horizontal bar
          in between joined them together; the third letter was similar to a curling
          lock of hair. Then the next letter appeared to be a trident on its side, and
          fifth came two wands of equal length up above, and these converged into a
          single base. Sixth came the letter which I mentioned before, the lock of hair.

F7   It is fitting to begin with the gods.

F8   If there is anyone among mortals who criticizes the gods for not going in pursuit of the unjust at once, but delaying it, let him listen carefully to this explanation: if punishments followed immediately on crimes, many people would honour the gods because of fear and not because of piety. But as it is, since punishment is far off, people obey human nature. Nevertheless, when they are apprehended and recognized as criminals, they pay the penalty late in the day.

F9   But, o wretched Thyestes, bear up with fortitude, taking anger's bit between your teeth. At this moment your rage is as a keenly-whetted knife, but I give you this advice: measureless Time brings all things to obscurity and takes them in its grip.

F10   O Helios – you who swiftly ply your flaming light with its glorious beams, the brightness that is dear to all mankind – did you ever see anyone else end up in a situation of such enormity, or facing a trial from which it is so difficult to escape? This woman is making a speech accusing me, and the person that she is addressing happens to be [my? her?] husband, and those who stand in judgement over me are also my accusers.

F11   A great deal of effort is necessary if one is going to obtain praise and glory. Indolence may achieve a short-term pleasure, but it is wont to beget sorrow in the course of time.

F12   Everything in human life naturally gets older and reaches its appointed end – with the sole exception, so it seems, of shamelessness. The more the human race increases, the more shamelessness grows day by day.

F13   Whenever a husband brings home a wife, he doesn't obtain merely a wife, so it seems, but together with her he also takes a daemon into his house, maybe a good one or maybe the opposite kind.

F14   Children are saved by their parents' advice.[50]

F15   I can never speak in praise of noble birth when it is exemplified by leaders who are unworthy of it.

---

[50]   The meaning of this fragment (Stobaeus 4.26.8) is clear enough, but the metre is problematic.

F16   It has long been known, old man, and the word travels up and down Greece
with a widespread fame, that human fortunes are not stable.

F17   As he approached these people [the Ethiopians], Helios, driving his chariot, discoloured the men's bodies with the dark flower of his smoky flame, and he caused their hair to curl into shapes that could not be extended, melting it together with his fire.

F18   What creature is it that does not fall among those that are born by the protecting earth or the sea, that doesn't have limbs that grow like those of mortals, but is biggest at the time of its first sowing and generation, small at the very mid-point of its prime, and in old age once again even larger than at all other times in shape and size?

Dionysius (*TrGF* 1.76)

Adonis

F1   ADONIS: As I bring the newly-born wild boar
beneath the covered cavern of the nymphs,
I am spoken of as a lucky hunter,
and I bring the boar's hooves to offer as first-fruits.*

Alcmene

F2   If you expect that nothing painful will ever befall you,
you are living in a state of blissful ignorance:
the sort of life that you are imagining you will have is the life of the gods,
not the life of humans.

Leda

F3   Let no mortal man ever judge anyone blessed,
before he sees him end his life well;
only when he is dead is it safe to praise a man.

* On the text and translation adopted here see p. 141 and n. 84 above.

From unknown plays

F4   Tyranny is the mother of injustice.

F5   The eye of Justice, looking out from a quiet face, as it were, always sees all things equally.

F6   Either say something better than silence, or keep silent.

F7   Don't you even understand this – that absolutely no one envies the dead?

F8   You may be poor yourself, but do not envy those who are rich.

F9   †Doris, the wife of Dionysius, is dead.[51]

F10   Alas! I have lost a useful wife.

F11   Foolish people make sport of themselves.

F12   *balantion* (javelin)
helkydrion (urn)
skeparnon (wool)
eriôlê (cloak)
thyestês (pestle)
menandros (young maiden)
menekratês (pillar)
mystêria (escape of mystic initiates)
garotas (ox)
iacchos (piglet)
karpotex (month)

F13   *Timaeus (FGrHist 562 F1) tells us that poets and other authors reveal their natures in their works by their choice of subject matter and by dwelling excessively on certain topics and details. For example, Homer is always showing his heroes eating, which indicates that he may have been a glutton ... and in the same way Dionysius the tyrant revealed his nature by his interest in bed-hangings and by the constant study he devoted to many different varieties and peculiarities of woven tapestries.*[52]

---

[51]   The text is not certain; I translate Hermann's *Dôris tethnêken* (rather than *Dôrikon hêken* as in Snell's edition).
[52]   Not strictly a fragment but a testimonium (from Polybius 12.24.1).

Cleaenetus (*TrGF* 1.84)

F1   It is a fine thing to die for the sake of one's parents.

F2   Anger and grief, when they come together in a single place within the
          soul,
          turn into madness for those who experience them.

Diogenes of Sinope (*TrGF* 1.88)

F1h   Those whose hearts have been stuffed full
          of the pleasures of effeminate and filthy luxury
          do not want to exert themselves even in the smallest way.

F2   I wish for a drop of fortune rather than a whole jar of intellect;
          if fortune is absent, intellect fares badly.

Fragments of doubtful origin

F3   *Heracles:* O wretched virtue! So you were a mere word, though I practised
          you as a reality – and yet all the time you were a slave to fortune . . . and
          so I gave up wealth-producing injustice and also licentiousness that gives
          birth to every sort of pleasure.[53]

F4   Cityless, homeless, deprived of [my] fatherland,
          a beggar, a wanderer, living from day to day.

F5   He who clothed me in rags and forced me
          to become a beggar and an outcast from my home . . .

F6   All those who practise philosophy and achieve something by hard work
          are thereby able to gain mastery over their bodily appetites;
          for simplicity is a teacher of the wise counsel, which is the best sort.

F7   If my father who begat me had possessed any sense,
          I would have understood that it is better to give up cultural pursuits
          and instead to do work, in order to enjoy good fortune and
          to fare less well from time to time. The first thing of all,

---

[53]   A mixture of quotation and paraphrase: see Chapter 5, pp. 157–8.

and the source of all things for mortals,
is to be of a good size, without having a full belly,
and to be content, just like an animal always drinking from streams,
and to train one's body in wintertime and to approve
the hot shafts of the sun's arrows, not hiding oneself away in the shade.
But as it is, not being habituated to this life,
I lack understanding – but one needs must bear up.
Taking Orpheus and the whole nine-voiced song of the Muses,
I do not choose to obey my belly; but life must be supported.

APPENDIX 2

Glossary

aetiological: explanatory (from the Greek *aition*, an explanation or cause). An 'aetiological' myth is one that goes back in time to explain how some familiar feature of modern life or religious ritual came about.

agôn: a contest of any sort; the word is commonly used in the context of tragedy to denote a formal, forensic-style debate between two central characters.

aulos: a woodwind instrument, resembling the modern oboe.

chorêgos: the producer or financial backer of a theatrical production.

didascalic: relating to *didaskaliai* (ancient records of theatrical performances, festivals and prizes). *Didaskaliai* was also the title of a (lost) work by Aristotle.

didaskalos: the normal Greek term for the director (literally 'trainer' or 'teacher') of a theatrical production; usually but not invariably synonymous with the author of the play.

Dionysia: festival of Dionysus, the god of theatre. Many of the tragedies and comedies we possess from antiquity were staged at the City (or 'Greater') Dionysia, a major spring festival which took place in Athens and attracted many visitors to the city. There were also a large number of smaller festivals known as the 'Rural Dionysia' which took place in the outskirts of the city or in the countryside of Attica.

dithyramb: a form of choral performance in honour of Dionysus. Some dramatic festivals (e.g. the 'City' Dionysia) included dithyrambic contests as well as tragic and comic drama.

ekkyklêma: a small portable stage on wheels (used to display scenes or tableaux from indoors).

episode: a scene, principally composed of spoken dialogue, placed in between songs.

fragment: a portion of a lost text (either a piece of papyrus or, more commonly, a word for word quotation in the work of another author)

gnôme (plural *gnômai*): a quotable maxim or proverbial statement, commonly found in tragedy. Many of the fragments of lost plays take the form of *gnômai*.

hypothesis: an ancient plot-summary (or summary of the play's myth) handed down in the manuscript tradition along with the text of a Greek play. The exact date and authorship of some hypotheses are unknown, but they can contain useful information about the play and the circumstances of its first production.

iambic trimeter: the verse metre most commonly used for dialogue in tragedy (and the ancestor of iambic verse in English); it was thought to be close to the rhythm of everyday speech.

intertextuality: the (often self-conscious) relationship between one literary text and another text or texts.

lacuna: a gap or hole in a papyrus text.

mêchanê: the mechanical crane or flying-machine that was used for the surprise entry of characters from time to time in tragedy. It was used especially for divine epiphanies (hence the Latinized expression *deus ex machina*, 'the god from the flying-machine').

mode: the tonality or tuning of a piece of Greek music, roughly equivalent to 'scale' in modern usage. Different modes (*harmoniai* in Greek) included, for instance, Aeolian, Phrygian, Lydian, Mixolydian and Dorian, each of which was associated with a particular musical or emotional effect.

monody: song performed by a solo actor (comparable to an operatic aria).

orchêstra: in the Greek world, this word refers to the flat area in the centre of the theatre, which was used for acting and dancing. The word 'stage' does not reflect the right meaning, since there was no raised stage in the classical Greek theatre.

proagon: an event that took place in the Odeon (next door to the Theatre of Dionysus) at the start of the Athenian Dionysia festival. Playwrights and their companies of actors and musicians took part in this preliminary event, but no one knows exactly what form it took.

prologue: everything that happens on stage before the first entry of the chorus.

satyr-play: a bawdy type of drama that was often included as the fourth and final play in a tetralogy (following a set of three tragedies): i.e. the tragedians wrote satyr-plays as well as tragedies. Satyrs are wild creatures, half-man and half-beast, thought to have a special connection to the god Dionysus.

sophist: a controversial type of philosopher and rhetorician who sprung up at Athens during the last few decades of the fifth century BCE. The sophists were not an official 'school' of philosophy but a loosely-connected group of individuals who had certain characteristics in common, including interests in epistemology, ontology, ethics and the philosophy of language. The most famous sophists were Gorgias and Protagoras; Socrates was often numbered among them, but he was keen to distinguish himself from the group.

stasimon: choral ode between scenes of dialogue.

stichomythia: rapid-fire dialogue in which each participant speaks one line of verse at a time.

tragôidia: the Greek word for the tragic genre; not quite the same thing as the 'tragedy' of later periods (e.g. Shakespeare).

tychê: chance, fortune or randomness.

APPENDIX 3

Chronology

This is not a comprehensive timeline of Greek theatre history: it relates only to playwrights, productions and events mentioned in this book. Note that many of these dates and other details (marked '?') are uncertain, especially those relating to the very earliest tragic productions: see individual entries in the Index to locate further discussion of the evidence.

534 BCE	? Thespis' first victory at the City Dionysia
c. 523–520	? Choerilus' first dramatic production
c. 511–508	? Phrynichus' first dramatic production
c. 499–496	? Pratinas competes against Aeschylus and Choerilus
494	Siege and destruction of Miletus
492	Phrynichus, *The Sack of Miletus*
c. 484–480	Birth of Achaeus
c. 483	Euetes wins first prize at the City Dionysia
c. 482–471	Polyphrasmon's first victory at the City Dionysia
480	Battle of Salamis
476	Phrynichus exhibits? *Phoenician Women*, with Themistocles as *chorêgos*
472	Aeschylus' *Persians*
after 469	? Choerilus competes against Sophocles
467	Aristias wins second prize at the City Dionysia with *Perseus, Tantalus* and *Wrestlers* (written by his father Pratinas); Polyphrasmon wins third prize with his *Lycourgeia* tetralogy (or shortly afterwards): Mesatus' first victory at the City Dionysia
c. 466–460	Aristias' first victory at the City Dionysia
c. 465–455	Mesatus wins third prize at the City Dionysia; Aeschylus' Danaid trilogy (including *Suppliant Women*)
c. 451–448	Ion begins competing at the Athenian dramatic festivals

446	? Carcinus the Elder wins first prize at the City Dionysia
438	Euripides' *Alcestis*
435	Iophon wins first prize at the City Dionysia
431–404	The Athenians are at war with the Spartans and Peloponnesians
431	Euphorion wins first prize at the City Dionysia, defeating Sophocles and Euripides; Carcinus the Elder serves as Athenian *stratêgos*
428	Euripides wins first prize at the City Dionysia (with plays including the extant *Hippolytus*), Iophon comes second and Ion third
427	The sophist Gorgias arrives at Athens from Leontini in Sicily
422	Menecrates wins first prize at the City Dionysia; Aristophanes' *Wasps*
421	Aristophanes' *Peace*
419	*Agamemnon* (author unknown) wins first prize at the Lenaea; Hera[cleides?] wins second prize with *These[us?]*
418	Callistratus' *Amphilochus* and *Ixion* win second prize at the Lenaea
c. 416	Agathon's first dramatic production and victory
415	Xenocles wins first prize at the City Dionysia (with *Oedipus, Lycaon, Bacchae* and *Athamas*), defeating Euripides (with *Alexandros, Palamedes, Women of Troy* and *Sisyphus*)
411	Aristophanes' *Women Celebrating the Thesmophoria*
c. 410	Meletus' *Oedipodeia*
c. 409	Aristophanes' *Storks*
c. 408	Aristophanes' *Gerytades*
406–367	Dionysius, tyrant and tragedian, rules over Syracuse
406	Death of Euripides
405	Death of Sophocles; Aristophanes' *Frogs*
404	The Peloponnesian War ends in Athens' defeat; rule of the 'Thirty Tyrants' (including the tragedian Critias)
401	Sophocles' *Oedipus at Colonus* is produced posthumously by his grandson Sophocles the Younger
c. 398–380	Polyidus wins the dithyrambic competition at the City Dionysia
388	Aristophanes' *Wealth*
387	Sophocles the Younger wins first prize at the City Dionysia
386	Programme at the Dionysia expanded to include category of 'old tragedy'

375	Sophocles the Younger wins first prize at the City Dionysia
372	Astydamas' first victory at the City Dionysia
c. 372–370	Theodectes' first victory at the City Dionysia
370	Astydamas wins first prize at the Lenaea
367	Dionysius wins first prize at the Lenaea and immediately dies
c. 372–365	Carcinus the Younger wins his first victory at the City Dionysia
364	? Nicomachus wins third prize at the Lenaea with *Amymone*
363	Theodorides wins second prize at the Lenaea with *Medea* and *Phaethon*;
	Cleaenetus wins third prize at the Lenaea with *Hypsipyle* and *Ph*[ ];
	Aphareus puts on his first dramatic production
c. 359–350	Philinus, Asclepiades, Caerius, Achaeus and [?Tim]ostratus win first prizes at the Lenaea
c. 353	Theodectes produces *Mausolus* at Halicarnassus
347	Astydamas wins first prize at the City Dionysia
341	Astydamas' *Achilles, Athamas* and *Antigone* win first prize at the City Dionysia;
	Euaretus wins second prize with *Teucer* and *Achilles* (and a third play);
	Aphareus wins third prize with *Daughters of Pelias, Orestes* and *Auge*
340	Astydamas wins first prize at the City Dionysia with *Parthenopaeus* and *Lycaon*;
	Euaretus wins third prize;
	Statue of Astydamas is erected in the Theatre of Dionysus
c. 339–330	[?Tim]ocles wins second prize at the Lenaea with *Phrixus* and *Oedipus*
338	Athenians are defeated by Philip of Macedon at the Battle of Chaeronea
c. 337–324	Lycurgus holds political power in Athens as treasurer and director of the Theatre; official state texts and commemoration of the three 'great' Athenian tragedians
323	Death of Alexander the Great and beginning of the 'Hellenistic' period
322	Athens' defeat by Macedon and the end of democracy

APPENDIX 4

Guide to Further Reading and Resources

A full guide to further reading and resources for the study of lost tragedies will be provided in Volume 2, where it will be immediately obvious that there is much more material relating to the fragmentary plays of Aeschylus, Sophocles and Euripides. Here I mention only works relating to the neglected tragedians, together with a few items of general bibliography: such items are dispiritingly few in number, but I hope that the current work may stimulate further study. For discussions of specific points relating to each individual tragedian, the reader is directed to the footnotes and the full Bibliography of Works Cited.

Editions

The standard modern edition of the remains of all the lost tragedies is the multi-volume *TrGF* (*Tragicorum Graecorum Fragmenta*), edited by Bruno Snell, Stefan Radt and Richard Kannicht and published in instalments between 1971 and 2004. The remains of the neglected tragedians, edited by Snell (who refers to them, misleadingly, as *Tragici Minores*), are to be found in Volume 1. Volume 2, to which I sometimes refer, contains the *adespota*, i.e. fragments which cannot be assigned to a particular author (including several important papyrus fragments). Volumes 3–5 are devoted to the 'classic' triad.

TrGF supersedes all previous editions of the same material, by Nauck, Meineke and others, mainly because of its exhaustive coverage of the evidence but also because it contains very full and careful annotation. However, these earlier editions sometimes contain interesting discussions, and it can be instructive to compare the earlier editors' methods and arrangements of the material with what is seen in *TrGF*. For illuminating analysis and discussion see R. Kassel, 'Fragmente und ihre Sammler', in H. Hofmann (ed.), *Fragmenta Dramatica* (Göttingen, 1991): 243–53 [translated into English by H.M. and F.D. Harvey as 'Fragments and their collectors' in F. McHardy, J. Robson and F.D. Harvey (eds.),

Lost Dramas of Classical Athens: Greek Tragic Fragments (Exeter, 2005): 7–20 and
F.D. Harvey, 'Tragic thraumatology: the study of the fragments of Greek tragedy
in the nineteenth and twentieth centuries' also in F. McHardy, J. Robson and F.D.
Harvey (eds.), *Lost Dramas of Classical Athens: Greek Tragic Fragments*: 21–48.

TrGF presents, in the case of each tragedian, (i) testimonia relating to the
poet's life and work; (ii) fragments, numbered according to earlier editions
with supplements here and there; (iii) details of the sources where the testimonia
and fragments are found; (iv) an *apparatus criticus* with details of textual
problems, variant readings and conjectures, supplements and other bibliographic
information. All of this material is presented with the utmost rigour and clarity.
However, it is designed exclusively for professional scholars. The introduction,
notes and apparatus are in Latin, and the texts themselves are in Greek without
any translations or aids to comprehension. Thus the student or general reader
will find *TrGF* difficult or impossible to use.

Translations

A generous selection of testimonia and fragments from *TrGF*, Volumes 1 and 2,
is available in German translation: Richard Kannicht et al., *Musa Tragica: Die
griechische Tragödie von Thespis bis Ezechiel* (Göttingen, 1991). But this edition
omits some of the material, and it is no use to those who do not read German.
The fragments of Agathon were translated into elegant French by Pierre Lévêque
in his monograph on that poet (Paris, 1955), but there is no English translation
available. In fact there has never been an English version of any of the fragmentary
tragedies until recent years. During 1996–2008 the Loeb Classical Library issued
parallel texts of the fragments of Aeschylus, Sophocles and Euripides, and
selected fragmentary plays of Euripides and Sophocles have appeared in the Aris
and Phillips Classical Texts series (Oxford, 1995–2010), but the remains of the
neglected tragedians have never been available in English.

General or introductory reading

There are many excellent modern books on Greek tragedy. The Blackwell
Companion to Greek Tragedy, edited by Justina Gregory (Malden/Oxford, 2005),
is perhaps the best and most comprehensive single-volume guide for the
beginner or the general reader: it contains thirty-one essays, by numerous

contributors, on different aspects of the genre, and includes a wealth of bibliographic guidance. Readers will also find a huge amount of stimulus and interest in Edith Hall's books *Greek Tragedy: Suffering Under the Sun* (Oxford, 2010) and *The Theatrical Cast of Athens: Interactions Between Ancient Greek Drama and Society* (Oxford, 2006). All of these works concentrate almost exclusively on the fifth century and the surviving plays, but see now E. Csapo, H.R. Goette, J.R. Green and P. Wilson (eds.), *Greek Theatre in the Fourth Century* (Berlin, 2014) for a variety of studies of later classical drama.

Evidence relating to the dramatic festivals is collected and discussed by E. Csapo and W. Slater, *The Context of Ancient Drama* (Ann Arbor, 1994). Performance and staging are discussed by David Wiles, *Greek Theatre Performance: An Introduction* (Cambridge, 2000); see also P.E. Easterling and E.M. Hall (eds.), *Greek and Roman Actors: Aspects of an Ancient Profession* (Cambridge, 2002) and M.L. West, *Ancient Greek Music* (Oxford, 1992). The question of the extent to which tragedy should be seen as political, or distinctively Athenian, is addressed by D.M. Carter (ed.), *Why Athens? A Reappraisal of Tragic Politics* (Oxford, 2011). For those who read Greek, Richard Rutherford's book *Greek Tragic Style* (Cambridge, 2012) is an excellent guide to the language and poetry of tragedy.

Reading matter specifically relating to the neglected tragedians is very thin on the ground. I have already mentioned Lévêque's book on Agathon, which is the only book devoted to a single 'non-canonical' tragedian. Bernard Knox devotes a mere six pages to 'Minor Tragedians' in P.E. Easterling and B.M.W. Knox (eds.), *The Cambridge History of Classical Literature I* (Cambridge, 1985): 87–93, but his discussion does not really suggest that these tragedians would repay further study. A.H. Sommerstein, *Greek Drama and Dramatists* (London, 2002) contains a few judicious (but very brief) remarks on the neglected tragedians in relation to the genre as a whole. Bruno Snell's *Szenen aus griechischen Drama* (Göttingen, 1971) discusses a few individual playwrights and their work (including Neophron, Astydamas the Younger and Chaeremon). Martin Cropp's chapter on 'Lost tragedies: a survey', in J. Gregory (ed.), *A Companion to Greek Tragedy* (Malden/Oxford, 2005): 271–92, is full of good things but is mainly devoted to the lost plays of the 'classic' triad. F. McHardy, J. Robson and F.D. Harvey (eds.), *Lost Dramas of Classical Athens: Greek Tragic Fragments* (Exeter, 2005) is a collection of essays mainly concerned with the lost plays of the triad, but it contains some interesting and suggestive discussions of methodology as well as the two chapters on fragmentologists by Kassel and Harvey (mentioned above, under 'Editions').

Reception

It is hardly worth pointing out the reasons why there has been virtually *no* reception of the lost plays (though there have been some interesting modern encounters with the fragments of Aeschylus, Sophocles and Euripides – see Volume 2). However, a seemingly unique example of a modern dramatic work which incorporates and revivifies the work of a neglected tragedian is Tony Harrison's play *The Labourers of Herakles*. This was first performed on 23 August, 1995, on an excavated site intended for the New Theatre of the European Cultural Centre of Delphi. Harrison's version incorporates all the fragments of Phrynichus' plays, transcribed and read out in ancient Greek straight from *TrGF* (untranslated and largely unexplained), and in particular Phrynichus' play *The Sack of Miletus* stands as a symbol of cultural destruction and as a brave work of art about genocide. The script, including a few photographs of the production, is published in Harrison's *Plays: Three* (London, 1996).

Bibliography of Works Cited

Listed below are all works which I have cited in the main text and notes. Abbreviations follow the normal scholarly conventions (as in *L'Année Philologique*).

Adair, G. (1997) *Surfing the Zeitgeist* (London).

Allan, W. (2004) 'Religious syncretism: the new gods of Greek tragedy', *HSCP* 102: 113–55.

Allan, W. (2014) 'The body in mind: medical imagery in Sophocles', *Hermes* 142: 259–78.

Arnott, W.G. (1959) 'The Greek original of the *Poenulus*', *RhM* 102: 252–62.

Arnott, W.G. (1996) (ed.) *Alexis: The Fragments* (Cambridge).

Austin, C. and Olson, D. (2005) (eds.) *Aristophanes: Thesmophoriazusae* (Oxford).

Bakola, E. (2008) 'The drunk, the reformer and the teacher: agonistic poetics and the construction of persona in the comic poets of the fifth century', *PCPS* 54: 1–29.

Bakola, E. (2009) *Cratinus and the Art of Comedy* (Oxford).

Barker, A.D. (1984) (ed.) *Greek Musical Writings, I* (Cambridge).

Bartalucci, A. (1970–71) 'Una probabile ricostruzione dell' *Eracle* di Diogene di Sinope', *SCO* 19–20: 109–22.

Barthes, R. (1970) *S/Z* (Paris).

Barthes, R. (1975) *Roland Barthes par Roland Barthes* (Paris).

Barthes, R. (1977) *Le Plaisir du Texte* (Paris).

Battezzato, L. (2003) (ed.) *Tradizione testuale e ricezione letteraria antica della tragedia greca* (Pisa).

Baumann, M. (2007) '*Mousa lesbiazousa*: Die Fellatio treibende Muse. Sexuelle Devianz und Poetologie in der Komödie des Aristophanes', in M. Baumann, D. Matzner, S. Matzner, Y. Nowak (eds.), *Wo die Liebe hinfällt . . . AMORalische Liebeskonzeptionen in der europäischen Geistesgeschichte* (Marburg): 5–20.

Bayard, P. (2007) *Comment parler des livres que l'on n'a pas lus?* (Paris).

Bélis, A. (2004) 'Un papyrus musical inédit du Louvre: identification, transcription et interpretation musicale', *CRAI* 3: 1305–1329.

Bierl, A. (1991) *Dionysos und die griechische Tragödie* (Tübingen).

Bloom, H. (1973) *The Anxiety of Influence* (Oxford/New York).

Blumenthal, H. (1973) 'Meletus the accuser of Andocides and Meletus the accuser of Socrates: one man or two?', *Philologus* 117: 169–78.

Borthwick, E.K. (1968) 'The dances of Philocleon and the sons of Carcinus in Aristophanes' *Wasps*', *CQ* 18: 44–51.

Bosher, K. (2012) (ed.) *Theater Outside Athens* (Cambridge).

Braund, D.C. and Wilkins, J.M. (2000) (eds.) *Athenaeus and his World* (Exeter).

Bühler, W. (1973) 'Tzetzes über die *Hektoros Lytra* des Dionysios', *Zeitschrift für Papyrologie und Epigraphik* 11: 69–79.

Burian, P. (1997) 'Myth into *muthos:* the shaping of tragic plot', in Easterling (1997): 178–208.

Burkert, W. (1966) 'Greek tragedy and sacrificial ritual', *GRBS* 7: 87–121.

Burkert, W. (1985) *Greek Religion* (Oxford).

Burkert, W. (1987) *Ancient Mystery Cults* (Cambridge, MA).

Caizzi, F.D. (1966) (ed.) *Antisthenis Fragmenta* (Milan).

Cameron, A. (2004) *Greek Mythography in the Roman Empire* (Oxford/New York).

Carrara, P. (1997) 'L'addio ad Andromaca e ad Astianatte nell' *Ettore* di Astidamante', *Prometheus* 23: 215–21.

Carter, D. (2007) *The Politics of Greek Tragedy* (Exeter).

Carter, D. (2011) (ed.) *Why Athens? A Reappraisal of Tragic Politics* (Oxford).

Caven, B. (1990) *Dionysius I, War-Lord of Sicily* (New Haven).

Centanni, M. (1997) *Atene assoluta: Crizia dalla tragedia alla storia* (Padua).

Clarke Kosak, J. (2005) *Heroic Measures: Hippocratic Medicine in the Making of Euripidean Tragedy* (Leiden).

Clay, D. (1975) 'The tragic and comic poet of the *Symposium*', *Arion* 2: 238–61.

Colesanti, G. and Giordano, M. (2014) *Submerged Literature in Ancient Greek Culture: An Introduction* (Berlin).

Collard, C. (1969) 'Athenaeus, the Epitome, Eustathius and quotations from tragedy', *RIFC* 97: 157–79.

Collard, C. (2007a) 'The *Pirithous* fragments', in *Tragedy, Euripides and Euripideans* (Exeter): 56–68 [original version published in J.A. López Férez (ed.), *Da Homero a Libanio* (Madrid, 1995): 183–93].

Collard, C. (2007b) 'On the tragedian Chaeremon', in *Tragedy, Euripides and Euripideans* (Exeter): 31–55 [original version published in *JHS* 90 (1970): 22–34].

Collard, C. (2013) 'Pratinas', in C. Collard and P. O'Sullivan (eds.), *Euripides: Cyclops and Major Fragments of Greek Satyric Drama* (Oxford): 242–7.

Collard, C. and Cropp, M. (2008) *Euripides: Fragments* (Cambridge, MA).

Conacher, D.J. (1981) 'Rhetoric and relevance in Euripidean drama', *AJP* 108: 3–25.

Corbato, C. (1948) 'L'*Anteo* di Agatone', *Dioniso* 11: 163–72.

Craik, E.M. (2001) 'Medical reference in Euripides', *BICS* 45: 81–95.

Crescini, V. (1904) 'Di Agatone poeta tragico', *RSA* 9: 7–30.

Cropp, M.J. (2005) 'Lost tragedies: a survey', in J. Gregory (ed.), *A Companion to Greek Tragedy* (Malden/Oxford, 2005): 271–92.

Cropp, M.J. and Fick, G. (1985) *Resolutions and Chronology in Euripides* (London).

Csapo, E. (2010) *Actors and Icons of the Ancient Theater* (Malden/Oxford).

Csapo, E., Goette, H.R., Green, J.R., Wilson, P. (eds.) (2014) *Greek Theatre in the Fourth Century BC* (Berlin).

Csapo, E. and Miller, M. (2007) (ed.) *The Origins of Theater in Ancient Greece and Beyond* (Cambridge).

Cusset, C. (2003) *Ménandre ou le comédie tragique* (Paris).

Dale, A.M. (1967) '*Ethos* and *dianoia*: "character" and "thought" in Aristotle's *Poetics*', in *Collected Papers* (Cambridge): 139–55.

D'Angour, A. (2011) *The Greeks and the New* (Cambridge).

Davidson, J. (2000) 'Gnesippus *paigniagraphos*: the comic poets and the erotic mime', in F.D. Harvey and J.M. Wilkins (eds.), *The Rivals of Aristophanes: Studies in Athenian Old Comedy* (Swansea/London): 41–64.

Davidson, J.F. (2003) 'Carcinus and the temple: a problem in the Athenian theater', *Classical Philology* 98: 109–22.

Davies, M. (1989a) 'Sisyphus and the invention of religion ('Critias' *TrGF* 1 (43) F 19 = B 25 DK)', *BICS* 36: 16–32.

Davies, M. (1989b) *The Greek Epic Cycle* (London).

Davies, M. (1998) 'Euripides' *Electra*: the recognition scene again', *CQ* 48: 389–403.

Deardon, C. (1999) 'Plays for export', *Phoenix* 53: 222–48.

Delcourt, M. (1959) *Oreste et Alcméon: Étude sur la projection legendaire du matricide en Grèce* (Paris).

Del Grande, C. (1934) 'Teodette di Faselide e la tarda tragedia posteuripidea', *Dioniso* 4: 191–210.

Depew, D. (2007) 'From hymn to tragedy: Aristotle's genealogy of poetic kinds', in Csapo and Miller (2007): 126–49.

Desmond, W. (2008) *Cynics* (London).

Dickey, E. (2007) *Ancient Greek Scholarship* (Oxford/New York).

Diggle, J. (2008) 'Did Euripides plagiarize the *Medea* of Neophron?' in D. Auger and J. Peigney (eds.) *Phileuripides: mélanges offerts à François Jouan* (Paris): 405–13.

Dihle, A. (1977) 'Das Satyrspiel Sisyphos', *Hermes* 105: 28–42.

Dillon, J. and Gergel, T. (2003) (ed., tr.) *The Greek Sophists* (London).

Dobrov, G. (2002) *Figures of Play* (Oxford).

Dolfi, E. (2006) 'Sul fr. 14 di Cheremone', *Prometheus* 32: 43–54.

Dover, K.J. (1968) (ed.) *Aristophanes: Clouds* (Oxford).

Dover, K.J. (1978) *Greek Homosexuality* (London).

Dover, K.J. (1986) 'Ion of Chios: his place in the history of Greek literature', in J. Boardman and C.E. Vaphopoulou-Richardson (eds.), *Chios* (Oxford): 27–37.

Dover, K.J. (1988) 'The freedom of the intellectual in Greek society', in *The Greeks and their Legacy* (Oxford): 135–58.

Duchemin, J. (1968) *L'agon dans la tragédie grecque* (Paris).

Dudley, D.R. (1937) *A History of Cynicism from Diogenes to the Sixth Century AD* (London).

Duncan, A. (2006) *Performance and Identity in the Classical World* (Cambridge).

Duncan, A. (2012) 'A Theseus outside Athens: Dionysius I of Syracuse and tragic self-presentation', in Bosher (2012): 137–55.

Easterling, P.E. (1985) 'Anachronism in Greek tragedy', *JHS* 105: 1–10.

Easterling, P.E. (1993) 'The end of an era? Tragedy in the early fourth century', in A.H. Sommerstein et al. (eds.), *Tragedy, Comedy and the Polis* (Bari): 559–69.

Easterling, P.E. (1997) (ed.) *The Cambridge Companion to Greek Tragedy* (Cambridge).

Easterling, P.E. (2007) 'Looking for *Omphale*', in Jennings and Katsaros (2007): 282–92.

Edmunds, L. (1975) *Chance and Intelligence in Thucydides* (Cambridge, MA).

Else, G. (1957) *Aristotle's Poetics: The Argument* (Cambridge, MA).

Else, G. (1965) *The Origin and Early Form of Greek Tragedy* (Cambridge, MA).

Ercolani, A. (2014) 'Defining the indefinable: Greek submerged literature and some problems of terminology', in Colesanti and Giordano (2014): 7–18.

Fowler, R. (2013) *Early Greek Mythography, Volume II: Commentary* (Oxford).

Fries, A. (2014) (ed.) *Pseudo-Euripides: Rhesus* (Berlin).

Freese, J.H. (1926) (ed./tr.) *Aristotle: The 'Art' of Rhetoric* (Cambridge, MA).

Gantz, T. (1993) *Early Greek Myth* (Baltimore).

Garland, R. (2003) *Surviving Greek Tragedy* (London).

Garvie, A. (1969) *Aeschylus' Supplices: Play and Trilogy* (Cambridge).

Garvie, A. (2009) (ed.) *Aeschylus: Persae* (Oxford).

Gekoski, R. (2004) *Tolkien's Gown* (London).

Gill, C.J. (1996) *Personality in Greek Epic, Tragedy and Philosophy* (Oxford).

Gill, C.J. (2005) 'Tragic fragments, ancient philosophers and the fragmented self', in McHardy et al. (2005): 151–72.

Gladigow, B. (1964) *Sophia und Kosmos* (Hildesheim).

Goldhill, S. (1990) 'The Great Dionysia and civic ideology', in J. Winkler and F. Zeitlin (eds.), *Nothing to do with Dionysos? Athenian Drama in its Social Context* (Princeton): 97–129.

Goldhill, S. (2007) *How to Stage Greek Tragedy Today* (Chicago).

Graf, F. and Iles Johnston, S. (2013) *Ritual Texts for the Afterlife: Orpheus and the Bacchic Gold Tablets* (2nd edn) (London).

Graham, D.W. (2010) *The Texts of Early Greek Philosophy* (Cambridge).

Green, J.R. (1990) 'Carcinus and the temple: a lesson in the staging of tragedy', *GRBS* 31: 281–5.

Green, J.R. (2003) 'Speculations on the tragic poet Sthenelus and a comic vase in Richmond', in E. Csapo and M. Miller (eds.), *Poetry, Theory, Praxis: The Social Life of Myth, Word and Image in Ancient Greece* (Oxford): 178–84.

Gregory, J. (1991) *Euripides and the Instruction of the Athenians* (Ann Arbor).

Gregory, J. (2005) (ed.) *A Companion to Greek Tragedy* (Malden/Oxford).

Griffin, J. (1998) 'The social function of Attic tragedy', *CQ* 48: 39–61.

Griffith, M. (1977) *The Authenticity of Prometheus Bound* (Cambridge).

Grossardt, P. (2005) 'Zum Inhalt der *Hektoros Lytra* des Dionysios I (*TrGF* 1, 76 F2a)', *Rheinisches Museum für Philologie* 148: 225–41.

Guthrie, W.C. (1971) *The Sophists* (Cambridge).

Hall, E.M. (1989) *Inventing the Barbarian: Greek Self-Definition Through Tragedy* (Oxford).

Hall, E.M. (1995) 'Lawcourt dramas: the power of performance in Greek forensic oratory', *BICS* 40: 39–58.

Hall, E.M. (1997) 'The sociology of Athenian tragedy', in Easterling (1997): 93–126.

Hall, E.M. (1999) 'Actor's song in tragedy', in S. Goldhill and R. Osborne (eds.), *Performance Culture and Athenian Democracy* (Cambridge): 96–122.

Hall, E.M. (2007) 'Greek tragedy, 430–380 BC', in R. Osborne (ed.), *Debating the Athenian Cultural Revolution* (Cambridge): 264–87.

Hall, E.M. (2010) 'The Pronomos vase and tragic theatre: Demetrios; rolls and Dionysos' other woman', in Taplin and Wyles (2010): 159–79.

Hall, E.M. (2013) *Adventures with Iphigenia in Tauris: A Cultural History of Euripides' Black Sea Tragedy* (Oxford).

Hall, E.M., Macintosh, F. and Wrigley, A. (eds.) (2004), *Dionysus Since 69: Greek Tragedy at the Dawn of the Third Millennium* (Oxford).

Handley, E. (1993) 'Aristophanes and the generation gap', in A.H. Sommerstein et al. (eds.), *Tragedy, Comedy and the Polis* (Bari): 417–44.

Hanink, J. (2010) 'The classical tragedians, from Athenian idols to wandering poets', in I. Gildenhard and M. Revermann (eds.), *Beyond the Fifth Century: Interactions with Greek Tragedy from the Fourth Century BCE to the Middle Ages* (Berlin): 39–67.

Hanink, J. (2014a) *Lycurgan Athens and the Making of Classical Tragedy* (Cambridge).

Hanink, J. (2014b) 'Literary evidence for new tragic production: the view from the fourth century', in Csapo et al. (2014): 189–206.

Harries, E.W. (1994) *The Unfinished Manner: Essays on the Fragment in the Later Eighteenth Century* (Charlottesville).

Harris, E., Leão, D. and Rhodes, P.J. (2010) (eds.) *Law and Society in Ancient Greece* (London).

Harris, W.V. (1989) *Ancient Literacy* (Cambridge, MA).

Harvey, F.D. (2005) 'Tragic thrausmatology: the study of fragments in the nineteenth and twentieth centuries', in McHardy et al. (2005): 21–48.

Havelock, E. (1982) *The Literate Revolution in Greece and its Cultural Consequences* (Princeton).

Hawes, G. (2014) *Rationalizing Myth in Antiquity* (Oxford).

Heath, M. (1989) *Unity in Greek Poetics* (Oxford).

Heath, M. (2009) 'Should there have been a *polis* in Aristotle's *Poetics*?' *CQ* 59: 468–85.

Heilmeyer, W.D. (2002) (ed.) *Die griechische Klassik: Idee oder Wirchlichkeit* (Berlin).

Henderson, G. (1998) (ed., tr.) *Aristophanes: II* (Cambridge, MA).

Henderson, J. (2007) 'The hocus of a hedgehog: Ion's versatility', in Jennings and Katsaros (2007): 17–44.

Herington, J. (1985) *Poetry Into Drama. Early Tragedy and the Greek Poetic Tradition* (Berkeley).

Hook, B.S. (2005) 'Oedipus and Thyestes among the philosophers: incest and cannibalism in Plato, Diogenes and Zeno', *Classical Philology* 100: 17–40.

Hornblower, S. (1982) *Mausolus* (Oxford).

Hunter, R. (1983) (ed.) *Eubulus: The Fragments* (Cambridge).

Hunter, R. (2014) *Hesiodic Voices* (Cambridge).

Hunter, R. and Russell, D.A. (2011) (eds.) *Plutarch, How To Study Poetry* (Cambridge).

Huxley, G. (1986) 'Aetolian Hyantes in Phrynichus', *GRBS* 27: 235–7.

Ireland, S. (2010) (ed.) *Menander: The Shield (Aspis) and The Arbitration (Epitrepontes)* (Oxford).

Janko, R. (2011) (ed.) *Philodemus: On Poems Books 3–4, with the Fragments of Aristotle, On Poets* (Oxford).

Jennings, V. and Katsaros, A. (2007) (eds.) *The World of Ion of Chios* (Leiden).

Jocelyn, H.D. (1969) (ed.) *The Tragedies of Ennius* (Cambridge).

Kaimio, M. and Nykopp, N. (1997) 'Bad Poets Society: censure of the style of minor tragedians in Old Comedy', in J. Vaahtera and R. Vainio (eds.), *Utriusque linguae peritus: studia in honorem Toivio Viljamaa* (Turku): 23–37.

Kannicht, R. et al. (1991) *Musa Tragica: Die griechische Tragödie von Thespis bis Ezechiel* (Göttingen).

Karamanou, I. (2003) 'The myth of Alope in Greek tragedy', *L'Antiquité Classique* 72: 25–40.

Karamanou, I. (2010) 'Aristotle's *Poetics* as a source for lost tragedies', *Actas del XII Congreso Español de Estudios Clásicos* (Madrid): 389–97.

Kassel, R. (1991) 'Fragmente und ihre Sammler', in H. Hoffmann (ed.), *Fragmenta Dramatica* (Göttingen): 243–53 [= 'Fragments and their collectors', tr. H.M. and F.D. Harvey, in McHardy et al. (2005): 7–20].

Kerferd, G. (1981) *The Sophistic Movement* (Cambridge).

Knox, B.M.W. (1979) 'Euripidean comedy', in *Word and Action: Essays on the Ancient Theater* (Baltimore): 250–74.

Knox, B.M.W. (1985) 'Minor Tragedians', in P.E. Easterling and B.M.W. Knox (eds.), *The Cambridge History of Classical Literature I* (Cambridge): 87–93.

Konstan, D. (2011) 'Excerpting as a reading practice', in Reydams-Schils (2011): 9–22.

Konstan, D. (2015) (ed./tr.) *Aspasius, On Aristotle, Nicomachean Ethics 1–4, 7–8* (London).

Kovacs, D. (1986) 'On Medea's great monologue', *CQ* 36: 343–52.

Kovacs, D. (2005) 'Text and transmission', in Gregory (2005): 459–71.

Kotlińska-Toma, A. (2014) *Hellenistic Tragedy* (London).

Krentz, P. (1982) *The Thirty at Athens* (Ithaca).

Krumeich, R., Pechstein, N. and Seidensticker, B. (1999) (eds.): *Das griechische Satyrspiel* (Darmstadt).

Krumeich, R. (2002) 'Die lycurgische Tragikerweihung', in Heilmeyer (2002): 542–6.

Lee, K. (1975) (ed.) *Euripides: Troades* (London).

Lada-Richards, I. (1999) *Initiating Dionysus* (Oxford).

Lefkowitz, M.R. (1981) *The Lives of the Greek Poets* (London).

Lefkowitz, M.R. (1984) 'Aristophanes and other historians of the fifth-century theater', *Hermes* 112: 143–53.

Lefkowitz, M.R. (1987) 'Was Euripides an atheist?' *Studi italiani di filologia classica* 5: 149–66.

Lefkowitz, M.R. (1989) ' "Impiety" and "atheism" in Euripides' dramas', *CQ* 39: 70–82.

Le Guen, B. (1995) 'Théâtre et cités à l'époque hellénistique', *REG* 108: 59–90.

Leone, P.L. (1995) (ed.) *Ioannis Tzetzae Carmina Iliaca* (Catania).

Leonhardt, J. (1991) *Phalloslied und Dithyrambos: Aristoteles über den Ursprung des griechischen Dramas* (Heidelberg).

Lesky, A. (1983) *Greek Tragic Poetry,* tr. M. Dillon (3rd edn) (New Haven).

Leurini, L. (2000) (ed.) *Ionis Chii Testimonia et Fragmenta* (2nd edn) (Amsterdam).

LeVen, P. (2014) *The Many-Headed Muse* (Cambridge).

Lévêque, P. (1955) *Agathon* (Paris).

Lloyd, M. (1992) *The Agon in Euripides* (Oxford).

Lloyd-Jones, H. (1964) 'The *Supplices* of Aeschylus: the new date and old problems', *Antiquité Classique* 33: 356–74.

Lloyd-Jones, H. (1966) 'Problems of early Greek tragedy', *Cuadernos de la Fundación Pastor* 13: 11–33.

Lobel, E. (1936) *Greek Poetry and Life: Essays Presented to Gilbert Murray* (Oxford).

López Cruces, J.L. (2003) 'Diógenes y sus tragedias a luz de la comedia', *Ítaca* 19: 47–69.

Loraux, N. (1987) *Tragic Ways of Killing a Woman*, tr. A. Forster (Cambridge, MA).

Lucas, D. (1968) (ed.) *Aristotle: Poetics* (Oxford).

Luppe, W. (2009) 'Zur Anzahl der an den Lenäen von den Tragikern aufgeführten Dramen', *Archiv für Papyrusforschung* 1: 36–9.

Luz, C. (2010) *Technopaignia: Formspiele in der griechischen Dichtung* (Leiden).

Macaulay, R. (1953) *The Pleasure of Ruins* (London).

McDonald, M. (2003) *The Living Art of Greek Tragedy* (Bloomington).

MacDowell, D.M. (1971) (ed.) *Aristophanes: Wasps* (Oxford).

McHardy, F., Robson, J., Harvey, F.D. (eds.) (2005), *Lost Dramas of Classical Athens: Greek Tragic Fragments* (Exeter).

Maitland, J. (2007) 'Ion of Chios, Sophocles, and myth', in Jennings and Katsaros (2007): 266–81.

Manuwald, B. (1983) 'Der Mord an den Kindern: Bemerkungen zu den Medea-Tragödien des Euripides und des Neophron', *WS* 17: 27–61.

Marti, B. (1947) 'The prototypes of Seneca's tragedies', *CP* 42: 1–16.

Mastronarde, D. (2002) (ed.) *Euripides: Medea* (Cambridge).

Meursius, I. (1619) (ed.) *Aeschylus, Sophocles, Euripides. Sive de Tragoediis eorum, Libri III* (Leiden).

Michelini, A.N. (1987) *Euripides and the Tragic Tradition* (Madison)

Michelini, A.N. (1989) 'Neophron and Euripides' *Medeia* 1056–80', *TAPA* 119: 115–35.

Millis, B. and Olson, S.D. (2012) (eds.) *Inscriptional Records for the Dramatic Festivals in Athens* (Leiden).

Monoson, S.S. (2012) 'Dionysius I and Sicilian theatrical traditions', in Bosher (2012): 156–72.

Moorton, R.F. (1988) 'Aristophanes on Alcibiades', *GRBS* 29: 345–59.

Morelli, G. (2001) *Teatro attico e pittura vascolare: una tragedia di Cheremone nella ceramica italiota* (Hildesheim).

Most, G. (2009) 'On fragments', in W. Tronzo (ed.), *The Fragment: An Incomplete History* (Los Angeles): 9–20.

Muecke, F. (1982) 'A portrait of the artist as a young woman', *CQ* 32: 41–55.

Müller, C.W. (2002) 'Der Sieg des Euphorion, die Zurücksetzung des Sophokles und die Niederlage des Euripides im Tragödienagon des Jahres 431', *RhM* 145: 61–7.

Nagy, G. (2007) 'Introduction and discussion', in Csapo and Miller (2007): 120–5.

Nauck, A. (1856) *Tragicorum Graecorum Fragmenta* (Leipzig).

Nervegna, S. (2013) *Menander in Antiquity: The Contexts of Reception* (Cambridge).

Nesselrath, H.G. (1995) 'Myth, parody and comic plots: the birth of gods in Middle Comedy', in G. Dobrov (ed.), *Beyond Aristophanes* (Atlanta): 1–27.

Nestle, W. (1901) *Euripides: Der Dichter der griechischen Aufklärung* (Stuttgart).

Nicole, J. (1884) 'Le poète tragique Carcinus et ses fils', *Mélanges Graux* (Paris): 163–7.

Nietzsche, F. (1872) *Die Geburt der Tragödie, oder Griechenthum und Pessimismus* (2nd edn) (Leipzig).

Noel, A.-S. (2012) 'La dramaturgie de l'objet dans le théâtre tragique du vᵉ siècle avant J.-C.: Eschyle, Sophocle, Euripide', diss. (Lyon).

Noussia, M. (2006) 'Fragments of "Cynic" tragedy', in M.A. Harder et al. (eds), *Beyond the Canon* (Hellenistica Groningana 11, Leuven): 229–47.

Nünlist, R. (1998) *Poetologische Bildersprace in der frühgriechischen Dichtung* (Stuttgart).

Oakley, J.H. (2009) 'State of the discipline: Greek vase painting', *AJA* 113: 599–627.

Ogden, D. (2013) *Drakon: Dragon Myth and Serpent Cult in the Greek and Roman Worlds* (Oxford).

Olivieri, A. (1950) 'Dionisio primo tiranno di Siracusa e Patrocle di Turi, poeti drammatici', *Dioniso* 13: 91–102.

Olson, S.D. (1997) 'Was Carcinus I a tragic playwright? A response', *CP* 92: 258–60.

Olson, S.D. (1998) (ed.) *Aristophanes: Peace* (Oxford).

Olson, S.D. (2002) (ed.) *Aristophanes: Acharnians* (Oxford).

Olson, S.D. (2007) (ed.) *Broken Laughter: Select Fragments of Greek Comedy* (Oxford).

Origa, V. (2007) *Le contraddizioni della sapienza: sophia e sophos nella tragedia euripidea* (Tübingen).

Orth, C. (2009) *Strattis: Die Fragmente: Ein Kommentar* (Berlin).

Ostwald, M. (1986) *From Popular Sovereignty to the Sovereignty of Law: Law, Society and Politics in Fifth-Century Athens* (Berkeley).

O'Sullivan, P. (2008) 'Aeschylus, Euripides, and tragic painting: two scenes from *Agamemnon* and *Hecuba*', *AJP* 129: 173–98.

O'Sullivan, P. (2012) 'Sophistic ethics, old atheism, and "Critias" on religion', *CW* 105: 167–85.

O'Sullivan, P. and Collard, C. (2013) (eds) *Euripides: Cyclops and Major Fragments of Greek Satyric Drama* (Oxford).

Pack, R.A. (1965) *The Greek and Latin Literary Texts from Greco-Roman Egypt* (2nd edn) (Ann Arbor).

Page, D.L. (1938) (ed.) *Euripides: Medea* (Oxford).

Page, D.L. (1942) (ed., tr.) *Select Literary Papyri III: Literary Papyri* (Cambridge, MA).

Page, D.L. (1981) (ed.) *Further Greek Epigrams* (Cambridge).

Papathomopoulos, M. (1981) 'Tzetzès sur les *Hektoros Lytra* de Denys le tyran', *Revue des Études Grecs* 94: 200–5.

Pappas, A. (2011) 'Arts in letters: the aesthetics of ancient Greek writing', in M. Swan and M. Dalbello (eds.), *Visible Writings: Cultures, Forms, Readings* (New Brunswick): 37–54.

Parker, L.P.E. (1997) *The Songs of Aristophanes* (Oxford).

Parker, L.P.E. (2007) (ed.) *Euripides: Alcestis* (Oxford).

Parker, R. (1996) *Athenian Religion: A History* (Oxford).

Parker, R. (2005) *Polytheism and Society at Athens* (Oxford).

Patzer, H. (1962) *Die Anfänge der griechischen Tragödie* (Wiesbaden).

Pendrick, G.J. (2002) (ed.) *Antiphon the Sophist: Fragments* (Cambridge).

Pelling, C. (2000) *Literary Texts and the Greek Historian* (London).

Perlman, S. (1964) 'Quotations from poetry in the Attic orators of the fourth century BC', *AJP* 85: 177–92.

Pfeiffer, R. (1969) *History of Classical Scholarship: From the Beginnings to the End of the Hellenistic Age* (Oxford).

Piatowski, A. (1981) 'La figure humaine dans le drame grec du IV-ème siècle av.n.ère', *Philologus* 125: 201–10.

Pickard-Cambridge, A.W. (1927) *Dithyramb, Tragedy and Comedy* (Oxford).

Pickard-Cambridge, A.W. (1962) *Dithyramb, Tragedy and Comedy*, rev. T.B.L. Webster (2nd edn) (Oxford).

Pickard-Cambridge, A.W. (1988) *The Dramatic Festivals of Athens,* rev. T.B.L. Webster, J. Gould, D.M. Lewis (3rd edn) (Oxford).

Pirrotta, S. (2009) *Plato Comicus: Die fragmentarischen Komödien – Ein Kommentar* (Berlin).

Pitcher, S.M. (1939) 'The *Anthus* of Agathon', *AJP* 60: 145–69.

Prauscello, L. (2006) 'Looking for the "other" Gnesippus: notes on Eupolis fragment 148 K-A', *CPh* 101: 52–66.

Rachet, G. (1973) *La tragédie grecque* (Paris).

Rau, P. (1967) *Paratragodia: Untersuchung einer komischen Form des Aristophanes* (Munich).

Rehm, R. (1994) *Marriage to Death: The Conflation of Wedding and Funeral Rituals in Greek Tragedy* (Princeton).

Reinhardt, K. (1957) 'Der Sinneskrise bei Euripides', *Eranos* 26: 279–317.

Reinhardt, T. (2010) 'Rhetoric and knowledge', in I. Worthington (ed.), *A Companion to Greek Rhetoric* (Malden/Oxford): 365–77.

Reydams-Schils, G. (2011) (ed.) *Thinking through Excerpts: Studies on Stobaeus* (Turnhout).

Ringer, M. (1998) *Electra and the Empty Urn: Metatheater and Role-Playing in Sophocles* (Chapel Hill).

de Romilly, J. (1992) *The Great Sophists in Periclean Athens*, tr. J. Lloyd (Oxford).

Rood, T. (1998) *Thucydides: Narrative and Explanation* (Oxford).

Roos, E. (1951) *Die tragische Orchestik im Zerrbild der altattischen Komödie* (Lund).

Rosen, R.M. (2006) 'Aristophanes, fandom and the classicizing of Greek tragedy', in L. Kosak and J. Rich (eds.), *Playing Around Aristophanes* (Oxford): 27–47.

Rosenbloom, D. (1993) 'Shouting "fire" in a crowded theater: Phrynichos' *Capture of Miletos* and the politics of fear in early Greek tragedy', *Philologus* 137: 159–96.

Ross, I. (2013) *Oscar Wilde and Ancient Greece* (Cambridge).

Rossi, L.E. (2000) 'L'autore e il controllo del testo nel mondo antico', *SemRom* 3: 165–81.

Rothwell, K.S. (1994) 'Was Carcinus I a tragic playwright?' *CP* 89: 241–5.

Ruffell, I.A. (2002) 'A total write-off: Aristophanes, Cratinus, and the rhetoric of comic competition', *CQ* 52: 138–63.

Russell, D.A. and Winterbottom, M. (1972) (ed., tr.) *Ancient Literary Criticism* (Oxford).

Rutherford, R. (2012) *Greek Tragic Style* (Cambridge).

Sanders, L.J. (1987) *Dionysius I of Syracuse and Greek Tyranny* (London).

Sansone, D. (2015) 'The place of the satyr-play in the tragic tetralogy', *Prometheus* 16: 3–36.

Scaliger, J.J. (1629) *De emendatione temporum* (3rd edn) (Geneva).

Schenkl, C. (1863) 'Die euripideische Literatur von 1850–1862', *Philologus* 20: 466–506.

Schmid, W. and Stählin, O. (1929) *Geschichte der griechischen Literatur* (Munich).

Schubert, C. (2013) 'Ein literarishes Akrostichon aus der ersten Hälfte des vierten Jahrhunderts v. Chr.? Zu Chairemon, *TrGF* I, 71 F14b', *GFA* 16: 389–97.

Scodel, R. (1980) *The Trojan Trilogy of Euripides* (Göttingen).

Scodel, R. (2006) 'Lycurgus and the state text of tragedy', in C. Cooper (ed.), *Politics of Orality* (Leiden): 129–54.

Scodel, R. (2010) *An Introduction to Greek Tragedy* (Cambridge).

Scullion, S. (2002a) 'Tragic Dates', *CQ* 52: 81–101.

Scullion, S. (2002b) 'Nothing to do with Dionysus: tragedy misconceived as ritual', *CQ* 52: 102–37.

Scullion, S. (2005) 'Tragedy and religion: the problem of origins', in Gregory (2005): 23–37.

Seaford, R.A.S. (1981) 'Dionysiac drama and the Dionysiac mysteries', *CQ* 31: 252–75.

Seaford, R.A.S. (1984) (ed.) *Euripides: Cyclops* (Oxford).

Seaford, R.A.S. (1987) 'The tragic wedding', *JHS* 107: 106–30.

Seaford, R.A.S. (1994) *Reciprocity and Ritual* (Oxford).

Seaford, R.A.S. (2003) 'Aeschylus and the unity of opposites', *JHS* 123: 141–63.

Seaford, R.A.S. (2005) 'Mystic light in Aeschylus' *Bassarai*', *CQ* 55: 602–6.

Seidensticker, B. (1982) *Palintonos Harmonia: Studien zu den komischen Elementen der griechischen Tragödie* (Göttingen).

Seidensticker, B. (2002) 'Wie die Tragiker zu Klassikern wurden', in Heilmeyer (2002): 526–9.

Sens, A. (2010) 'Hellenistic Tragedy and Lycophron's *Alexandra*', in J.J. Clauss and M. Cuypers (eds.), *A Companion to Hellenistic Literature* (Malden/Oxford): 297–313.

Silk, M.S. (2000) *Aristophanes and the Definition of Comedy* (Oxford).

Sluiter, I. (2005) 'Communicating Cynicism: Diogenes' gangsta rap', in D. Frede and B. Inwood (eds.), *Language and Learning: Philosophy of Language in the Hellenistic Age* (Cambridge): 139–63.

Small, J.P. (2003) *The Parallel Worlds of Classical Art and Text* (Cambridge).

Snell, B. (1953) *The Discovery of the Mind: The Greek Origins of European Thought,* tr. T.G. Rosenmeyer (Cambridge, MA).

Snell, B. (1964) *Scenes from Greek Drama* (Berkeley).

Snell, B. (1971) *Szenen aus griechischen Drama* (Göttingen).

Sommerstein, A.H. (1983) (ed.) *Aristophanes: Wasps* (Warminster).

Sommerstein, A.H. (1987) (ed.) *Aristophanes: Birds* (Warminster).

Sommerstein, A.H. (1994) (ed.) *Aristophanes: Frogs* (Warminster).

Sommerstein, A.H. (1996) 'How to avoid being a *komodoumenos*', *CQ* 46: 327–56.

Sommerstein, A.H. (2003) *Greek Drama and Dramatists* (London).

Sommerstein, A.H. (2008) (ed., tr.) *Aeschylus: I* (Cambridge, MA).

Sommerstein, A.H. (2010) '*Sherlockismus* and the study of fragmentary tragedies', in *The Tangled Ways of Zeus and Other Studies In and Around Greek Tragedy* (Oxford): 61–81.

Sourvinou-Inwood, C. (2003) *Tragedy and Athenian Religion* (Lanham).

Stevens, A. (2007) 'Ion of Chios: tragedy as commodity at the Athenian exchange', in Jennings and Katsaros (2007): 243–65.

Stevens, P.T. (1956) 'Euripides and the Athenians', *JHS* 76: 87–94.

Stieber, M. (2011) *Euripides and the Language of Craft* (Leiden).

Stoessl, F. (1945) 'Die *Phoinissen* des Phrynichos und die *Perser* des Aischylos', *Museum Helveticum* 2: 148–65.

Storey, I.C. (1977) '*Komodoumenoi* and *komodein* in Old Comedy', diss. (Toronto).

Storey, I.C. (2011) (ed., tr.) *Fragments of Old Comedy* (Cambridge, MA).

Stroheker, K. (1958) *Dionysios I: Gestalt und Geschichte des Tyrannen von Syrakus* (Wiesbaden).

Suess, W. (1966) 'Der ältere Dionys als Tragiker', *Rheinisches Museum für Philologie* 109: 299–318.

Sutton, D. (1981) 'Critias and atheism', *CQ* 31. 33–8.

Sutton, D. (1987) 'The theatrical families of Athens', *AJP* 108: 9–26.

Tanehisa, O. (2009) 'Friedrich Schlegel and the idea of the fragment: a contribution to Romantic aesthetics', *Aesthetics* 13: 59–68.

Taplin, O.P. (1986) 'Fifth-century tragedy and comedy: a *synkrisis*', *JHS* 106: 163–74.

Taplin, O.P. (1993) *Comic Angels and Other Approaches to Greek Drama through Vase-Painting* (Oxford).

Taplin, O.P. (2007) *Pots and Plays: Interactions Between Greek Tragedy and Vase-Painting of the Fourth Century BC* (Oxford).

Taplin, O.P. (2009) 'Hector's helmet glinting in a fourth-century tragedy', in S. Goldhill and E.M. Hall (eds.), *Sophocles and the Greek Tragic Tradition* (Cambridge): 251–63.

Taplin, O.P. (2014) 'How pots and papyri might prompt a re-evaluation of fourth-century tragedy', in Csapo et al. (2014): 141–56.

Taplin, O.P. and Wyles, R. (2010) *The Pronomos Vase and its Context* (Oxford).

Taràn, L. (1981) *Speusippus of Athens: A Critical Study with a Collection of the Related Texts and Commentary* (Leiden).

Thomas, R. (1992) *Literacy and Orality in Ancient Greece* (Cambridge).

Thompson, E.A. (1944) 'Neophron and Euripides' *Medea*', *CQ* 38: 10–14.

Thumiger, C. (2013) 'Mad *eros* and eroticized madness in tragedy', in E. Sanders et al., *Eros in Ancient Greece* (Oxford): 27–40.

Torrance, I. (2013) *Metapoetry in Euripides* (Oxford).

Trendall, A.W. and Webster, T.B.L. (1971) *Illustrations of Greek Drama* (London).

Tronzo, W. (2009) (ed.) *The Fragment: An Incomplete History* (Los Angeles).

Van Gennep, A. (1909) *Les rites du passage* (Paris).

Wachsmuth, A. (1881) *Studien zu den griechischen Florilegien* (Berlin).

Wardy, R. (1996) *The Birth of Rhetoric* (London).

Wartelle, A. (1971) *Histoire du texte d'Eschyle dans l'antiquité* (Paris).

Webster, T.B.L. (1936) 'Sophocles and Ion of Chios', *Hermes* 71: 263–74.

Webster, T.B.L. (1954) 'Fourth-century tragedy and the *Poetics*', *Hermes* 82: 294–308.

Webster, T.B.L. (1956) *Art and Literature in Fourth-Century Athens* (London).

Webster, T.B.L. (1970) *Studies in Later Greek Comedy* (Manchester).

West, M.L. (1977) 'Notes on papyri', *ZPE* 26: 37–43.

West, M.L. (1989) 'The early chronology of Attic tragedy', *CQ* 39: 251–4.

West, M.L. (1992) *Ancient Greek Music* (Oxford).

West, M.L. (2000) '*Iliad* and *Aethiopis* on stage: Aeschylus and son', *CQ* 50: 338–52.

West, M.L. (2007) 'A new musical papyrus: Carcinus, *Medea*', *ZPE* 161: 1–10.

Whitmarsh, T. (2014) 'Atheistic aesthetics: the Sisyphus fragment, poetics and the creativity of drama', *CCJ* 60: 109–26.

von Wilamowitz-Moellendorff, U. (1875) *Analecta Euripidea* (Berlin).

Wilde, O. (1880) '*Encyclopaedia Britannica* Vols. x and xi', *Athenaeum*, 4 September: 301–2.

Wilson, N.G. (1983) *Scholars of Byzantium* (London).

Wilson, P. (1996) 'Tragic rhetoric: the use of tragedy and the tragic in the fourth century', in M.S. Silk (ed.) *Tragedy and the Tragic* (Oxford): 310–31.

Wilkins, J.M. (1991) 'Euripides' myths', *CR* 41: 17–18.

Wimmel, W. (1960) *Kallimachos im Rom* (Wiesbaden).

Wise, J. (1998) *Dionysus Writes: The Invention of Theater in Ancient Greece* (Ithaca).

Woodward, C. (2002) *In Ruins* (London).

Wright, M.E. (2005) *Euripides' Escape-Tragedies* (Oxford).

Wright, M.E. (2006) '*Cyclops* and the Euripidean tetralogy', *PCPS* 52: 23–48.

Wright, M.E. (2009) 'Literary prizes and literary criticism in antiquity', *Classical Antiquity* 28: 138–77.

Wright, M.E. (2010) 'The tragedian as critic: Euripides and early Greek poetics', *JHS* 130: 165–84.

Wright, M.E. (2012) *The Comedian as Critic: Greek Old Comedy and Poetics* (London).

Wright, M.E. (2013a) 'Comedy *versus* tragedy in *Wasps*', in E. Bakola, L. Prauscello, M. Telò (eds.), *Greek Comedy and the Discourse of Genres* (Cambridge): 205–25.

Wright, M.E. (2013b) 'Poets and poetry in later Greek comedy', *CQ* 63: 603–22.

Wright, M.E. (forthcoming a) 'A lover's discourse: *erôs* in Greek tragedy', in R.A. Seaford, J.M. Wilkins, M.E. Wright (eds.), *Selfhood and the Soul: Essays in Ancient Thought and Literature in Honour of Christopher Gill* (Oxford).

Wright, M.E. (forthcoming b) 'Euripidean tragedy and quotation culture: the case of *Stheneboea* F661', *AJP* 138.

Xanthakis-Karamanos, G. (1979) 'Deviations from classical treatments in fourth-century tragedy', *BICS* 26: 99–103.

Xanthakis-Karamanos, G. (1980) *Studies in Fourth-Century Tragedy* (Athens).

Yunis, H. (2003) *Written Texts and the Rise of Literate Culture in Ancient Greece* (Cambridge).

Zeitlin, F. (1980) 'The closet of masks: role-playing and myth-making in the *Orestes* of Euripides', *Ramus* 9: 51–77.

Zeitlin, F. (1994) 'The artful eye: vision, ecphrasis and spectacle in Euripidean theater', in S. Goldhill and R. Osborne (eds.), *Art and Text in Ancient Greek Culture* (Cambridge): 138–96.

Zuntz, G. (1965) *An Inquiry into the Transmission of the Plays of Euripides* (Cambridge).

Index